SMOKY JOE WOOD

SMOKY JOE WOOD

The Biography of a Baseball Legend

GERALD C. WOOD

University of Nebraska Press · Lincoln & London

Library of Congress Cataloging-in-Publication Data
Wood, Gerald C.
Smoky Joe Wood: the biography of a baseball
legend / Gerald C. Wood.
p. cm.
Includes bibliographical references and index.
ISBN 978-0-8032-4499-3 (cloth: alk. paper)
1. Wood, Howard Ellsworth, 1889–1985. 2. Baseball
players—United States—Biography. I. Title.
GV865.W66W66 2013
796.357092—dc23 [B]   2012040000

Set in Minion by Laura Wellington.
Designed by Roger Buchholz.

For Edra

Contents

Illustrations

Acknowledgments

First thanks go to Robert K. Wood, Joe's youngest son and keeper of the Smoky Joe flame. Bob shared his archives and, despite suffering from emphysema, courageously endured a rainy, exhausting trip to Shohola, Pennsylvania, and the Baseball Hall of Fame. While deeply concerned for the health of his wife, Connie, Bob supported this book, providing essential information and images. Baseball lost a warm-hearted advocate when Bob died on May 31, 2009.

Once oriented in my research, I retraced the path of Smoky Joe's career. Good friends Andy Hazucha and Emily Hester offered their home in Lawrence, Kansas, as a launching pad for my side trips in Kansas and Missouri. Traveling west to Ness City, Kansas, I enjoyed a day at the Ness County Historical Society and places associated with the John F. Wood family. Michele O'Toole at the Ness City Public Library provided pictures and articles from local papers. In Hutchinson, Kansas, Barbara Ulrich-Hicks of the Reno County Museum introduced the town and its baseball. Crucially, in Kansas City, after visiting the Kansas City Public Library, I met Jim Swint. After we explored baseball sites, including Blues Park, he shared his seminal research on Joe Wood. Thanks, Jim, for your generosity.

In anticipation of a trip to Ouray, Colorado, I contacted the Ouray County Historical Society, whose members invited my wife and me to the dedication of Joe Wood Park there. Alas, we missed that ceremony by two weeks, but when we arrived in Ouray, representatives of the County Museum had rounded up local artifacts, including the *Ouray Times*, edited by Joe's father. (Years later archivist Glenda Moore and director Maria Jones kindly answered further inquiries.) On our way to Ouray, we visited Durango, where Duane Smith, history professor at Fort Lewis College, shared his expertise on Joe's days in Colorado.

Trips to Boston and New England were essential to understanding Smoky Joe's Red Sox years. Dick Johnson, author and curator of the New England Sports Museum, opened the Bill Carrigan scrapbooks and talked brilliantly of Smoky Joe. At the Boston Public Library, Roberta Zonghi and Aaron Schmidt gave access to the McGreevey collection. Geoff Zonder, former sports archivist at Yale, kindly granted access to Joe Wood materials at the university. While I was in New Haven, Leo Cooney, chief of geriatric medicine at Yale Medical School, described Joe's final illness. Connecticut's Smoky Joe Wood Chapter of the Society for American Baseball Research (SABR) and its president, Steve Krevisky, gave unqualified support.

I am especially thankful to the Joe Wood family. Rob, Bob's older son, and his wife, Lucy; his brother Jeffrey of Monterey, California; and their sister, Durinda, a costume designer in Hollywood, have repeatedly shared their time and memories. In Milford, Pennsylvania, David Wood and his wife, Cyndi, discussed family history and even let me hold Joe's hunting rifles. Richard Wood of Juneau, Alaska, who (like David) is a son of Joe Frank Wood, offered vivid impressions by phone and mail. Sensitive reflections were also offered by Carol Wood, Virginia Wood Whitney, Gary Whitney, and Sandy Theimer, daughter-in-law of Zoë, Joe's sister. Thanks to the many other helpful Woods I met at Bob's memorial.

Phone interviews aided immensely. Crucial were Fay Vincent Jr. on his father's Yale years under Coach Joe Wood and the 1926–27 controversy and former Yale secretary John Wilkinson on the honorary doctorate. Frank Durham remembered summers in the Twin Lakes area; George Fluhr re-created the history and myths of Pike County, Pennsylvania;

Tim Gay discussed the Speaker-Wood relationship; Ken Berg shared his enthusiasm for Smoky Joe's legacy; and Roger Angell reflected on his visits with Smoky Joe. Joe's appearance in *Field of Dreams* was explained by writer/director Phil Alden Robinson, and John and Tom Begin reminisced about life with Joe Wood on Marvel Road.

Many others helped remove specific roadblocks. Kevin Johnson of Sports Artifacts and Drew Boyd of CMG aided initial contacts in the Wood family. Robert T. Lord gave useful directions to the Wood family cemetery. The Kansas Historical Society researched Logan Galbreath and the Kansas City Bloomer Girls, and I profited from the sage advice of Leslie Heaphy, Barbara Gregorich, and Deb Shattuck on the Bloomer Girls. The Levi Travises, senior and junior, helped me locate Indian Camp and referred me to Mike McConnell, who brought the camp alive. The Chicago History Museum helped find the Wood family in the Windy City. I also appreciate Dorothy Moon, archivist at the Zane Grey Museum, and author Thomas Pauly for background on Zane Grey. In Milford, Pennsylvania, Lori Strelecki opened files at the Pike County Historical Society, and Reverend David A. Repenning and Carolyn Krejmas introduced me to Milford United Methodist Church, where Joe and Laura were married.

Special thanks to those who helped with remote material. Mary Ellen Kollar of the Cleveland Public Library gave access to the Murdock papers and tapes. At the Giamatti Research Library at the Cooperstown Hall of Fame, Claudette Burke organized my search, and Tim Wiles offered suggestions over many baseball seasons. Deb Stephenson and the Carnegie-Stout Library, Dubuque, Iowa, facilitated access to electronic resources. At Notre Dame George Rugg provided the unedited tapes of the Lawrence Ritter interview with Joe Wood. Glenna Dunning at the Los Angeles Public Library determined the residences of Joe and Pete Wood in LA. At the Boston Public Library, Katie Devine helped identify Paul Shannon's first use of the nickname "Smoky," and Linda MacIver helped with images in Boston papers. I gained access to Joe E. Brown materials at the Margaret Herrick Library, the Academy of

Motion Picture Arts and Sciences, Beverly Hills, California, with the assistance of Kristine Krueger. Similarly, I thank Nancy Miller of the University of Pennsylvania Archives and Liz Hibbard, associate director of development at Wyoming Seminary, Kingston, Pennsylvania, for information on John F. Wood as a lawyer.

Some helped more personally. Kathleen and Harvey Brandt offered reminiscences in Ness City, as did Bob and Pauline Duda about Joe in New Haven. Bill Hickman led me to Pat Flaherty and his daughter, Frances, who was taught golf by Joe Wood. Roger Abrams sent me primary materials on the 1926–27 hearings before Judge Landis. Statistics and convincing interpretations of Joe's career by Doug Roberts, Dick Thompson, and Frank Williams were inspirational. Matt Gladman found Joe Wood–related material at Ohio University. Carl Vogt remembered Joe and John Wood in Shohola, Pennsylvania, and Roger Henn resurrected early Ouray for me. Similarly, the late John Jamieson of Greer, South Carolina, shared memories of Joe and Charlie Jamieson, John's father. I also briefly talked with Tris Speaker Scott in Hubbard, Texas.

I am obviously indebted to interviewers — particularly Bob Wood, Richard Wood, and Lee Goodwin — who kept Joe's voice alive for me, a late addition to the lineup. At the Cleveland SABR National Convention in June 2008, Bill Nowlin discussed Joe on religion, and Dave Bohmer offered valuable opinions on the Dutch Leonard accusations. Most helpful with various reproductions were Donnie Newman, Glenn Cragwall, Bruce Kocour, Ami Hartsock, and Shelia Gaines. Linda Gass performed magic in genealogical research, Shawn O'Hare was always ready with nonsense about the Mets, and Jim Burke shared his love of Smoky Joe stories. Special thanks to baseball scholars Glenn Stout, Charles Alexander, Peggy Gripshover, and Rick Huhn for vital suggestions on the middle chapters. Jane Winton of the Boston Public Library helped with images. Rob Taylor, Courtney Ochsner, Kyle Simonsen, and the staff at the University of Nebraska Press handled the manuscript expertly.

Final thanks go to my wife, Edra, and our children and grandchildren. You are my emotional home base.

SMOKY JOE WOOD

Introduction

Bart at 90 Marvel Road

History, experts, and all the instruments agree. It was an unusually pleasant day on Thursday, January 3, 1985, in New England, Connecticut, and New Haven itself. The nice suburban neighborhood of Westville was quiet as usual, except for the lines of cars on both sides of Marvel Road, in front of number 90. The house was, as it is now, unpretentious, comfortable, and thoroughly middle class, like all the homes on the surrounding streets. The front door was, and is, on the right side, facing, opening onto a small porch, which is a couple of easy steps from the small driveway.

The living room, to the left, was crammed with friends, relatives, reporters, TV cameras, and some medical people, including attending physician Leo Cooney, stationed unobtrusively. The dignitaries kept the path to the wheelchair open. Nothing was missed by the family, especially Bob, the child most committed to his father's legacy. Steve, the middle boy, had been dead for ten years. Laura, the beloved wife, had been gone for more than five, though her picture as a fiancée stood sentinel on the mantel. Her ashes were there as well. Bob's twin sister, Virginia, and her husband, Clarence, were vigilant, always looking after the honoree and this home, one of two. The other (in the family for 140 years) was in the foothills of the Poconos.

The subject of all the hoopla sat in the wheelchair, slightly slumped to his right, in glasses that didn't do much good anymore. His right arm, the one that Walter Johnson had praised above the Big Train's own, rested in his lap. The left worked better, as Red Sox fans observed when he had thrown out the first ball at the second old-timers' game at Fenway Park the previous spring — May 27, 1984. That day, sitting in a golf cart, he had lobbed the pitch southpaw. Reduced to a spectator was the right arm, which had fired fastballs past Fletcher and Crandall in the last inning of the first game of the 1912 World Series. Crandall probably didn't even see it, the aging pitcher once suggested with rare bravado. But this day failing health claimed such heroics, even as memories, along with nearly every other sign of dignity.

At this unique event in baseball history and that of Yale University, the celebrant was mostly emotionally absent, hard of hearing and visually impaired, often confused about his surroundings. It was a time when both son Bob and the legend himself admitted, neither with bitterness, that he "shouldn't have been alive." But those who crowded into that room could remember, even if he couldn't. He had been so great that the president of Yale, having heard his father's wondrous stories about the Smoke King, had been afraid to approach such an idol of Bart's beloved team, the Boston Red Sox. Truth to tell, even on this day he was a bit hesitant, still in awe of the man seated next to him. Not yet the commissioner of baseball, not yet the man who banned Pete Rose, Bart Giamatti forced a practiced smile while standing to the right of the ex–Major Leaguer. Gazing at the declaration in his hands in order to hide deeper emotions, he began the ceremony.

Under the leadership of Richard Lee, the mayor of New Haven, and the secretary of Yale, John Wilkinson, this was only the second honorary doctorate given outside the hallowed walls of Yale (the first given to composer Cole Porter in his New York apartment). With these words A. Bartlett Giamatti hooded the legendary baseball player: "Best known as 'Smoky Joe Wood,' a name synonymous with baseball, your life has paralleled the development of that noble sport. You became one of the game's greatest pitchers, one who 'threw smoke' for the Boston Red Sox, with the remarkable achievement of thirty-four games won in 1912. Lured from the professional ranks by Yale, you coached Yale baseball for twenty years, 1922–1942, beloved by your players and an inspiration to New Haven youth. Yale is proud to confer upon you the degree of Doctor of Humane Letters."[1] Miraculously, those words returned Joe from the profound absence of Alzheimer's to the drama of the moment, and he cried, his upper body shaking as he adjusted his glasses with his left hand.

Such a sadly beautiful scene demands a series of questions for even the most casual observer, then and now. The first is the most obvious. Why would Yale give an honorary degree to this high school dropout, born in Kansas City and raised even farther West, in places like Ness City, Kansas, and Ouray, Colorado? Joe Wood was no New England Yankee, and though a man of strong conviction and disarming directness, he was no intellectual like his father, John F. Wood. But Joe's baseball skills were legendary and thus familiar to anyone at Yale who followed sports in the early years of the twentieth century. And Wood's friendship with teammate Tris Speaker, from the plains of central Texas, was portrayed by Hub sportswriters as a gathering of attractive roughnecks. Though the stories were often exaggerated, Smoky Joe had observed white settlers wrestle with Indians and bandits, and Wood's father twice panned for gold, in the Yukon and the desert Southwest. Shades of the Joe Wood persona — a mad, bad, and dangerous cowboy — haunted the 1985 proceedings.

More obviously, Joe received such a prestigious award because for twenty years he successfully coached Yale baseball, grooming a half-dozen players for the Big Leagues, including his son Joe Frank Wood, who played briefly for the Boston Red Sox in 1944. But not all was sweet during the Yale years. After some soul-searching by the administration, the university decided to retain Joe's services in 1927 following accusations by a former teammate, Dutch Leonard, that Joe conspired with Tris Speaker and Ty Cobb to throw a baseball game in Detroit, just days before Chicago White Sox players fixed the 1919 World Series. Even the commissioner of baseball, Judge Landis, stood ready to travel to New

Haven in support of Joe, but Yale's final decision made intervention unnecessary. More difficult was the dismissal of Smoky Joe Wood in 1942 as part of retrenchment for World War II. Despite the support of alums, he was released with only a limited pension. That action left Joe somewhat bitter because he had retired from professional baseball at thirty-two for the security of college work. Yale and Giamatti, aware of the uneven past between the Elis and Wood, wanted a happier ending.

But why, so many years after his boyish love of this star, would A. Bartlett Giamatti, a brilliant man comfortable with making melodramatic flourishes in public, be intimidated by this frail, sick man? From his father and research, Bart knew the mystique of the man first tabbed "The Kansas Cyclone" and later "Smoky Joe." Endearing is the true story that Wood earned his first paychecks as a member of the Kansas Bloomer Girls. Within two years, having quickly journeyed from Hutchinson, Kansas, to Kansas City, eighteen-year-old Wood was pitching in the Major Leagues alongside Cy Young and Tris Speaker. At twenty-one he won twenty games for the Red Sox. At twenty-two he enjoyed one of baseball's greatest years, winning sixteen consecutive games and going 34-5. He capped the year with three wins in the 1912 World Series, the last against Christy Mathewson. Plagued by injuries, including a torn rotator cuff, Wood still threw whenever he could lift his arm, posting the lowest ERA in the American League (1.49) in his final season as a pitcher, 1915. Maybe those amazing eight years with the Sox made Bart Giamatti shy.

But there was an equally compelling second act in the story of Smoky Joe Wood, familiar to students of baseball like A. Barlett Giamatti. After a year away from baseball—in 1916 a salary dispute with the Red Sox management left him free to experiment with rehabilitating his arm—Joe Wood was sold to the Cleveland Indians. But 1917 wasn't a comeback year. The injury made it impossible for Wood to pitch. Then in 1918 a suggestion from an Indians official inspired his shift to the outfield. A naturally gifted fielder, Smoky Joe dedicated himself to hitting and made himself into an excellent everyday player. Platooning as a member of the World Champion Indians of 1920, Wood joined Babe Ruth as the only players to start a World Series at both pitcher and outfielder. In his next-to-last year in the Majors Joe hit .366, and in his final one, 1922, he had ninety-two RBI, in the top ten in the AL. By then his courage and resilience made him once again famous, with fans and sportswriters. Wood's return with the Indians, when added to his remarkable time with the Red Sox, made Joe an imposing figure for President Giamatti.

After the Yale years Smoky Joe Wood retained his residence at 90 Marvel Road, near the Giamattis. But he wasn't always at home. Contributing most to his later security was a six-year excursion to Los Angeles from 1946 until 1953, where he and his brother Pete ran a Wilshire Boulevard golf range that catered to the rich and famous. Profits and financial tips from that enterprise allowed Joe and his wife, Laura, to enjoy a comfortable lifestyle when they returned East. Eventually he sold the Pennsylvania home he had built for his bride in 1913, but he and Laura continued to use the family homestead only a few hundred yards away. Joe didn't often reconnect with baseball, except over radio and television, but he became a scratch golfer and an outdoorsman. While Bart didn't know all these details, he knew Joe lived, and thrived, well into old age.

Ironically, the hated Yankees were first to rediscover Smoky Joe Wood. In Joe's time he was known as a Highlander (later Yankee) killer. He regularly beat them when pitching, and his greatest game as a position player was at the Polo Grounds in 1918 when he hit two home runs, the second in the nineteenth inning, to give Stan Coveleski a complete game victory, 3–2. By the seventieth anniversary of Fenway Park and the advent of Red Sox old-timers games, Smoky Joe Wood's history and celebrity were recovered in Beantown as well. Bart, by then president of Yale and still a passionate fan and brilliant interpreter of baseball, was well aware of the revitalized legend of Smoky Joe Wood. A literature teacher, Giamatti read the references to Wood in baseball writing, from Ring Lardner to Eric Greenberg, from James Farrell to Roger Angell. But Bart most likely didn't know all Joe's losses, for example, the deaths of brother Pete, son Steve, and Laura. But, intuitive and sensitive, Giamatti must have felt the devotion of Virginia and Bob, twins and youngest of the Wood children, as well as oldest son, Joe Frank Wood, on that January day in 1985.

Even if he knew that Joe's wife, Laura, was from a family of Irish and Catholic background, Bart Giamatti most likely didn't investigate the Boston press's linking of Joe to the Protestant side in sectarian squabbles, displaced from European countries to the Massachusetts Commonwealth. Lacking intimacy with his hero, Bart had no way of understanding the impact of the sudden loss of Steve Wood, the charming, fun-loving, but finally self-destructive son. And then there was the onset of dementia, another drama surely unknown to Bart. Many details of Joe Wood's professional life were also lost to Bart. For example, Wood had a complex understanding of Babe Ruth, who played a major role in Joe's final at-bat in the Majors, facts accessible to only the most dogged baseball scholars. Only in tapes preserved by son Bob does Joe tell of his visits to Bonesetter Reese and an illegal chiropractor as he became desperate to heal his injury. Equally unavailable to Bart that January was Joe's influence on 1930s baseball films and the homage to granddaughter Durinda in *Field of Dreams*, released much later, four and one-half months before Bart's own death.

Also remote from Bart's experience were the everyday affairs in Shohola, Pennsylvania, where the Wood family first settled and Joe's life became a part of local folklore. The family's interest in lumbering and the religious zeal of Joe's grandfather, Bradner Wood, were distant from Bart's city ways. Even more removed were the dreams of Joe's father, John F. Wood, a brilliant lawyer, who practiced in Chicago for ten years and then took fits of gold fever in the Alaska Yukon and the Southwest. After John brought the family back to the family acres in 1910, stories of fishing trips on the Delaware River between Pete—Joe's brother—and the author Zane Grey as well as nighttime card games between Joe and Babe Ruth were whispered across the Parkers Glen area. Joe's real hunting trips with his baseball buddies from a cabin called Indian Camp refueled such myths across the woody hills of northeastern Pennsylvania.

Such stories served as background for that day at 90 Marvel Road in January 1985. By the end of the following summer, Joe Wood was dead, of old age, dementia, and dehydration doing their ugly final business. He died in Soundview Convalescent Home in West Haven, Connecticut, a suburb of New Haven not far from the Wood and Giamatti homes. The man born Howard Ellsworth Wood, who legally didn't become Joe Wood until almost 1950, was buried in a private ceremony at the Wood family cemetery near Shohola. Soon afterward Bart Giamatti exited academia for baseball, first as president of the National League and then in 1989 as the commissioner of baseball. A champion of fairness and integrity, Giamatti was responsible for banning Pete Rose. Bart knew similar charges had been leveled against Joe Wood in the Leonard/Speaker/Cobb controversy of 1926 and 1927. Although Bart didn't argue the case in public, in private he strongly advocated Joe's innocence. Despite historical documents implicating Wood in betting on baseball and Wood's admission that he was an agent for bets, Bart was a loyal defender of the idol he shared with his father.

As commissioner of baseball and a man of intense desire for justice, Giamatti, like his predecessor Judge Landis, could see the need to protect the game and preserve the heroic image of players like Speaker and Cobb . . . and Wood. For Bart Giamatti, who loved Edmund Spenser and parables of transcendent order, Joe Wood's story seemed a paradigm of talent, desire, perseverance, and courage. Consequently, the man who conferred the honorary doctorate in that early January, usually a gregarious and expansive soul, hid his deepest feelings in the business of the ceremony, knowing much of what had come before and sensitive to what was being lost. He stood a bit rigid in the presence of such a hero, carrying the sadness with a willed grace so that he could serve the man in a wheelchair beside him. Some of what follows in this biography A.

Barlett Giamatti knew well. Other facts and stories were unavailable to him and much of popular American culture. But the history recorded here was all there, directly or indirectly, that day on 90 Marvel Road, and it made Giamatti, the president of Yale University, speechless in the presence of such a bittersweet and arresting scene.

ONE

John F. and Howard E.

They talk about this being an on-the-go society today, what with
the automobile and super highways and all that, but it seems to me
that Americans were always a restless people. Back then those wagon
wheels were always grinding, and wherever you went you met people
going in the opposite direction.

—JOE WOOD, quoted in Honig, "Joe Wood"

It is a truism of psychology and a cliché of popular sports writing that
a boy's identity is traceable to his relationship with his father. That
certainly was the case with Joe Wood. Smoky Joe Wood's father, John
F. Wood, was brilliant. He was a lawyer and two-time newspaper editor, as well as a politician, gold rusher, chicken farmer, wood- and met-
alworker, even a bit of an inventor. His eccentricities even outstripped
his intelligence. A schoolteacher for one year, he eventually married
one of his students. John F. made a lot of money in land speculation.
Then he lost it all the same way. Joe's father felt no need to learn to drive
when he bought his first automobile. He named his cows after characters in Shakespeare plays. Refusing to change with the times, John kept
his wood-burning stove and shunned electricity. Such stubbornness
eventually drove his wife away. She took their daughter and retreated to rooms above the streets in a nearby town. The couple was only
reunited in the Wood family cemetery near Shohola, Pennsylvania.

Young Howard Ellsworth Wood, the second child and middle of three, loved this man, though often from afar. He proudly and repeatedly asserted that his father never lost in a juried courtroom, rubbed elbows with future governors, and was the companion of Death Valley Scotty. John F. was, the son asserted, an atheist who knew more about the Bible than the righteous Christians. Even as an old man, Joe Wood became prickly if anyone suggested there was something unfinished, dark about John F. Joe's combativeness on the baseball field grew naturally in imitation of his father. But it is equally clear that Joe's defensiveness toward John masked the hurt of a boy orphaned twice by his father's lust for gold. Joe's letters to his father in 1898 while John F. was in the Yukon are sad and a bit desperate. The absence of John F. left Joe insecure, isolated, and preoccupied with routine. Luckily, when John F. took off again three years later, leaving his family in Ouray, Colorado, Joe was diverted and calmed by his necessary chores and, most crucially, a newfound passion for baseball.

Brainy John F. Wood and his athletically gifted son descended from pioneers deeply rooted in Orange County, New York, bounded by the Delaware River on the west and the Hudson River on the east, at the southern tip of New York and just above New Jersey. Originally the land of the Minisink Indians, from the Munsee tribe of the Lenni-Lenapes, the county (one of the original twelve in New York) was named for the Prince of Orange, husband of England's Princess Mary. By the eighteenth century the Indians had been displaced by a diverse group of English, French, Dutch, German, and Swiss colonists and African slaves (emancipated between 1791 and 1827) on small, modest farms. During the War of Independence, when the British forces tried to seize the area and cut off the New England colonists from their brothers and sisters to the south, the Delaware/Hudson Valley, especially the hills at West Point, became hotly contested. Once West Point was secured, the Americans made east Orange County, New York, a strategic center of the war, a place from which they could monitor, and implicitly control, the Hudson River.

The decisive major offensive of the revolution began at Newburgh, Orange County, New York, just north of West Point. From there George Washington engineered the entrapment of the British at Yorktown, Virginia. After the war Washington and the victors returned to Orange County and established permanent headquarters that winter in New Windsor, between Newburgh and West Point.[1] Fighting for the victorious insurgents as a member of the Orange County Militia was Jonathan Wood, Joe Wood's paternal great-great-grandfather. Jonathan, the proprietor of Lapstone Tavern, and his wife, Mary Durland, were both from Orange County, where all nine of their children were born.[2] Although he didn't fight at the Battle of Minisink Ford on July 22, 1779, where the Americans were soundly defeated up the road from the future home of the Woods, Jonathan died there in 1801, when it had been renamed Greenville, in western Orange County, New York.

The key figure in the exodus of the predecessors of John F. and Howard E. from Orange County was Charles, the sixth child and fourth son of Jonathan and Mary Wood.[3] Although all six of his children with Phoebe Cole were born in New York, in 1830 Charles Wood bought land just across the Delaware River and the Pennsylvania-New York state line, in Pike County, Pennsylvania, an area the Lenni-Lenape Indians called Shohola, "Place of Peace." It had been peaceful when William Penn controlled the land, but in 1737 his heirs used a questionable 1680s agreement to seize Lenape-Delaware Indian land at the junction of the Delaware and Lehigh Rivers "as far west as a man could walk in a day and a half." After provincial secretary James Logan hired three runners, who set out on September 19, 1737, and stopped only for a night's rest, the whites gained seventy miles and over a million acres, including Shohola.[4] Most of the early colonial settlements supported travel along the Wyoming Road and the turnpike between Milford and Owego, which featured the Shohola House Inn and Tobias Hornbeck's hotel. By the nineteenth century sawmills appeared in the area, and the opening of the Delaware and Hudson Canal in 1829 led to a ferry crossing at Shohola, which certainly aided Charles Wood.

When the Wood family crossed the river, they found a heavily forested, rolling terrain dotted with lakes. After purchasing acreage from Hornbeck and David Case, Charles helped his son Reeves build a sawmill on Brush Creek. On the cleared land they established farms, where they raised cattle and chickens in addition to their crops. Reeves eventually left the area, but Charles stayed on land later inherited by Decatur Wells, Charles' son-in-law. Meanwhile, a younger brother of Reeves, Bradner (born on February 1, 1816), purchased adjoining property, on which he built a fanning mill.[5] The fourth child of Charles and Phoebe, Bradner, Joe Wood's paternal grandfather, purchased the land, which became the Wood homestead. The deed notes, "William Phillips and Archibald McCall of the City of Philadelphia Gentlemen of the one part and Bradner Wood of Milford Township Pike County Pennsylvania Farmer" exchanged a parcel of "240 acres" on the "14th day of March in the year of our Lord one thousand eight hundred and forty three" for "480 dollars."[6] On October 28 of that year, Bradner married local girl Elizabeth Middaugh and built a cabin on his property. A staunch abolitionist, Bradner profited from selling firkins of butter during the Civil War. In Joe's words, he "didn't realize automobiles would turn the country right around" and gave valuables, including Twin Lakes land, to those who shared, or pretended to share, his religious notions.

The first of the seven children of Bradner and Elizabeth was Jerusha, born July 7, 1844, who eventually married William Cortwright, from whom Joe's brother took his middle name. The third child, and the first male, was Joe's father, John F. Wood, born June 28, 1854, into a changing Shohola. Just two years earlier, on September 25, 1852, the township had been incorporated by sectioning neighboring townships: Milford, Lackawaxen, and Westfall. But during John F.'s early years, the greatest catalyst for industrialization was the Erie Railroad, especially after a suspension bridge was constructed over the Delaware River in 1855, making most points in the new township accessible. The price for such progress was horrible train wrecks: during the Civil War, on July 15, 1864, 300 soldiers were wounded or killed, and in April 1868, another

120 were killed or injured. Despite the tragedies eventually more than twenty small villages were established in Shohola, including Shohola Falls, Bee Hollow, Pond Eddy, Twin Lakes, and Woodtown.

John F. Wood, Joe's father, was the most educated of the children of Bradner and Elizabeth Wood. He attended Wyoming Seminary, whose records show him as a second-year student in 1874–75; he most likely graduated in 1877. Although family oral history says he took a law degree from the University of Pennsylvania, there are no records of his attending that institution as an undergraduate or a law student. Most likely he apprenticed with a lawyer, still a common practice in the 1870s. By John's own description, he began law in 1878. Soon afterward (local history says 1879), following the path of his uncle Samuel and Sam's adopted son, John (formerly a Williams), John F. Wood ventured west to Ness City, Kansas, a small town on the threshold where middle Kansas hills give way to the tabletop flatness of the Kansas plains.[7] Today it radiates a few blocks in every direction from the intersection of roads 96 and 283. The demographics of Ness City changed in the last twenty-five years with the discovery of oil. But signs of the Old West remain at establishments like the Cactus Inn and Trails End.

In Ness City John F. Wood practiced law, representing, as Joe remembered for Lawrence Ritter, "the Missouri Pacific and Santa Fe Railroads."[8] On January 22, 1880, John F. Wood also started a newspaper, the *Ness City Times*, calling himself "editor and proprietor" and charging $.50 per copy or $1.50 for a year's subscription, which soon included the eight-page literary journal *Monthly Nation*. In his paper, which he called the "Official Paper of Ness County," John regularly advertised his law business, land "broken and ready for crops," and "improved Homestead and Timber claims." He added a third profession to his résumé that fall as the teacher in the first Ness City school, inside the temporary courthouse.[9] Among his students was Rebecca Stephens (sometimes spelled "Stephans"), who, according to family oral history, received high marks for deportment, not attendance. She turned fourteen that fall.

John F. Wood also ran for county attorney in late October 1880 and lost by a mere eighteen votes — 262 to 244 — to George Redd. The loss brought out a bitterly competitive side, later inherited by his son Smoky Joe. In the spring of 1881, John F. attacked, declaring Redd was tied politically to a sheriff implicated in record-keeping controversies. Then, in the political wrangling over the establishment of a county seat, Ness City won easily. But folks from Sidney objected that land given for the new county buildings by Ness City's Ross Calhoun (a friend of Wood) amounted to a bribe of the voters. When sitting county attorney George Redd took up the prosecution, John F. wrote in his paper on May 5, 1881, that Redd had "succeeded in saddling several hundred dollars cost upon the already burdened county of Ness, by one of the most insane prosecutions that could be well conceived of." Two weeks later he called Redd "altogether unfit" and "a tool in the hands of men more cunning that himself." Still enraged, John F. directly challenged Redd "to prove, take back, or eternally shut up."

Finally, on February 9, 1882, the county seat was settled in favor of Ness City, with district judge Peters decreeing that there was "nothing in the donation as made by Ness City which could amount to bribery." By then John had solidified his position in the Kansas Republican Party by becoming a delegate to its Judicial Convention at Kinsley. And he continued his land speculation, offering over 1,300 acres for sale, in claims of 160 and 320 acres (with and without houses) priced from $25 to $650. That fall Wood's friend Sam A. Smith was elected county attorney, by a vote of 372 to 5, and Sam Sheaffer (also spelled "Sheffer"), who would play a major role in the life of the Wood family, became secretary of the county Republican Party and the clerk of the court for the Third District. For his part John F. Wood was named secretary of the Building Association. In a lighter vein the *Times* noted on December 14, 1882, that the drive for a city Christmas tree would include a committee on music, including Mrs. Ross Calhoun and two others, named in a Freudian typo slip as "Miss Beckie Stephens John Wood."

As the family Bible records, John Wood and "Beckie E. Stephens were married at Ellis ᴋs, evening of Dec. 25th, 1884." He was thirty, she eighteen. The Stephens family that John married into was influential in western Kansas. John Stephens was one of the first settlers in the Ness City area when he built a dugout on Sunset Lake, and over the years Stephenses acquired significant tracts of land.[10] As Joe later explained, Becky's father owned a six-section (almost four thousand acres) ranch, with between two hundred and three hundred horses; Joe rode a bicycle to the ranch for baseball games. Significant for later Irish-Protestant wrangling in Boston, which implicated Smoky Joe, Beckie claimed Irish heritage, telling Tim Murnane, in the 1913 article "It Is the Simple Life for Farmer Joe Wood in the Winter Time," that her grandfather (named McDowell) owned a country home in Ireland and her Massachusetts bloodline included Benjamin Butler, a Union general in the Civil War and a U.S. congressman from and governor of Massachusetts.

In the mid-1880s the couple remained in Ness City, Kansas, where John F. practiced law and edited his newspaper. For the most part John became a less controversial figure after marrying. But in June 1885 a Sidney, Kansas, newspaper famous for opposing alcohol reported that John F. Wood had been seen drinking whiskey. Wood responded in his paper that such charges indicated the "cussedness, deceit and hypocrisy" of publisher Joseph Langellier. Eventually the controversy faded, and John F. retreated from the limelight as the *Times* merged with the *Ness City News*, run by J. K. Barnd.[11] The following summer, in 1887, the Ness City baseball team (supported by Beckie's family) became western Kansas champs.

But John and Rebecca were focused less on baseball than on the birth of their first child, on September 7, 1887, a boy they named Harley Cortwright Wood. Although it isn't clear why or exactly when John and Becky relocated to Kansas City over the next two years, it seems likely that it was business of the lawyering kind that required the transition. Whatever the cause, they were in Kansas City, Missouri, when their second child, also a boy, was born on Friday, October 25, 1889. The Department of Health record file A 351, number 3334, says that Howard Ellsworth was born at 2512 East Eighteenth Street. The parents are listed as John H. [*sic*] Wood, whose birthplace is identified as Pennsylvania, and Becca Wood, born in Iowa.[12] Remarkably the first home of Howard was within two blocks of where he would play in 1908, the year he was called up to the Boston Red Sox.

Within three years the young family moved again. This time John F. took them to Chicago, where he established himself as a lawyer and reconnected with Rebecca's brother-in-law, Samuel Sheffer, who later claimed to have taught Joe to pitch on the South Side of the city. The *Chicago Tribune* notes the filing in superior court of a ten-thousand-dollar case between Paul Wolfom and Max Monhehner, on March 23, 1892, with John F. Wood as an attorney. And Samuel A. Sheffer is listed in the 1890 census as a "driver" who lived at 3658 State Street. Also a John Wood is noted as working at 3900 State and living at 5349 Dearborn. Although not definitive these details suggest Joe correctly remembered that his father had an office on State Street, where Joe would meet John F. for ice cream. It also seems true, as Sheffer claimed, that Smoky Joe Wood first played baseball in the Windy City.[13]

While in Chicago the Wood family attended the World's Columbian Exhibition (commonly called the Chicago World's Fair). Named in honor of Christopher Columbus and located on 686 acres south of downtown, the exhibition opened on May 1, 1893, and entertained over 21 million visitors before it closed on October 30. Although it ostensibly celebrated world cultures, the exhibition sang the praises of technological progress, including electric lights, ballooning, and the Yerkes telescope. Most impressive was a Ferris wheel, 264 feet high, which dominated the skyline. The main entrance was called the Midway Plaisance, stretching for a mile from Jackson Park to Washington Park and including a water-driven railway. It is probably along this pathway, congested with seedy characters, from belly dancers to pickpockets, that John F. and Rebecca met clowns Joey and Petey, whose antics recalled their rambunctious boys, at the time aged six and three. When the couple returned home, they rechristened Howard as Joe and Harley as Pete, names that took root as if they were the originals.[14]

Next to the Columbian Exposition was the Wild West Show of Wild Bill Cody, where the parents and boys welcomed Rebecca's brother, Rattlesnake Pete, one of nine riders in the Great 1,000-Mile Cowboy Race. Wearing a headband of rattlesnake rattles, Stephens rode from Chadron, Nebraska, in pursuit of first prizes: two hundred dollars, a Montgomery Ward saddle, and a Colt pistol. Forty miles from Sioux City, Iowa, one of Pete's horses developed colic, and Rattlesnake started spitting up blood. But he continued by riding another horse, General Grant, while brandishing a whiskey bottle for the cough. When he finished on Tuesday, June 27, 1893, in front of ten thousand spectators, Pete claimed the winner had cheated. But, alas, Rattlesnake was declared fourth by Cody.[15]

All seemed well as the family became more settled, establishing domestic rituals in Chicago that included clowning, ice cream, and baseball, as Joe told Lee Goodwin, "out on the lots there." Then, just before the end of the decade and the century, John F. Wood caught his first case of gold fever. Never a man to let his family stand in the way, he took his wife and children back to the family homestead near Shohola, Pennsylvania, and then headed for Alaska and the Yukon. Though the home itself hadn't changed much since John left for Kansas twenty years earlier, the surrounding area had begun to embrace commerce. In 1879 Chauncy Thomas, who had constructed the Shohola suspension bridge, the Shohola Glen Hotel, and the Shohola depot on the Erie Railroad, started planning an amusement park. When Thomas died in 1882, the property was purchased by John Fletcher Kilgour, who in 1886 added the Shohola Glen Switchback Gravity Railroad to facilitate passage to the new Shohola Glen Amusement Park, which attracted the affluent from New Jersey and New York. Kilgour also mined bluestone, earning the title of "Blue Stone King" and modifying the demographics of Shohola.

For the young Wood boys, the area was no longer primarily a place for farming and logging. As Joe later told his grandson Richard, most everyone had become stonecutters, some walking fifteen miles round-trip to jobs. But the old Wood homestead remained primitive, with just a wood-burning stove and no indoor water. To get to school Pete and Joe walked two miles along a hard-top road to Walker Lake, a trip of half to three-quarters of an hour. When snow rose above their knees, Pete and Joe would ride a bobsled, a single-horse cutter for six to eight passengers, also used to pick up their grandmother in nearby Parkers Glen or retrieve flour from a gristmill in Milford, Pennsylvania, twelve miles to the south.[16] More thrilling was the twenty-mile mountain express train ride to Port Jervis, New York. Though a skilled hunter as an adult, when given his first gun in these years, Joe felt lost about how and where to use it.

Meanwhile, as John F. Wood's journal records, he missed his family but never let an adventure pass him by. His notes begin on March 16, 1898, when he "Set Sail from Seattle on schooner Lily and Maud." By April 8 his schooner had anchored at Alert Bay, Cormorant Island, British Columbia, where the next evening, Easter eve, he attended church with "3 whites & 34 indians" and heard scripture in Siwash, the Indian language. Smitten by Hope Island, on the fifteenth John F. "Sold interest in Schooner for $130 & left party" to stay at a cabin there and three days later traveled in an Indian chief's canoe to Galiano Island, where he spent a "day & nite in wigwam with 12 indians." The next day he was "Picked up by riverboat Courser," which the following day anchored at Port Rupert, British Columbia.

Taking a few days in Port Rupert, John F. Wood had time to catch up on his mail, including a letter from Joe, with the inside address "Parkers Glen, February 16, 1898." A dutiful son, the boy reported, "Manuel may [*sic*] is going to make a new handle for my axe," and explained why he hadn't worked the woodpile: "It is awful cold here to-day it is to [*sic*] cold to go out and chop wood to-day." Not wanting to appear a slacker, Howard/Joe wanted John to know that he had "washed the dishes to-day." Though just nine, he was well aware of issues with the hired help, noting to his father, "Butcher got drunk to [*sic*] times since you have gone." Imagining his father concerned over his mother's health,

Joe declared, "Grandma [about to turn eighty] is better now." Caretaker Joe reminded him: "Grandma says the next time you write you must write to her she said she would be very anxious to hear from you." It is signed "Howard E. Wood."

After a week in Port Rupert to rest and write his family, on April 27, 1898, Joe's father crossed into Alaska. He stopped at Ketchikan for water on the twenty-eighth and then continued to Wrangell Island, where he boarded the steamer *Alki*, out of San Francisco. After arriving in Juneau, at 2:00 a.m., on May 2, 1898, John ate a "good dinner for 25 cents," boarded a tug to Dyea, and quickly moved on to Skagway, the popular staging point for gold seekers. After three days on the summit trail, he reached Bennett, the launching place, on May 7. In the company of nearly ten thousand residents, mostly in tents, John F. Wood reported on May 10 that the snow was still five feet deep. With no railroad links completed yet, he took two weeks to build a sailboat. As soon as the ice broke, he was sailing on Lake Linderman, the river to Lake Bennett, and then Lake Tagish on June 7, where the trees and flowers bloomed but mosquitoes had become "a problem."

The hard prospecting began when John F. passed customs at the foot of Lake Tagish, entered the Yukon Territory on June 8, 1898, and "camped halfway down 5-Mile River." In less than a week, he moved down Marsh Lake and Twenty-Five Mile River, camped at the head of Miles Canyon, passed through Whitehorse, and headed northwest. After crossing Lake Labarge, John tested for gold at the mouth of the Teslin River and staked a claim at Lake Creek on June 19. Two days later he passed through Little Salmon Lake and Five Finger Rapids. He prospected below the Tatchum River rapids and on the south branch of Lake Tatchum, then zeroed in on Dawson, where he expected "letters from wife and boys." But he diverted again, turning west to Selwyn Creek, then up to Stewart River and the mouth of Indian Creek, where he set up base camp on July 3, 1898. Unable to celebrate the Fourth of July because they "could not afford to waste any ammunition," for the next three weeks Wood prospected south of Dawson, in Irene Gulch,

Squaw Creek, Nine Mile Creek, and Nugget Gulch. On the fifteenth of July, he was mesmerized by "French Gulch with its fabulously rich hill claim." After unsuccessful prospecting July 16–21 "around French Gulch," John made Dawson on the twenty-second at "5:30 a.m."

In Dawson he had time to receive the expected letters, including surviving notes from Howard. Though not dated, they were written near the end of the school year, following reports that Howard E. (alias Joe) was doing well, especially in arithmetic and spelling. In addition to casting doubts on the accuracy of the spelling scores, the boy's words indicate that his anxiety over money had increased that spring. Joe barely got beyond the direct address when finances jumped into his fearful head: "Dear old Father Will you send me sume [*sic*] money have you any money? Howard Wood." In another note he was calmer; aware of his father's respect for learning, Joe reported, "Dear pa, I thought I would write you a few lines tonight before I go to bed. I got put up in school and Mary is going to get me a knife for passing." Controlling his sibling rivalry, he added simply, "Pete got put down," before noting, "I went to swimming pool with Marshall Myers."

By the end of July, John F. had decided to build a cabin "near Dawson." But the Yukon diarrhea put him down for two weeks. Finally, on August 15 and 16 he began cutting logs and "fording down river" "to cabin site." He laid the foundation on August 22, had built the walls and rafters by September 2, and added a roof of dirt and moss on September 5, 1898. His final push began on September 12, when he started up the Klondike River to the mouth of Rock Creek ("50 miles into the wilderness primeval") in search of meat. But on October 2, when he declared, "Hunt ended in failure," the final chapter was predetermined. He "Sold rifle and ammunition for $22" and headed back to Dawson, where he witnessed the famous fire on October 14: "Fire broke out in Green Tree Saloon about 6 this a.m. and before it could be stopped, burned the whole block." (Lost were the post office, the Worden and Vancouver hotels, the Empire Bakery, and the New England Saloon.) The next day John F. Wood began work at the Chicago Hotel for lodging and $7.00 a day, until October 21. By November he had given up and sold the cabin for $77.50.

When John F. finally trudged back from Alaska to reconnect with his young boys, he had stories to tell. Most memorable to young Joe was John F.'s bout with Yukon diarrhea and his thirty-miles-per-day exit with legs covered up to the knees in gunny sacks for protection against snow and icy water. As John F. reported, and Joe explained in later tapes, those leggings would "save his life." But the reunion was only brief. As the new century began, John F. Wood loaded up the family and headed for Colorado, via (once again) Ness City, Kansas. At times Joe later gave material for a romantic view of this journey, portraying himself as riding high on a prairie schooner, already deeply in love with baseball, a ten-year-old exhibiting his ball glove on the front seat to, in his words, "show anybody who was interested where he wanted to go."[17] But the trip from Kansas, across Colorado, and into Ouray was much more complicated.

In his interview with grandson Richard Wood, Joe reported that they picked up Becca's youngest sister, Allie, and her husband, Doc Barker, along with a Ruth Barker Veranda, Doc's sister, in Kansas City.[18] After they had negotiated the 350 miles from Ness City to Denver, the exciting part began when the party boarded prairie schooners, drawn by two horses, for the trip to southwest Colorado. From Denver they would have followed one of two passages. To the south they might have turned west at the village of Symes, below Mount Evans and above the Tarryall Mountains, through Coal Branch Junction to Fairplay, then negotiating Mount Sheridan, through Buena Vista to the south, and then on to Leadville. The northern route to Leadville passed through Golden, south of the Boulder Pass and Bald Mountain, turning south through the Loveland Pass to Dillon, and then almost directly south through the Tennessee Pass to Leadville.

Then they had another choice. They might have followed the southern, more direct route south of Red Table Mountain above Aspen, turning back north at Emma to Glenwood Springs. Or they could also have

journeyed north out of Leadville, through the Mountain of the Holy
Cross and Redcliff, where they would have angled westward below the
Red and White Mountains and then west to Glenwood Springs. From
there they followed the main highway down. West below The Great Hog
Back through Rifle and Balzac, they turned to the southwest, along the
Grand River (not the Colorado until 1921) to Grand Junction. Then it
was southeastward along the Gunnison River to Delta, sixty miles north
of Ouray, where the Doc Barker party exited to start farming. John F.
and his family continued along the Uncompahgre River on to Dallas,
Colorado, which Joe remembered being "5 or 10 miles from Ouray"
(actually almost thirteen miles).[19]

They stayed the winter there in a place Joe called "a shack," actually
a small house that was part of the hastily reconstructed ranch of David
Wood (not a relative of John and Joe).[20] It was on this property that the
John F. Wood family ushered in the new century, with John and Pete
working the hay crop for their room and board. When the spring arrived, John F. and family moved into town. Ouray, surrounded on three
sides by the San Juan Mountain range (east of Telluride and north of
Silverton), in 1900 was a rough and exciting town. In *The Glory of Their
Times*, Joe explains, Ouray was "in the southwestern part of Colorado,
not far from places with names like Lizard Head Pass and Slumgullion
Gulch. And every day I'd see these big stage coaches go by, drawn by
six horses, two guards sitting up there with rifles, guarding the gold
shipment coming down from the mines."[21] Although there were barely two thousand people there, its frontier ruggedness supported fifteen
to twenty saloons, wide-open gambling, and whorehouses with main
attractions Stringbean Annie and Loco Lil.[22] Declaring his total property one clock valued at eighteen dollars, John F. Wood found work at
the Ashenfelter Livery, where he honed skills he would use later back
in Pennsylvania.[23]

But Alaska hadn't cured John F. Wood's itch for adventure and riches.
Joe's father again rushed for gold—this time in the deserts of Nevada
and California. Partially financing his trip by selling his home back in

Ness City, he left the family in a safe Ouray house, just up the hill to the east of the main street, the third house behind 342 Seventh Avenue (no longer in existence). John had an amazingly creative justification for his new venture. He claimed an Ouray doctor told him that to recover feeling in his legs, injured by frostbite in the escape from the Yukon, he needed to go barefoot in sand for long periods. The prescription was obvious to Joe's dad: walk the deserts of the Southwest. Although there is no logbook of this trip, John claimed that he traveled with Death Valley Scotty, described by Wood as entering cities with money but never leaving with any. Unlike Walter Scott, John periodically earned money from legitimate sources, usually lawyering, so eventually he and Death Valley Scotty parted ways. The result of this trip was the same: no luck, gold, or security for his family.

Those years, 1901–3, were tough in Ouray. In Joe's words, "We did everything we could do to make a dime or a quarter, and we got by with what he [John F.] could send us."[24] As Joe remembered, Harley (Pete) went "in cahoots with George Holmes with a laundry service, where they shipped laundry in a basket out to Denver, and it was done there and shipped back—they then would collect." He also washed dishes at the Bird Mine and eventually drove rigs to Silverton for travelers at three dollars a trip.[25] In another scheme Pete brought burros from Ridgway to sell in Ouray. Joe picked raspberries, which he sold to drugstores at one dollar a bucket, carried "special deliveries for the post office, 10 cents a piece after school," and worked "in a butcher shop for $4.00 a week"—as he said, "anything I could to turn over a little money, here and there," including selling popcorn and shining shoes. The boys even scavenged "up and down the alleys before school in the morning, picking up bottles [they] could sell, and old copper and brass and rubber."[26] And Joe at twelve made five to seven dollars with the baseball team.

As Joyce Jorgensen summarized years later, "When [Joe's] father returned to Ouray after a couple of years' fruitless search for gold in the desert country, he resumed the practice of law." Reflecting the younger son's worship, as well as the influence of family stories, Joe proudly declared, "He [John F.] put in all his days then as a criminal lawyer, and he never lost a case in front of a jury in those years. A judge at that time was Judge Henry Rathmell, who was rather a tricky bird as a judge, and my Dad kind of showed him up, sometimes."[27] Beginning in 1903, when John F. Wood decided to start another newspaper, Joe set type for his father and other papers, the *Ouray Herald* and the *Plaindealer*, sometimes skipping school to do so. Strategically John F. Wood established his new business across from the city hall and the library, named after Camp Bird Mine owner Thomas Walsh. Joe's summary is accurate: "Dad started the paper himself, got the press — and the fellow who made up the paper and did the job work at the time was named Grant Turner."[28]

John F. called his Ouray paper the *Times*, though there had already been a paper called the *Ouray Times*, first published in 1887. As Wood made clear in the first issue, on Thursday, May 21, 1903, this version would be controlled by a single individual; it headlined "Published and Edited by John F. Wood." In a long editorial Joe's father explained that this was his second venture in publishing, following "a calling" "most remote" from his "intention." He then explained that after taking his law degree in Pennsylvania in 1878, he had traveled to Kansas to practice law, but "within a year, besides attending" to "professional business" he found himself "in charge of a county newspaper" because "the people of the town" had selected him "to own, operate and control it." As John remembered, he "for seven years labored for the upbuilding of the Ness City Times and the community in which it circulated." In his humble estimation, his Ness City "newspaper grew and prospered" under his "management."

Continuing, John F. declared his motives were not just the improvement of the writing and the uplift of his Colorado town. With the support of the "Citizens party Committee," he intended to oppose boss politics in Ouray. In an obvious reference to the other two papers, he planned to establish "a newspaper to be run without fear or favor, backed by sufficient courage to advocate what it conceived to be true and right and to denounce what it believed to be wrong, and any and all interests to the contrary notwithstanding." After bragging that there would be "not a better equipped newspaper and job office in Colorado, west of the Continental Divide, than [the *Ouray Times*]," John F. Wood got into politics. He claimed the Republican reformist tradition: the paper "will be Republican in politics, because the doctrines and policies of the Republican Party are more in harmony with our own notions than those of any other party. We will stand true to that party so long as, in our humble judgment, it stands true to the best interests of this great Nation." Remarkably, after five years of risking his life and his family's well-being and (according to Joe) gambling heavily himself, John then took a righteous stand against gaming.

Less than a week after the first issue of the *Ouray Times*, gambling was banned in the city, on May 26, 1903. Wood immediately declared victory, printing as the headline for Thursday, June 11, 1903, "The Games Ended!" In John F.'s words, "Part of the gambling dens removed their gaming paraphernalia last Saturday at noon. At noon Monday the edict went forth that the police would seize and destroy gaming devices to be found in the city. Thus Ouray is rid of the greatest evil that ever afflicted her people." Reveling in the moment, John F. expressed concern about gambling's effect on the disadvantaged, who were more likely to become addicted: "There is no degradation so degrading, no humiliation so humiliating, no slavery so servile as that into which public gambling hurls its victims." After attacking the other newspapers for public stands that contradicted their private dealings, Wood declared on Thursday, July 23, 1903, "Gambling has practically ceased both in Ridgway and Ouray. In Ridgway its passing was comparatively tranquil and peaceful. In Ouray it died hard and with many struggles accompanied by much agony."

Unfortunately, the next month, August, was cruel to labor and its Ouray supporter, John F. Wood. The battle lines between owners and workers were drawn in Idaho Springs, thirty miles west of Denver, where workers had struck for an eight-hour day. Governor James H. Peabody exacerbated conditions by banning the unions, which were reinstated by a district judge. And then a supporter of the workers blew up the Sun and Moon Mill there. In the August 6 edition of his paper, Wood expressed no "sympathy for the dastard who did [the bombing], or with his advisers, if he had any." But in Wood's opinion the response of authorities—the wholesale arrest, without cause, of citizens who supported labor—was equally despicable. Two weeks later, on August 20, 1903, the editor developed his position: "Until the methods of handling capital and carrying on gigantic industrial enterprise in this country are radically changed, it may as well be set down as a fact that the labor organization is here to stay." Attempts to discredit unions drive a wedge between "capital and labor" when "friendly relations" are "necessary to the prosperity and happiness of both."

For John F. Wood these principles had obvious application to Ouray, where local workers were considering striking in sympathy for issues "back East." He felt "self-serving leaders" and "a short sighted press" led to irresponsible "independence" among capitalists and reactive "hostility" by labor. Wood's alternative: recognize the unions and negotiate peace. His approach was both logical and philosophical, he said, because (1) the "organization [of unions was] inevitable," and (2) since "Colorado's population [was] largely made up of wage earners, Colorado's employers of labor must deal with labor Unions." Locally, the "owners and operators of Mines, Mills and Smelters" must "treat with the Western Federation of Miners for an adjustment of existing differences." Wood predicted a peaceful conclusion if both sides proceeded without "arrogance." On August 27, 1903, John F. Wood argued that since there was "a real grievance" against "eastern smelter interests," local workers would be "less than true men" if they did not follow the union, which he trusted would take a reasonable position.[29]

As politics started to turn against his views and the paper began to lose its urgency, John F. Wood sold an interest in the *Times* to Amel Lundberg on September 5, 1903, but Joe's father and Grant Turner apparently stayed involved for a few more months. In the meantime the paper didn't totally ignore local news. In a lighter moment John F. noted a request by the Women's Christian Temperance Union for advertising space in his paper. Despite being an atheist, Wood said he was glad to accommodate them, in the spirit of equality, but he couldn't avoid the sly comment that the Bible says wine might be good for indigestion. (Homemade wine was also regularly advertised in the *Ouray Times*.) In the Local Mention section of the *Times*, baseball (which was organized and supported by Wood's partner, John Barnett) was portrayed as an expression of civic pride and economic progress. The *Ouray Times* happily encouraged "a base ball club" because "this harmless sport" would "make possible many gala days in this and adjoining towns the coming summer, with the profit to the business of the town."

Baseball in Colorado had not always been so easily tied to festival and financial packages. Initially, "most adults were too busy pursuing gold nuggets to have much interest in chasing bouncing baseballs." Free time "was dominated by more earthy pursuits: drinking, gambling and whoring," "horse racing, cockfights, boxing, foot races, billiard and ten pins."[30] Nevertheless, organized baseball was established in Colorado by the Civil War, in imitation of eastern sport for gentlemen who "dressed in neat uniforms and engaged in only mildly competitive, genteel 'matches.'" Such civil ideals were most valued in Denver, where in March 1862 the Colorado Baseball Club was organized.[31] The Civil War initially reduced the number of players, but eventually returning veterans declared that "baseball had been very popular in the army camps, where soldiers often had to entertain themselves for weeks at a time between vicious battles. In friendly competition with easterners, they practiced some of the emerging fine points of the game, and they also learned that in some eastern cities the game was being taken more seriously, even becoming commercialized." Indicative of the revived interest, the Colorado Baseball Club was reestablished in February 1866 as the Young Bachelors Baseball Club of Denver.[32]

In Colorado, as elsewhere, the game was interpreted as an invigorating activity in support of community standards. The Young Bachelors believed it inspired "that healthy tone and vivacity to the physical system, so necessary to the perfect working of the mental." Better yet, baseball inspired "an open, honest manhood . . . without that hypocritical trade and dicker spirit." It was, simply, "a matter of hygiene."[33] Before the year was out, the club was playing other teams from the territory, ten years before Colorado became a state. The following year there was even a championship between the Bachelor's Club and the victorious Rocky Mountain Club, with the final score 79–43.[34] During the 1870s Colorado baseball welcomed gamblers and professional players, known to play to win and throw curve balls, without warning or guilt.[35] Driven by the nostalgia for *their* game, between 1877 and 1881 gentlemen incorporated the Denver Brown Stockings, Queen City Baseball Club, Eclipses, Metropolitans, and Athletics. More influentially, in 1882 moneyed people established the Denver Baseball Association and the Colorado Baseball League.[36] Inspired by the success of the Leadville Blues, Denver initiated the Denver Baseball and Athletic Association, eventually calling their team the Athletics and featuring David E. Rowe, who played in the National League both before and after his time in Denver.[37]

By the mid-1880s professional baseball had arrived in Colorado with the Rocky Mountain League, which featured recruited players and played exhibitions against such distant teams as the St. Joseph Reds, the St. Louis Enterprise, and the Chicago White Stockings (later the Cubs), with as many as four thousand in attendance.[38] Among the players was George "White Wings" Tebeau, who two years later played for the Cincinnati Red Stockings of the Major League American Association (and would later own the Kansas City Blues when Joe played for them in 1908). Looking for more financial stability and a wider representation, the Rocky Mountain League morphed into the Western League in 1886. But the national depression in the 1890s was especially hard on silver economies like Colorado, and bicycling became a serious competitor of baseball.[39] The turnaround came in 1900, when Tebeau resurrected a Denver team in the Western League. Called variously the Grizzlies, Cubs, Teddy Bears, and Bears, it featured Joe Tinker, "Kid" Mohler, Henry Schmidt, and Charles "Babe" Adams.[40]

More than three hundred miles from Denver, Ouray didn't sponsor clubs "for the purpose of making a profit. Players received no salaries [and] were local men who held other regular employment."[41] But their history was almost as long as Denver's: "Baseball had arrived almost on the heels of the first prospectors who ventured into the towering, craggy San Juan Mountains back in the 1870s. The little mining camps, nestled in canyons and valleys, wished to give visitors the impression of being settled communities with many of the refinements and entertainments they had known at home. They also wanted to build community pride for all."[42] By the beginning of the twentieth century, such villages were implicated in the emerging belief that baseball captured "many of the finest traditional American qualities," "competitiveness, honesty, patience, respect for authority, and rugged individualism" developed "on the frontier over many generations."[43] Thus Ouray offered a double dose of myth. Like a natural ore those values remained in frontier life. They also came secondhand in the baseball baggage carried by the easterners encountering wilderness for the first time.

But as Joe Wood himself later clarified, "community pride" could hide less-than-refined impulses. What Joe said, in words shaped by Lawrence Ritter, about games in Kansas also applied to the more contentious battles in the Rocky Mountains: "The smaller the town the more important their ball club was. Boy, if you beat a bigger town they'd practically hand you the key to the city. And if you lost a game by making an error in the ninth or something like that, well, the best thing to do was just pack your grip and hit the road, 'cause they'd never let you forget it."[44] In places like Ouray the "teams carried, with their bats, the town's honor," followed by a "lot of local money," which was "bet on them, too."[45] Baseball thus had a complex identity in Ouray. For those nostalgic for past joys, it became a rural idyll. For others it became the occasion for raw competition, fueled by pioneer aggressiveness.

As Joe later described it, in the previous years, while he wandered the streets longing for the return of his father, he had been mostly a mascot for the Ouray team. In 1903, the year his father was resurrecting the *Ouray Times*, the game had evolved into something approaching a job for the young Wood, as it was the following summer, when Joe was nearing fifteen years of age. But it was in 1905, the last year the Wood family lived in Ouray, that Joe first hit stride as a baseball player even though he was still not sixteen. That year "the Ouray boys had the easiest times with those 'cornhusker' nines from the farm country north of them — Olathe, Montrose, and Grand Junction. They had the most trouble, losing four out of five games, with Silverton, a team sponsored by the noted politician and saloonkeeper, Jack Slattery."[46] On the Ouray team Joe Wood played shortstop, third base, and outfield, but not pitcher, almost always against much older players.

Early in the season Joe was a marginal player on a team that, as reported in the *Plaindealer*, struggled. When Montrose won on Sunday, May 14, 1905, by a score of 16 to 5, there were rumors that Ouray had thrown the game. In the May 28 rematch, the whiny chronicler noted that the only break in the monotony came when "a fierce snow storm ensued and kept up for two hours." Unfortunately for the locals the snow quickly melted, and Ouray lost again, 5–4. When Ouray finally won a game, on June 4, there was almost nothing to report except "Peeping Toms" getting to watch the game free from a hillside. Still no Joe Wood sighting. That came on Sunday, June 11, 1905, when Ouray fell again, this time 28–18 to Hotchkiss. But the *Plaindealer* found hope in the play of "Young Joe Wood," "the only one who [did] not deserve a good roast. . . . He did fine, but could not win the game single handed." The rest of the Ouray nine played a game that would "go down in base-ball history as one of the rankest travesties on an inflicted public." On June 25, in a game won 16–5 over Montrose, "'Little' Joe Woods [*sic*] played a good game on short — his throwing to bases was perfect. Joe also drove a hot one through centre [*sic*] field for a home run."

On July 7, 1905, the *Plaindealer* noted that in a Fourth of July game

Wood batted seventh at an unnamed position, going 1 for 4 while scoring two runs. The writer declared Joe "the 16 year old wonder of the San Juan" (though he was only fifteen) whose performance "endeared him to the hearts of every 'fan.'" On Sunday, July 23, he played left field, where he threw out a runner at home and doubled against Silverton. As the *Ouray Herald* explained, "Our little man Woods came to the front and made the hit" that drove in Ouray's first run in a two-out, ninth-inning rally. He also scored the second run, but Ouray fell short and lost 3–2. The August 4 report from the *Herald* praised him for "catching a long fly." He was in the outfield again, according to the *Plaindealer*, on August 20 and 27, and made a good catch as he joined Pete in "the brotherly act in Ouray's outfield," where "they [could] sure eat 'em up." The *Herald* apologized for Joe's error on Labor Day, September 4, 1905, speculating that he was "thinking of the new home in Kansas and the girl he left behind." Maybe that was the same malady that got him the "collar," 0 for 7, in his last two games. He is not mentioned in the final game the next day, made noteworthy by a $250 bet between managers of the Ouray and Denver teams.[47]

Today there is still a park in Ouray where Smoky Joe Wood played his games. A ball field remains as well, on the only large flat grounds in the town. As longtime resident Roger Henn clarifies, home plate then was deeper into the southwest corner, with a grandstand that would seat about one hundred people made from remnants of an old lumberyard. Instead of the 1905 watery enclosure made from a quarry, with a fountain and goldfish in it, Ouray now has a pool, opened on July 4, 1927, sporting a water slide and other updates. Baseball is still played, and swimming remains big, along with basketball, skating, and volleyball. The Fourth of July celebration is, as in Joe's time, a major event at what has become Fellin Park. But there is a significant change: the ballpark is Smoky Joe Wood Field, so dedicated in May 2007.

As the 1905 summer came to an end and the John F. Wood family prepared to return to Ness City, Kansas, Joe Wood filed away images that enlivened later interviews. As Duane Smith has explained, "Wood later remembered that, after a winning game, fans would push money through the backstop for the players, and they would get free drinks at the saloons. Being too young to drink, Joe would get a meal at one of the restaurants." Joe added: "Chase and Hebler had a saloon and gave me a meal ticket at the restaurant—at so much a game according to the gate receipts." Ouray was where Joe first played pool. Hiram Herr, Joe explained, "started up a pool and beer room" where Joe "learned to play pool . . . so well Hi let" him "play for the house." When six-horse teams of big buck horses, with armed men atop, brought gold bullion down from the mine, the town got, in Joe's words, "wild and wooly." But only on weekends, when the miners sought "hooch" and the town got "boisterous." Once it even snowed on a Fourth of July up at Camp Bird Mine.[48]

Joe preferred discussing such literal details about Ouray. But in rare moments he left hints of his emotional life. Off-balance from poverty and the wanderlust of his father, Joe Wood often walked the streets of Ouray feeling orphaned. In his words he was "a little snot-nosed kid" who "knew who all the people were, but they didn't know" him. Such invisibility freed him to observe the condescension of the wealthy, as when rich Thomas Walsh "along with his daughter, Evalyn [who would later own the Hope Diamond], would throw out nickels and dimes to the kids who would follow their rig up and down the street."[49] Not surprisingly the catalyst for his transition from isolated critic to engaged citizen was baseball. In 1940, during the Wood family's last grand tour of the West, Smoky Joe vividly recalled "the feeling of importance" he got when he received "$5 for a game and walked with the rest of the team to eat a meal furnished by Barney at the Office Café."[50] The game allowed Joe to earn his share, join a surrogate family, and be fed, both physically and emotionally. No wonder years later Smoky Joe Wood insisted that he would have played baseball for nothing. In Ouray, Colorado, the game at times became his best home.

During his formative years Joe knew firsthand—from his father—the American restlessness he described in the epigraph of this chapter. As difficult as it was for Joe when John F. set off for Nevada and California with Death Valley Scotty and others, at least it was the last wild hare of the father. The remove of the Wood family to Ouray would be as far west as they would locate. When times got tough, the boys rose to the need, working at many jobs essential to their mother's well-being and the family finances. Joe, always loyal to his father (as he would later be to Tris Speaker and Ty Cobb), didn't get angry or rebel. Instead he admired John F.'s risk taking and filled the void with baseball. Joe's success on the town team offered acceptance and prestige while his father roamed the Southwest, trying to get rich quick. Although not yet smoking on the mound, Howard E. (most often called "little Joe") proved himself as a boy among men. The effect of this drama, centered on his relationship with John F., would be revealed as the Wood family packed up to move back eastward.

TWO

Bloomer Girl and Minor Leaguer

I t is impossible to know exactly why the Woods returned from Ouray. The boys were probably not included in decisions about such relocation. And even if he knew the reasons, Smoky Joe Wood rarely revealed such personal details. But two realities seem clear. Rebecca had more familiar connections in Ness City (the home of her extended family) than she ever had in Colorado. Even the sister who accompanied them westward remained a good distance from Ouray in times of limited travel and finances. Whether or not Becca expressed unhappiness over John's absence, he took flight before she established firm grounding in the San Juan Mountains. For his part John was unhappy with the political climate, in Colorado and nationally, so essential to his contentment. With unions not doing well after 1904, John F. went into default mode and headed back to Kansas to practice law (advertising with Harry D. Stidger for work "in the Supreme and Inferior Courts of the State").

Before the snows arrived in 1905, the Wood family was back in Ness City, their once and future home, designed (consciously or not) to bring stability to the family. Both Alaska and the desert were finally behind John, and his wife would again be surrounded by comforting faces. There were unforeseen changes for the Woods, but they were mostly for the good. Always a talented athlete, hard-working, and ambitious, Pete soon enrolled at the University of Kansas at Lawrence. Called Harley in the more formal surroundings of college, he joined the Sigma Chi social fraternity at KU and Phi Delta Phi, a law fraternity. Once settled, he joined the football and baseball teams. Pete played right guard and tackle on the 9-0 (Missouri Valley Conference Champion) 1908 University of Kansas football team (though injuries to his shoulder and knee limited his play) and centerfield on the baseball diamond in 1909 (as H. C. Wood). More immediately, sixteen years after the birth of Joe, Rebecca Stephens Wood became pregnant again. On September 6, 1906, Zoë Alice Wood (who hated being called "Zozie" or "Zozo") was born.

Meanwhile, dramatic changes were afoot for their second child. A veteran of town ball at fifteen, Joe easily made the transition to the Ness City team, which played competitions with nearby towns (especially to the north). In Joe's words, during both 1905 and 1906, "We'd play all the surrounding Kansas towns, like High Point, Ransom, Ellis, Bazine, Wa Keeney, Scott City—nearby places like that." Even though Ness City was a "little hick town of about 1,000 people," its residents "thought a lot of their baseball in those days. I used to ride from Ness City to a town called Beeler, about sixteen miles, pitch a ball game, then ride a bicycle back. I'd get $2.50 if I lost; $5.00 if I won" in front of "quite a few sports fans," except on a "working day."[1] As in Colorado, Ness City games often were the centerpiece of weekend festivals and social and patriotic affairs.

But baseball could also be a diversion, designed as novelty rather than territorial battle. One such game in Ness City late that summer became part of baseball lore: "In Ness City no game was more eagerly anticipated than a game advertised in the *Ness County News* to be played August 27, 1906, at 3:00 p.m. sharp between the Ness City nine and the barnstorming Kansas City Bloomer Girls. Owned and managed by Logan Galbreath, the Bloomer Girls team would travel from town to town playing men's teams while unbeknownst to most, the Bloomer Girls would have three or four young men dressed in wigs playing on their side."[2] Though Joe recalled playing shortstop that day, not pitching, Ness City won 23–3 before an unusually large crowd. Even the Ness City paper on September 2, 1906, tabbed the game disappointingly lopsided. At least it made $150 in gate receipts, 75 percent going to the Bloomer team.

Despite their slapstick setup, such games were essential to the growth of women's baseball. Soon after female teams formed at women's colleges like Vassar and Smith, the contests deteriorated into oddities; by the 1870s spectators and reporters were more interested in the clothes or comedy than the competition. The rise of the Bloomer Girls in the 1890s, while still identified popularly with their outfits, encouraged some reformist ideals championed by Adelaide Jenks Bloomer back in the 1850s. Not part of organized leagues, teams barnstormed, with men playing on the squads: "By the late 1890s bloomer teams were popping up throughout the country. There were the Boston Bloomer Girls, Chicago Bloomer Girls, Star Bloomers, and All-Star Bloomers, as well as the Texas, Tennessee, and St. Louis Bloomer Girls." Crucially, in the early twentieth century this trend evolved into major women's squads, playing in Boston, Philadelphia, and New York.[3]

But it wasn't women's rights that motivated Joe Wood's entry into professional baseball in 1906. When Logan Galbreath asked Wood to join the Bloomer Girls after the game on August 27, the choice was John F.'s, not his teenaged son's. In Joe's view a "sense of the absurd" and the twenty dollars for the remaining three weeks of the season led the father to permit his son to play as a girl. Although called the National Bloomer Girls, Galbreath's team was from Kansas City, playing in rural Kansas as a curiosity like the House of David or Native American squads. For example, the *Daily Item* from Great Bend, Kansas, advertised a game on Sunday, July 1, 1906, between the Ellinwood Greens and the National Bloomers Girls, "that famous organization of woman ball players." A more noteworthy game was a rematch between those teams, an afternoon game on Labor Day, Monday, September 3, 1906. As the *Ellinwood Leader* reported, the locals made the only run, in the top of the sixth off left-hander "Lady" Waddell. On the other side Ellinwood pitcher Baumhart carried a no-hitter into the ninth. With two outs and the count 0-2, the next hitter "laid out a nice single, the only hit." "It was a real girl who made the hit," assured the *Hutchinson News* on March 26, 1907. Joe Wood was a Bloomer in that game.

As Joe explained in future years, traveling by bus, he played pitcher, catcher, or shortstop, with most of the players (and always the battery) being men. Many of the women "just sold programs." But one remarkable girl was thirteen-year-old Ruth Egan, from Kansas City, who played first base with a catcher's glove. As Joe explained to Lawrence Ritter, the

> third baseman's real name was Bill Compton, not Dolly Madison. . . . Fact is, there were four boys on the team: me, Lady Waddell, Dolly Madison, and one other, the catcher. . . . We dressed in our uniforms at the hotel and rode out to the ball park from there. I think everybody except maybe some of the farmer boys must have known some of us weren't actually girls, but the crowds turned out and had a lot of fun anyway. In case you're interested, by the way, the first team Rogers Hornsby ever played on was a Bloomer Girls team, too.[4]

Joe told Ritter that he played wigless but never mentioned his name on the Bloomer Girls, though the *Indianapolis Star* on January 26, 1913, named him "Lucy Totton."[5] When the season ended in Wichita, Kansas, during the second week of September, Joe Wood received a train ticket back to Ness City, where his sister was just a week old.

As Joe told Eugene Murdock, Rebecca wanted him to follow Pete to the university. But Howard Ellsworth lived only for baseball, and his brief time in 1906 with the Bloomer Girls, classified as professional since he was paid, supposedly made him ineligible for college athletics. So when Pete met an older player at the University of Kansas, the ball started rolling. He was Clarence Holmes, a pharmacy student, who played pitcher for the baseball team in 1906–7. Born April 2, 1882, in Fredonia, Kansas, Holmes turned twenty-four in the spring of 1906. He had pitched forty-six games in the 1903–4 seasons for the Cedar

Rapids Rabbits of the Class B Three-I League. And he was the "Lefty" Holmes that Jay Andrews, the player/manager of the 1907 Hutchinson Salt Packers, recruited at KU on the strength of a no-hitter Holmes threw (according to Andrews) in 1905, one of four wins with Great Bend of the Class D Kansas League. He and Pete were roommates.[6]

In the Ritter interview the transitional figure is only identified as "a friend of [Harley]." Fortunately, we have Joe's words at opening day of the 1982 season in Boston. In a videotape he described the process, calling Holmes "Duffy" (in other instances Joe named Holmes "Ducky"):

> My brother, who was two years older than I, was going to Kansas
> University at that time, at Lawrence, Kansas. And while there, he met
> an old-time player who I think had big league experience, and I think
> his name was Duffy Holmes. Well, my brother told Duffy Holmes
> that he had a brother who was a pretty good little baseball player and
> if he wanted, he could hook him on professionally someplace. He got
> in touch with a friend of his who happened to be the owner of Cedar
> Rapids, in the Three-I League, which I imagine was a Class C club [ac-
> tually Class B], named Belden Hill . . . . I signed up as an infielder.[7]

Most likely Holmes told Hill of Joe because Lefty/Ducky had played for Hill at Cedar Rapids. If so Ducky Holmes was an ex-professional who pitched for KU, a common practice in college circles at the time.[8]

On the recommendation of Holmes and without seeing Joe play, Belden Hill took a flyer on the boy and offered him a contract for ninety dollars a month to play for Cedar Rapids. Joe (and presumably his father) signed in the first few weeks of 1907 with the expectation that he would become an infielder for the Rabbits. But he never left Kansas for Iowa. Instead, "two or three weeks before the season" (as he told Eugene Murdock) he "got a letter from the owner [Belden Hill] saying that he was pretty well filled up with infielders" and wondered if Joe "minded if [Hill] turned [the] contract over to Hutchinson, Kansas, where [Belden] had a friend who was managing there by the name of Jay Andrews." Without any compensation (Wood told Ritter: "He didn't sell me, he just *gave* me away"), Hill sent his untried player to friend Jay Andrews, the new manager (and third baseman) of the Hutchinson Salt Packers of the Class C Western Association — for the same salary.[9]

Since Joe was still only seventeen years old in the spring of 1907, his father accompanied him on the train from Ness City to Hutchinson. John "wanted to make sure this was a proper environment. So he came to Hutchinson with [Joe] to make sure everything was all right. Hutchinson's only a little over a hundred miles from Ness City, so it wasn't too far from home."[10] John F. then put his son and another Salt Packers player under the protection of Becca's brother James, formerly known as cowboy Rattlesnake Pete, by then a barber who lived downtown behind the Midland Hotel in Hutchinson. John F. wasn't particularly interested in baseball, but the father supported Joe's pursuit of a dream and was willing to ignore Pete's history of bootlegging. John F. and Rebecca where also, as Joe declared in the Joe Wood Archives (JWA) tapes, "glad to have me turn my money over to them."

By 1907 Hutchinson, Kansas, the seat of Reno County, had established a long history of amateur and professional baseball. According to baseball historian Jim Swint, the game was accepted from the establishment of the city in 1871 by Indian agent and staunch Baptist C. C. Hutchinson, and the first official baseball game was played on July 4, 1872. Within five years, in the summer of 1877, a team was established when pitcher and captain Arthur Hutchinson led the local team against the Halstead Terribles in an away game on August 25, a contest hailed as the championship of Goose Creek Township. Hutchinson lost 29–4. More successful was the Hutchinson Baseball Association, chartered on November 10, 1886, by twenty citizens who paid $125 each. The next year Hutchinson played in the Western Baseball League and quickly constructed a Northside Field for the 1888 season. Soon they played teams from cities like Leavenworth, Denver, and Lincoln.[11]

The next two decades are summarized neatly by Swint: "Even when professional baseball came into existence, local teams were often organized to play one another based on a person's occupation. . . . To get a game organized, a challenge was often issued through *The Hutchinson News*. . . . One such challenge in 1906 stated [that] 'the employees of the News Company . . . issues a challenge for a contest to the winners of yesterday's game; or in case they have had enough, would take on the barbers nine, the bankers, or any other team that is anxious for a try for amateur championship honors.'"[12] Burgeoning interest in the game led to the building of Athletic Park, between the rail lines of the Missouri Pacific and Rock Island companies, dedicated on June 6, 1905.[13] Fans were charged thirty-five cents to park their carriages and just twenty-five cents for admission to the games, thirty-five cents for the grandstands. Despite being soaked for parking and wooden seats, as many as two thousand spectators frequented the new grounds, allowing the team to pay their pitchers and catchers, though not others. A year later, one before Joe's arrival, "when the St. Joseph franchise of the Western Association experienced financial difficulties, Hutchinson had a [professional] team—The Salt Packers."[14]

Aided by Andrews's willingness to embellish, the local paper at times was misleading about the future star they tabbed "pretty" Joe Wood. On March 15, 1907, the *Hutchinson News* introduced Joe to sports fans of the Kansas town with the assertion: "Doc Andrews is very jubilant over being able to land Joe Wood, the base ball player recently secured from the Cedar Rapids team which won the pennant in the I.-I.-I. league last year." So far, correct on all points, except that "secured" might've been replaced by "passed along." Then the *News* turned fact into myth, claiming that "Wood pitched the season through, showing great ability," when Joe had played for only Ness City and the Bloomer Girls, not Cedar Rapids. The article then accurately predicted Andrews's choices for the upcoming year: "Wood is also a good infielder, being able to play almost any position on the diamond. He has played a good deal at shortstop and may be put at this position a good bit of the time."

The first practice was the next Wednesday, March 20, 1907, with regular sessions scheduled at 10:00 a.m. and 2:30 p.m. daily. That day the local paper argued that the Salt Packers might have a "claim to a first division" finish under the leadership of Dr. Jay Andrews, "the jolly fat doctor" whose fans would "have the utmost confidence in his ability both as a player and as a manager."[15] The same article identified Wood as one of three candidates for shortstop and pitcher. In passing the paper corrected its previous claim of the achievements by the seventeen-year-old; he was "a pitcher of great promise who was drafted last year by Cedar Rapids in the Three I league. The manager thought he was getting an infielder but when he found he was a pitcher turned him over to Andrews, there already being more pitchers on the Cedar Rapids team than could stay there." (Cedar Rapids actually had too many infielders.)

In later years Joe often remembered that the key to his becoming a pitcher was old players coming up lame. That memory was supported by Jay Andrews in a 1912 article in the *Kansas City Journal*. In Andrews's cartoonish memory, a "weakened" "pitching staff" gave Wood and his powerful arm a chance on the mound. As Andrews recalled, Joe "came in on his own hook" to play an exhibition game against the White Sox, a "little slender fellow just out of short pants who looked as though a Kansas wind would blow him away. He sat around for a while on the bench and finally asked [Andrews] if he couldn't get out on short and practice a bit." After Joe's "wonderful arm" nearly toppled "the first sacker, a big Swede," Jay played him at shortstop "until one day [his] pitching staff weakened." He recalled, "I put Joe in. He hit the first man up in the first inning, smack in the ear. Three days in the hospital for the player." That day, Andrews said, "Joe struck out 17 . . . and won his game 2 to 0."[16] At least the strength of Joe's arm and the debilitated pitchers have the ring of truth.

Joe was a hit with the Salt Packers fans on April Fools' Day, playing shortstop for the "Regulars" in an intrasquad game against the "Colts." The *Hutchinson News* claimed, "Wood gets more favorable notices than any one else. He has already fully demonstrated his ability to field fast and clean and to throw well. His youth too is all in his favor. When many of the tryouts are gone and forgotten, Wood will still be with

Doc's team." Joe batted sixth, going 1 for 3. He also pitched two innings in relief, giving up no runs. Maybe because he made an error in three chances at short on April 1, Wood was in right field the next day for the first of three games against the Denver Grizzlies, won by Hutchinson 4–3. Joe went 0 for 2 and made a put-out in the field. He also successfully sacrificed and was hit by a pitch. Then in the second game of the three-game series, Joe started on the mound and threw three innings of one-hit ball, demonstrating what the *News* called an ability to get himself into "bad corners . . . but each time the kid would pull himself out." Hutchinson won 14–7. Joe also had a single in his only at bat.

After playing right field flawlessly on Saturday (April 6) against Pittsburg, Kansas, going 1 for 4 and knocking in the lead run as the Salt Packers won 6–1, he got the start against Pittsburg on Sunday. In a hint of things to come, Joe Wood was both wild and effective, giving up a walk, three hits, and a hit batter while striking out six in three innings of one-run ball, in a game won by Hutchinson 11–4. He also singled in both at bats. "Young Joe," as he was often called, also pitched well in the following April preseason games. On Friday, April 12, 1907, his complete-game four-hitter against Independence, won 9–2, got him highlighted the next day in the *Hutchinson News* as "the 17-year-old wonder" who "got away with the goods" by allowing "the smallest number of hits made of Hutchinson's twirlers this year."

The following Wednesday, April 17, Wood pitched another full game and won against Chanute 15–3 on a three-hitter. Then on Sunday, April 21, 1907, he topped even the previous two outings, pitching a one-hit 5–1 victory against the Wichita Junior Jobbers, affiliated with a gas company. The next day the *News* gushed: "Joe Wood, the youthful wonder, was a complete puzzle to the Wichita aggregation, for only one scratch hit was made by them and nineteen of them fanned the air three times and were told to sit down. Three of Wichita's players struck out every time they came to bat. Every Wichita player struck out at least once. During the first three innings Wood struck out seven men in succession." It was, of course, a strikeout record for the Salt Packers.

When the roster came out on May 2, the official beginning of the 1907 season, Joe Wood (written as "Woods") was listed as one of six pitchers, not a position player. After two rain outs, on a windy and cold Sunday, May 5, 1907, he pitched the second Hutchinson game of the regular season against a strong Wichita team. Joe tossed four perfect innings before allowing five runs over the next two frames, giving up just five hits but losing 5–0. Wood struck out seven in his debut, walked none, and gave up just three earned runs. Wood's second game was a week later at Topeka. Joe allowed four runs and was a bit wilder, giving up five walks in a game that Hutchinson lost in the twelfth, 5–4. At least the *Topeka Journal* saw potential in the ex-Bloomer: "Woods [*sic*] is a little boy 17 years of age and he gathered his first baseball experience by traveling over the country last summer working as a pitcher on a team of bloomer girls. . . . He looks young enough to be the son of Dr. Andrews. . . . He has nice curves and smoke to back them up."

Such praise seemed well placed on Sunday, May 19, 1907, when Wood handed Wichita only its second loss in fifteen games, 4–1. Joe walked three and threw a wild pitch, but he also struck out seven while beating Kid Speer. As the *Hutchinson News* summarized, "Joe Wood, the 17-year-old phenom had the Jobbers on his hip yesterday and didn't give them a ghost of a show. He was master of the situation at all times. The six hits made off him were wisely scattered, only one of them resulting in a score." He also went 1 for 4 at the plate. For the next few games, against Topeka and Joplin, Joe Wood was at second base, where, as the Hutchinson paper described, his play "brought many a round of applause." In the four games he batted 4 for 12, hitting seventh, eighth, and ninth. Over the four days he had sixteen assists and eleven putouts, though he made two errors in the first game.

He was still at second and batting eighth in the historic series against the Oklahoma City Mets. In the first two contests Joe played well, handling eleven chances flawlessly in the field and batting 3 for 6 plus a walk. Hutchinson won both games, 4–0 and 9–3, with Wood getting a double and scoring in the second game. The next contest at Athletic Park in Hutchinson, Kansas, on Wednesday, May 29, 1907, required twenty-three innings to decide. Though Hutchinson lost 2–1 when the potential tying run was called out at the plate in the bottom of the twenty-third, the game drew curious locals to the field as it progressed and prompted a national syndicated press release. Joe made one error, batted 0 for 6 (dropping his batting average to .231), and was lifted for a pinch hitter in the crucial eighteenth when both teams scored a run. The following day he pitched a three-hitter against the same team. But one was a home run, and Hutchinson had a single hit as the Salt Packers lost 1–0.

By early June Joe Wood was still playing some third base and outfield, but his batting declined as he found himself as a pitcher. On Wednesday, June 5, 1907, he lost to Springfield, 4–0. With his family in the stands, he pitched well, especially in the first four innings, giving up only six hits over the nine innings, striking out five, walking three, and hitting a batter. In the strained metaphors of 1907 Hutchinson sportswriting, he became a "poor table waiter" in a baseball meal while his family watched as the hurler "fainted in the fifth course": "His father, mother and brother were all in the gallery looking on at the banquet, so he was anxious to show off well. But their presence made him nervous, and in the fifth course he dropped his tray breaking three dishes." He also went 0 for 3 and was taken down for a pinch hitter in the ninth.

Over the next week he showed strength against the Webb City Goldbugs. On June 9 at Webb City, Missouri, Joe Wood entered in the sixth with two runners on and one out. He struck out two, but between them he gave up a squeeze that scored the tying run. He also surrendered a run in the seventh on two hits, giving Webb City the lead, 3–2. But the Salt Packers rallied for three in the eighth, making Joe Wood the winning pitcher in the 5–3 game. Over the three and two-thirds innings, he gave up just two hits and a wild pitch while striking out seven. The next day the two teams continued a home-and-home series in Hutchinson, with Joe back on the mound. He started a bit slowly—a tendency throughout his career—giving up three runs in the first four innings, but in the last five Joe faced the minimum. He allowed just four hits and two walks and struck out five. Again a late Hutchinson rally beat Webb City, 4–3. Joe Wood made it three in a row over the Goldbugs on the fifteenth, pitching a three-hitter, on four walks and six K's, winning 3–2 with both runs unearned.

By mid-June Joe was slumping at the plate, hitting just .191 on June 13. Then in the last game of the Webb City series, he was 0 for 4. On the mound June 20 he was rocked at Springfield, Missouri, pitching just one inning and giving up three doubles for two runs before Hutchinson came back to win 7–5. In a show of confidence in his young pitcher, Doc Andrews sent Joe Wood back out the next day, in Leavenworth, Kansas, against the Convicts; Wood was dominant, winning 3–1 on another three-hitter. He struck out seven but was wild, walking five and throwing a wild pitch. The only run was unearned as Joe's fielding also impressed local writers. When the two teams returned to Hutchinson, on June 25 Joe again easily beat the Convicts, 9–0, on a one-hitter. This time he had good control, giving up just one walk while striking out ten, the only hit a single in the seventh. While 0 for 2 at bat, he scored a run. The *Hutchinson News* quipped that Joe "had all kinds of steam and more beautiful curves than the fair Venus ever boasted of."

The wildness of the youthful Joe Wood returned before the end of the month. On Sunday, June 30, he struck out nine of the Topeka White Sox. But he also walked six, which combined with three timely singles for five unearned runs and a Salt Packers loss, 5–3. Back in left field on July 3 against Wichita, batting eighth, Joe made two errors and was 0 for 2 as his batting continued its slide. On the Fourth of July he also was ineffective in relief against the Jobbers in Hutchinson, giving up eight runs while walking four over seven innings. Wichita won easily, 11–1. The next day, a Friday, he was in right in yet another game against the Wichita Jobbers, where he made five putouts and played errorless baseball, including an impressive one-handed catch. But batting eighth he again was shutout at the plate, 0 for 3. At least this time Hutchinson won 3–0.

His mediocrity and wildness continued against the Topeka White

Sox that weekend. Although he hit a double on Saturday, July 6, 1907, on the mound he gave up five runs on five hits and five more walks and struck out only three, as Hutchinson lost 6–4. The next day he played right field and batted eighth, going 0 for 2 and playing errorless ball in three chances. Still not hitting with consistency, Joe was replaced late in the game by a pinch hitter as Salt Packers pitcher Earle Fleharty hit a grand slam to right-center field in the bottom of the ninth, giving Hutchinson a 5–3 win over Topeka. When Joe went hitless in his only at bat on July 11, his average dropped to .160, next to last on the Hutchinson team. In a sixteen-inning game on July 12, again versus the Joplin Miners, Wood entered in the twelfth as a second baseman; he went 0 for 1 and turned a double play as the Salt Packers scored two in the sixteenth to win 5–4.

Beginning the next day, Saturday, July 13, Joe Wood started to turn things around. That day he won 2–1 in a fourteen-inning complete game. He walked five and gave up eight hits, but he also struck out eight against the Oklahoma City Mets. Still struggling at the plate, he was 0 for 5 as the Salt Packers won on a suicide squeeze in the bottom of the fourteenth. On the fourteenth, in a 4–1 loss to Oklahoma City he pinch-hit in the ninth and walked. Two days later, after entering as a pitcher in the sixth, he gave up a run in that inning but blanked the Mets the rest of the game. Hutchinson won 7–6 by scoring three in the eighth, with Wood singling in the winning run. Joe gave up just one hit and two walks as he struck out three over the four innings. He was even better on July 20 against his cousins, the Leavenworth Convicts, striking out eleven while giving up five hits, three walks, and a wild pitch as the Salt Packers won 4–1. He was also 2 for 4, with a run and a stolen base. Recognizing Joe's dominance of that team, Doc Andrews sent him in two days later after Leavenworth had scored four in the ninth. Wood struck out the only batter he faced to preserve an 8–5 win.

For the most part Joe Wood played well the rest of the year, even as a hitter. On Tuesday, July 23, playing third base and batting ninth against Leavenworth, he doubled in three at bats. The next day, still in

Hutchinson against the Convicts, he again was 1 for 3, with a run. And he was even better on the mound, pitching a two-hit, 6–1 win, striking out eight and walking five. When the news accounts on July 25, 1907, noted "the sawing of the ozone by the Leavenworth players," the "ozone" nickname stuck. From then until the 1912 season, Joe was most often tabbed "Ozone" Wood or the "Kansas Cyclone." His hot streak continued on Saturday, July 27, at Webb City, Missouri, where he struck out ten Goldbugs while walking four in a ten-inning 1–0 victory. Joe then won two games against the Springfield (Missouri) Midgets, but not as convincingly. On July 31 in Hutchinson, he gave up five runs in the last two innings to blow a 3–0 lead, on ten walks, a wild pitch, and nine hits (only one run earned) as the Salt Packers scored two in the ninth to win, 6–5. He had two sacrifices and was 0 for 2. Joe was a bit stronger at home against the Midgets on August 5, winning 4–3, giving up just five hits while walking one and striking out twelve. He also was 2 for 3 at the plate.

Manager Andrews used him regularly and effectively the rest of August 1907. On the mound August 9, he gave up two runs to the Joplin Miners in the first inning on an error by his left fielder. But then he settled in, subsequently giving up just three hits and two walks while striking out eight in a 6–2 win. After losing to Wichita on the thirteenth 4–1, to Clyde Milan and the Jobbers, despite giving up just six hits and a walk, he had one of his best games in the Minors. Against Oklahoma on August 14, 1907, he pitched a ten-inning 1–0 victory, striking out every Mets player (five in a row and the side in the third), seventeen in all, while walking no one. He gave up no hits until the seventh inning and only two overall. Joe was also 1 for 3 at the plate. He pitched well on Monday the nineteenth, without a decision, as Hutchinson got two in the ninth to beat Oklahoma City 2–1. On August 25 his record was 14–7. The next day Joe won again 1–0 over Topeka. He gave up four walks, four singles, and struck out eight White Sox, leaving the tying run on third base in the ninth. He also went 1 for 3.

The following day he was playing shortstop, batting seventh, in a

6–4 loss to Topeka. Joe made no errors and had a triple and two runs scored in two official at bats. Back on the mound on August 29 against Leavenworth, he suffered a rare loss to the Convicts, 5–4. Joe struck out eleven prisoners but walked four and hit a batter. Three crucial errors by his middle infielders sealed his fate. He was 0 for 3. His better hitting resumed the next day when he played second base against Leavenworth and batted eighth at Hutchinson. Although he made an error, Joe was 2 for 3, with a double, as the Salt Packers won 4–1. Back at second the next day, but Joe made another error and was 0 for 4. On Saturday, September 7, Joe gave the Springfield Midgets a lot of chances early. In the first a run was cut down at home, and Joe filled the bases before retiring the side. In the second a windblown home run by opposing pitcher Fred Olmstead (with the Chicago White Sox the next four seasons) gave the visitors two runs. But Joe allowed no others, walking five and allowing seven hits but striking out nine as the Salt Packers won 3–2.

The pattern was repeated on the eleventh, again in Hutchinson, when he gave Webb City a run in the first, on two hit batters and a bases-loaded walk, and another in the third. But once again he gained composure and allowed no more runs and only two hits, though he walked six. Joe struck out eight Goldbugs and scored a run as the Salt Packers won going away, 8–2. On the sixteenth he couldn't overcome the early troubles. At home versus Webb City again, he only lasted two-thirds of an inning, giving up five hits, a walk, and four runs. At least Hutchinson won 11–5. Then Joe Wood moved to the outfield. On the twenty-first he played left and batted sixth, to go 0 for 2 as the Salt Packers lost to the Springfield Midgets 9–5. Again in left during the first game of the doubleheader in Springfield, Missouri, that ended the season, he batted eighth and hit two home runs in three at bats as Hutchinson won 4–0 behind Earle Fleharty. In the second game after Earle gave up three runs through six innings, he and Wood switched positions. Though Joe gave up no runs, walked one, and struck out two, the Midgets won 3–1. Wood was 0 for 3.

The Hutchinson Salt Packers finished the 1907 season with a 77-59 record, good enough for third place in the Western Association. The Wichita Jobbers won the league easily, by fourteen and one-half games over the Oklahoma City Mets. But Hutchinson showed strength on the mound. The workhorse was Earle Fleharty, who won twenty-eight games that year and was rumored to make the jump to the Cincinnati Reds that fall.[17] But "little Joe" wasn't far behind, winning eighteen while losing eleven, most of his losses coming, according to the *Hutchinson News*, during two weeks when he had a cranky arm. Already he was known as a strikeout pitcher, striking out 224 batters in 196 innings, and he gave up just 6.8 hits per game. But wildness was a problem as he walked four and one-half batters per game, which raised his WHIP to 1.245. He hit better, and with power, in the second half of the season. But he hit .190 for the year. Joe also showed promise defensively, especially in the outfield.

The next day the Hutchinson papers, still calling Joe Wood "the Kid," admitted that the young star probably wouldn't remain with the Salt Packers in 1908.[18] But it wasn't clear where he would play as Joe kept active after the season. On September 30 he pitched for Ellinwood, Kansas, in the first game of a doubleheader at Larned, Kansas. He lost that day, 3–0, to his Hutchinson teammate Earle Fleharty. Two day later, on Wednesday, October 2, he was back in Hutchinson, playing right field and batting eighth, in an exhibition game against the Omaha Rourkes of the Class A Western League. Though he made an error, Joe was 1 for 3, batting eighth as the visitors won 6–2. The next day, also against Omaha, he played flawless outfield but was 0 for 4. Hutchinson lost 2–0. Once the weather made baseball impossible, the negotiations for Joe's services, overseen by John F. Wood, began in earnest. It took all fall, but eventually the owner of the Kansas City Blues paid $1,000 to Hutchinson (according to Jay Andrews) for the services of the Kansas Cyclone. The next season Joe would get $250 a month for Monte Cross's team.[19]

By the time Joe Wood arrived in Kansas City, the city had enjoyed a long history of baseball. The first team, the Antelopes, was organized in 1866, and the first professional team, the Unions, played in 1884 as part of the Union Association. Other teams, all called the Cowboys, played in two versions of the Western League and in the National League during the 1886 season, finishing 30-91. Equally unsuccessful was a Kansas City entry in the Major League American Association. Also called the Cowboys, they were 43-89 and (last in the eight-team league) in 1888 and 55-82 (next to last) in 1889. Meanwhile, other Kansas City Cowboys played fitfully in the Western Association, changing their names to the Blues (the uniform color) in 1888 and 1890. Throughout the nineties, Kansas City fielded teams in the Western Association and the Western League.[20]

The city's entry in the 1900 Single-A American League was also called the Blues; the team finished in the middle of the pack at 69-70. The next year George Tebeau, ex-player with the Cincinnati Red Stockings and Cleveland Spiders (called "White Wings" for his speed) and investor in the Denver Grizzlies of the Western League and the Louisville Colonels, moved to Kansas City to manage the Blues in the Western League. Focused on the money side of the game, in 1902 he recruited ex–Major Leaguer (and lawyer) Dale Gear as part-owner, president, and playing manager of the new independent team, again the Blues. That year things didn't go well as the Kansas City Blue Stockings, the name of the Western League team that year, suddenly were excellent. Their new manager, Kid Nichols, who had already won more than three hundred games with the Boston Beaneaters (and was elected to the Hall of Fame in 1949), also pitched, posting a 26-7 record. With such a leader the Blue Stockings also raided the Blues for players. While the Blues fielded a team with essentially a .500 record, the rivals were champions of the Western League.

But Tebeau had an alternate plan. On land he had leased three years earlier, George built Association Park at Twentieth Street and Olive Avenue. It was modern, seating eight thousand, with a lounging area under the grandstands and easy access to three streetcar lines. Major railroads were adjacent on the north. Most quirky was a right-field wall only 245 feet from home plate, with a ten-foot fence thirty feet long to reduce home runs. The new facility opened with an exhibition versus the White Sox on April 11, 1903; with the first official game on April 22, 1903, the Blues defeated the Minneapolis Millers 8–4.[21] By then the Kansas City Blues, that year called the Cowboys, had been reclassified with the rest of the American Association to Class A. Though their record wasn't any better, the Cowboys were able to attract fans to their ten-thousand-dollar park. When the Kansas City Blue Stockings folded in 1904, the Gear/Tebeau team once again became the Blues. In following years they were managed by a series of ex–Major Leaguers: Pop Schriver (1904), Arthur Irwin (1905), Sunset Jimmy Burke (1906 and 1907), and then Monte Cross.

The Sunday, January 26, 1908, edition of the *Kansas City Star* said two new pitchers had signed the previous week with Cross and the Class A Blues. One was Frank Kinsey, from Hackettstown, New York, and the other Joe Wood, described as "another Brandom," referring to Chick Brandom, whose life soon would become entwined with Joe's, on and off the field. Back in Hutchinson, as late as March 13 the paper imagined Joe wouldn't stick with Kansas City and might return to the Salt Packers. But after the first team meeting of the Blues on Sunday, March 15, and initial practice the next day, hope died in Hutchinson as the *Kansas City Star* noticed Joe's "bundle of fancy hoists," naming him "the pellet-manipulating parcel of adolescence from Hutchinson, Kansas." Also noted were his difficulty holding runners on base and his ability to play the middle infield. The youth of Wood and Brandom would be complemented, the paper observed, by the experienced arms of Clyde Goodwin, who had pitched four games for the Senators as a nineteen-year-old, and Wish Egan, with Detroit in 1902 and the St. Louis Cardinals in 1905 and 1906.

Joe Wood made as quick a start in Kansas City as he had in Hutchinson, demonstrating excellence in exhibitions. By mid-March the Kansas City papers were comparing him with George Upp, then playing for the Columbus Senators, who in the previous year (1907) had led the American Association with a 27-10 record and a WHIP well under 1.00.[22] The comparison seemed justified on Sunday, March 22, when Joe started and pitched three innings against the Denver Grizzlies of the Western League, giving up just one hit and no runs. He struck out three while walking two, showing good curves but an inability to hold runners in the 4–3 win. After another successful workout against the Grizzlies midweek, in which he gave up just one hit over six innings, Joe was even more impressive against the Chicago White Sox second team on Sunday, March 29. On a cold day he and Chick Brandom combined to beat the Sox 5–2. Wood threw four innings, giving up just one hit (and no runs) while striking out two and walking two. By then the nickname "Ozone Wood," transferred from the Hutchinson papers, was being used regularly in Kansas City.

Joe started the regular season with a splash, beating the Indianapolis Indians at Washington Park on April 16, 4–2. Despite wildness he gave up only five hits and was 1 for 3 at the plate. The *Kansas City Star* called it a "steady and cool" performance. He wasn't as fortunate on April 19 in Louisville against the Colonels. He pitched six perfect innings. But one bad one, in which he gave up two walks and three hits, led to a loss. In the same series, on Wednesday the twenty-second he entered a game at shortstop, replacing Monte Cross when the player/manager was ejected in the sixth inning for arguing a play at the plate. But the next day he went home for not being "in good condition." (A cartoon in a Kansas City paper suggested he had a stomach ailment.) While Joe was recuperating, George Tebeau predicted a Major League career for Joe, comparing him to the "little chap, Johnny Fisher," a recent top pitcher with Indianapolis who would play outfield in 1910 for the St. Louis Browns.

His first day back, April 30, Wood started in the home opener against the Toledo Mud Hens. There was the usual hoopla, including the Third Regiment Band (called Hiner's Band after Dr. Edward Hiner, a pal of John Philip Sousa), a parade of players, and a speech by the mayor of

Kansas City, Thomas Crittenden Jr. Initially Joe pitched well, holding Toledo scoreless for the first four innings, before giving up five runs between the fifth and seventh innings. Eventually the Blues lost 6–5 in thirteen, with Joe getting no decision. He also lost 6–4 to the Columbus Senators on May 5 at Association Park in a game typical of his year in Kansas City. He struck out seven and gave up just two runs through eleven innings. But he also walked eight and threw a wild pitch while permitting ten hits. In the eleventh he caved, giving up the four runs that beat the Blues. The summary of the early season published on May 10 told the story. He was 1-2, giving up only fifteen hits in three games. But he had twice as many walks, twenty-two, as strikeouts, eleven. A sportswriter for the *Kansas City Star* insisted that Joe Wood had "the goods" and was "hard to hit" but lost "control in pinches."

While Joe's record was uneven, the star of the early season was twenty-one-year-old Chick Brandom.[23] He was most impressive on May 14, 1908, throwing the first no-hitter at Association Park, 5–0 over the Indianapolis Indians. But Joe's competition with Chick Brandom wasn't just on the field. After a game in Kansas City, Joe Wood relieved his fellow pitcher of a date, a girl named Laura O'Shea, as described by Joe to Lee Goodwin:

Joe: She and her sister and another friend came out to a ball game one time. And they sort of hung around after the game was over and I met them, myself and Chick Brandom.

Bob Wood: Did he date mom before you did?

Joe: There was no dating to it. We walked home with them, or got a car and took them home, or some darn thing. Chick Brandom was with your mother [to Bob] and I was with the other girl [Mary Dasbach]. But I soon changed.

Goodwin: Did you like her as soon as you met her?

Wood: Like her? Oh, yes, she was a beautiful girl. And just as nice as she was beautiful.[24]

Laura's sister Edith, the baseball fan in the O'Shea family, initiated many such trips.

Meanwhile, in mid-May against the Indians again, Joe was again effectively wild in relief. He hit a batter and threw a wild pitch, but he also struck out one and gave up no runs. On May 18 and 19 Monte Cross inserted Joe at shortstop. The papers praised his skill with pop-ups and his strong arm, though he didn't have the range of veteran Cross. And then, almost in response to Chick Brandom's feat of a week earlier, on May 21, 1908, Joe was masterful as the Blues beat Milwaukee on the road 1–0, with ex–Major Leaguer and future Hall of Famer Jake Beckley tripling in the seventh and scoring on a sacrifice fly.[25] Joe walked no one and struck out nine; he had a perfect game in the ninth before, with one out, manager and shortstop Cross made a throwing error. Joe then completed his no-hitter just a week after Chick's. Typical of youth, in Joe's next appearance, in relief two days later, he was wild. Entering in the seventh against the St. Paul Saints in Minnesota, he gave up four walks and a wild pitch, allowing the tying run to score in the eighth. But he also struck out two, including the last batter of the game, as Kansas City came back to win 9–7.

As the weather heated up, Joe's control improved, but not always his luck. On May 26 he gave up only three hits and walked just one against the Minneapolis Millers, but the Blues were one hit themselves and Joe lost 4–0. On Decoration Day, May 30, 1908, he and Chick Brandom, by then called roommates, combined for a doubleheader sweep against St. Paul. Chick won in the morning game, 5–2. In the afternoon Wood threw a two-hitter, striking out seven while walking two and throwing a wild pitch. The *Star* this time was more uniformly positive about Joe, calling him the "pride of Hutchinson" (of course, he was from Ness City) and, more to the point, an "eminent young finisher and decorator." As June began, Joe was hitting like a pitcher (only .171), but he was fielding his position pretty well (at .943) and showing (reporters said) "remarkable improvement in his recent games," especially in a newly acquired "excellent control." His record was just 3-4.

As summer arrived, Joe settled in as a pitcher, though he was used in the field, sometimes out of necessity. On June 1 he replaced Monte Cross when the player/manager was thrown out in eighth inning. After being hit by a pitch, Cross was ejected for retrieving the errant ball and throwing it back at the Milwaukee pitcher. As a replacement in the 7–2 loss, Joe didn't bat and made an error. Two days later Joe pitched, and lost, to the Brewers, 2–0. Again wildness was the culprit. In the fifth inning he walked four batters to force in the first run, and in the sixth a walk, followed by a stolen base and a hit, scored the other. That day Wood struck out six and only gave up four hits, but five walks did him in. By the end of the first week in June, Kansas City papers declared Wish Egan the best Blues pitcher (he would finish 7-9 and be out of baseball two years later) with Brandom also in the running. Wood, 3-5, was considered uneven. By June 7 in ten games he had fifty strikeouts but thirty-five walks.

Joe's record moved to 4-5 when he beat the Mudhens 5–2 in Toledo, giving up runs in the first and ninth while striking out five, walking two, and throwing a wild pitch. That contest had ramifications beyond the field of play. Speculation ran high that an offer would be coming from the Boston Red Sox because Fred Lake, a scout (who would manage the Red Sox later that year and for the 1909 season), was seen at the game. The *Kansas City Times* reassured Blues fans that Joe would remain until the end of the 1908 season. But the drama intensified when Wood was named in a controversy between Washington Senators' manager Joe Cantillon and the Blues. Pitcher Clyde Goodwin had been with the Senators briefly near the end of 1906 but was returned after the season Milwaukee, where he also pitched in 1907. Kansas City picked him up for the 1908 year, with the Washington Major League team claiming that if Clyde didn't stick, the Senators had the right to draft Joe Wood. Cross argued that Goodwin might be returned, thus nixing any deal for Wood. Meanwhile, the Red Sox and many other teams continued to watch young Joe.[26]

The attention from Major League clubs didn't help Joe's performance.

On June 11 in Columbus he again started slowly, giving up four runs in the first, eventually walking five, giving up ten hits, and losing 5–2. Nearly a week later, on June 17, a game in Indianapolis featured two budding stars. Joe relieved in the third inning, followed by Rube Marquard, who entered in the ninth. Wood pitched well, only giving up runs in the seventh and the tenth. But a walk-off home run by future Major Leaguer Donie Bush in that last inning gave Wood the loss, despite his seven strikeouts, no walks, and just four hits over seven and two-thirds. Joe had a double. In Kansas City on June 22, he blew a lead in relief of Chick Brandom, giving up two in the ninth, permitting three hits, and walking in a run. More important than the 3–2 loss was the presence of George Huff, who had managed the Boston Americans for eight games the previous year, reviving speculation about Wood being signed by Boston.

Despite uneven play Joe showed signs of brilliance for a couple of weeks as June came to an end. On the twenty-fourth he pitched well, though he lost 2–0 to Indianapolis in a six-inning game. He was even better on the twenty-ninth, beating Louisville 3–2 on a four-hitter, striking out nine and giving up just two bases on balls. He had a single and scored the winning run on a hit by Monte Cross in the ninth. In the meantime the politics surrounding Joe heated up again as Clyde Goodwin was sent from Kansas City, where he had a 13-13 record, to Columbus of the same league. (Still only twenty-one in 1908, Goodwin would pitch until 1914 but never return to the Majors.) Joe again looked good in the second game of a doubleheader on the Fourth of July, beating the Milwaukee Brewers 2–1 on a seven-hitter, walking four and giving up a wild pitch but striking out six. By July 4 Joe was only 6-7 with fifty-two walks. But he had eighty-five strikeouts. He was hitting just .151.

The rest of his last month in the Minors, he won only one game. On July 8 he pitched a single inning in St. Paul against the Saints, giving up two doubles and three singles, plus a walk, leading to five runs as the Blues lost the second game of a doubleheader, 10–0. He returned the next day and pitched better. But he again lost, 3–2 in thirteen innings, giving up ten hits while striking out six and walking one. After pitching two innings in relief on the eleventh at Minneapolis, Joe returned on the thirteenth at St. Paul and won 10–5 while striking out twelve and giving up eight hits and three walks. He was shelved with a sore wrist in mid-July but returned on July 21, when he lost to Toledo 3–1, striking out six but giving up seven hits, a walk, and two hit batters. After playing left field as a substitute for an injured player on July 26, Joe completed his Minor League career on the twenty-eighth by losing to the Columbus Senators 2–1, giving up runs in the eighth and tenth while permitting eight hits, walking none, and striking out just two.

By August 5, 1908, the Kansas papers reported that Joe had left the Blues "for good." But Joe Wood didn't exit Kansas City quietly. When his sale to the Boston Americans was made official on August 9, Senators' manager Joe Cantillon argued that he should have been able to acquire Wood for $1,500 and Clyde Goodwin, who had been released to Columbus. Feeling the pique of losing Joe, the *Kansas City Star* declared, "Brandom is better than Wood," noting that Wood "refused to report to Boston unless he gets more than the minimum $400/month, which has been offered him." Accompanying the story was a cartoon of Joe with a "swelled head" as he turned down Boston. Meanwhile, Joe returned to Ness City. Within a couple of weeks John Taylor had, in Joe's words, "met my terms." Reportedly the Red Sox agreed to pay the Blues $3,500, not the normal minimum of $2,400, and Joe received $500 rather than the usual $400 a month. If Joe remembered correctly later, he also took "Kansas City to court to get [his] money from them." Apparently, with the support of John F., Joe got paid on both ends.[27]

At first it might be hard to see why Boston was so anxious to purchase Joe Wood. His record was only 7-12 in thirty-two games. But Joe gave up only 118 hits in 178 innings, and his ERA was a very respectable 2.38. He permitted only forty-seven earned runs, and he also struck out 116. During the video at opening day of 1982 in Boston, Joe summarized the pattern that got him to the Majors:

Several of the big league teams coming up from South stopped at Kansas City [for] exhibition games . . . before they opened the season. . . . I went pretty good against them. . . . They reported me to different places, and one of them that I was mentioned to was the Boston Red Sox. So it wasn't very long before a fellow by the name of Fred Lake, who was later manager of the Red Sox in Boston, came on as a scout to look me over. . . . There was a little argument about what the salary was going to be, and so on, so I went back to western Kansas and stayed home until I heard more from the Red Sox and finally got what I wanted to break in.[28]

As he exited for Boston, Joe Wood was already known as the Kansas Cyclone and Ozone Wood. But even before he joined the Red Sox, he ruffled feathers when Joe and his father, John F. Wood, played hard-ball on the business side. The Kansas City newspapers felt it was presumptuous of the youngster to hold out. Later there would be a similar sentiment from Beantown papers, most predictably the *Boston Globe*, whose owners were literally invested in the Red Sox. The Sox front office met the demands of Joe and John, but the reputation of Wood as a difficult negotiator, with a chip on his shoulder toward management, was established before he threw a pitch in the American League. When injuries eventually diminished his production, the pattern would resurface. But that conflict was half a decade away. In the meantime the Hub awaited the Cyclone and his smoke ball.

THREE

Rookie and More

The Boston Red Sox that purchased the rights to Joe Wood in 1908 had only been a Major League team since 1901, experiencing dizzying highs and lows in those seven seasons.[1] Ban Johnson and his upstart American League initially deferred to major NL strongholds, including Boston. But when the senior league supported an American Association franchise in the Hub, Johnson and his cohorts (most influentially bankroller and AL vice president Charles W. Somers) reversed field. Forcing a confrontation Ban focused on recruiting players from Boston's National League team for Boston's AL franchise. With the help of Connie Mack, Johnson's people also built a new stadium, the Huntington Avenue Grounds, across the railroad tracks from the field of the Nationals (aka the Beaneaters), where on opening day, May 8, 1901, they outdrew the NL team.

In these early years the Boston Americans went by various names, none of them the Red Sox: Pilgrims, Puritans, Plymouth Rocks, and (after owner Somers) the Somersets. Whatever their nickname, they were good primarily because key players, most significantly third baseman/manager Jimmy Collins, centerfielder Chick Stahl, outfielder/first baseman Buck Freeman, and pitcher Parson Ted Lewis, jumped from the Boston NL team, not unusual since 111 of 182 new leaguers came from the old one. The inhabitants of the Huntington Avenue Grounds also purchased thirty-four-year-old Cy Young and his catcher Lou Criger from St. Louis of the NL. Despite a shaky start, the Bostons nearly won the first AL pennant, finishing only four games behind the White Sox. Better yet, in their inaugural year the Americans drew almost two hundred thousand more fans than the Boston Nationals.

In their second year — 1902 — the team added another key player from the Boston Nationals, pitcher (and future umpire) Bill Dinneen, as well as first baseman George LaChance (a trade with Cleveland), outfielder Pat Dougherty, and pitcher Tom Hughes (purchased from the Baltimore Orioles). They finished third, six and one-half games behind the Philadelphia Athletics, despite Cy Young's 32-11 (2.15 ERA) year and the yeoman 21-21 record (2.93 ERA) of Dinneen. The following year, 1903, as the AL and the NL made peace, Somers sold his interest to Henry J. Killilea, former owner of the Milwaukee Brewers, who spruced up Huntington Avenue Grounds and raised the price of left-field bleacher seats from twenty-five cents to fifty cents.

With the only substantial change at backup catcher, where Garland "Jake" Stahl replaced Duke Farrell, Boston was just two games ahead of the Athletics in early August. But the team pulled away in the final two months, winning by sixteen and one-half games. They did so by ranking first in the AL in hitting and by pitcher thirty-six-year-old Young going 28-9 and Long Tom Hughes and Bill Dinneen both winning twenty games — with a team ERA under 2.60, also first in the AL. After negotiations by the Boston and Pittsburgh front offices, the 1903 Boston team represented the American League in the first "modern" World Series. The Americans defeated the Pirates five games to three in a nine-game format, thanks (as legend has it) to the playing of the song "Tessie" by the Royal Rooters beginning in Game Five at Pittsburgh.[2] Truth to tell, injuries to Pirate pitchers were as determinative.

The following year, 1904, John I. Taylor, the son of *Boston Globe* owner Charles Taylor, took ownership from Killilea. While the team's batting slipped to fourth in the league, the pitching was once again tops. Cy Young and Bill Dinneen both lowered their ERAS, and Jesse Tannehill, traded to Boston from New York for Tom Hughes, won twenty-one, with a 2.02 ERA. Despite fading down the stretch, Boston had another pennant-winning year, highlighted by Young's perfect game on Thursday, May 5, 1904. But there was no Series in 1904 because John T. Brush, owner of the NL champion New York Giants, refused to play the "inferior" league. In 1905 despite a 1.82 ERA, thirty-eight-year-old Cy Young was 18-19, and no Boston regular hit even .280. The team finished fourth. In 1906 (Jimmy Collins's last), Boston finished in the cellar, losing twenty games in a row and finishing 49-105. The team won ten more games in 1907 but only moved to seventh place. At least they had a new name: the Boston Red Sox.[3]

The year Joe arrived in Boston, Cy Young managed to win twenty-one games, pitch his third no-hitter on June 30, and finish with an amazing 1.26 ERA. The hitting improved in 1908, and the team had added Eddie Cicotte to the rotation. But the other starters, Cy Morgan and Fred Burchell, weren't first-line players. Although the Red Sox climbed to fifth place, at 75-79, they needed to rebuild and get younger. That year youngsters Amby McConnell, Tris Speaker, and Larry Gardner got time in the field. On the mound the Sox also had Elmer Steele and brought up Frank Arellanes in late July. Joe was next, though still not well known in Boston. The *Boston Globe* reported on July 26, 1908, that Wood was left-handed, nineteen (not until that October), born in Hutchinson, Kansas (actually Kansas City), and had "two brothers who are promising ball players" (just one, Pete). More accurately the paper identified Joe's excellent exhibitions against Major League teams and his good fast ball but inconsistent control.

Joe Wood first pitched on Monday, August 24, 1908, against the Chicago White Sox, who were in fourth place, eight games ahead of the Red Sox. When he stepped into Huntington Avenue Grounds, he found a mix of the industrial and the artsy. Over the first base bleachers, to Joe's left on the mound, sat railroad tracks linking New York with Hartford and New Haven. Conspicuous behind and parallel to the bleachers sat the round house and repair shops, not the most attractive buildings on the line. In contrast behind him over the left-center-field fence stood the new opera house, with the Boston storage warehouse to the opera's right. As Joe walked onto the field, the weather was fair but a bit cool for August, with light westerly winds. Renovation had left the center-field wall well over six hundred feet from home and the right-field fence back from 280 to 320 feet, still a short porch. The dimensions were similar to those of Association Park in Kansas City. In both venues Joe needed to keep the ball up the middle, avoiding long drives to the right side. Typical for a weekday only half the seats were filled for a game lasting just two hours and four minutes.

The first batter Joe Wood faced in the Major Leagues was right fielder Ed Hahn, a thirty-two-year-old outfielder, who reached on an error by rookie second baseman Amby McConnell. Joe then walked veteran Fielder Jones. A sacrifice by George Davis put both runners in scoring position. But Joe struck out Pat Dougherty (who failed to run when catcher Lou Criger dropped the ball), and Jiggs Donahue grounded to Jake Stahl at first base, unassisted. Wood also managed a scoreless second, giving up a one-out walk before getting a force out and a ground out, this time fielded cleanly by McConnell. However, in the third lead-off hitter Hahn walked, followed by a single to center from Jones. Wood fielded a sacrifice from Davis but threw low to Harry Lord at third, who let the ball roll away, scoring the first run (unearned) for Chicago. The other two runners moved up. Another hit, to center by Dougherty, scored two more runs. After a sacrifice a throwing error by catcher Lou Criger gave Chicago their fourth run, on just two hits.

Joe got a run back in the bottom of the third when he singled off the glove of third baseman Lee Tannehill and scored after consecutive hits by Harry Lord and Jack Thoney. In the top of the fourth, a lead-off hit by Tannehill, another walk to Jones, and a double by George Davis got two more Chicago runs. Though he finished the fourth without further damage, Wood was relieved by Elmer Steele, who gave up only one hit and no runs the rest of the game. The final tally in Joe Wood's first Major League game: four hits and four walks, one strike out, the losing pitcher in a 6–4 game. His first day in the Majors he was 0-1 as a pitcher but hit 1.000. The next day, August 25, the *Globe* said that "things broke badly for him" and he deserved "another chance" "before judging," though the writer saw "no particular speed," "control," or "curve equipment." The same day the *Boston Post* disagreed, saying Joe had "nice curves and a pretty drop ball." Aware of Joe's recent negotiations, Paul Shannon added, "Pitcher Wood, late of Kansas City, thinks he is worth a whole bunch of money more than the Boston team is willing to give him."

For most of the rest of the season — basically the month of September — Joe was used in relief. But before Joe pitched again he had a new manager. On August 28 Deacon McGuire resigned (amid rumors of discord with President Taylor) and was replaced by Joe's recruiter, Fred Lake, the fifth manager for Boston in two years. Before Fred saw Joe Wood in a Major League game, the youngster had appeared in exhibition against Waterbury of the Connecticut League on August 30. Wood relieved Doc McMahon (who won his only game in the Majors on October 6 that year), giving up five hits and two walks. Joe was 1 for 1. Wood's third appearance, second in the Majors, was at Washington on September 9, 1908, where he pitched a scoreless eighth inning, giving up a hit and striking out one.

Joe got more responsibility two days later. In the first game of a doubleheader against the New York Highlanders, he relieved Frank Arellanes in the sixth inning with Boston down 4–0. Even though the Red Sox lost 4–2, Wood gave his best outing to date, called by the *Globe* on September 12 "showing up to good advantage." Over the final four innings Joe gave up only a single, a walk, and a hit batter. Joe Wood came close to his first win on September 19 in Cleveland. Entering for Elmer Steele in the third, Joe allowed three runs in that inning and another in the fifth and pitched through the seventh. The Red Sox tied the game before losing, 6–5, in the ninth. At the plate he went 0 for 2 and was removed for a pinch hitter in the eighth inning.

It was ten days before he pitched again, in Chicago on September 29, 1908, the day Ed Walsh of the White Sox won both games of doubleheader,

5–1 and 2–0. Joe relieved in the sixth of the first game. He pitched two-plus innings, giving up two runs on two hits and a walk. Wood next played a day after Addie Joss's perfect game over the White Sox. On October 3, 1908, at Philadelphia, with the Red Sox in fifth place, Wood started in the second game of a doubleheader. In a contest shortened by darkness to six innings, he pitched a one-hit shutout, 5–0, with the only hit by pitcher Jack Coombs. Boston capitalized on five errors by Philadelphia and two Red Sox double plays, one started by Wood himself. As the *Globe* sportswriter summarized, "There was nothing to the second game but Boston. Wood had the entire Athletic outfit on his staff."[4]

When the season ended four days later, on October 7, Joe Wood returned to Ness City, Kansas, where later that month he would celebrate his nineteenth birthday. His first games for the Boston Americans had been typical for a young pitcher. His fastball wasn't overpowering, and he was plagued by wildness, giving up sixteen walks in fewer than twenty-three innings. But Joe made progress. For starters the press had figured out that he wasn't left handed. And the league's youngest player showed flashes of brilliance. Though his record was just 1-1, his ERA was lower than 2.40, and he twice mounted impressive innings, including the one-hitter. Joe played with Cy Young and pitched a shutout. Back home he enjoyed his toddling sister and the "Ever Victorious" 1908 football games of his brother and KU.

During his brief 1908 season, Joe gathered some valuable memories. Later he testified to experiencing no hazing as a rookie, and though he became an extremely loyal friend of Tris Speaker, they didn't choose each other as roommates in 1908. They were placed together by the team secretary, Eddie Reilly. Many of the Red Sox stayed at Putnam's Hotel, at Huntington Avenue and Gainsborough Street, in Joe's words, "only a hop, skip, and a jump" from the Conservatory of Music. They lived upstairs in rooms for six or eight players. Downstairs were a drugstore and restaurant, where the players would sit outside on pleasant nights. [5] At Putnam's Joe attended a farewell dinner for Cy Young, with the food named after the players: Wood celery, Higgins potatoes, and Speaker solid nuts. According to Joe, "The Red Sox had been finishing in last or next to last for quite a while. But even in those days, when they were having the tough luck that they were having, they never got any razzing out of any of the fans in Boston. They were too loyal." And, yes, very friendly women followed the players, including Joe.

Joe's reputation as a difficult negotiator (with support from his father, John F.) grew that off-season. Joe was the next-to-last player to sign with the Red Sox. He submitted his contract a couple of days before the end of February and didn't report to the first practice in Hot Springs, Arkansas, on March 1. When the players left the Majestic Hotel at 9:30 a.m., riding for ten minutes on a streetcar and then walking five more minutes to the new grounds, they faced incomplete construction and a grassless infield. But the weather was fine, warm with broken clouds. Tim Murnane reassured his readers the next day in the *Globe* that "Pitcher Joe Wood," though a day late from Ness City, was "looking well" and would "be out with the bunch tomorrow." Speaker, on the other hand, was in "Little Rock to pay his respects to one of Arkansas' fair daughters."

Recognizing Joe's natural ability, manager Lake used Wood in the outfield that spring, where he was brilliant. On March 9, in the first game of spring training, he played right for the Regulars, batted fourth, and homered to lead off the fifth inning. On March 10 and 12 he shifted to center for the Yannigans, where he made a game-saving catch in the first game and a difficult play on a Tris Speaker drive in the second. But he wasn't seriously considered for the outfield, or shortstop, where he played on March 14. Finally, the next day, March 15, 1909, he took "the box" for the Regulars and showed a fastball that Murnane compared with those of Kid Nichols and Cy Young. But Joe was also wild, hitting two batters and walking one while striking out four. At the plate he had a hit and two RBI.

His hot hitting continued with a home run the next day and 2 for 3 with a double on the seventeenth while playing third and left for the Yannigans. But Joe's future as a pitcher became perfectly clear March

25 in a 9–0 victory over Memphis of the Southern League on the trip north. Wood pitched five perfect innings, striking out eight of fifteen batters, including two in the first inning and the side in the fifth, walking none. The key, Wood explained later in his life, was the work of a little-known catcher, just twenty-five, in his only year for the Sox: Edward "Tubby" Spencer. Not one for exaggeration in anything but friendship, Joe declared he didn't "believe a better catch ever lived" than Tubby. Although others, including Bill Carrigan, claimed that they had tamed wild Joe Wood, Joe named only Spencer, who had a spotty career in the Major Leagues from 1905 to 1918, as his greatest backstop in the early years.[6]

There was a hiccup in Joe's last warmup, in Cincinnati against the Reds on April 4. With Pat Donohue catching Wood gave up three walks and five hits in just three innings, for seven runs (five of them unearned) in the 7–3 loss. But that performance was not the cause of Joe's absence from the opening games in Philadelphia and Washington or the home opener on April 21 against the A's. It was more serious. Joe and Tris Speaker were, in Joe's words (to Eugene Murdock), "monkeying around" in a hotel room when Tris opened a door on Wood's right foot, breaking a toe. The injury, the first of many, required surgery two days before the first game at Huntington Avenue Grounds. The official news, reported on April 21, 1909 in the *Boston Globe*, read, "Dr. William A. Brooks, who performed an operation on Joe Wood of the Boston Americans Monday [April 19], says the pitcher will take light practice by the end of the present week. This is good news to Manager Lake, who is banking on the Kansas City boy for important work early in the season."

Lake would need to be patient. After a light workout in Boston, Joe (ten pounds underweight) was activated on May 29 and joined the team in Philadelphia. But he didn't return to action for another three weeks, on June 21 in the second game of a doubleheader against the A's, in Boston. With Tubby Spencer as his catcher, Joe pitched a two-hitter, the only run unearned following an error by Amby McConnell, a hit batter, and a single. Boston 4, Philly 1. After that game the *Globe* on June 22 declared Joe "a general favorite and a fine all-around ball player." A week later, on June 28, against the Senators in Washington, on the strength of a bloop RBI single by Joe and a hit by Spencer, the Red Sox led 5–2 in the eighth. But Wood, weakened by his injury, gave up three hits in the bottom of the inning and was replaced by Elmer Steele, who allowed the tying runs before Boston won 6–5. Joe had more endurance on July 2 in Boston against the A's but lost 1–0 on a home run by Eddie Collins. Noteworthy to reporters was the "jump" on Joe's fastball.

Once fully healed from his broken toe, Joe was able to throw regularly in 1909. On July 6 he won a complete game 3–2 in the first game of a doubleheader against Washington at Boston, scattering seven hits and walking just one. But his control eluded him four days later against the White Sox; Joe gave up six hits and walked another half dozen, and Boston lost in Chicago 6–1. With a little more rest, Joe pitched a complete game on July 15 in the second half of a doubleheader against the Browns in St. Louis. But he lost a four-hitter 1–0, for the second time in less than two weeks, the only run on a throwing error by the Sox catcher Pat Donohue as Wood's record slipped to 2-3. Two days later there was a pivotal game for Wood — in relief. On July 17, 1909, he outpitched Addie Joss in Cleveland, 6–4, while demonstrating potential as a power pitcher. Joe struck out the side in the sixth, seventh, and ninth innings, totaling ten strikeouts and no walks in four innings. Halfway through Joe's first full season, Paul Shannon in the *Post* the next day requested, "Hats off to Wood. This afternoon the youngster gave an exhibition of pitching that has never been seen before in Cleveland."

Wood continued his dominance as a starter on July 20, still at Cleveland, winning 4–0 on two days' rest, as Shannon declared Joe Wood "the idol of the Boston camp." Despite the newfound praise, Joe's winning ways stopped three days later at Detroit, where he lost the first game of a doubleheader, 5–2, on a cold and overcast day. Joe got revenge on August 3 in Boston, winning 2–1, after giving up a run in the first on a ground-rule double from Cobb into what Tim Murnane in the *Globe* the next day called the "largest crowd that ever attended a ball game in New England." More importantly, the dean of Red Sox baseball in the same article named Joe "a pitcher of nerve and staying qualities." Joe allowed just three hits (two to Cobb), two walks, and two hit batters while striking out seven. Still in Boston on August 7, Wood pitched a 3–0 shutout of the White Sox, striking out seven (four in a row) while walking only one. In Murnane's words on the eighth, "The chief attraction was Joe Wood, the Kansas cyclone, who pitched an air-tight game, refusing to allow a visiting player to put his foot on third base," by controlling "remarkable speed" and "a slow ball that was a pippin." Joe Wood's second straight three-hitter raised his record to 6–4.

Within a week, on August 12, Joe started at the Huntington Avenue Grounds against Cy Young but got knocked out after four innings, leaving behind 3–2. August 18 was a better day for Boston and Joe Wood. The Red Sox won both games of a doubleheader in New York, moving them into second place. With his family attending Joe pitched the first game, giving up just three hits and winning 3–0 as his record improved to 7–4. The next day his picture was on the front page of the *Boston Post*. Joe's fourth consecutive win of the 1909 season came three days later at St. Louis, where he cruised to a 9–3 victory. Before his next start Joe replaced Ed Karger in Chicago on August 25, giving up three runs prior to being replaced by Eddie Cicotte. Luckily the Red Sox rallied, and the game ended 4–4. In his next start, on August 30, he threw three costly wild pitches in his only loss to the Naps in 1909, at Cleveland, 4–2. He was 8-5.

From that point until the end of the 1909 season, Joe Wood ran hot and cold. On September 6, in a doubleheader at Huntington Grounds, he was both. Entering the first game in the tenth inning, Wood walked a batter but retired the side before Amby McConnell's triple and a wild pitch gave Boston the win 10–9. Wood was also leading in the second game, 6–4 in the ninth, when four errors, one by Joe, allowed the Highlanders runs and a 9–6 win. On September 11 Joe rebounded at Philly in the second game of a doubleheader, shutting out the A's on four hits in a 1–0 win. As the Red Sox entered the final weeks of Joe's first full season, manager Lake rested his young pitcher.

He threw on the eighteenth as the White Sox shut out the Red Sox in Boston 7–0. Joe pitched only four innings, giving up four runs. The one light moment was Joe's participation in a 9-4-2-5-3-5-6-1-5 double play in the fourth inning. Still in Boston four days later, Joe started his final game of 1909, against Cleveland. It was a complete game 3–1 victory, the only run unearned. A day after the 1909 Red Sox season, Joe gave up a run and tripled in an exhibition at Berkeley, Rhode Island, against the champions of the Woonsockett Mill League. The game was called after eleven innings, 4–4. Two days later, in Portland, Maine, Joe pitched the middle three innings against Maine All-Stars, throwing hitless ball, doubling, stealing third, and scoring as Boston won 3–0.

Although the Red Sox would not match their 1909 record over the next two years, the foundation was established for the 1912 season. The team moved from fifth to third in the standings, from four games under .500 to twenty-five over, their first winning year since 1905. From August 4 through 18, they won eleven in a row—with youth. In addition to Wood at nineteen, on the mound they had Eddie Cicotte (twenty-five) and Larry Pape (twenty-three), as well as Charley Hall (twenty-four) and Ray Collins (twenty-two). In the field Speaker and Hooper were both twenty-one, as was Steve Yerkes. Larry Gardner was twenty-three and catcher Bill Carrigan twenty-five. The next year they added Duffy Lewis, the same age as Speaker and Hooper, to complete one of the great outfields in baseball history. Even their nickname, the Speed Boys, indicated their youth and intense play.[7] And Fred Lake, their leader, knew this young talent well.

Later Boston writers characterized Wood's play as untamed, cowboy aggressiveness. He *was* very young. But except for a couple of games, he had more trouble with hit batters than walks. During 1909 he reduced his walks per game from 6.4 (in 1908) to 2.4. Despite signs of brilliance, he wasn't a strikeout pitcher, averaging under five strikeouts per game.

The most accurate impression is that of Chet Hoff, who played for the New York Highlanders in 1911 and lived to be 107. In an interview with supporters of Joe for the Hall of Fame, Hoff remembered young Joe Wood as a "great pitcher" with "good control" who "wasn't a strike-out king, but he could strike you out when he wanted." The positives in Wood's 1909 season were obvious: nine games of no or one run, a two-hitter, and three three-hitters. Despite losing two months to injury and two games 1–0, he finished the year 11-7 with an ERA of 2.18, though he hit just .164.

On September 30, 1909, the National Commission in Cincinnati announced a postseason series between the third-place teams in the two leagues: the Red Sox and the New York Giants. It would be a seven-game series, designed to imitate the traditional White Sox-Cubs series as well as the 1909 World Series between the Tigers and the Pirates. It was destined to become a preview of the 1912 World Series. Though the Red Sox lost in New York to the Giants in the first game 4–2 on October 8, 1909, both Tris Speaker and Joe Wood starred. Speaker played flawlessly in the field (with a put-out at home from deep center field), had 3 for 4 (one a long home run to right), and stole two bases. A surprise starter for Cicotte, Joe gave up just six hits and a walk over eight. But the Sox defense was shaky (including a crucial throwing error by Joe), leading to a run in the first and three in the fourth, all unearned. Consolation was offered on the ninth by the *Washington Post*, which reported that Wood had "outpitched" Christy Mathewson. Joe didn't return in the series, but Speaker was the star, hitting 12 for 20 as Boston won four games to one.

On November 1, 1909, President John I. Taylor announced that Fred Lake, so successful in the previous season, would not return. Money and lack of appreciation were the issues. Lake was replaced by Patsy Donovan. Keeping the hot stove stoked that winter, the January 5 *Boston Globe* declared Joe to be a "great young pitcher." In addition to lauding his baseball skills, the paper reproduced images from Joe's life in Ness City, Kansas, with a letter written by Wood, describing his love of the outdoors: "I have been having some great times since coming home, hunting, fishing and skating. I also have put in some spare time horseback riding." He then narrated a local crisis. Since the "rabbits have been unusually thick around here this winter," men in Ness City "have gone out several times in the afternoon for a couple of hours and three or four of us have brought in from 150 to 200." A picture of Wood and friends on the main street showed the remains of the rabbits. Typical of a rural boy, Joe also noted "the longest cold stretch here this winter that [had] been known for a long time." He signed on January 28, 1910.

On the evening of March 3, 1910, as the train from Boston began the trip south, Joe was in Kansas City visiting Laura O'Shea. Nevertheless, he was included in Donovan's early assessment of his team. On March 4 the manager listed Wood as his third right-hander, behind Frank Arellanes and Eddie Cicotte, declaring Joe "not in the best condition last season, and yet his marvelous pitching at times was the talk of the American League." His fastball was Joe's greatest strength, according to Donovan: "When it comes to speed, no pitcher in the game today can compare with the Kansas cyclone." The main contingent arrived at 5:00 p.m., Sunday, March 6, and transferred to the Majestic Hotel. Joe appeared on the afternoon of March 8, after the 3:00 practice. Wood reported ten pounds heavier, a healthy addition given his build and medical history. Once again the Red Sox rode a trolley to the park, improved by grass in the infield, a fence in the outfield, and five hundred new bleacher seats along first base.[8] Joe began two-a-days, one-and one-half-hour workouts mornings and afternoons.

After a light shower on the morning of March 9, Joe pitched his first batting practice in the afternoon. Typical of Wood's enthusiasm for baseball — anytime, anywhere — on the twelfth Joe played second base in the morning workouts. With no baseball on Sundays, on the thirteenth he took an afternoon automobile ride into the country, indulging his softer side by returning with wild flowers. Joe Wood pitched for the first time on March 17, 1910, throwing the final three innings of a 6–4 victory over Cincinnati, giving up one run and striking out two of the last three batters he faced. He returned on Friday, March 25, and struck out five in five innings while walking only one and permitting one unearned run. But Joe was roughed up on March 31 in a 12–6 loss to the Reds, giving up ten hits, four walks, and ten runs in eight innings. He also threw into center field on an attempted pick-off at second, allowing two runners to score.

During the first stages of the northern tour, Joe didn't play against either the Memphis Turtles or the Nashville Volunteers. Given free time in Nashville, he indulged his fascination with automobiles, joining Ray Collins, Larry Gardner, and Tom Madden on a ride to the Hermitage, home of Andrew Jackson. Finally Joe returned to the mound in Cincinnati on Saturday, April 9, 1910. He pitched seven innings and gave up four of the five Reds' runs as Boston lost 5–2. In 1910 Joe Wood was rested during the exhibition games on April 12 against Worchester of the New England League and Harvard, as well as the final intrasquad game the next day. He was being groomed for the opener, on April 14 at Hilltop Park in New York, where he relieved Eddie Cicotte in the eighth, with Boston ahead 4–2 and runners on first and third, no outs, and Hal Chase at bat. On his first offering, Joe made a wild pitch, scoring a run and sending the runner on first to third. Chase then hit a sacrifice fly, tying the game. From there Joe pitched six scoreless innings, giving up just two hits, walking none, and striking out six. The game ended after fourteen innings, a 4–4 tie, because of darkness.

Joe's bad luck against the A's in his first start in 1910, April 25 in Boston, an especially cold, damp day, set the tone for a frustrating year. He pitched well, giving up only four hits in eight innings while striking out five. But Eddie Collins hit a wind-assisted home run into the left-field stands to lead off the fourth, and the next inning Philadelphia scored three more, on walks, two Red Sox errors, and a passed ball; the Sox lost 4–2. Four days later, in even wetter conditions at Washington, he relieved Sea Lion Hall in the bottom of the third inning, after Boston scored six runs to take a commanding 8–2 lead. Over the last seven innings, Joe gave up only one unearned run; the Red Sox won 9–3, and

Joe evened his record at 1 and 1. But misfortune returned at Philly on May 3. Harry Krause two-hit (one by Joe) the Red Sox for his second consecutive shutout against Boston, with both runs against Wood unearned on an error by second baseman Charlie French. Joe struck out six and walked none but lost 2–0.

His luck temporarily improved in his next three outings at the Huntington Avenue Grounds. After shutting out New York 10–0 while permitting just five singles and winning easily over the lowly Browns 8–1, giving up only four singles and an unearned run, his third win in a row was in relief, against the Tigers on May 17. After Detroit took a 6–5 lead in the fifth, the Sox scored three in the seventh, with Joe singling in Larry Gardner before scoring himself. No-hitting the Tigers in his five innings of the 8–6 victory, Joe raised his record to 4-2. He extended it to 5-2 when he beat Addie Joss in Boston on May 24. Joe gave up just four hits, striking out nine, in a complete game as Boston held on 4–3. But his four-game winning streak ended on the twenty-eighth against the mighty A's when, as usual, the problems came early. A walk, two errors, and Jack Barry's hit, the only ball to leave the infield, led to four unearned runs. Joe gave up three more runs and exited as Philadelphia won 9–3.

More bad luck seemed to follow on May 30, when Joe bruised his finger in batting practice and was expected to be sidelined indefinitely. But for once he healed quickly and returned to the mound on June 4 at Sportsman's Park in St. Louis, where he pitched a three-hit shutout, 6–0, striking out eight while walking only two. Indicative of his better hitting than in 1909, Joe went 3 for 4, with a double and two runs scored. His next two mound appearances were in relief, both in Chicago. On June 7 Wood beat Ed Walsh. Joe entered in the sixth; he gave up an unearned run and just five hits and two walks in seven and two-thirds, moving his record to 7-3. Joe wasn't as fortunate the next day. He entered in the ninth and pitched hitless baseball until the twelfth, when three White Sox hits gave Chicago a 5–4 win. On the fourteenth in Cleveland, Joe got no decision in a fourteen-inning 6–6 tie with the

Naps. Over his six and two-thirds innings, Joe gave up just five hits and no runs, striking out six while walking one and hitting another.

Even with the loss and the tie, Joe seemed on schedule for twenty wins in 1910. But Detroit and injury sent things south during the rest of June. On the eighteenth he again gave up a first-inning run, on a single by Sam Crawford, followed by five more in the fifth, on a Ty Cobb triple and Jim Delahanty's home run, which bounded into the right-field stands. The Red Sox lost 6 to 2. Joe relieved the next day in the seventh with Boston ahead 9–8. But in the ninth, with two out and Sam Crawford on third, he threw a wild pitch to tie the game. In the tenth Cobb singled to center to drive in the winning run; Joe's record fell to 7-6. Before Joe could return to the mound, the injury bug bit again. While pitching batting practice, he was struck in the left ankle by a Harry Hooper line drive. Though the bone wasn't broken, he was sidelined for a month with arterial damage. Joe went shoeless most of the rehab time.

When his leg healed, the poor luck of 1910 returned, on July 29 against the Highlanders in Boston. Joe dominated for eight innings, despite being wild (five walks and a hit batter); the only run scored on an error by Carrigan. But Wood tired in the ninth and gave up three hits around a two-base throwing error by Larry Gardner. Joe drove in the only Boston run and pitched a four-hit complete game. But he lost 3–1. After relieving in Detroit on August 2, giving up two runs on two hits and a hit batter (with no decision), on August 6 at Cleveland's League Park his wildness was the downfall. In the first inning Joe hit a batter, walked another, and threw two wild pitches, which led to three runs, the Naps winning 5–2, and Joe's record sliding to 7-8 after five straight losses. Wisely manager Donovan shelved Wood for two weeks, allowing his ankle to heal and his wildness to settle. He returned on August 23 in Boston against the St. Louis Browns.

He entered in the seventh of a hitting contest, with the Red Sox down 11–9. Joe gave up a walk in that inning but no runs. More dramatically, with one out and Bill Carrigan on first in the bottom of the seventh, Joe drove a home run into the center-field bleachers to tie the score at eleven. When Boston again scored two in the eighth, on doubles by Lewis and Engle, Wood evened his record at 8-8. The results were similar two days later, still in Boston, against the Naps. In relief of Charlie Smith, Wood pitched masterfully for six innings, permitting just five hits and no walks. When Boston scored six in the eighth, coming back from a 4–1 deficit, Joe had his ninth win. But in New York on September 2, he relieved Cicotte; Joe gave up a walk, single, and wild pitch for the two runs that allowed the Highlanders a 6–5 win. Joe was 9-9.

When Joe started again, on September 5 in Boston against the Senators, he pitched a shutout in the second game of a doubleheader. In the sixth, after a ten-minute rain delay, the Sox used walks and RBI singles from Speaker and Wagner for five runs, the only ones of the game. Gaining momentum from this shutout, Joe won again at home against the Highlanders five days later. In another complete game, he gave up three runs on six hits, two walks, and a hit batter, but his teammates scored in each of the first five innings to win 5–3.

With the Highlanders still in town on September 12, Joe relieved Loose Ed Karger in the eighth of the second game of a doubleheader, with two on and one out. Joe struck out the next batter, but Jake Stahl misplayed a ball into the two runs that tied the game 5–5. Over his two and two-thirds innings, Wood gave up one hit and struck out five. When Speaker was hit on the arm by a 3-2 pitch with the bases loaded in the tenth, Boston won 6–5, and Joe moved to 12-9. Boston papers were predicting a strong finish for Joe.

But like the young Boston team, Joe faded down the stretch. He pitched well on the thirteenth, replacing High Pockets Ben Hunt, surrendering no runs in the last two innings against New York. But the Red Sox lost their last home game 7–5. The rest were road games, which were not kind to Joe or the Sox. On the nineteenth they even lost in St. Louis. Joe once again gave up runs early, two in the first on a walk and two hits and another in the second on an error by third baseman Billy Purtell and two more hits. Boston lost 6–3. Wood had a triple but was out trying to stretch it into a home run. On September 25, the day the Red Sox slipped into fourth place, Joe gave up thirteen hits, three walks, a hit batter, and a wild pitch as the Tigers won 4–2. On September 30, Wood lost to the A's and Coombs, 4–1, as errors by Purtell and Gardner led to three unearned runs.

In his next appearance Joe entered a game in Washington on October 5 in relief of six-foot-five High Pockets Hunt. With the bases loaded, no one out, and the score 5–2, he got a fielder's choice grounder to first and another roller to Engle at third. But Clyde fumbled the ball, panicked, and threw wildly toward home, allowing two runners to score and tying the game. A double play on a fly to Duffy Lewis ended the scoring. But the game was called for darkness, a 5–5 tie. The next day Wood relieved against the Senators in the sixth with two outs, the bases loaded, and the score 5–4. On the first pitch Bill Cunningham's grounder was misplayed by Jake Stahl, giving Washington the lead 6–5. Joe gave up no more hits, but the Sox didn't score on Walter Johnson, and the game was called after eight, again for darkness.

Joe pitched the first game of a doubleheader at Hilltop Park in New York that ended the 1910 season on October 8, with the Red Sox finishing 9-23 after the first of September.[9] Once again he started slowly, giving up a run on Hal Chase's hit in the first and two more in the third, primarily because of Duffy Lewis's error. The Sox lost 4–1 as twenty-year-old Joe Wood finished bad-luck 1910 with a 12-13 record, despite his best ERA until 1915, 1.69. Though not a regular starter, he had fourteen complete games and three shutouts. While he struggled against the best teams, going 0-4 against the A's and 1-3 versus the Tigers, and preferred the Huntington Grounds, finishing just 3-10 on the road, the rest of his record spoke for itself. His ERA and WHIP were second—barely—on the Red Sox to Ray Collins, and his strikeouts were up from 4.9 to 6.6 per game. Joe also hit .261 with two doubles, a triple, a home run, and five RBI.

During this hard-luck year on the baseball field, the Wood family made some major changes. Soon after the death of his mother, on

December 30, 1909, John F. decided to return to the family farm in Shohola, Pennsylvania, at the request of Aunt Jerusha (who lived in Parkers Glen, where her husband was postmaster), executor of the estate.[10] So, as Joe remembered, his father used Joe's income from baseball to rent two boxcars for the trip from Ness City, Kansas. Pete, the elder brother, was selected to watch over the livestock in transit, which involved feeding and watering the four horses, a couple of cows, and a few chickens. John F. intended to become a chicken farmer, with trial law on the side. Unfortunately, he found none of the courtroom drama he had tasted in Kansas, Chicago, and Colorado. Instead, in Joe's words, his father did the "searching records kind of thing." John F. also milked four to six cows, mostly for the farmhands but also so that the family could be "raised on ice cream" at Woodtown. When a disease decimated the chicken population, John switched to dairy farming and churned butter on a treadmill driven by dogs and mules.

October 25, 1910, was Joe's twenty-first birthday. To mark the occasion, his mother gave him a fourteen-carat Longines watch, which broke against the side of a trunk he took to spring training. But the young man replaced the crystal and repaired the hands and face; he declared proudly as an old man that it worked "same as ever." In the off-season between 1910 and 1911, Joe worked the farm, which helped him gain weight and strength. For Red Sox fans the big news was that first baseman Jake Stahl, who had played 144 games the previous year and led the team in home runs (ten) and RBI (seventy-seven), left baseball to work in a Chicago bank with his father-in-law. Joe sympathized, feeling that the financial insecurity of Major League baseball made other employment smart, especially after one's baseball career. After a mediocre year, marked by a precipitous decline in September, manager Patsy Donovan was rehired by Taylor in a poor non-move. This time Joe gave the Sox little trouble, signing for John I. Taylor and the Boston Americans on January 9, 1911.

Spring training came early that year. In order to train at Redondo Beach, a town of just nine hundred eighteen miles southwest of Los

Angeles, the first contingent left Boston at 1:00 p.m. on February 18.[11] Joe boarded in Jersey City, New York, at 7:40 the next morning. After stops in Philadelphia and Chicago, the team arrived in Kansas City at noon on Tuesday the twenty-first, where fans of local hero Joe Wood stood in deep snow.[12] Surprisingly, given Joe's work in the off-season, on the ride West the Red Sox organization expressed concerns that Joe looked thin and thus not in ideal shape. It didn't help anxieties over Joe's health that, after the Red Sox arrived February 23, 1911, Joe was excused from the initial intrasquad game because he had taken a "jar" on the long, curving "chute slide" at the saltwater baths. He was healthy enough for a rifle contest on the practice field, losing to Ed Karger and Tris Speaker.

After Joe's first appearance, on February 26, in which he gave up a walk and a hit batter in the fifth inning for the Regulars in a 3–2 win over the Yannigans, the team moved north, rain set in, and Joe came down with a cold. Between his illness and even more rain, Joe didn't play again until March 11 against the San Francisco Seals. In a 6–4 win, Joe was wild, giving up three hits, six walks, a hit batter with the bases loaded, and four runs over five innings. Once the Regulars returned to the LA area, Wood settled in against the Vernon Tigers of the Pacific Coast League on March 16, 1911, pitching five innings, winning 3–1, striking out five without walking a batter. The run was unearned. On St. Patrick's Day key players, including Speaker and Wood, were given the day off to watch boxer Ad Wolgast of Milwaukee, the lightweight champion, successfully defend his title against George Memsic.

On the nineteenth when Wood pitched the final five innings of a ten-inning victory, 6–3, over Vernon, he was effectively wild, striking out four while giving up two walks, a wild pitch, and a hit batter. The Tigers got just two hits. Joe pitched against the Los Angeles Angels of the Pacific Coast League on the twenty-fourth and dominated in his six innings by striking out nine and giving up only four hits, a walk, and no runs as Boston won 11–4. He also drove in a run. On getaway day, March 26, he tossed an inning in the 12–4 win over Los Angeles before the Regulars headed out on the southern route to cities like Yuma, El Paso, Oklahoma City, Wichita, and Joe's Kansas City. That way the older players could expect better weather and players from the South, like Tris Speaker, would attract larger crowds.

In Yuma, capitalizing on their cowboy image, Joe and Tris mounted "Indian ponies" in a parade while other Sox rode in autos before a lopsided win, 17–5, against the Yuma team. In Joe's first work on the southern tour, Tuesday, March 28, versus the El Paso Mavericks, he gave up one unearned run on three hits over five innings while tripling for two RBI, scoring a run, and stealing a base. The score was 9–1. In his most dominating game of the 1911 spring season, on March 31 at Fort Worth in 100 degree heat, Wood pitched the Red Sox Regulars to their fourteenth straight win, 4–2, over the Fort Worth Panthers of the Texas League. Joe struck out fifteen, eleven in the first five innings, and gave up two unearned runs. On April 2 in Wichita, cheered on by Kansas supporters, Joe pitched the sixth and seventh innings, striking out three and allowing no runners, as Boston beat the Jobbers of the Western League 5–4. The stage was set for a weekend return to Kansas City, the home of the Blues and Laura O'Shea, his regular correspondent. He arrived a day early, probably to do some courting of the Irish girl.[13]

In the first game, on Saturday, April 8, Joe appeared late in the game, but not as a pitcher. At Association Park Joe ran on the field at umpire McKee, protesting that the Blues were getting to hit clean balls while the Red Sox had to swing at dirty, soft ones. When "the umpire swung a right-hand punch at Wood's face," Joe responded by "hooking and jabbing with both fists" before a Blues player managed a "hammer lock and a double strangle hold."[14] Police were called, and the fans had to be restrained by wires around the field. The next day, Sunday the ninth, with McKee behind the plate, and facing Chick Brandom (back with the Blues), Joe entered in the seventh and pitched three innings of nohit ball, walking one and striking out six. Joe won 4–3 on hits in the ninth by Lewis, Wagner, and Rip Williams.

Joe Wood's breakout year, 1911, began in Washington DC. He was just twenty-one on April 12, 1911, when he took the mound at National Field to face the Senators' lefty Dolly Gray. (Walter Johnson was holding out for a long-term contract.) Before a sold-out crowd, President Taft threw out the first ball (to the pitcher) as fans sat in new seats, rebuilt after a major fire three weeks earlier had leveled the grandstands and bleachers. On a cold and breezy day, Wood dominated early, using strikeouts to overcome weak fielding by Boston. With Joe doubling in his only official at bat, the Red Sox built a 4–0 lead. But the misfortune of 1910 returned in a disastrous sixth, due to Heinie Wagner's two misplays. The Sox lost 8–5, with Joe throwing five and one-third innings and giving up seven unearned runs. The next day, April 13, Tim Murnane of the *Globe* declared, "Wood displayed rare form and should have won in a walk."

The rest of April was hit and miss. In his second game, at Philadelphia on April 18, Joe tested his luck again when he fell behind 1–0 after six. But the Sox scored seven in the seventh and another six in the ninth, with Joe picking up another hit, two runs, and an RBI to win 13–5. He seemed to gain momentum in his second consecutive complete game a week later at the Huntington Grounds, against the Highlanders. Three runs in the third and Speaker's two-run homer to the flagpole in the fifth gave the Red Sox all they needed to win 5–3. Joe struck out ten, all in the first seven innings. On April twenty-sixth Murnane gushed: "Joe Wood never looked better." But on April 29 things reversed again. Speaker's homer to center in the fourth and Joe's triple in the fifth gave Boston a 2–1 lead. But in the bottom of the seventh, Sox first baseman Rip Williams made two errors and Senators back-up catcher Eddie Ainsworth tripled. Joe pitched a three hitter, striking out eight, but lost 4–3. He was 2-2.

He heated up in May, winning four consecutive games, starting with back-to-back shutouts at Hilltop Park in New York. On May 4 he threw a two-hitter, striking out seven and winning 2–0. Four days later Joe only struck out two but gave up just a bunt single, to pitcher Ray Caldwell; the game was called for rain and darkness after six, with

Boston winning 4–0. Wood extended his record to 6 and 2 by winning two games in relief on the road. On May 11 in Cleveland Joe stranded two inherited runners in the ninth. After Bill Carrigan's single put the Red Sox ahead 7–6 in the tenth, Joe left runners on second and third by striking out Neal Ball and inducing a ground out. In Detroit on the thirteenth, the Tigers led 10–4 in the ninth when the Sox rallied for seven, including a grand slam by Duffy Lewis. Joe then gave up the tying run and loaded the bases with one out in the bottom of the ninth. But he struck out Charlie Schmidt as Ty Cobb was doubled up trying to steal home. The Red Sox got two in the tenth before Joe struck out two of the last three batters for the win, 13–11.

Joe alternated between wins and losses over the next three weeks. His four-game winning streak ended on May 15 in Detroit. In a typical slow start, Joe fell behind 3–0 in the third, from walks, a wild pitch, and a key double by Ty Cobb, before settling in and facing the minimum from the fourth through the ninth. Meanwhile, the Sox tied the game, aided by Detroit errors from Delahanty and Bush, plus a bases-loaded hit batter. Boston could have won it in the tenth when Larry Gardner tripled to deep center and scored on another boot from Bush. But in the bottom, with two out and one on, Duffy Lewis made a three-base error, Wood intentionally walked Cobb and Crawford, and Delahanty singled to left for the winning—unearned—runs. Detroit 5, Boston 4.

Four days later in Chicago, after Joe entered in the sixth and allowed the tying run in the eighth on a wild pitch, he responded by striking out the next five batters. In the twelfth, after Wagner's double led to a Sox run, Joe gave up a triple with one out. But Joe, a good fielder, leaped to grab a high-bounding squeeze attempt and tagged the runner trying to score. The game ended with a runner caught stealing. In seven innings Wood struck out ten. On May 19 the Red Sox beat the White Sox 4 to 3 in the twelve-inning game.

May 24, 1911, in St. Louis was one of those rare days when Joe Wood lost to the Browns. He pitched a complete game, giving up only four hits, but lost 1–0. This time the slow start killed; with two out in the first, he gave up a double against the right-field fence and a bloop over second for the run. Following the pattern of wins after losses, revenge was Joe's the next day. Still in St. Louis Joe relieved in the sixth with the score tied 5–5 and pitched four innings, striking out eight as the Red Sox won 9–5. He gave up three hits and walked two, but the strikeouts put out all fires.

Joe squeaked out one more win in May, beating the Senators and Walter Johnson 5–4 at Washington on the thirtieth. Again early innings put the Sox in jeopardy as Washington scored in the first on Clyde Milan's speed and third on an error by Clyde Engle. But in the ninth Larry Gardner's bases-loaded Texas League single into center while batting for Joe and Duffy Lewis's double gave Boston a three-run lead. Charley Hall gave back two runs before making Joe Wood a winner. But Joe still couldn't pick up steam in Boston against the White Sox on June 2. Two throwing errors on the same play, by Rip Williams and Clyde Engle, gave away two runs in the first. Chicago added another two in the second before Joe left in the fourth. Hall wasn't any better as the White Sox won 13–8.

Finally, beginning on June 5, Joe put together a winning streak. That day, also against the White Sox, he pitched two and one-third innings in relief, striking out four of the last six batters, including three consecutive pinch hitters in the ninth. The Red Sox won 5–4, Wood's tenth victory against five losses. Five days later he persevered for a ten-inning 6–5 win against the Tigers in Boston. The Red Sox scored five runs by the fourth, with Wood leading off that inning with a homer to the back of the left-field bleachers. But the Tigers chipped away, with Steve Yerkes's error allowing the tying run in the ninth. Fortunately, in the tenth Boston catcher Les Nunamaker singled for the winning run. Joe was stronger in his third straight victory, against the Naps in Boston on June 15. He held Cleveland to six hits, striking out seven, walking just two, and retiring the last fifteen Naps as the Sox won 4–2.

Four days later Joe won in New York, as he did during all of 1911.

He gave up three runs to the Highlanders in the third, one unearned when nineteen-year-old first baseman Tracy Baker, playing his only game in the Majors, failed to corral a throw from shortstop Wagner. Meanwhile, Joe's RBI double to right and Harry Hooper's inside-the-park homer to the same field led Boston to a 6–3 win. On the twenty-third, back in Boston, Joe ran his record to 14-5 by beating the A's 7–3 in the first game of a doubleheader. The key inning was the fourth, when Boston scored six times, with Joe hitting a three-run homer to right and Speaker a two-run round-tripper deep into the same stands. Joe gave up eleven hits, but weak fielding led to all the A's runs.

Four days later, on June 27, the winning streak was stopped at five as Joe completed just three innings, giving up five hits and a run in each frame. The A's won 7–3. With such a short outing he was able to return two days later against New York and pitch a complete game. But he lost again, this time 3–1, as Boston made four errors, three by Clyde Engle and another by Hap Myers, making a clumsy transition from the outfield to first base. Even with that loss Joe's record at the end of June stood at 14-7. His win-loss percentage got even better on the Fourth of July in Boston against the Senators. Joe relieved after a stomach disorder required Cicotte to be carried from the field by four teammates. In the ninth Joe gave up a walk and two hits to tie the game at three. But in the bottom of the inning, Harry Hooper scored on Duffy Lewis's short fly to left when the Washington catcher dropped the ball in the collision at home. Boston won 4–3.

Three days later, on July 7, 1911, Joe pitched his second-best game of the year, at St. Louis. He struck out fifteen Browns in an easy 6–1 win, a one-hitter. The only runners to reach base before the last inning were Al Schweitzer, on a throw from third baseman Larry Gardner dropped by Hap Myers, and Bobby Wallace, who walked before being erased in a double play. But Joe made a mess in the ninth, when he walked Wallace and Dode Criss. With two on, Burt Shotton broke up the no-hitter with a single to right, filling the bases. It looked like Joe would salvage the shutout when he struck out Jimmy Austin and Al Schweitzer. But then he hit Frank LaPorte to force in the only Brown before retiring the side. Joe's record: 16-7 a week into July.

But as the pressure increased and the innings piled up, Joe's play became uneven. He lost the next two games, in Chicago and Detroit. Against the White Sox on July 11, he and the Red Sox were shut out 4–0 by Doc White, with Clyde Engle getting the only three hits by Boston. Joe lost another shutout in the eighth, with a hit batter and back-to-back hits leading to the four runs. Four days later his early-inning issues returned against the Tigers. At Bennett Park in the first Joe gave up two walks, a bunt hit by Ty Cobb, and two more hits before exiting without getting an out and being charged with five runs. The Tigers won 9–4.

His pattern of hot and cold continued during the rest of July. On the nineteenth in Cleveland, he beat forty-four-year-old Cy Young, pitching in his final year, 10–2. Joe gave up nine hits and threw two wild pitches, but he had three hits himself, including a triple. He wasn't as strong the next day in relief of Ray Collins. Joe gave up a single, walk, wild pitch, and the game-winning hit to Terry Turner as Boston and Joe lost 8–7. Three days later, in an eleven-inning game, still in Cleveland, the heavy workload started to show. Ahead 2–1 in the eighth, Wood struck out Jack Graney and Ivy Olson with runners on second and third to preserve the lead. But in the ninth Joe Jackson bunted safely, moved to third when Joe threw wildly to first, and scored on a wild pitch to tie the game. In the eleventh Jackson again singled, moved to third on Ted Easterly's single, and scored on Neal Ball's infield hit. The Naps won 3–2.

The next day, July 24, 1911, Tris Speaker and Joe Wood didn't leave with the rest of the Red Sox for Boston. They remained in Cleveland for the Addie Joss benefit game. A pitcher with a lifetime ERA of 1.89 who became a Hall of Famer via the Veterans' Committee in 1978, Joss had died at thirty-one that April 14 of tubercular meningitis. The game between the Naps and the AL All-Stars raised money for Joss's widow and children. Many believe the lineup for the stars was the greatest ever: Tris Speaker, center field; Eddie Collins, second base; Ty Cobb, right field; Home Run Baker, third base; Wahoo Sam Crawford, left field; Hal Chase, first base; Bobby Wallace, shortstop; and Gabby Street, catcher. Joe started the game and gave up two hits and a run in his two innings before giving way to Walter Johnson and Russ Ford. Starter Cy Young gave up three runs in three innings for the Naps as the All-Stars won 5–3. For the stars Hal Chase had three hits, with Speaker, Milan, Collins, and Cobb getting two each. Joe had a sacrifice fly in his only at bat. The receipts were $12,914.[15]

The five-day rest did wonders for young Joe Wood in his next game, at the Huntington Grounds. Something good was expected against the Browns since he had thrown a one-hitter July 7, the last time he had faced them. But this day, July 29, 1911, was even better. In the first game of a Saturday doubleheader, Joe pitched his only no-hitter. Just three batters reached base: in the second Willie Hogan walked with one out and was erased on a double play; with two outs in the next inning, Wood walked pitcher Joe Lake before Burt Shotton flied out to Speaker; and in the fifth Hogan was hit by a pitch, advanced on a sacrifice and a ground out, but was stranded at third when Joe struck out player/manager Bobby Wallace, looking. The Red Sox were backed by a two-run triple to right from Larry Gardner and Tris Speaker's slicing home run into the stands in left. Joe struck out twelve Browns, with the Red Sox winning 5–0 as only two hits reached the outfield. Defensively Larry Gardner played a strong third base.[16]

Joe returned to the mound in the first game of a Wednesday doubleheader against the Detroit Tigers on August 2. He got off to his typical start, giving up two runs on an RBI double from Cobb and single by Sam Crawford. It took a pick-off of Crawford at second base to end the scoring in the first. The only other Detroit run was unearned, on two Sox errors in the sixth. Boston seized the lead in the second when they scored four runs, thanks to three Tigers errors and a bases-loaded walk. Joe's double into the roped-off crowd in left helped the Sox score two more in the sixth. They won 7–3. With his record 19–11, twenty-five victories, maybe even thirty, seemed possible for the young star.

But he stumbled on magic number twenty, losing his next three starts without pitching well. On August 7 in Boston he lost to Cleveland 8–3, giving up thirteen hits to the Naps, including three doubles and a home run to Napoleon Lajoie. Four days later, on August 11 in Philadelphia, Joe was even less effective, lasting only two innings. After giving up eight hits and five runs, he exited with no one out in the third. The Red Sox lost 11–5. On August 17 Joe relieved in the ninth at Detroit and got a fly to right and a ground out to preserve the Boston 4–3 win. But he lost two days later, 6–3, in Detroit, his third loss while stuck on nineteen wins.

Finally, on August 25 Joe got his twentieth win, against the Browns in the first game of another doubleheader in St. Louis. He struggled with his control, walking five and hitting a batter, and, typically, gave up a run in the first, on a walk and a double. Crucial was the sixth, when Joe struck out pinch-hitter Dode Criss on three pitches, all looking, with the bases loaded and the Sox ahead 3–1. In the ninth St. Louis scored and had the tying and winning runs on base. But Joe got Frank LaPorte on a come-backer to win 3–2. Once Joe got number twenty, however, he went on another losing streak.

He pitched well on August 29 in Chicago, surviving a walk and a single in the first by striking out the side. Later Chicago got only single runs in the third, sixth, and eighth. But spitballer Death Valley Jim Scott threw a shutout, 3–0. On September 4 Joe pitched another complete game, against the Highlanders in Boston, in the first game of a doubleheader. He started well, taking a 2–0 lead into the fifth. But New York scored four in the inning on three hits, a walk, and three errors. In the ninth a walk and two more errors allowed two more unearned runs. Though Wood scattered six hits, he also walked six and hit a batter as the Red Sox porous defense made the final score 6–3. Two days later at Philadelphia Joe relieved in the ninth inning of the second game of a doubleheader, with the scored tied at two. He gave up only a walk that inning. Yerkes tripled and Speaker singled him home in the tenth. But a single and two bunt hits set up a two-out single by Jack Barry, giving Philadelphia a 4–3 win. The sixth loss in the last seven decisions dropped Joe's record to 20-17.

Just when it looked like Joe would end the 1911 season on a major skid, manager Donovan gave him valuable time off. Joe responded by giving up only two runs the rest of the season. After a ten-day hiatus he beat Cleveland 6–0 at Boston on September 16 in the first game of a doubleheader, allowing just four singles while striking out seven. After another long rest he struck out even more Browns, eleven, in Boston on September 25, 1911, including the side in the first. Despite being wild (four walks, a hit batter, and a wild pitch), Joe extricated himself from trouble; in the seventh, after four consecutive singles, he struck out the side. Boston won easily, 9–2. Wood was even better in his last game of 1911, on October 3 at New York's Hilltop Park. In the second game of yet another doubleheader, called after eight because of darkness, he struck out thirteen Highlanders and allowed just two singles after carrying a perfect game into the sixth. Boston won 7–0.

That year he was also chosen for the American League All-Star team that played a series of exhibition games the second week in October while the A's waited for the NL season to end. Joining Joe were Hal Chase, Larry Gardner, Clyde Milan, Ty Cobb, Tris Speaker, and Walter Johnson. Like Ray Collins and Gardner, Wood was a substitute when White Sox stars were held back by Charles Comiskey for the Chicago championship series. Joe won the first game, a warmup against Newark of the Eastern League, 2–0 on a four-hitter. He also stole home for the first run. After the All-Stars and the A's split two games in Washington and the All-Stars won 13–8 in Richmond, Virginia, Joe pitched the final game on October 12 in Philly. He gave up only five hits (four of them singles) but lost 3–2 because he also walked three, threw two wild pitches, and made a throwing error that allowed one of the A's runs. He had a single in two times at bat.[17]

Joe Wood tired as the 1911 season wore on; 14-5 by June 23, he went 6-12 before winning his last three games. Nevertheless, the 1911 season showed Joe's potential when healthy. Four complete game wins at

Hilltop Park, three of them shutouts (a one-hitter and two two-hitters), solidified his reputation as Highlander/Yankee killer.[18] At twenty-one Joe Wood became the workhorse of the Red Sox, throwing over seventy-five more innings than in 1910 and fifty-five more than any other Boston pitcher. His 2.02 ERA was third in the AL. He threw a no-hitter against the St. Louis Browns, nearly two in a row against them. Emerging as a power pitcher, Joe averaged 7.542 strikeouts per game, an AL best. His 231 strikeouts were second only to Ed Walsh's 255. Though his .261 batting average was identical to 1910, Joe in 1911 had four doubles, two triples, and two homers, along with eleven RBI. His slugging percentage moved from .362 to .420 between 1910 and 1911.

When Joe Wood returned to the Shohola farm, he found a blend of the old and the new. The nineteenth-century barn remained. But added were a corncrib and a chicken house, both two stories. Eventually John F. used skills learned in Ouray, Colorado, to build a blacksmith shop, an ice house, and a shed for wagons; the place became, in Joe's words, a "village . . . all his own," with Joe "paying the bill all the time." Despite his irritation over John F.'s sponging, Joe was proud of his father's abilities to "take a piece of metal and make any damn thing with it he wanted," including horseshoes and braces for the bobsled. John even made a boat to ferry the family across the lake for picnics. The ideal for John and Joe was a man named Bill who lived deep in the woods, eating deer, growing vegetables, cutting wood, even flying his own plane; in Joe's words, it's a "pretty smart hombre" who is "self-sufficient" and lives the "life that he loves."

Farm life came with some life lessons. The Woods paid their help $10 a month plus room and board in the summer, only room and board in the winter. Many hired men had drinking problems. Joe remembered particularly Christopher Miller, called "Butcher" (referenced in a Yukon letter) who under the influence would declare, "My name is Christopher Miller, and my name is just as good as yours is." Observing such vulnerability taught Joe moderation, which he tried to instill in his children. But self-control allowed joyful eccentricities. John F. named cattle after Shakespeare characters and loved to argue religion. In Joe's words, "swarms" of fifteen-twenty people would gather "just to hear him talk." A "first class atheist," John F. could, according to his adoring son, quote every passage in the Bible. To his dying day, Joe's father "defied them if they said he was going to live after death."

Although Joe loved the Pennsylvania farm, he didn't romanticize its conditions, naming it a "pretty dull existence," full of "tough going." As he told grandson Richard, "When you went to bed at night, you'd sneak into your nightgown, or whatever you're wearing, and get upstairs and get into bed. In the morning you'd run down to the stove." Chores went with the territory: "All winter long they'd cut wood and throw it into the wood house, using two-man crosscut saws, no power saws." Eventually sixteen-volt Delco batteries powered lights, and when kitchen appliances became available, Joe installed a Kohler plant to power them. But John F., stubborn and independent, balked at conveniences, lighting kerosene lamps and burning wood until his death in 1944. In winter Joe skied from the hill behind the graveyard down to the house. He preferred ten-foot hickory skis, but chestnuts were better for jumping stone walls, which in warmer weather he flew over on a one-eyed palomino.

These country idylls were interrupted by an announcement in national papers that Joe would be married in Philadelphia on December 20, 1911, to one May Perry, a "light-hearted," "very attractive," and popular former student at Burdett College, a Boston business school. They had met the previous summer at Huntington Avenue Grounds, where she was a rabid fan. There was no marriage. But decades later, in an interview with Lee Goodwin and Joe's son Bob, Joe hinted at his love life in 1911:

Bob: May Perry.

Joe (in strong, deep voice): She was a call girl. (Bob and Lee laugh.)

Lee: She was supposed to be a debutante.

Joe: Yeah . . . I got congratulations from my real wife for that.

Bob: That's really true. Mom was kind of disappointed, and she sent you a telegram or something, from Kansas City.

Joe: "Congratulations."

Bob: . . . And then what happened? How did you fix that up?

Joe: I didn't fix it up. I just didn't say anything more about it, that's all.[19]

A politic man who was fond of fishing, Joe knew what to keep quiet and when to cut bait.

In the meantime there were chores to be done on the Shohola farm and a little sister, just five years old, to know better. But even Zoë, as worshipful as she was, couldn't imagine the baseball season awaiting her brother, just turning twenty two years old. Since 1907 he had been Ozone and the Kansas Cyclone. Within a year he would be Smoky Joe, the equal of the Big Train, and a hero of the 1912 World Series.

FOUR

The 1912 Regular Season

Before Joe Wood and the Red Sox could realize their dreams, the Boston organization needed to get its house in order, starting with three substantial changes at the top. John I. Taylor agreed to sell 50 percent of the team to two men: James McAleer, a longtime player with the Cleveland Spiders of the National League and (since the creation of the American League) manager of Cleveland, St. Louis, and the Washington Senators; and Robert McRoy, the secretary to AL president Ban Johnson. The second change was in player personnel. By mid-October there was speculation that Jake Stahl, friend to the new owners, would return from banking to play first base for the Sox. On November 6 the rumor was upgraded to a better fact. Jake would also become manager, a popular move with the players. Once McAleer was appointed president, John I. Taylor was free to develop the third change, a new facility to be completed by the 1912 season, eventually named Fenway Park.

Unlike catcher Nunamaker and Tris Speaker, and despite Wood's reputation as a difficult negotiator, twenty-two-year-old Joe had signed a contract by mid-February. The new Boston management, remembering the maddening rain and exhausting travel to Redondo Beach, California, in 1911 didn't ask the Red Sox players to report to Hot Springs, Arkansas, until Sunday, March 10. The Boston Americans would use Majestic Park, four blocks from the trolley with a field likely to hold water after unwelcome spring showers. Most of the players and coaches joined Sox supporters, including Nuf Ced McGreevey, in a circuitous train ride from Boston, down to New York and Washington, then over to Cincinnati, picking up a few Red Sox at each stop. They were due in Hot Springs at 10:50 a.m. on Sunday, the tenth, but were delayed by the wreck of an Illinois Central freight near Louisville and a subsequent missed connection in Memphis. The Rock Island Line added the Sox to its train for Little Rock and then attached the team's Pullman and baggage cars to a local for Hot Springs. They made it late Sunday night. Waiting for them were Nunamaker and Wood, who both had arrived on Saturday evening. Joe, like his father, was stubborn and independent. But mostly he was anxious to get the season started.

The next day the first bad weather set in. The rain on Monday, March 11, 1912, allowed the players to experiment with changing into their uniforms at the new bathhouses rather than the hotel. The next morning was dry but cold and windy, so they revisited the baths. That afternoon California pitchers Hall and Leonard (presumably better conditioned in the western sun) pitched the first batting practice. Joe Wood, reporters noted, was also in good form after winter workouts at the Pennsylvania sawmill, where he had cut timber for a new house. Tim Murnane observed, "Wood has never started a season in as good shape as he is this spring."[1] Joe was hobbled briefly in the first days when he gathered a nail in a shoe. But the setback was minimal.

In anticipation of games against the Phillies the following Saturday and Monday (no games were played on Sunday), the Red Sox began an intrasquad series between the Regulars and the Yannigans. On Wednesday the Regulars won 8 to 6, with Wood limited to throwing batting practice. The next day he was still gimpy from the nail wound and his first throwing session, but a major storm caused the cancellation of all workouts anyway. On Friday, the fifteenth, it was clear but chilly, so for precaution Wood stayed on the sidelines as O'Brien, Cicotte, and Bedient threw to the batters. Joe was still off the mound in the first game with the Phillies, won by Philadelphia 12–2.

Joe's first work in "the box" came the next day, on Tuesday, March 19, in a scrimmage won by the Yannigans 8–6. He started and pitched three innings, giving up three singles and two doubles but only one run, striking out the side in the second after runners reached second and third with no outs. Joe also got a hit and scored a run. Then the rains returned, along with high winds and the Sabbath, leading to four days of inactivity. On Monday, the twenty-fifth, after the team worked out in the morning, Wood entered an afternoon practice game and struck out the first two batters. But then Marty Krug hit a home run. Wood went five innings, giving up three singles and a double in addition to the first-inning homer, a total of three runs, two unearned, in the 7–3 victory by the Regulars. He found a groove on March 27, in a game won by the Regulars 3–2. Joe pitched hitless ball the last four innings, employing what Tim Murnane of the *Globe* called "fine speed and perfect command." The next day the same paper declared Wood the "Hardest Pitching Proposition of the Spring."

Then another rainstorm arrived, forcing the team to work out between showers. Finally, on Saturday, the thirtieth, Wood and O'Brien pitched for the Regulars against Cicotte and Hall for the Yannigans. Joe was again superb . . . after the first inning, in which Olaf Henriksen's double was followed by Bradley's RBI single. Wood gave up only that run and five hits over five innings. The Regulars won 2–1. At Hot Springs in 1912, Joe demonstrated the command that would serve him well in the regular season. In four games between March 19 and 30, he gave up only one walk and one wild pitch over sixteen innings. With so many rainouts the team considered working out on Sunday, but heavy rains lasted all day. The Sox prepared to head for Nashville on Tuesday, April 2.

But McRoy, noting the flooding throughout the South, canceled trips to Nashville and Dayton and rearranged a direct train for Cincinnati, leaving on Thursday, April 4, and arriving on Friday. In the meantime the rains continued on Monday, canceling the twelve-mile walk through the mountains to Ozark Lithia Springs. The baths were a welcome alternative. The Sox played a scrub game on soggy Majestic Park on Tuesday, with Wood working three hitless innings. The last two days in Hot Springs, the weather finally turned sunny and warm for an intrasquad game and a practice on Thursday morning before the team boarded at 1:30 p.m. for Cincinnati. But before the Sox left Arkansas, the Friday game in Cincinnati was canceled because the new park wasn't ready. McRoy also failed to get Norwood Inn Park for a Friday scrimmage, the trip took twenty-four hours because of flooding around Memphis, and forty bags of clothes and equipment got lost. At least they were welcomed at the Havlin Hotel, a classy ten-story structure on Vine Street, by August Herrmann, chairman of the National Commission.

In previous incarnations the home of the Reds at Western Avenue and Findlay Street had been called League Park and the Palace of the Fans. But Redland Field, which later would be renamed Crosley Field, was a complete rebuild.[2] At a cost of $400,000, it had a capacity of twelve thousand. Though Cincinnati would officially open the park the next Thursday against the Chicago Cubs, the first game in Redland Park, on April 6, 1912, featured Joe Wood pitching for the Red Sox. The weather was good, and the field was playable though soft because of the new grass and rains. The game was a smear. Both Speaker and Hooper had three hits, and player/manager Jake Stahl registered five RBI. Joe went six scoreless innings, giving up four hits and walking one while striking out six. He also had two hits, one a double. With Joe's brother, Pete, in the stands, Joe and the Sox won 13–1.

The following day the Reds evened the series by winning 6–2, with Eddie Cicotte losing, partly because of two costly errors by Marty Krug, who later that year would become infamous for another drop with Joe on the mound. Seven and one-half years later in that same park, Cicotte, playing for the Chicago White Sox, hit the first batter, Reds' second baseman Morrie Rath, and the fix of the Series was on. But this day the Red Sox hurried to make a 6:20 p.m. train back to Boston, where a dusting of snow was visible on the way to Back Bay Station, next to nearly abandoned Huntington Avenue Grounds, where they arrived on the morning of April 9, 1912.[3] That afternoon the 1912 Boston Red

Sox traveled as a team for their first view of Fenway Park, which had been in construction since the late fall of 1911.

Built on reclaimed land, the park was designed to support the Fenway Realty Company, owned by General Taylor, John I.'s father. It stimulated nascent Kenmore Square and trolley service to the surrounding area. From an engineering standpoint, it was concrete and steel, not a wooden structure that tended to catch fire. The shape was a bit odd. It kept the orientation of the old Huntington Avenue Grounds, with the third baseline pointing almost due north. But the left-field fence was a mere three hundred feet from home plate, squeezing against Lansdowne Street. The wall there was twenty-five feet high (to obstruct the view by fans outside the park), with a hill, twenty-five feet long and rising nearly ten feet off the normal playing surface, to seat overflow. In Fenway's first version the only roofed section was down the right-field line. For automobile aficionados like Joe Wood, there was a parking area outside right field. Fenway Park also featured an electric scoreboard and a brick facade entrance. With nearly thirty thousand seats, twice as many as the Huntington home, it cost about $650,000.[4]

The first game in the new Fenway Park was an exhibition against Harvard on April 9, 1912. The start was moved to 3:30 to conform to rules against class-time athletic events at the university. The grandstands of Fenway and even some runways were incomplete. The right- and center-field bleachers welcomed fans, but the field, including infield sod replanted from the Huntington Grounds, was soft because of the rain and primitive conditions. A light snow fell as Casey Hageman pitched a one-hitter over seven innings for the Sox in a game called because of darkness, won by the Sox 2–0. Key was the wildness of the Harvard pitchers, who walked ten. Among the three thousand attendees were Governor Eugene Foss and Boston mayor John F. "Honey Fitz" Fitzgerald. President McAleer presented Cardinal O'Connell with a permanent pass to Fenway "engraved on a solid gold plate."[5]

The weather was surprisingly much better for the first game of the season — in New York, at Hilltop Park on April 11, 1912. Because of Joe's dominant spring, it was easy for Jake Stahl to name his young pitcher the starter. As usual opening-day festivities abounded. New York's new manager, Harry Wolverton, was presented with a large floral display and a loving cup in hope of improved fortunes for the Highlanders. A military band furnished the musical salute, and the first ball was thrown out by Supreme Court justice Edward E. McCall. Charles Somers, who had bankrolled much of the early expansion of the American League, was there as the president of the Cleveland Indians. The weather was almost balmy, though attendance was low, about fifteen thousand, because the popular Giants were playing in Brooklyn against the Dodgers, still often called the Superbas.

Joe was his slow-starting self that day. After the Red Sox scored a run in the top of the first, he walked two and gave up a hit in the bottom as New York countered with two, one unearned on a throw into center field by catcher Les Nunamaker and the other on a fielder's choice. Another runner was thrown out at the plate by Duffy Lewis. Then Wood settled down and allowed no runs for the next seven frames. Most of the action came in the ninth, with the score still 2–1 Highlanders. After Stahl walked to lead off and was sacrificed to second by Larry Gardner, the Sox hit four consecutive singles — one by Joe (driving in two) — for four runs. But the drama wasn't over. In the last of the ninth, the home team used two singles and a fielder's choice to make it 5–3 before Wood induced a ground out to short and foul fly to first baseman Stahl to end the game. It was a victory, though fireballer Joe Wood only struck out two while walking three and giving up seven hits.

Despite this come-from-behind victory, there was little indication in April or early May of the greatness to come in 1912 for Joe, not yet Smoky, Wood. He won his second start, 9–2, at Philadelphia on April 16, striking out eleven and giving up only one walk. But he also served up twelve hits. Again Wood started slowly, giving up a run in the first. He was rescued by Larry Gardner at third base, who made spectacular double plays on line drives in both the first and the second inning. Meanwhile, the Red Sox scored seven runs in those initial frames for an early cushion. Actually, early in the season Joe's bat was as dominant as his arm. In this game he had two doubles, including one for an RBI in the ninth. That gave him 4 for 8 for the season. But his winning streak ended at two as he lost his next start to Washington, on April 23, 6–2.

By then Joe and Tris Speaker were settled in a rented home in nearby Winthrop, far more comfortable than the field on Tuesday, April 23, Joe's Fenway debut.[6] The ground had been softened again by rain, and it was cold and very windy, all of which contributed to weak support. For example, in the third inning the Senators scored three runs on errors by Wagner and Speaker. The visitors repeated that number in the eighth, on miscues by Stahl and Speaker. Washington was also generous; both Red Sox runs came on an error by shortstop Ray Morgan and a wild pitch. This time Joe lacked command, walking seven and giving up eight hits. The Red Sox also had no timely hitting, loading the bases in both the second and the third inning without scoring. After Joe gave up three runs in the eighth, Olaf Henriksen batted for him in the ninth as the Senators won 6–2.

Joe won for the first time in Fenway Park on April 27, 1912, 6–5 over the Athletics after being behind as much as 5–1. Timely hitting by Larry Gardner and Duffy Lewis saved the day as the Red Sox got two in the sixth and three in the eighth. Wood struck out six, walked only one, and had another double. Back on the road in Washington, he pitched better on May 1, but his efforts were sabotaged by a very unusual ending. Going into the eighth Wood trailed 1–0 when the Sox tied the game on two walks and a wild pick-off throw to first that would have scored both runners but hit the Sox base coach, backup catcher Chet "Pinch" Thomas.

With the score still tied 1–1, the bottom of the ninth started with shortstop Wagner making a two-base error. Joe retired the next two batters and intentionally walked catcher John Henry to get to Dixie Walker, the Washington pitcher, who also walked on a 3-2 pitch, with Wood objecting violently. Composing himself Joe quickly got two foul strikes on left fielder Danny Moeller. But when Moeller chased a waste pitch in the dirt, the ball caught the edge of the plate and flew into the stands. As John Flynn scored from third and Moeller ran to first, Joe's seventh strikeout became the wild pitch that gave the Senators a 2–1 win.

Joe Wood didn't pitch again until May 7, at Fenway against Detroit; he won in another shaky outing, 5–4. Boston scored in the first on Harry Hooper's lead-off single and a two-out error by Detroit short-stop Donie Bush. Joe got through the first three innings unscored upon, with Harry Hooper throwing out Jim Delahanty trying to score from second on a single in the second. In the top of the fourth, Detroit took the lead on Ty Cobb's double, two singles, and a fielder's choice RBI from Paddy Baumann. The turning point came in the bottom of the sixth, when a sacrifice fly by Duffy Lewis, a double by Heinie Wagner, and a single by Hick Cady netted two runs. Joe gave back single runs in the seventh and the ninth, but Davy Jones popped out to third base-man Larry Gardner (with Ty Cobb on deck) to end the game. Quietly that game began a streak of 14 of 15 wins.

The long home stand continued with two victories against the Browns. On May 11, after walking Burt Shotton to start the game, Joe pitched perfectly until, with two out in the sixth, Shotton blooped a single into center. The game was essentially over when the Red Sox scored their eight runs in the first three innings as Clyde Engle and Tris Speaker each had three hits. The Browns' run came on back-to-back doubles in the eighth as Joe pitched a three-hitter, striking out eleven while walking only two. He also had an RBI single to right. Wood repeated his domi-nance of St. Louis four days later, still in Boston, winning 2–1, the only Browns' run unearned when Joe dropped a relay that allowed Jimmy Austin to tie the game in the sixth. Boston scored in the first and the last inning, the initial one on a Speaker double and the winner on a two-out Wagner single.

Joe's dominance at Fenway continued on May 20 when he shut out the White Sox and future Hall of Famer Big Ed Walsh 2–0. The only Red Sox runs came in the second, aided by an errant pick-off attempt at first base by Walsh. In very cold weather, driven by strong winds from the northeast, Joe struck out eight Chicago batters while giving up only five hits and a walk. Jake Stahl brought back Wood in relief on May 23 against Cleveland. He entered after Eddie Cicotte had blown a 5-to-2 lead by allowing the first three batters to reach and two runs to score. Although Joe gave a game-tying single to Jack Graney, he got Joe Jackson on a long fly to Lewis in left to keep the game tied. Wood gave up a double to Art Griggs to lead off the tenth. But he got Griggs in a rundown on a come-backer and then retired the Naps. In the bottom of the inning, Tris Speaker singled, advanced to third on a sacrifice, and scored when a throw from first baseman Eddie Hohnhorst sailed over Ivy Olson at third. That gave Joe victory number eight as the Red Sox won 6–5.

The string of six victories ended on May 25. Though it would be the last game Joe would lose at Fenway that regular season, it was not pretty. The defending champion Philadelphia Athletics, led by Colby Jack Coombs, beat Wood and the Red Sox 8–2. The problem was wildness, with the three batters Joe walked and the one he hit all scoring. His teammates didn't help either, gathering only three hits. It was Wood's first loss since May 1 and only his third of the year. After the disappointing game on May 25 against the A's, Joe Wood began one of the most remarkable streaks in the history of baseball. He would lose only one game over a period of nearly four months. But there was little in the next outing, on May 29 at Fenway, to predict such a run. The Red Sox beat Washington by thirteen runs, but Joe gave up eleven hits and eight runs, winning 21–8. He also struggled at Cleveland on June 2, needing ten innings to beat the Indians 5–4. After a relief appearance on June 5 at Detroit, he won four hard-fought games on the road, requiring good run support from his teammates to keep the streak alive.

Despite Joe's giving up his usual run in the first inning, at Detroit on the eighth the Red Sox defeated the Tigers 8–3, primarily because Wood held Ty Cobb hitless in key situations. Boston controlled the game throughout, getting four runs in the first and another in the second, led by three hits from Harry Hooper and two each by Krug, Speaker, and Wagner. It was a bit more difficult when Wood started four days later, on June 12 (the day after the Red Sox moved into first place) in St. Louis. This time Joe needed his own two-run homer in the fifth and three hits from Larry Gardner, as well as some fine defensive play from all his infielders, to defeat the Browns 5–3. In Chicago on June 16 he got good offensive support after giving up three runs in the first, two on a home run from Harry Lord that passed under a gate in right field. But Boston scored a run in the first and three in the fifth. Chicago tied the game in the bottom of the seventh, on a two-base throwing error by Heinie Wagner, but the Red Sox responded with two runs, on an RBI single from Stahl and a redemptive double from Wagner. Joe retired the final six White Sox in order to win 6–4.

It was easier on June 21 back in New York. Duffy Lewis took care of things with 3 for 3, including a triple and a home run to center field. Boston scored five runs in the second inning to take a commanding lead, then added three in the seventh and two more in the eighth. Sensing the game was no contest, Joe gave up single runs in the sixth, eighth, and ninth, and the Sox won 11–3. More predictive of Joe's dominance were two shutouts at the end of June. The first was the second game of a doubleheader on June 26 in Washington, a preview of the September Johnson-Wood match-up. On a hot early summer's day, the Big Train pitched perfect baseball until one out in the fifth when Larry Gardner singled and then circled the bases as both the right fielder and the catcher misplayed the ball. Tris Speaker's two-run double to the center-field wall in the next inning sealed the victory. Meanwhile, Joe struck out nine and gave up only three hits and a walk, winning 3–0. Three days later, back at Fenway, Joe shut out the Highlanders 6–0 in a game called after seven innings for darkness. Joe gave up only one hit and two walks, allowing no runner to second. The Sox scored three in the second, on a Gardner triple and a Stahl double, and two in the third on a Stahl double and Wagner's single.

All the "what iffers," including Joe Wood himself, have focused on

Marty Krug's error in Detroit late in the 1912 season. But the most dramatic game in Wood's streak, and the one most neglected, was played on the July 4, 1912, in Philadelphia. It was morning/afternoon doubleheader, famous at the time for attracting a record crowd of over fifty-five thousand. Joe pitched the morning game against Eddie Plank, enjoying the seventh of his eight twenty-win seasons. Wood had a no-hitter through four, apparently on his way to his tenth consecutive victory. Boston led 1–0 on Wood's double to right leading off the third, a sacrifice by Hooper, and an RBI single from Steve Yerkes. Maybe because of the base running, Wood weakened in the fifth, giving a walk, four hits, and two runs. Boston nearly scored in the fifth, when Joe doubled after Hick Cady singled, but Hooper struck out and Yerkes grounded out. The sixth was crucial. The Sox had runners on first and third with no outs after Speaker doubled and Lewis reached on an error. After Gardner popped to second, Stahl hit a long fly to center, but Speaker, after tagging, failed to score before Lewis was doubled off first on a throw from Rube Oldring to Stuffy McInnis.

In the bottom of the sixth, Joe apparently survived a lead-off double by Home Run Baker. But with two out he threw a wild pitch that gave Philadelphia a two-run lead. Boston got within a run in the seventh when Harry Hooper's single drove home Heinie Wagner, who had reached on an error. But Joe, after walking, was thrown out at third after a hit to left by Hooper. Joe then gave up the winning run in the bottom of the inning on a single, double, and sacrifice fly by Oldring. The Red Sox got their final run in the eighth, when Speaker singled, stole a base, and scored on a fielder's choice. But the Sox were three up, three down in the ninth, including Joe's fly to right, and the streak stopped at nine, with the Red Sox losing 4–3. As a disgusted Tim Murnane in the *Globe* on July 5 summarized, "A wild pitch by Wood allowed the home team one run, and . . . Lewis was doubled at first on a long fly to center, and Speaker failed to score from third on the play, taking it easy." Without those miscues that Fourth of July, Joe could have won twenty-six consecutive games in 1912.

Even so that was the last game Joe would lose in the next nineteen times he took the mound. Joe was especially effective in the next two games. On July 8 (the day Rube Marquard's NL streak of nineteen consecutive wins was halted by the Cubs) at Fenway, Wood easily defeated the Browns 5–1, striking out eight and scattering seven hits. He gave up a run in the first, but the Red Sox answered with three in the inning and added runs in the sixth and the eighth. Much more taxing was his game four days later against the Tigers in Boston, in the second game of a doubleheader. He gave up only five hits and struck out ten over eleven innings in a 1–0 shutout. But there was trouble along the way. Detroit had runners on first and second with two out in the first, when Joe picked off Ty Cobb to end the threat. In the second a double by Jim Delahanty and a hit batter put two on with no outs. But Joe struck out the side. Cobb also opened the sixth with a double but was stranded on second. With one out in the ninth, Delahanty doubled off the left-field wall, but catcher Hick Cady picked him off at second.[7] The game was won in the eleventh when with two out, Speaker tripled to left center and Lewis hit the first pitch to center, scoring Tris.

After finishing the ninth inning of the fourth game of the series with Detroit, lost by Charley Hall and the Sox 6–4, Joe pitched a complete game two days later against the White Sox in Fenway. In the second game of a doubleheader, Joe got off to a typically slow start. He gave up two singles before an error by Larry Gardner scored a run. A strike out and a grounder to first limited the damage. After Joe retired the White Sox on three pitches in the top of the fourth, the Red Sox took the lead with two runs on a double by Yerkes, a single and a stolen base from Speaker, and a Gardner clutch single. With one out in the fifth, Boston added another run when Joe doubled in Cady. But the White Sox tied the game in the bottom of the sixth on only a lead-off single when Gardner and Wagner misplayed balls and Cady was unable to hold a strike-out pitch in the dirt. Luckily in the eighth the Red Sox scored four on a barrage of singles by Hooper, Yerkes, Speaker, Gardner, and Wagner. In the ninth Buck Weaver doubled with one out, but Joe handled two consecutive ground balls himself, improving to 19-4 with the 7–3 win.

Joe enjoyed almost a week's rest before he started again. This time Cleveland, his most troublesome team that year, came to Fenway Park. Yet again Joe got into trouble in the first inning, with a walk and two singles putting him behind 1–0. Only a double play kept things from getting worse. A single by Gardner and a couple of errors by the Naps tied the game in the second. In the next inning Joe tripled and scored on Steve Yerkes's sacrifice fly to left. The Sox took the game over in the sixth when an error was followed by triples from Larry Gardner and Jake Stahl, both to deep center. Joe gave up runs in the seventh and the ninth, but Boston got two in the seventh on doubles from Cady and Yerkes and singles from Hooper and Lewis. That day Wood gave up eight hits, walked a batter, and hit another, but the Red Sox won 6–3. With that victory the Boston lead moved to eight games in the AL, and Joe Wood had his twentieth win of the season . . . on July 23. But he needed luck and a technicality in pursuit of the consecutive-win record. Both came on July 28 in Chicago.

Wood was unusually strong early as the Red Sox beat up on ex-team-mate Eddie Cicotte. Hooper walked to start the game, and Yerkes followed with a hit to center. When Tris Speaker legged out an infield single, the bases were loaded with none out. After Hooper scored when Duffy Lewis hit into a double play, Gardner singled, putting the Red Sox ahead 2–0. They added a run in the third when Jake Stahl hit a two-out triple after Speaker had doubled to lead off. Crucial were two runs in the top of the fifth. Speaker scored on a fielder's choice after reaching second on a two-base error to start the inning. With two out Stahl homered into the left-field stands to make it 5–0. But in the bottom of the fifth, with one out, Joe hit a batter, gave up a hit to Cicotte, and threw wildly to first on a sacrifice bunt, scoring a run and putting runners on second and third. Wood seemed close to getting out of the inning when Rollie Zeider hit a sacrifice fly to Harry Hooper in right field. But Joe walked Shano Collins, and two singles drove Wood from the mound. Luck arrived when Hugh Bedient held Chicago scoreless. The final score was the same as at the end of five, 5–4. Today Joe wouldn't win because he didn't finish the fifth. But in 1912 he left with the lead and was declared the winner.

Joe Wood got a breather in St. Louis on August 2, the usual case against his cousins, the Browns. A last-minute substitution for Ray Collins, Wood breezed to a 9–0 victory in another complete game. It was scoreless until the fourth, when the Red Sox put it away quickly, thanks to a grand slam by Jake Stahl, doubles by Cady and Joe, and a single from Harry Hooper. Speaker stole another in the seventh as he walked, swiped second, and scored when Browns catcher Paul Krichell threw the ball away as Tris also stole third. The most frightening moment came in the fourth, when St. Louis second baseman Del Pratt hit a line drive off Joe's right wrist; the ball caromed to Gardner at third, who made the out at first. But Joe was able to finish, with Charley Hall in the pen. The Sox added a run in the seventh on Hooper's lead-off home run into the right-field bleachers and another in the eighth, when Joe singled in Wagner. The three-hitter was Joe's twenty-second win, sixth in a row.

Then the Red Sox traveled to League Park in Cleveland, where Joe needed another exhausting effort to defeat the Naps. In the fourth the Red Sox scored two runs, on walks to Lewis and Gardner, a sacrifice, and a two-run single by Wagner. When they added another in the sixth, Cady doubling in Stahl, who had singled, it looked like Boston might cruise since Joe was pitching a shutout. However, the bottom of that inning was nearly disastrous. After two singles Joe Jackson bunted safely to fill the bases with no outs. Napoleon Lajoie hit a sacrifice fly to left, giving the Naps their first run. After being enraged that his fastball wasn't called strike three on Art Griggs, Joe gave up another hit, which scored two and tied the score at three. Worse yet, when Joe Birmingham singled to left, Lewis fumbled the ball, and the runners moved to second and third. Then fortune smiled again. Roger Peckinpaugh hit a fly to Hooper in right, deep enough to score Griggs easily, but Wagner cut off the throw and immediately ran to third, protesting the runner had left too early.

The third-base umpire denied the appeal. But after the Red Sox stormed the field, the home-plate umpire, Jack Egan, overruled the call.

Both teams had chances before regulation was over. In the eighth, after a single to center by Griggs, Tris Speaker made a perfect throw to Cady, who blocked Joe Jackson trying to score from second. In the top of the ninth, Joe and Harry Hooper singled with two out, but Steve Yerkes grounded to Napoleon Lajoie for the final out. In the decisive eleventh Joe had a chance to put the Red Sox ahead, but he struck out with runners on second and third with one out. After Hooper was walked intentionally, Yerkes singled to center, scoring Stahl and Wagner. For a while the bottom of the eleventh seemed a replay of the sixth. With one run in, Art Griggs was once again on third with one out. But Joe struck out left-handed batter Ted Easterly, pinch-hitting for Peckinpaugh. With two strikes on another left-handed hitter, rookie Bill Hunter batting for Steve O'Neill, Griggs broke for home, but Hunter, protecting against a strikeout, fouled off Joe's pitch. On the next pitch Joe struck out Hunter for the win. Joe walked no one, but he gave up thirteen hits in the 5–4 win, raising his record to 23-4.

Once Joe and the Boston Red Sox crossed Lake Erie from Cleveland to Detroit, the streak of seven games gained momentum. On August 10 he showed few ill effects from the Cleveland marathon, throwing a complete game victory over the Tigers. Under persistent rain he started slowly and hit first batter Red McDermott in the shoulder. After a passed ball, walk, and fielder's choice, Detroit scored on the double steal, with Wahoo Sam Crawford running to second and Wagner's relay to Cady too late. Though the Red Sox threatened repeatedly in the first five innings, the Tigers led 1–0, with rain threatening to end the game. Fortunately play continued on the soggy field, and the Sox broke through in the sixth. After Yerkes and Speaker singled, Detroit first baseman Eddie Onslow tried to get Yerkes at third on Duffy Lewis's bunt, but his throw was wild, and both runners scored. Cady's double was followed by Hooper's triple for another run in the seventh, and they added insurance when Lewis walked to open the eighth and scored on

Wagner's two-out hit. Joe finished in a flourish, with two strikeouts and a fly to center, for win eight in a row, 4–1. Afterward there was some concern when Joe reported his arm a bit lame, with expectation that he might not pitch again until the fifteenth or the sixteenth.

But back home in Boston on August 14, Joe only needed to throw his glove on the mound because the Browns were in town. Once again he started by walking a batter, this time Burt Shotton, who stole second. But two strikeouts and a grounder to short took care of St. Louis. The game was decided in the third when Joe doubled home Wagner, who had walked, Hooper singled Wood home, and Harry also scored when Shotton misplayed the ball into a three-base error. The total came to five in the inning when Compton dropped Neal Ball's fly, Speaker was hit by a pitch, and Duffy Lewis doubled to left, scoring both runners. Boston added two more in the fourth (on a triple from Stahl, a walk, a stolen base, and Joe's single) and another in the seventh. Joe faced no significant threat until the eighth, when the Browns loaded the bases with one out on a hit batsman, single, and walk. But Wood fielded a grounder from Del Pratt, threw to Cady, who touched home and threw to Stahl at first for the double play that ended it when umpire Bill Dinneen called the game for darkness. Number nine.

It was common in the Deadball Era to use excellent pitchers in relief between starts. Joe next was called upon twice in that role. The first time was against the Browns two days after his 8–0 victory, when he relieved Buck O'Brien in the eighth after the Red Sox had scored in the seventh to pull within a run, 3–2. He walked Gloomy Gus Williams in that inning but gave up no runs, striking out four over the two innings, including the side in the ninth. But the Sox didn't score, and Joe got no decision. The next day, August 17, he was called upon in the eighth, against the Detroit Tigers at Fenway. This time he replaced Ray Collins after the Red Sox, trailing 3–0, rallied for five runs in the seventh. The Red Sox added an insurance run in the eighth. Joe retired the first two in the ninth before Oscar Stanage tripled, Wabash George Mullin hit him in, and Davy Jones flied to Wagner to end it, 6–4, a save for Joe.

Three days later, on August 20, 1912 (the day Walter Johnson beat Cleveland 4–2 to set a new AL record of fifteen straight wins), Joe started at Fenway against the Tigers, with a chance to win his tenth in a row. That day he faced Chauncey Dubuc, who won twelve consecutive games that year for the Tigers (and would be involved in the Black Sox scandal in 1919). It was a sloppy game, played on a wet field. Joe got in trouble in the top of the third, with Ty Cobb up and the bases loaded after a single and two errors by Larry Gardner. But Ty hit back to Wood, who threw to Cady, who relayed to Engle at first for the double play. The Red Sox responded in the bottom when Neal Ball doubled, scoring Wood, and then Ball scored on a double steal executed with Speaker, who had walked. The Tigers got a run in the fourth on a Ball error and Wagner's wide throw to first on an apparent double play. The game was preserved in the sixth when Speaker, playing shallow, made a diving catch of Crawford's liner with Cobb moving on the hit and run. After sliding on the wet ground, Tris recovered in time to double Cobb at first.

The Red Sox took over the game in the bottom of the sixth. Speaker scored on a sacrifice fly by Duffy Lewis, and then Clyde Engle walked, stole second, and scored on Wagner's single. Just to be sure, Boston also added another two runs in the seventh. Neal Ball hit his second double off the left-field fence, scoring Harry Hooper, and then scored himself when Speaker followed with a single. After both teams went out in order in the eighth, Sam Crawford opened the Detroit ninth with a single. After the Red Sox showed indifference to his advances on the bases, he scored on Cady's passed ball. But Wood ended things with a strike out and a fly out to Harry Hooper. The final was Boston 6, Detroit 2 in Joe Wood's tenth consecutive win of 1912. Next in Boston were the Cleveland Naps, on August 24, 1912, who gave Joe Wood the most trouble since, well, the last time he had faced the Naps, in Cleveland. The day before, Walter Johnson won his sixteen straight, 8–1, against Detroit in Washington.

With the Red Sox in first place by eight games and Vean Gregg (who had shut out the Sox 1–0 in his last start against them) on the mound for Cleveland, there was an overflow crowd of more than twenty-two thousand at Fenway Park that Saturday. This time Joe got off to a smooth start in the first, with the Red Sox jumping on Gregg for three runs in their half. With one out Neal Ball singled and Speaker walked, followed by a double steal, putting runners on second and third. On Lewis's grounder to first, Ball slid around the throw to home, and the Sox had a run. Speaker tried a similar move on Gardner's roller to Lajoie, but Tris was out easily at home. Clyde Engle's single to center scored Lewis; when Joe Birmingham threw wild at home, Gardner also scored, the third Red Sox run. Joe gave up an unearned run in the fourth when Wagner misplayed Lajoie's grounder and Napoleon stole second and scored on Doc Johnston's single.

The resilient Red Sox answered with four more in the bottom of the fourth. After Wood followed Wagner's single and Cady's sacrifice with an infield hit, Hooper bounced a ball off Lajoie's shoulder for a double, scoring Wagner. Ball struck out, but Speaker picked him up with a hit to center for two more runs. Tris scored when, after Lewis walked, catcher Steve O'Neill threw poorly to second trying to get Lewis, who took third on the play. The Indians continued to score off Joe, on Lajoie's single in the sixth, but Boston answered on a double to left by Hooper and a single to the same field by Tris Speaker. Cleveland scored again in the eighth and the ninth when Wagner threw wildly to first trying to turn double plays. Joe gave up seven hits to the Indians and walked two more, but he struck out eight; the Red Sox won 8–4, his eleventh victory in a row. Two days later Walter Johnson's streak ended at sixteen games.[8]

As Joe Wood closed on that record, his next start was August 28, 1912, at Fenway against the White Sox. It was a joyous day in Boston as the Red Sox took a midweek doubleheader from the Pale Hose and extended their lead to ten games over the Washington Senators. After Buck O'Brien won the first game 5–3, Joe was masterful in the nightcap. Never walking a batter Joe faced no threat until the eighth. Meanwhile, the Red

Sox batters got all they would need in the fourth. With one out Speaker walked and took third on Lewis's hit to center. Larry Gardner's double scored Speaker and put runners on second and third. Clyde Engle's Texas Leaguer to right scored both Lewis and Gardner. The eighth began with rookie Buck Weaver's infield single, knocked down by Larry Gardner at third. Pinch-hitter Ted Easterly, purchased from the Naps on August 7, followed with a single. Ernie Johnson's hit filled the bases. But Wally Mattick grounded to second baseman Yerkes, who tagged Johnson and threw to Clyde Engle to complete the double play. In the ninth Joe retired the side in order for the fifth time, striking out Shano Collins and Ping Bodie to end it. The game was Joe's seventh shutout, 3–0, and his twelfth consecutive win.

Joe had a tougher struggle when he faced the Highlanders on September 2 at the rebuilt Polo Grounds, which would be the site of that year's World Series. Again he pitched the second game of a doubleheader. The only run came in the first, when Hooper led off with a single and, after an error and a sacrifice by Steve Yerkes, scored on Tris Speaker's sacrifice fly. Wood never allowed more than one runner until the fifth, when a two-out walk and two singles filled the bases. But Joe induced Hal Chase to ground to Yerkes to end the threat. In the sixth the first batter, Bert Daniels, lined a double off the left-field wall and was sacrificed to third by Dutch Sterrett. But Joe struck out Jack Lelivelt and got Hack Simmons to hit back to the mound for the final out. The Highlanders went down in order in the seventh, but in the eighth Tommy McMillan led off with a single, stole second, and moved to third on Chase's grounder. After Daniels popped to Wood, McMillan was out trying to steal home. Joe retired the first two batters in the ninth. But a single, walk, and grounder that Gardner could only knock down at third filled the bases. Joe then struck out Slats McConnell to end the game in which, according to Tim Murnane in the *Globe* the next day, "never was a pitcher put to a greater strain." The 1–0 victory gave Joe back-to-back shutouts and his thirteenth consecutive win.

Meanwhile, the drama was building for the most exciting regular season game of Joe Wood's career, on Friday, September 6, 1912, at Fenway Park. Although Washington was a perennially weak team, that year they were good and eventually finished second to the Red Sox. There was added suspense because two of Joe Wood's four losses that year had been to Johnson's team, bunched on April 23 and May 1. The game was hyped by both teams. Clark Griffith suggested that the Sox wanted to avoid Johnson to ensure that Wood broke the record. Manager Jake Stahl responded that Joe would pitch on any day named by Griffith. Although there was talk that Stahl was hoodwinked into pitching Joe on short rest, both pitchers had started on the second; Johnson lost to the A's 9–7 while Wood beat the Yankees. More fuel was added to the fire by the controversy over the Boston victory on August 17 against Detroit, the game Joe entered with the score 5–3 and completed with a 6–4 victory. Some scorers wanted a victory rather than a six-out save. But on the day before the showdown, Ban Johnson declared that Wood didn't win that game.

The press contributed to the hype. As Joe later explained (without identifying the date), his nickname Smoky was originated by sportswriter Paul Shannon of the *Boston Post*. Impressed by Joe's speed while warming up, Shannon declared, "That young man sure does throw smoke." That happened in late August (most likely the twenty-eighth, when Joe shut out Chicago at Fenway), with Shannon first calling him "Smoky Joe Wood" in the *Post* on September 3. But it wasn't picked up in other papers until this game. The *Hartford Courant*, for example, used the phrase for the first time in its analysis following the game.[9] Most comical to Joe were the boxing metaphors that flowed from the writers. Their physical stats, like height and weight, were given, with Johnson listed as "The Champion" and Joe "The Challenger." Sometimes, in more hyperbolic language, they became the "gladiators of the mound." The papers gladly reprinted Clark Griffith's inciting words: "I feel sure my man can win the honors. Johnson's record this season was against all comers, and I want to see Joe Wood matched up with our man."[10] The game made page 1 of the *Globe*.

For the season Joe Wood had pitched in thirty-seven games, going 29 and 4, while Johnson had cooled off after his streak, standing at 28-10 in forty games before September 6. Though the Red Sox had won nine straight and seventeen of twenty, their season record against Washington stood at only 9 and 8. Of course Fenway was filled beyond capacity. As reported by Melville E. Webb Jr. in the *Globe* on the seventh, they "packed the stands and the bleachers, and trooped all over the outfield inside the stand and bleacher boundaries. In the grandstand the broad promenade was packed solid ten rows deep with fans on tip-toes to see what was going on. The playing field was surrounded completely by a triple, even quadruple, rank of humanity, at least 3,000 assembling on the bank in left field, and the mass of enthusiasts extending around in front of the huge concrete stand." On a clear and pleasant day, the 3:15 p.m. game was delayed as police ordered crowds back from the field to make room for play. Even though it cost seventy-five cents just to stand on the field, fans were turned away.

Two interviews by Bob Wood and others in support of Joe's candidacy for the Hall of Fame (in May 1993) offer vivid impressions of the game. Elmer Colcord, ninety-seven years old at the time of the interview, graduated in 1913 from a high school in Canton, Massachusetts, the home of Sox player Olaf Henriksen. To make money to attend Tufts University that fall, Elmer worked for the Boston Streetcar Co. and was called to the East Boston "barn" to drive an extra car to Fenway. Once he conducted his "dinky," a smaller car, to the game, Colcord watched by climbing onto the top of his trolley, where he took a very slippery stance. He remembered the atmosphere as "very excitable, except that it was a pitcher's duel." With the help of Jack Slattery, the Tufts coach who had caught Walter Johnson, and Horace Ford, captain of the Tufts team who later played fifteen years in the NL, Colcord studied the difference in the pitchers. In his words Walter had a "long armed" delivery, while Joe's was "a very active drive, not that long sweep that Johnson had."

As one would expect, the Boston fans were very excited when they returned to Elmer's streetcar for the ride home or to a local bar. Equally interesting is Colcord's impression of Joe Wood: "Magnificent. I've never seen any thing like him. At that time there was Big Chief Bender, Eddie Cicotte, Grover Alexander, Three-Fingered Brown." But Wood was "absolutely tops . . . in a class by himself." Believing the story that Joe had once bent the backstop support on a passed ball by Bill Carrigan, the "kids" and "young men" of the time only considered two players "really two superstars. One was Honus Wagner, the Pittsburgh shortstop, and the other was Joe Wood." Similarly Joe Derba, who sold popcorn at both the Wood/Johnson game and the World Series of 1912 (making a dollar, which he would give to his mother), said that Walter and Joe had "about the same speed." He added that Joe was "the number one pitcher of his time," including Cy Young, and a "great clutch hitter."

Unlike the games in the World Series that year, this one was a defensive gem. Neither team made an error, and the pitchers were in top form. Joe had significant early trouble but repeatedly helped his own cause. The very fast Clyde Milan started the game with an infield hit to deep shortstop. Joe, not good at holding on runners, threw seven times to Engle at first, which paid off when the next batter, Kid Foster, hit back to Wood, who threw to Wagner at second, with the relay to Engle completing the double play. Joe then struck out Danny Moeller on a 3-2 pitch. Things were even tighter in the third, when George McBride opened with a double into the crowd in left field and Dorf Ainsmith sacrificed him to third. But with one out Joe got Walter Johnson to hit back to the mound. Wood, Cady, and Gardner got Ainsmith in a rundown, while Johnson continued on to second. That still didn't settle matters. Pitching carefully Joe walked both Milan and Foster to fill the bases. Two quick strikes set up crucial pitches to Moeller: ball, foul, ball, foul, and then a strike to end the third.

In the fifth Ainsmith walked with one out, and Johnson followed with an infield hit. But Joe got Milan to fly to Lewis and Foster to fly to Speaker. With two out in the sixth, LaPorte doubled into the right-center-field crowd, but Joe struck out Charley Moran. In the eighth Foster singled with one out and stole second when Cady dropped Joe's pitch and could make no throw. After Moeller popped to shortstop Wagner, Gandil hit a liner down the right-field line that went barely foul before flying to Speaker in shallow center. There was one thrill left, in the ninth, when LaPorte hit over third to lead off and Milan sacrificed him to second. But Joe hitched up his belt, pulled on his pants, and struck out McBride (called) and Ainsmith (swinging), both on 1-2 pitches, to give Smoky Joe Wood his third consecutive shutout.[11]

The game was decided in the bottom of the sixth, when, with two out, Tris Speaker, on a 1-2 pitch, drove a ball down the left-field line to the edge of the crowd for a double and Duffy Lewis followed on a 2-1 pitch with a bloop double to right off a diving Moeller's glove. For the game Walter Johnson threw 98 pitches while walking only one batter. Joe threw 108 (mostly because he walked two more batters), left nine Senators in scoring position, and retired the side in order only in the second, fourth, and seventh innings. Wood struck out nine, Johnson only five, though the Big Train whiffed the Boston side in the fifth inning.[12] The result was a fantasy come true for new Red Sox president McAleer, who had predicted "a great fight between two great pitchers" and hoped "the score might be 1 to 0 and that [the Red Sox] might make the 1."[13]

The loss hit many Washington players in their wallets. In his later testimony before Commissioner Landis in the Leonard/Speaker/Cobb scandal (see chapters 9 and 10), Joe remembered the confident betting by members of the Senators:

> Wood: I can recall one instance when the whole Washington ball club went broke. I say broke, that is they lost all the cash they had with them on a ball game that I pitched and beat Walter Johnson, they lost one day and they won it back the next day on a game when Bob Groome [sic] beat our club.
>
> Q [from Landis]: They lost their money one day and won it back the next?
>
> A: Yes.

Q: Who did they bet on?

A: They bet on Washington.[14]

Records verify Joe's memory, in this as is most cases. The next day, September 7, 1912, Washington beat Boston 5–1 behind pitcher Bob Groom, who won twenty-four games that year. Also a syndicated cartoon by Sid Greene, portraying Joe as "The New White Hope" in beating Johnson, had a funny box imagining the Washington players eating beans out of cans because "the Washington team bet five hundred on Johnson."

Often a letdown follows such a dramatic game. And it did, on September 10 in Chicago. The strain that rainy day at Comiskey Park was so intense that Joe needed help finishing the game. He struggled from the beginning, giving up singles to Harry Lord and Shano Collins with two out in the first before he got Babe Borton to ground to Gardner. Joe also gave up two hits and a walk in the second but was bailed out when Cady's throw to second got Buck Weaver in a rundown. After getting the White Sox in order in the third and the fourth and permitting only a single in the fifth, he carried a shutout into the sixth, when Rollie Zeider doubled home Collins with two out. After scoring himself in the top of the seventh, on a single, sacrifice, and hit by Speaker, he got the White Sox in order in the bottom of the inning. But then he tired. In a replay of the first inning, Lord and Collins opened the eighth with singles. Borton's infield hit loaded the bases with none out. It looked good when Ted Easterly, batting for Zeider, hit a grounder to Yerkes, but the second baseman booted it and two runs scored.

Joe struck out Cuke Barrows, batting for Buck Weaver. But then he hit Ray Schalk to reload the bases. Ping Bodie's grounder toward shortstop Wagner hit Ernie Johnson, who was running for Easterly, and all runners had to return to their bases. Morrie Rath tried a surprise bunt, but Gardner made the play. So Boston had a two-run lead going into the ninth, with Joe Wood still on the mound. But Wally Mattick led off with a double, and Harry Lord followed with a single, putting runs on first and third with no outs. For the second time all year, but the second time in Chicago, Joe was taken from a game. Charley Hall got Collins to pop to Engle at first base and Borton to hit a sacrifice fly to Lewis, scoring Mattick. Cady then ended the game by throwing to Wagner, getting Lord trying to steal second. Boston 5, Chicago 4. An exhausted Wood had his fifteenth in a row, though he gave up twelve hits and walked a batter. Only his patsies, the Browns, stood in the way of the new record.

That game would come in St. Louis, where they played Sunday baseball. And a Sunday it was, the second game of a doubleheader. Joe Wood once again started slowly, giving up hits in the first and the second, and then two more and a walk in the third to fill the bases with two out. But he struck out Willie Hogan to end that inning. Joe then settled down and retired the Browns in order in the fourth and the fifth. By then the Sox had scored on a Gardner walk, a Wagner single, and a sacrifice fly to deep center by Hick Cady. In the sixth Joe walked a batter, who was erased by a good throw from Cady. Del Pratt led off the Browns' seventh with a double off the right-field wall, moving to third on George Stovall's fly out. Pinch-hitting for Doc Shanley, Wood's nemesis Pete Compton then drove in Pratt with a single to center. Wood gave up another single in the inning, but he struck out Earl Hamilton to keep the 1–1 tie. In the eighth Joe walked, advanced on Hooper's single, and after an intentional walk to Speaker, scored on a wild pitch. St. Louis went quietly in the eighth, on a fly ball to center and ground balls to short and third. When darkness ended the game, Joe had his sixteenth consecutive win, 2–1.

It was inevitable that the fates one day would conspire against Joe Wood. That day was September 21, 1912, in Detroit. Though the Red Sox had been swept by the Naps in a four-game series in the intervening days, they also had clinched the pennant as the second-place A's also lost. After a difficult boat ride from Cleveland to Detroit on the morning of the twenty-first, there were complications. Jake Stahl had to begin a three-day suspension for arguing a play in the Cleveland series, and Wood was suffering from a cold. Joe was also tired from the Johnson game, short rest before the White Sox series, and the tough outing in St. Louis. But Wood decided to take the ball and was doing well into the third, with two outs, when he walked Tex Covington, Donie Bush, Red Corriden, and Sam Crawford in succession, forcing in a run. The next batter was Ty Cobb, who popped to Marty Krug, substituting at shortstop. But the rookie dropped the ball on an easy chance, scoring two more runs.[15] While that is often retold as the end of the story, the Red Sox actually scored a run in the fourth, when Hooper scored on the throwing error by the pitcher Joe Lake, followed by three more in the fifth, on two walks, singles by Krug and Wood, and a throwing error on a grounder by Tris Speaker.

So even after Krug's gaffe, the Sox still had a chance to win and were ahead by a run. But in the bottom of that same inning, the fifth, the Tigers responded with two runs, on three singles. Feeling the strain Wood was unusually demonstrative, repeatedly yelling at home-plate umpire Silk O'Loughlin. But Detroit earned their final run, in the eighth, when Cobb singled, Veach doubled, and Ty came home on a fielder's choice. The Red Sox went quietly, making no hits over the last four innings. Joe gave up seven hits in addition to five walks. He struck out eight batters, but he and Hick Cady allowed three stolen bases by the speedy Tigers, and the Sox made just four hits. Manager Stahl was both fatherly and positive, declaring the defeat would relieve Joe's worry about the record and improve his general health. Krug's error was crucial, allowing two runs, but Detroit outplayed Boston, winning 6–4.

After four days of rest, Joe took out his frustration at Fenway Park on his favorite victims, the Highlanders/Yankees, shutting them out 6–0. This game was over in the bottom of the first, when the Red Sox scored four runs after no one was on and two were out. Speaker walked, Lewis singled, and Engle was safe on an error by second baseman Tommy McMillan, scoring Tris. After Lewis and Engle pulled off a double steal, Jake Stahl and Heinie Wagner hit back-to-back doubles to score three more runs. In the sixth after Engle, Stahl, and Wagner walked, and Cady popped to third base, Joe hit into a force at second, beating the wide throw to first for a fielder's choice RBI. With two out in the eighth, Cady tripled off the right-field fence, and Joe singled him in. Meanwhile, Joe gave up only a single in the fifth before a bizarre finish. A walk and a single put two New Yorkers on with no outs. Joe then struck out Ezra Midkiff before Hal Chase hit a high fly to right field, which Hooper temporarily lost in the sun. Williams tagged and jogged home with apparently the first run for the Highlanders. But pinch runner Dutch Sterrett, believing Hooper wouldn't recover, ran toward second. When Hooper sprinted deep into right field for the catch, he doubled Sterrett at first, preserving the shutout, Joe's thirty-third win.

In the long break before his final start against the A's on October 3, some major personal news hit the papers. The previous December, Joe was supposedly engaged to May Perry, described as a debutante, former student at a Boston business college, and Red Sox fan. That engagement disappeared as quickly as it had flashed in the papers. Now a second engagement was noted (on October 1), to Laura O'Shea, whose address was listed as that of her father, S. F. O'Shea, 2641 Forest Avenue, Kansas City. Articles explained that they had met while he was playing for the Blues in the 1908 season, maintained regular correspondence, and were planning to be wed after the baseball season. The most sweet, and suggestive, quotes were Laura's, in the October 2 papers: "I don't like to hear anybody call him 'Smoke' though. He's just plain Joe to me, and always will be, although I will admit he has some speed — both on and off the diamond." She also bragged that Joe wrote her before the Johnson game: "He knew he would beat him and told me so. And he did, too."[16]

Back in Kansas City, a reporter for the *Kansas City Post* the next day had an equally charming story to tell. Having heard of the engagement, he went to the O'Shea home. At first Miss O'Shea said "she didn't know a thing about it," but the sparkle from a huge solitaire on the third finger of her left hand flashed a contradiction. Miss O'Shea at first wouldn't talk until "she had heard from Joe," but assured that the report was authentic, "she finally admitted she and the pitching marvel were to be married soon." The same article also described, in cheesy metaphors, the earlier drama when Joe joined the Blues in 1908. At first Laura O'Shea "kept company" with "Chick" Brandom. "But Joe stuck around pretty close. As the course of true love always reaches the right destination, Brandom did not succeed in making a safe hit and was thrown out at first, while Wood landed with what turned out to be a home run." Mercifully, the article ended there.

In Philadelphia on October 3, in a game scouted by Christy Mathewson and Rube Marquard for the NL champion New York Giants, the Athletics held a 3–0 lead through four innings, on Frank Baker's long home run to left field and a triple by Jimmy Walsh in the third. But in the top of the fifth, the Red Sox scored eight runs, on five walks, a single by Wagner, doubles by Cady and Stahl, and a grand slam to the center-field fence by Duffy Lewis. Philadelphia got two more unearned runs in the sixth. But the Red Sox added single runs in the sixth, seventh, and eighth innings (Wood scored after leading off with a double), and then six in the ninth on Clyde Engle's triple, a walk to Hooper, and a bunch of singles, to win 17–5. Although the layoff weakened Joe's command, he finished the season 34-5.

The stage was set for the 1912 World Series, one of the most dramatic ever. Before it began, Smoky Joe Wood became the subject of human interest stories, often focusing on his sister. An article syndicated by the International News Company began, "When Joe Wood arrives here to face McGraw's clan in their first game of the world series, the Boston Red Sox premier pitcher will be accompanied by the most attractive mascot that ever 'mascotted' a well know athlete." Despite the difference in their ages, Zoë "trails with him and the two are always together." She was the "most keyed-up spectator in the big throng" at the Johnson game. In good times "she snuggles up even closer and a charging army couldn't drive her away." In bad "all he needs is to hear a certain small voice in the stand or catch the flutter of a waving handkerchief, and a combination of Cobb, Jackson and Lajoie up in turn would have no terrors."[17]

But most baseball fans wanted harder baseball stories. Both the American and the National Leagues had won four previous Series. The NL representative Giants, led by McGraw and Mathewson, were talented, confident, even arrogant. New York won 103 games, the Red Sox 105. Boston had rising stars, including the outfield of Lewis, Hooper, and Speaker. But center stage was "Smoky" Joe Wood, the most popular of the Red Sox. The Rooters even sang his song, which Giants fans loved to parody, "Knock Wood":

> If you think you will win all the tin with a grin,
>> Knock Wood, watch Wood.
> If they tell you, too, say to you, you will do,
>> Knock Wood, watch Wood.
> If you guess you've got the Red Sox right,
>> Guess again for you will have to fight.
> The "Speed Boys" are the noise, they're the "Joys"
>> Ship ahoy!
> Knock Wood, watch Wood![18]

1. Joe's parents, John F. Wood
and Rebecca Stephens Wood.
Courtesy of David Wood.

KANSAS CITY, MISSOURI

A-No. 3334

DEPARTMENT OF HEALTH
Bureau of Vital Statistics

Certified Copy of Birth Record

Surname __Wood__   Sex __Male__   Color __White__

Date of Birth __October 25, 1889__   Place of Birth __2512 East 18th St.__

Name of Father __John H. Wood__   Birthplace __Pennsylvania__

Name of Mother __Becca Wood__   Birthplace __Iowa__

Birth reported by __A. Donaldson__

File Number __A 351__   Date of Filing __October, 1889__

State of Missouri, }
City of Kansas City {

   I hereby certify that the above is a true and correct copy of the certificate of birth of __Howard Ellsworth Wood__ filed in the office of Vital Statistics of Kansas City, Missouri; that the above certificate is filed in said office and is a part of the permanent records of the Bureau of Vital Statistics of Kansas City, Missouri.

Witness my hand as Director of Health, Kansas City, Missouri this __12th__

day of __May__, 19 __47__.

Hugh L. Dwyer, M.D.
DIRECTOR OF HEALTH

Geraldine Holmes
Registrar.

An affidavit filed in this office states that this child was named __Howard Ellsworth Wood__

Fee 50c
FORM NO 5,000

2. (*Above*) Birth certificate of Howard Ellsworth Wood, born October 25, 1889, in Kansas City, a couple of blocks from where he would play baseball in Kansas City in 1908. Courtesy of Joe Wood Archives and Rob Wood.

3. (*Opposite top*) Ouray, Colorado, baseball team, Joe Wood's surrogate family, with him cradled by an older player (*second from left*). Courtesy of Joe Wood Archives and Rob Wood.

4. (*Opposite bottom*) 1906 Ness City, Kansas, baseball team with a serious-minded Joe (cross-legged, *lower right*). Courtesy of Joe Wood Archives and Rob Wood.

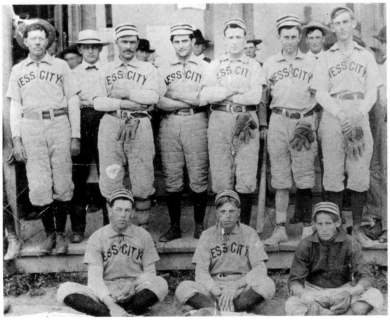

BALL ∴ GAME
MONDAY, AUGUST 27
BLOOMER GIRLS
VS.
NESS CITY

COME AND SEE THE GIRLS PLAY BALL!
Game Called at 3 o'clock Sharp

This is one of Best Attractions of the Season. Don't Miss It!

Ness County News.	CHIT-CHAT.

TRAIN TIME AT NESS CITY

GREATBEND BRANCH

EAST BOUND.

No. 576—Passenger.......................... 7:58 A. M.
No. 578—Freight............................ 3:10 P. M.

WEST BOUND.

No. 577—Passenger.......................... 3:10 P. M.
No. 579—Freight............................ 4:05 P. M.

NESS CITY, - KANSAS
Saturday, August 25, 1906.

A chiel's amang you takin' notes.
And, faith, he'll prent it!
—Burns.

Bloomer Girl base ball Monday.

A light sprinkle Sunday morning.

WANTED:—Everybody to use Ness City flour.

Stereoscopes and stereoscopic views at Brassfield's.

For music rolls and music satchels see Mrs. C. J. Bills.

5. Local advertisement for a game between Ness City and the Bloomer Girls, after which Joe was recruited to play for Logan Galbreath and the Bloomers. Courtesy of Jim Swint.

6. Joe (*third from left in top row*) on the 1907 Hutchinson, Kansas, baseball team, for which he first rose to fame as a pitcher. Courtesy of Joe Wood Archives and Rob Wood.

7. The typically well-groomed Joe Wood as a
rookie for the Boston Red Sox. Courtesy of Joe
Wood Archives and Rob Wood.

8. Joe Wood and men of Ness City, Kansas,
reducing the rabbit population, winter 1909–10.
Courtesy of Joe Wood Archives and Rob Wood.

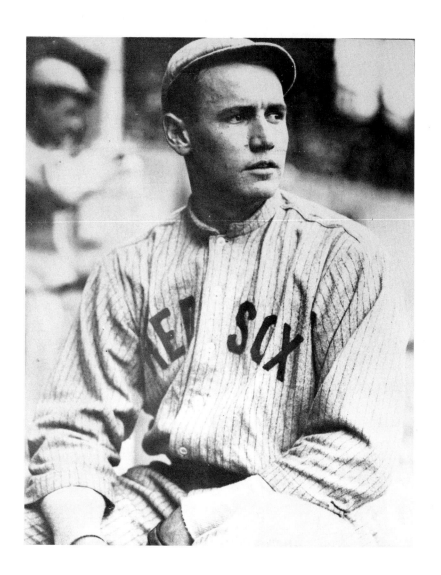

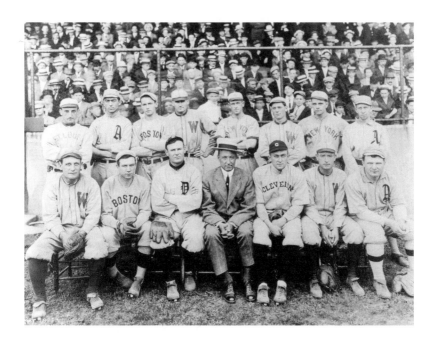

9. The highly competitive and courageous side of Joe Wood, star for the Red Sox. Courtesy of Joe Wood Archives and Rob Wood.

10. Joe with Cobb, Speaker, Johnson, Hal Chase, Home Run Baker, Sam Crawford, Eddie Collins, and others at the Addie Joss Benefit Game, July 24, 1911, in Cleveland. Courtesy of Joe Wood Archives and Rob Wood.

11. Smoky Joe Wood pitching as the ace of the 1912 Boston Red Sox, his cap typically angled toward his left ear. Courtesy of Joe Wood Archives and Rob Wood.

12. Joe and Walter Johnson before their crucial
game, portrayed in the press as a battle of
heavyweights, September 6, 1912. Courtesy of
Joe Wood Archives and Rob Wood.

Smoky Joe Wood in 1912:
"Was he ever something!"

A 1912 advertisement

M. Qiggo, Putman Ave. N. Y.

Joe Wood,

Boston Am. League Pitcher,

c/o Detroit Am. League Base-ball Grounds,

Detroit, Mich.

$229

Joe Wood,

Say your final farewells to friends and mates at once.
You will be no more within a short time. You will be in danger all
the time now on. Our method never fails. We always warn our
victims fefore hand but so far they have never escaped us.
With you go two others in your crowd a man higher up and one lower
Eight menbers of our gang took up your trail yesterday. Two men
from New York base-ball will accompany you sooner or later , and
one from Washington. Remember we warn you and we never fail. You
may be gone before this reaches you as we do not give no time
after our warning. This easy money getting business must be stopped.
ped. We never fail.   Return ad. is false.

13. Joe in an advertisement for Regal shoes
during the 1912 season, for which he received five
pairs of Regals. Courtesy of Joe Wood Archives
and Rob Wood.

14. A death threat letter to Smoky Joe before the
1912 World Series. Courtesy of Northeastern
University Libraries, Archives and Special
Collections Department, Boston.

15. Joe and Christy Mathewson, not good friends then or later, during the 1912 World Series, in which Wood beat Mathewson in Game 8. Courtesy of Joe Wood Archives and Rob Wood.

16. The 1912 World Champion Boston Red Sox, with Joe's sister, Zoë, standing next to him (*in top row*). Courtesy of Joe Wood Archives and Rob Wood.

FIVE

The 1912 World Series

The drama of the 1912 World Series was served by many backstories. Red Sox supporters believed that the first championship in the twentieth century, against the Pirates in 1903, was won by the Boston Royal Rooters singing "Tessie." Those rooters and their song were still around in 1912, as loud or obnoxious (depending on your point of view) as ever. There wasn't a series in 1904 because John McGraw, the Giants' manager, and owner John T. Brush wouldn't lower themselves to play the supposedly inferior American League and its first-place team from Boston. From the Red Sox point of view, both of those bastards, still leading the Giants, needed to be punished for their sins. The greatest hero in the "modern" Series was Christy Mathewson, who in 1905 threw three shutouts as New York defeated Philadelphia and remained a frontline pitcher for the Giants. He was called the Christian Gentlemen. But some Red Sox, including Joe Wood, weren't enamored of Mathewson. After the Series they would find more reason to hate him.

For many New York and Boston fans, the series between the Giants and the Red Sox following the 1909 season was reimagined as a prelude to the 1912 Series. The first game in October 1909 featured pitchers Joe Wood and Christy Mathewson. Since those two greats were expected to start Game One of this Series, it would be a rematch. Other major players were also the same. For New York Larry Doyle was still at second base and playing better than ever, indicated by his winning the Chalmers Award in 1912 as the most valuable player in the NL. Red Murray was back in the outfield, and Moose McCormick was available as well. Although some were at new positions, all the infielders on the 1912 Giants team had been on the 1909 roster. Hooks Wiltse and Rube Marquard, much improved, also remained Giants. Similarly the whole Red Sox infield was with Boston in 1909, and the outfield that year was only minus Duffy Lewis. Sea Lion Hall and Ray Collins had pitched well in the 1909 games. Tris Speaker was the hitting star that year. Like Doyle Tris won the 1912 Chalmers Award (in the AL), hitting .383 with an on-base percentage of .464 and a slugging average of .567.

More recently the rivalry between the leagues was heating up since both the Americans and the Nationals had won four previous Series. Furthermore, the Giants needed redemption, if not revenge, for being defeated in 1911 by the A's, with Mathewson losing back-to-back games and the score of the final game 13–2. Red Murray, the Giants' star outfielder, had gone an impossible 0 for 21, and the team hit just .175. In reaction the New York Giants came out of the blocks fast in the 1912 season. After losing three of their first four games, they enjoyed winning streaks of nine, seven, nine, and six games. Then they topped those marks by winning sixteen games in a row and went into the Fourth of July with an amazing record of 54-11. Most remarkable was Rube Marquard, who had won his first nineteen decisions. But before the season was over, Rube and the Giants gave their fans worry. Marquard went 7-11 the rest of the year as the lead of New York slipped to just four games by September before they turned things around. As the Series began, the New York Giants were playing lukewarm baseball, even with their 103 wins.

The Red Sox had even more wins — 105. They were more consistent than the Giants, only losing three games in a row one time before a five-game skid as they clinched the pennant in mid-September. They also had their revenge story. Shortstop Heinie Wagner first played in the Majors in 1902 as a twenty-one-year-old with the Giants. He appeared in seventeen games before being sent to the Minors, by John McGraw in one of his first moves as a manager. But the Red Sox had worries too. Like the Giants they cooled off near the end, especially at the plate. And their clutch hitter Larry Gardner was recovering from a broken pinky finger on his right hand. It was painful for him to bat, and there were questions about his ability to throw accurately. Also some analysts, like Hugh Jennings in a ghosted article, said that the Giants were a fastball-hitting team and might do well against a hard thrower like Smoky Joe Wood.

Even the weather added to the drama of the 1912 World Series. Fans remembered that the 1911 Series had taken thirteen days to complete because of delays, once for a whole week, between New York and Philadelphia. Anxieties over a repeat of such irritating stoppages were intensified when heavy rains hit the East at the end of September and then unseasonable cold arrived in New York just prior to the start of the Series. No matter what the weather, the fields of the two teams were expected to play in the 1912 postseason theater of baseball. At the Polo Grounds Boston's Lewis in left might have trouble with the notorious afternoon sun. Any of the outfielders, but especially Hooper in right, could be bothered by the shadows cast by the rooflines on the fancy marble facades at the Giants' park. On the other hand, shadows on cloudy days or boundaries between light and dark would make hitting difficult against serious heat, like that exhibited by Smoky Joe Wood. At least the Red Sox had played the Highlander/Yankees at the Polo Grounds late in the regular season, gaining some familiarity with the renovated park.

Fenway was just as problematic. New in 1912 the park had offered even American League players limited experience. But the National League teams had none in a park that required some getting used to. First, there were the odd dimensions. The foul lines, as now, were relatively short, creating sharp diagonals from the foul poles into left- and right-center fields. Right field was already a scary sun field, fueling anxiety that fielders would lose track of flies hit that way. And even though there was no Green Monster, in left field the grass took a steep upslope before it reached the wall. It was called Duffy's Cliff for the Boston left fielder's uncanny ability to run up the slope and find the ball as he descended again. A Giants outfielder might make a fool of himself either stumbling up or down Duffy's angles. Also, as the Wood-Johnson game had shown, overflow crowds across the outfield or down the baselines could turn normal fly balls into doubles and leave little ground for catching foul flies.

Preparations for the large World Series crowds only magnified the potential for trouble in Fenway. Just when the Sox felt that Duffy's skills in left would give them an advantage, additional seats were built along his cliff. Lewis would have to negotiate more than a new, low fence. Long but routine fly balls to left could, and would, easily land in the added seats for ground-rule doubles. Temporary fences in right center and right made it more likely that balls hit that way would catch the two corners and carom sharply away from fielders. Those three-foot fences were also odd, with only eighteen inches of planking beneath a top railing, allowing balls to hop through or over the boundaries. As Glenn Stout has estimated, such modifications reduced the playing area by 10 percent and the foul territory, especially behind home plate and down the left-field line, even more. Players on both sides faced a radically reconfigured park. New conditions promised unseen challenges and miscues.[1]

Drama also grew from the teams being well matched. At first base Fred Merkle and Jake Stahl were both capable of rescuing errant throws from anywhere in the infield. While Merkle could cover a bit more ground, hit for more power, and batted a career-best .309 that year, Stahl was the leader of the Red Sox and didn't have a "bonehead" play in his past. Steve Yerkes had become a solid defensive player at second for the Red Sox. But the Giants' Larry Doyle hit .330 that year and even beat out Honus Wagner for the Chalmers Award. Both shortstops were considered skilled players. Art Fletcher of the Giants, converted from the outfield, had neither the experience nor the aggressiveness of Heinie Wagner, who was also the captain and leader of the Red Sox. Wagner had the uncanny ability to get a foot in front of second base on steals and pick-offs, wearing a famous torn shoe to prove it. Although neither shortstop hit for a high average, Wagner was considered a more patient and powerful hitter as well as a better base runner. At third Buck Herzog of the Giants had better range, especially to his right, than Larry Gardner and was strong at fielding bunts. Buck was also more adept on the bases. But Gardner had a stronger arm, was a clutch hitter, and batted .315 in the 1912 season.

The Giants' outfield, while hitting for neither exceptional averages nor power, had speed. They could run down balls in the outfield, and the top four players — Murray, Snodgrass, Devore, and Becker — averaged almost thirty-five stolen bases, with Snodgrass stealing forty-three. But the Red Sox were unparalleled. While Speaker was famous for his assists, making thirty-five in 1912, Hooper also had twenty-two and Lewis twenty-three. On the offensive side Speaker stole fifty-two bases that year, and Hooper had twenty-nine. Lewis, a free swinger who didn't hit for a high average, nevertheless had power and, like Gardner, was good in the clutch. Like Murray of the Giants, Hooper in right field had an excellent arm. Chief Meyers was the best catcher, hitting .358 and placing third in the Chalmers voting that year. He also had a stronger arm than either Bill Carrigan or Joe Wood's personal catcher Hick Cady, though Chief's delivery was considered slow, and he sometimes had trouble handling spitballs. Always slow afoot Meyers was even slower after he suffered a sprain late in the year. But the major subplot was whether Cady could help Wood keep the speedy Giants runners from stealing, especially second base.

Both teams also had strong pitching. For the Giants Mathewson was still effective, winning twenty-three games in 1912 with an ERA of 2.12. But Matty, who had thrown sixty-eight shutouts in the previous eleven years, didn't have any in 1912. After very disappointing years in 1909 and 1910, Rube Marquard finally had two good seasons, going 24-7 with an ERA of 2.50 in 1911 before a phenomenal start in 1912. But he didn't have the control of Mathewson; he walked twice as many batters as Matty in fewer innings. The wild card was Charles Monroe "Jeff"

Tesreau, a product of the trolley leagues in St. Louis who had jumped from the Class A Toronto Maple Leafs of the Eastern League after posting a 14-9 record and a 2.7 ERA in 1911. Big for his age and time, six feet two inches and weighing around 240, the Bear Hunter in 1912 road his spitball to 17-7 and a 1.96 ERA. But Jeff walked almost as many (106) as he struck out (119), and he hit ten batters that year, more than twice any other Giants pitcher.

The Red Sox in 1912 had two twenty-game winners besides Smoky Joe Wood. Rookie Hugh Bedient, only two days older than Joe, had been brought up after a mediocre year (8-11) for Jimmy Collins's Providence Grays in 1911. Surprisingly, in 1912 he was 20-9, with nineteen complete games and a 2.92 ERA. The other was thirty-year-old Buck O'Brien, a spitball pitcher, in only his second year in the Majors and his fourth in professional baseball, having first pitched for the Evansville River Rats of the Central League in 1909. Ray Collins was also expected to see major action in the Series. Although his record in 1912 was only 13-8, Collins's crossfire was very effective against left-handed hitters. At twenty-five he had established himself as a control pitcher, with an ERA consistently around 2.5. Also on the Sox staff was Charley "Sea Lion" Hall, who sported an ERA of 3.02 while winning fifteen games that year. But Hall had almost as many walks (seventy) as strikeouts (eighty-three).

Recent substitutions and soft play by both teams also made Giants and Red Sox fans nervous as the World Series approached. On October 1 Manager McGraw of the Giants traveled to Washington to scout the Red Sox, where Little Napoleon saw Hugh Bedient pitch a complete game win, 12–3. Stahl played backup catcher Pinch Thomas and Clyde Engle at third, so Cady, Carrigan, and Gardner weren't on display for Mugsy. Worse yet for New York, that day neither Rube Marquard nor Jeff Tesreau was effective, and the Giants lost to the second-division Phillies 9–2. Worries over defensive lapses continued as even usually reliable Larry Doyle made an error that day. Concerns on the Boston side focused on Gardner's condition and whether Joe had worn himself out pursuing the consecutive-win record. More generally doubters felt Boston, despite its impressive record, was only in the Series because Philadelphia had slumped, the result of poor team discipline and the off year by Chief Bender.

As before any major athletic contest, there was concern with injuries. On the Red Sox side, Larry Gardner had broken his little finger at the first joint on his throwing hand while trying to field a ground ball during a game on September 21 in Detroit. By the end of the season, the finger was healing. But the trainer had to tape that finger to the ring finger for stability. As the Series started, the injured finger still looked disfigured. The Sox were encouraged when in the final tune-up, on Saturday, October 5, Larry had two hits, one a double, and three assists against the A's. Catcher Bill Carrigan suffered a contusion on the index finger of his right hand from a foul tip against Washington on Saturday, September 28. He also was healing normally, though he had an ugly yellow and purple discoloration under the nail. For New York, their main offensive threat, Larry Doyle, was spiked on the ankle in a game on October 3. But he was able to play the next day against Brooklyn and apparently had no lingering effects. Both teams could honestly say they were at nearly full strength.

There was agreement among experts that pitching would be the difference. The Sox had two twenty-game winners and a thirty-four-game winner. Their team ERA was 2.76, but the Giants' was 2.58, even lower. Most experts felt Wood's speed would play to the Giants' weakness, though it was well known that Smoky Joe could be wild and sometimes got rattled if he hit a batter, as he had against the White Sox during the 1912 season. Reporters also wanted to scoop the unexpected, the hidden causes of crucial outcomes. There was little news with Boston. But in the final weeks of the season, John McGraw experimented with pulling his starting pitcher when he suspected a "blow up" was imminent. Although it wasn't called relief pitching, McGraw seemed quite willing to call on his bullpen, though writers speculated McGraw wouldn't use such radical tactics in a championship. Also there was a rumor in baseball circles that Christy Mathewson had been working on a spitball.

Again observers were doubtful of such a change. Astute analysts also noted that umpire Bill Klem didn't give the corners, which might contribute to Wood's control issues.

This attention to players and strategy attracted unprecedented audiences because of the quantum leap in media attention. There was the traditional newspaper coverage. The *Boston Post*, for example, shouted that it had "Gathered Together" the "Greatest Corps of Expert Writers" for the game. On its front page were pictures and the accomplishments of writer Paul Shannon, baseball cartoonist Morris Scott, and funny man Newton Newkirk. Sam Carrick, the statistician, would be ready with facts. And then there were the heavy hitters: Old Cy Young, Ty Cobb, John McGraw, and Heinie Wagner as "Captain of the Red Sox." The October 6 *Atlanta Constitution* bragged that its reporting of the Series by Giants manager McGraw marked "a new epoch in baseball journalism." But the most remarkable changes were electronic. An estimated ten thousand telegraph operators would send messages across all states and into most small towns, even to Canada, Cuba, and Mexico. Visible in major cities were electronic scoreboards, placed at major public venues, including Times Square, New York parks, the Boston Theatre, and Madison Square Garden. Some devices replicated the fields and featured movable images of individual players.

The administrative side of baseball even came into play in the 1912 World Series. In New York only three thousand advanced tickets were sold, leaving more than thirty thousand seats available on the day of the game, a dollar for bleachers and two dollars for grandstands. The predictable result was people camping out for those tickets when they went on sale Monday morning, October 7. Lines stretched for over twenty blocks, with some long-suffering fans willing to bribe policeman for better positions. Out in the city fans from across the United States had to be accommodated, and children were rumored to have abandoned their homes for the streets, ready to sneak into the Polo Grounds if necessary. Even before the first game in Boston, hysteria developed there over ticket sales. A minor fire on October 4 at the office of John I. Taylor on Washington Street led to anxiety that applications for tickets, or even tickets themselves, had been lost. Red Sox officials reassured fans that the tickets were safe. But Sox staff had to promise seats to victims of forged seat reservations.

The Red Sox were early favorites, primarily because of their consistency and slightly superior record, plus the fact that the Giants had faltered down the stretch. Joe Wood had also had good rest since pursuing the streak. Writers like John R. Robinson noted that the Sox had won four of five games in 1909, had more superstars, Matty wasn't as dominant, and Marquard was "too high strung." Hugh Fullerton added that the Giants lost season series to the Pirates and the Cubs, indicating New York maybe wasn't the best team in the NL. Fullerton even accused the Giants of quitting against first-rate opposition. But in the last days before the Series, the odds started to shift as National Leaguers, even Charles Murphy of the Cubs, reluctantly showed public support for the Giants. The odds had shifted from almost two to one for Boston to more like ten to eight. The wagers, like the nerves the teams' supporters, were tightening in the final hours.

For Smoky Joe Wood there was even more drama before he threw a pitch in the 1912 World Series. It came from frightening "black hand letters." Joe recalled receiving two particular ones. But there may have been as many as six. The threats were general: "You will never live to pitch against the Giants in the world's series! We are waiting to get you as soon as you arrive in town," and "You better stay in Boston where you are safe among friends." There were some graphic details as well. One declared, "Look out for us! We're gunning for you" and had a knife and gun drawn on the bottom in red ink.[2] Two letters in the archives at Northeastern University, dated September 16 and posted by a fictitious M. Giggo of Putnam Avenue in New York, were sent care of the Red Sox, one to Cleveland and the other to Detroit. Class-based, they mention revenge for "easy money," not the teams playing the Series. According to Joe the Red Sox management contacted the New York City police, who laughed off the threats. Joe said he was unfazed. He

felt the situation came with his public character, no different from issues common to politicians.

The Boston Red Sox left Boston's Back Bay Train Station on special cars of the Knickerbocker Limited and pulled into Grand Central
Station at 6:00 p.m. on Monday, October 7. They transferred to the
fashionable but out-of-the-way Bretton Hall Hotel, at Eighty-Sixth and
Broadway, on the Upper West Side. The players were strongly encouraged to respect curfews and keep their distance from the action down
around Forty-Second Street. Most, if not all, met those expectations.
The next morning, October 8, 1912, the Red Sox made the first of their
two and one-half mile taxi rides to the Polo Grounds. The Sox didn't
wear their caps and shirts to avoid inciting the aggressive Giants fans.[3]
Joe also remembered pulling down the shades in the taxis so that New
Yorkers wouldn't throw rocks at the Boston players. He insisted in interviews that he was too young to be nervous. But Harry Hooper told
Lawrence Ritter that "tension on Joe was just terrific all that season,"
and before one game Joe was wound so tight he "couldn't say a word."[4]

That day most fans and writers assumed that veteran Christy
Mathewson would pitch for the Giants against Joe. Matty hadn't pitched
since September 28, in a move designed, most felt, to rest him for pitching the first game and eventually as many as three games. But a surprise
starter for New York was Jeff Tesreau, like Wood a quite young pitcher.
While compiling his impressive rookie record at twenty-four, Tesreau
pitched a controversial (the scorekeeper changed a hit to an error after the game) no-hitter 3–0 at Philadelphia on September 6, the same
day Joe outpitched Walter Johnson 1–0. Giants' manager McGraw explained that he wanted Tesreau home for his initial World Series game,
in a more familiar park and with more-supportive fans. What McGraw
didn't say but worried informed Giants fans was Jeff's control issues.
Despite his sub-2.00 ERA, he had averaged almost four walks per game
and threw six wild pitches, in addition to the ten hit batters.

There was the usual hoopla before the game. The teams arrived on
the field, first the Giants and then the Red Sox, both in long sweaters,

maroon for the Giants and red for Boston. But the warmups weren't just for display. The cool, almost cold, weather of the previous days remained for the game. The mayors of the respective cities arrived with political pomp. After publicizing manly challenges to each other, they sat down together as embodiments of their cities' pride. Admiral Oosterhaus was present, as was Governor Eugene Foss of Massachusetts. Before the game Larry Doyle received his Chalmers auto as most valuable in the NL. To build suspense and confuse the Red Sox, McGraw warmed up both Mathewson and Tesreau. But all these rituals were trumped by the entrance of three hundred Royal Rooters, accompanied by a thirty-member brass band, sporting hatbands declaring, "Oh, you Red Sox" and sashes fashioned from red socks. In an act of literal grandstanding, Mayor Fitzgerald ran across the field to incite Sox fans in their section. Finally, Mayor Gaynor of New York threw out the first ball, to Giants catcher Chief Meyers, at 2:03 p.m. Surprisingly, it wasn't a capacity crowd; many fans had stayed away at the last minute believing tickets would be unavailable.

For the first five innings of the game, Jeff Tesreau seemed an inspired choice by John McGraw. The Red Sox made no hits, but Jeff was wild, walking four in the first three innings. Harry Hooper led off the game with a walk and made it as far as third after two ground outs to Doyle at second base, by Yerkes and Speaker. But Duffy Lewis flied out to center to end that rally. In the second Larry Gardner reached on an error by Art Fletcher, the Giants' shortstop. Player/manager Jake Stahl forced him at second and tested the quickness of Chief Meyers's delivery to second. Both Chief's foot and arm worked fine. Stahl was out. Heinie Wagner walked, but Hick Cady flied out to right field, ending Boston's chances. When Joe began the third with yet another walk, the Sox had a lead-off hitter on for the third consecutive time. He was sacrificed to second by Harry Hooper and took third on Yerkes's groundout to second. But Lewis popped up to short, ending another scoring opportunity. When Boston went down one, two, three in both the fourth and the fifth innings, Tesreau seemed to be getting stronger.

Meanwhile, Joe wasn't as effective as Jeff. With two outs in the first, he gave up an infield hit to Snodgrass and a walk to Red Murray before getting Merkle to pop out to Wagner at short. He breezed through the second, striking out Meyers and Fletcher after Buck Herzog flied to first baseman Stahl. But trouble came in the third. After striking out Tesreau, Smoky Joe walked Josh Devore. Larry Doyle hit a pop-up to left. But apparently work in the sun at Fenway hadn't prepared Duffy Lewis for the Polo Grounds. He lost the fly, and the ball dropped in left, near the foul line, allowing Devore to take third and Doyle second on the throw. When Joe struck out Snodgrass, he seemed close to extricating the Sox from another jam, as he had done all that year. But in 1912, unlike 1911, Red Murray was up to the test. He drove a hit into center, scoring both runners before Cady cut down Murray trying to advance to second. Smoky gave up a single to Herzog in the fourth but struck out Fletcher. Doyle also singled behind third in the fifth but was out trying to stretch it into a double, ending that inning. Through five innings the Giants had five hits and were ahead of the hitless Red Sox 2–0.

The momentum shifted in the sixth. With one out Speaker hit a drive to deep left-center that Snodgrass couldn't corral as he and left fielder Josh Devore closed ground, giving Tris a triple. He scored on Lewis's grounder to second before Larry Gardner struck out. In the bottom of that inning, Snodgrass reached on an error by Wagner but was erased when Murray, attempting a bunt, popped into a double play, with Jake Stahl to Joe covering first base. Merkle's fly to Wagner ended the sixth. In a non-move for which McGraw was second-guessed, Tesreau stayed in to pitch the seventh, which seemed wise when Stahl grounded to second. But Wagner and Cady followed with singles to center, with Heinie moving to second. Joe then grounded to Doyle, who fell trying to hurry a double play and could only get a force at second. Joe was at first as Wagner took third. With two out Harry Hooper on a 0-2 pitch delivered a double down the right-field line, tying the game at two and sending Joe Wood to third. Steve Yerkes followed with a single to left, scoring both Wood and Hooper before Speaker struck out. In two innings the Red Sox surged from losing a 2–0 no-hitter to a 4–2 lead.

In the bottom of the seventh, after striking out Herzog, Wood hit Chief Meyers. But Joe composed himself and got Fletcher to ground to second for a force out. Moose McCormick, batting for Tesreau, then flied out to left fielder Duffy Lewis to end the seventh. Both teams went down in order in the eighth, leading to one of the most dramatic innings faced by Wood as a pitcher. In the top of the inning, he had a chance to give himself and the Red Sox a cushion. After Heinie Wagner's double to left, Cady bunted the shortstop to third. But Wood hit back to Doc Crandall, who had replaced Tesreau in the eighth, and Harry Hooper lined to Doyle at second.

In the bottom of the ninth, the Giants employed a new strategy: swing at first pitches. Red Murray hit Joe's initial delivery for a fly out to Hooper in right. But then Joe softened and gave up three consecutive singles—to Merkle, Herzog (Hooper lost a blooper in the shadows), and Chief Meyers (against the concrete wall in right field)—scoring one run and putting the tying run on third (Herzog), the winning run on second (Beals Becker running for Meyers). All on just four more pitches. In what became his most memorable sequence, Smoky Joe then struck out Art Fletcher on three pitches and Doc Crandall swinging at a high fastball on a 3 and 2 count. In later life in a rare moment of braggadocio, Wood said it was the fastest pitch he had ever thrown and, possibly, Crandall never saw it.[5]

Smoky Joe Wood struck out eleven Giants, eight of them looking. But he also gave up eight hits and two walks, plus the hit batter. More significant for the rest of Series, he had thrown 122 pitches, mostly fastballs. Indicative was the final sequence to Crandall, where he had wasted two curveballs, leaving them outside, in order to set up the last fastball, too fast and close to take. The Red Sox made only six hits, but they received four walks. And in a prelude of things to come, both shortstops made errors. The biggest surprise was the lack of adventurous base running. Repeatedly the teams resorted to sacrifices, or attempts at sacrifices, being careful between bases. For all its speed the Giants outfield was a bit suspect, especially when Snodgrass called off Devore and then let Speaker's drive through for a triple. Initially it looked like Boston's defense was better than the Giants'.

The Red Sox fans were, of course, delirious. They shouted, "Good old Joe Wood!" on the return trains and in the streets of Boston. And they had a new, more player-specific chant sung to the rhythms of "Tessie":

> Carrigan, Carrigan,
>   Speaker, Lewis, Wood and Stahl,
> Bradley, Engle, Pape and Hall;
>   Wagner, Gardner, Hooper, too,
> Hit them, hit them, hit them, hit them
>   Do, boys, do!

Equally celebratory were Damon Runyon's words the next day. The writer for the *New York American* declared: "A stripling with a braided arm and a fighting heart carried the Boston Red Sox through to victory over the New York Giants in the opening game of the world's series at the Polo Grounds. . . . It was the chilled steel nerve of 'Smoky Joe' that lifted the Sox across to the 4 to 3 victory." For the Sox the game had gone according to script. Their team had shown defensive skill, hit in the clutch, and Smoky Joe Wood once again rose to the occasion. They would've liked more offense. But Game One was theirs.

Joe rested for Games Two and Three, both at Fenway and almost as dramatic as Game One. Christy Mathewson started the second game in the first of his hard-luck performances. The Red Sox scored three unearned runs in the first on an error by Art Fletcher. But the Giants scored runs off Ray Collins in the second and the fourth. The Sox got some breathing room when Yerkes tripled in Hooper in the bottom of the fifth. But Duffy Lewis's error led to three unearned runs for the Giants in the eighth, with Charley Hall replacing Collins during that pivotal inning. In the bottom of the same inning, another error by Fletcher, on a grounder by Larry Gardner, scored Duffy Lewis.

Three walks loaded the bases for the Giants in the ninth, but Hall got

Red Murray to ground to Wagner, who forced Doyle at second. After Boston went quietly in the bottom of the ninth, the teams traded triples and runs in the tenth. For the Giants, with one out, Moose McCormick, pinch-hitting for Fletcher, hit a sacrifice fly, scoring Merkle, who had led off with a triple to center. With one out the Red Sox responded with a triple by Speaker, also to center, and an error by Art Wilson. Boston catcher Carrigan threw out two runners to keep the Giants scoreless in the top of the eleventh, but the Sox went down on three grounders before the game was called for darkness. All six Red Sox runs were unearned, on five Giants errors, three by shortstop Art Fletcher.

At first many thought the game, a 6–6 tie, would be counted. But the decision finally came to play an eight-game series if necessary. Before Game Three Speaker received his Chalmers car and took a sporty spin around Fenway. The game, a replay of Game Two, was a pitching duel between Rube Marquard and Buck O'Brien. Red Murray's lead-off double, followed by a bunt and a sacrifice fly from Buck Herzog, gave the Giants a run in the top of the second. New York scored again in the fifth on a double from Herzog and a single from Art Fletcher. They also loaded the bases in the same inning before Snodgrass flied out to Lewis in left. Then, typical of the 1912 World Series, the ninth inning got more interesting. Hugh Bedient, replacing O'Brien, hit a batter and gave up a single. But Hick Cady, who had replaced Carrigan, threw out Herzog, and Fletcher hit into a double play.

The Sox almost pulled it out in the bottom of the inning. After Speaker popped out to shortstop, Lewis got an infield single, and Gardner doubled to right, scoring the first run for Boston. But when Stahl hit back to Marquard, Gardner was thrown out trying for third. The game seemed over when Wagner grounded to Fletcher, but first baseman Fred Merkle dropped the throw, with Olaf Henriksen (running for Stahl) advancing to third. With Hick Cady batting, Wagner took second. Cady then lined to deep right center, where left-handed right fielder Josh Devore made a leaping, over-the-shoulder catch. On that play the Giants won 2–1 and evened the Series.

After another quick turnaround, the teams moved back to the Polo Grounds for a game on the fourth consecutive day, Friday, October 11. Joe returned to the mound where he had struck out Fletcher and Crandall to win Game One and where he would again face rookie Jeff Tesreau. Game Four was considered crucial by both teams. The Red Sox needed to bounce back; a second win from Smoky Joe would set the momentum flowing their way once again. The Giants felt that if they could win against Wood, they would gain the upper hand with Mathewson, who had given up no earned runs in his first outing, on the mound in the next game. In the meantime there was some question over whether Game Four would be played. Heavy rains in the morning left the skies dark and threatening, but at noon the officials decided to start on time. It was still misting in the first inning. But the rains held off, and the only effect was a slow field, which helped the infielders get to balls hit on the heavy grass.

At first it looked like the Red Sox would jump all over the Giants when Harry Hooper led off the game with a single to center and Giants catcher Chief Meyers made a bad throw to second on a bunt by Steve Yerkes. But equally unusual was Speaker's grounder to shortstop Fletcher, who stepped on second and threw to first for a double play to kill the rally. Joe snuffed out a minor threat in the Giants' first by picking Snodgrass off first to end the inning. In the second Larry Gardner led off with a triple to deep right center, and with Stahl batting, a Tesreau wild pitch gave Boston a 1–0 lead. In the bottom of the second, Fred Merkle got to third, after a single, a stolen base on a bad throw from Cady, and a ground out. But Joe got Meyers to fly to Lewis, ending the inning. The Red Sox almost scored in the third, after Joe singled and Hooper walked. But Yerkes failed to sacrifice before grounding back to Tesreau, who forced Joe at third. Two other ground balls failed to score a run. In the fourth, with two outs, Cady's single to left scored Stahl (after a walk, force out, and stolen base) with the second Boston run.

Meanwhile, Joe was cruising. He retired the Giants in order in the third and fourth innings while striking out half the batters. In the fifth,

after Speaker was out stealing second to end the top of the inning, Joe gave up the third Giants hit, a one-out single by Herzog. But no damage was done. The Sox went down in order in the top of the sixth. In the bottom Joe started to show some vulnerability. After Tesreau singled to left, Devore hit a liner back at Joe, who knocked it down, but both runners were safe. Again Joe found what he needed, getting Doyle to pop up to Gardner and both Snodgrass and Murray to ground out to Yerkes. The score remained 2–0 Boston.

After the Red Sox again went down 1-2-3 in the top of the seventh, Joe struck out Fred Merkle to lead off the bottom half of the inning. But after Buck Herzog fouled off a pitch, he hit a new, whiter ball for a single to left. Wood seemed to be in the clear as Meyers flied out to Speaker. But Art Fletcher doubled down the right-field line, scoring Herzog. It looked like the Giants might tie the game when Moose McCormick, pinch-hitting for Tesreau, singled off Yerkes's glove, but Steve recovered in time to thrown out Fletcher at home. Both teams threatened in the eighth. For Boston Tris Speaker doubled to left with two down, but Duffy Lewis grounded out to short for the third out. In the Giants' half, Fred Snodgrass reached on an error by Wagner and then raced to third when Red Murray drove a hit to right-center field. But Joe struck out Fred Merkle, on a slow curve, to end the inning.

The Red Sox added an insurance run in the ninth off Red Ames, working his second inning of relief. Joe stroked a two-out hit to right, over Fred Merkle, driving in Larry Gardner. Then Wood induced fly balls to end the game: Herzog sent one to Speaker, Chief Meyers fouled to catcher Cady, and Fletcher popped to first base. More easily than the first outing, Smoky Joe Wood had his second victory of the 1912 Series. Joe did bend, giving up nine hits (seven in the last five innings), but he walked none and struck out eight. He also was supported by better defense, especially by Wagner at shortstop and Yerkes at second. Boston won 3–1.

Red Sox fans in New York were again ecstatic. Previous banter between fans turned on Joe Wood's invincibility, with the New Yorkers mimicking the Boston songs like "Knock Wood." Now as they left the Polo Grounds, the Sox fans mimicked the parodies, singing sarcastically, "Old Joe Wood! / He's no good! / Oh, yes, / I guess, / That he's no good!" For Ring Lardner the decisive moment came when "two Giants got on base in the eighth when two were out and then Joe gave an exhibition of his very best brand, striking out Fred Merkle on pitching that nobody could have hit." Others named Joe's retiring of Meyers in key situations. But Lardner's summary was most poetic: "Under a dark sky that boded rain, the right arm of the marvelous Smoky Joe Wood thrashed the ball through the muggy air with speed that brought it up before the eyes of Giant batsmen no larger than a pea."[6]

On the surface the game was a replay of Game One. Again Joe gave up more hits than the Giants pitchers, 9 to 8. Again Tesreau walked more than Joe, 2 to 0. Again they both pitched well, and Joe won with his strikeouts. As in the first game, two fast teams didn't steal much; both had just had one stolen base. The Red Sox again tried sacrificing and failed. But there were subtle shifts. Joe relied on curves, suggesting either a strategy to keep the Giants off stride or the loss of hop on his fastball. While Tesreau was again wild early, this time he got stronger, striking out five of the six batters in the sixth and the seventh innings. Joe, on the other hand, gave up seven hits in the last five innings. Wagner made two excellent plays at short for Boston. But he also made two errors, indicating that the Sox were capable of defensive lapses equal to the Giants' in Game Two.

The next day, Saturday, October 12, the teams were back in Fenway for the fifth game in a row. This time Mathewson had better defensive support and retired the last seventeen Red Sox, eleven on ground-outs. But three of the five hits he allowed were triples, including lead-off back-to-back ones to Hooper and Yerkes in the third inning, followed by the only Giants error, by second baseman Larry Doyle. Those two runs, one unearned, were all Hugh Bedient needed. He pitched a three-hitter, with the only run in the seventh, when, with two out, Larry Gardner couldn't make a play on a ball hit by Moose McCormick, pinch-hitting for Fletcher. Like Joe Wood the previous day, Bedient sent the Giants down 1-2-3 in the ninth. The final score was 2–1. With the next day off, Stahl had options. But most felt that Joe would finish things off in New York on Monday.

Then things got messy. It was widely reported that President McAleer of the Sox had put pressure on Stahl to start O'Brien. Stahl first objected and then finally relented. There was also speculation that McAleer wanted to prolong the Series to ensure more money for the teams (the players' share had tapped out) and bring down the curtain in Boston. Stahl only said that he chose O'Brien over Collins because it was overcast. That left Joe Wood glaringly significant in his absence. Whatever the reasons, the game was decided early.

In front of 30,622 at the Polo Grounds, Harry Hooper led off with an infield single but was picked off. Speaker walked and stole second, where he was stranded when Duffy Lewis flied to left. In the bottom of the inning, after Devore grounded out to third, Doyle reached on an infield single and stole second. Snodgrass struck out. Wagner knocked down a ball hit by Red Murray, with Doyle advancing to third with two out. After O'Brien balked, scoring Doyle and giving Murray second base, Fred Merkle doubled to right, plating Murray. Herzog doubled to left, bringing in Merkle. Chief Meyers singled, with Herzog stopping at third. With Fletcher at bat, the Giants pulled the double steal of second and home, with Meyers moving to third when Yerkes missed Cady's throw. Fletcher's bunt scored the fifth run.

The Red Sox fought back in the top of the second with two unearned runs when Rube Marquard misplayed a grounder by Larry Gardner, Jake Stahl singled to center, and with two out, Clyde Engle, batting for Buck O'Brien, doubled to left, scoring both runners. Ray Collins took over on the mound for Boston and held the Giants the rest of the way, giving up five hits and no walks over the next seven innings. The problem was Rube Marquard. The Red Sox got only one runner past first for the rest of Game Six. In the fourth hits by Stahl and Cady put runners on the corners with one out. But Marquard got Boston's Collins to ground into a 6-4-3 double play. Although he gave up seven hits, Rube only walked one and lowered his ERA to 0.50 in the Series. Ray Collins was equally masterful, giving up no runs over seven and lowering his ERA to 1.88. Unfortunately, O'Brien was miserable from the start; the final score was 5–2, and the Giants were within a game of tying the series.

After the game there was a coin flip to determine the site of an eighth game, if it were necessary. Monitored by the National Commission, Jake Stahl called "tails," and the coin came up tails. The makeup game would be at Fenway. But according to Boston papers, on the way back from New York to Boston, things were already heating up . . . off the field. A rumor was floated, traceable to the wife of a Red Sox player, that Wood, O'Brien, Carrigan, and Cady had been in a tag-team shouting and pushing match on the ride back to Boston. The most popular version was that O'Brien blamed Cady for the melt down in the first inning that day, Wood called O'Brien a quitter, O'Brien swung at Wood, Cady used his fists to defend Wood, and finally the two catchers got into a real tussle. There was also a variation in which Joe's brother, Pete, had confronted O'Brien about his shoddy pitching.[7] In yet another version, O'Brien, not expecting to pitch, had gotten drunk and thus was hung over for Game Six, to the anger of Wood and others.

President McAleer denied the stories of dissension, as did many Red Sox players. At a press conference McAleer and Stahl even exhibited Wood and O'Brien to reporters, showing that they had no marks indicating a scuffle. A few months after the Series, in an interview with Tim Murnane, Joe declared that on his "word as a man, there never was the least foundation for the story" about him and O'Brien fighting on the train.[8] But Joe's most heated response came in an audiotape within a year and a half of his death: "My brother never met Buck O'Brien." He further speculated that the lies made good copy and insisted, "Nobody hit O'Brien. My brother probably could've beat up anybody on the ball club. But he never even met any of them." In the Murdock tapes, Joe also claimed there was no fight, by Joe or Pete.

Meanwhile, off the record even darker stories were told. People said, and others repeated, that Pete and other of Joe's friends had bet large amounts of money on the Red Sox in Game Six, believing that Wood was going to be on the mound. The motive given for the supposed fight, according to these storytellers, was financial loss, not just the score at the Polo Grounds. The implication, repeated with even more passion a day later, was that people, some close to and influential with Smoky Joe Wood, were in substantial debt over New York's victory in Game Six. Seven years before the Black Sox scandal, conspiracy theorists smelled gamblers. Those willing to believe were put on alert for indications of a fix or other suspicious actions on and off the field, especially ones involving Smoky Joe Wood.

In Boston this intrigue had even more resonance. Rumors of conflict between players named O'Brien and Wood revived the image of the 1912 Boston Red Sox team as deeply conflicted. Players like Tris Speaker and Joe Wood were portrayed as hard-living westerners, with a taste for a good fight. Their skills with sharpshooting, horse riding, and hunting contributed to this image, as did their racially tinged language and humor. But the most sensitive point was religion, with the press magnifying differences between local "insiders" and western "outsiders" into warfare between the Protestants (Masons), primarily Speaker and Wood, versus the Catholics (Knights of Columbus), including O'Brien, Hooper, Carrigan, and Lewis.[9] Purported fisticuffs between Joe and Buck gained credibility in this context. Joe never discussed the topic, most likely because he had no religious agenda and was engaged to a girl of Irish Catholic background. His issues with Carrigan were about passed balls and throws to second, not worship. But that complex explanation made poor copy.

There were more than city/country dichotomies and religious antagonisms on the minds of Red Sox fans in October 1912. Problems with tickets at Fenway before the Series were ignored, almost forgotten, once the Red Sox won early and often. Especially indifferent to that history were the noisy, prestigious fans in this Series (as in every

Boston season), the Royal Rooters. But when they arrived at Fenway for Game Seven, their tickets had been sold. They did what any entitled supporters would do: they rioted. After storming the park they stationed themselves near accustomed seats, obstructing the view of their replacements. When spectators behind them objected, the Rooters moved onto the field. As the police forced them back, the twenty-five feet of fence closest to the foul line collapsed. At that point about half a dozen cops on horseback cleared the playing surface between the break and the Giants' dugout. Not understanding why the police were attacking the crowd, people in the grandstand threw trash, food, and scorecards, even canes, onto Fenway Park.

Eventually order was restored. First, Captain Wagner of the Red Sox warned the Sox fans that their team would have to forfeit if they didn't stop the shenanigans. Then management found seats down the left-field line for the Royal Rooters. In the process the most expressive Boston fans were dispersed, rendering them less organized and demonstrative during the game. Unfortunately for the players, this ruckus broke out during the warmups for the game. Although the game started only ten minutes late, Smoky Joe had to sit down and then resume his limbering while many officials (as well as Tris Speaker, according to Joe) sorted out the fans and rebuilt some of the outfield wall. Such interruptions could tighten Joe Wood's muscles, resulting in loss of flexibility, rhythm, and speed, all the more likely when the temperature dropped and the winds came up just as the game started. It was a clear day, but dust whipped around the dirt on the infield.

And then something even more unthinkable happened. As bad as Buck O'Brien had been in the first inning the day before, Smoky Joe Wood was worse on Tuesday, October 15. Josh Devore led off with an infield hit, followed by a single to center by Larry Doyle, with Devore stopping at second. Inexplicably Joe didn't hold the runners, and they stole second and third bases, without a throw. Fred Snodgrass followed with a double to right scoring both runners. Red Murray sacrificed, to Stahl unassisted, as Snodgrass advanced to third. Merkle followed with another single, to left, taking second on Lewis's throw home. On a come-backer by Buck Herzog, Joe was able to trap Merkle in a rundown between second and third, though Herzog advanced to second on the play. Chief Meyers added a single to left, scoring Herzog with the fourth Giants run. The inning seemed over when Harry Hooper retrieved Fletcher's single to right and made an accurate throw to third to get Meyers. But Gardner dropped the ball. Tesreau singled off Wood's glove, with Meyers scoring and Fletcher moving to third. With Devore batting again, the Giants executed the double steal; Tesreau got into a 2-4-3-6 rundown while Fletcher scored. Six runs, on seven hits . . . all on thirteen pitches.

Charley Hall replaced Joe in the top of the second. Hall was a bit better, giving up single runs in the second, seventh, and ninth, as well as two in the sixth, including a home run to right by Doyle. Boston managed a run in the second, on Larry Gardner's homer into the right-field stands, two more in the seventh, and another in the eighth, thanks to two unearned runs, with the Giants making four errors in the game. But the game was never in doubt after Joe's disastrous inning. The final was 11–4, and with the six runs, Wood's ERA rose from 2.00 to 4.74. And he panicked when he went into the wind up with men on base. Paul Shannon was funereal in the *Post* on October 16: "The laurel wreath intended for the brow of peerless Joe Wood was thrust aside with ruthless force by a vengeful band of Giants," the "penalty of undue familiarity" with "the bats of the McGraw clan."

When the game was analyzed in the press, reasonable explanations were given for the performance of Smoky Joe Wood. Most obvious was that the Giants had capitalized on strategies first tried at the end of Game Four. They noticed early in the Series that Joe tried to establish the advantage by getting first pitches over the plate without regard for location. So they swung at the first good pitch whenever possible. That happened for seven of the ten batters he faced. The New York team had also decided that their conservative tactics on the bases were failing; they planned to steal at every opportunity, forcing the

Red Sox to react. That also happened. But stories of a fix were gaining legs. Whether it was Joe's money, his brother's, or that of people connected to him, including gamblers, the speculation followed one train of thought. Joe didn't play well so that the people who lost money betting on the previous game could recoup their wagers.[10]

Joe adamantly denied such charges for the rest of his life. His best defense is that he had the perfect excuse and cover-up, the long delay and repeated warmups, but never played that card. He once referred to the rumor that the Giants may have stolen his signs. But repeatedly he said some version of "I just didn't have it that day." His most complete discussion came in a taped interview in JWA:

> There was a mix-up in the ticket sales so when the Nuf Ced gang of Royal Rooters came in to get their seats, their seats were occupied. And the fence broke down out in left field. . . . I was already warmed up ready to go into the game. And when they broke the fence down, they had to stop and fix the fence up. . . . They [the Giants] knocked me out of the box in the first inning with six runs. A lot of them [reporters] related it to the idea of being warmed and then laying off and going in later. But I don't think that had anything to do with it. Just one of those days that we had every once in a while. Just couldn't get a ball by them.

Now 2 and 1 in the 1912 Series, Wood could only hope that he would get a chance to redeem himself. Such a low pitch count made a return the next day a viable option for manager Stahl. But the Giants had Mathewson ready. The tide seemed to have turned against the Boston Red Sox. The atmosphere for the final game, on Wednesday, October 16, 1912, was anticlimactic, even a bit spooky. It was still cool, with some wind again, but the sixteenth was actually milder than the fifteenth. Fenway didn't turn strange because of the weather. When disgusted Red Sox fans boycotted the game, dramatically lowering the attendance (officially only 17,034), Fenway assumed an eerie, dead feeling as the Sox rooters were scattered, defensive, and petulant. Down the third-base line more than half the seats were unused. The stands down right field were nearly empty in some places as Hugh Bedient went to the mound. The right-hander had pitched well in relief during Games Two and Three and won Game Five over Christy Mathewson. At least the wind was blowing from the northwest, possibly helping the pitchers.

As Wood looked on, another pitching duel developed. The Red Sox were a bit loose in the field. In the top of the first, after two ground outs, Fred Snodgrass walked and tried to steal second. Cady, an excellent defensive catcher, threw to Wagner in plenty of time, but the shortstop dropped the ball. Fortunately for the Sox, Bedient was able to get Red Murray on a ground out to Larry Gardner at third. The Giants returned the favor in the bottom of the first, when second baseman Larry Doyle dropped a throw from catcher Chief Meyers, allowing Tris Speaker, who had singled to right, to advance to second. But Duffy Lewis struck out to end the inning.

Still nervous and tight, the Red Sox made two errors, both by Gardner, in the top of the second. With two out Meyers's grounder was fumbled by the third baseman, and Art Fletcher followed with a line-drive single to center, advancing Meyers to second. When the Sox, on a throw-through from Cady, picked Meyers off at second, in desperation the Giants catcher ran to third, where he was an easy out, except that Gardner dropped the ball. Fletcher also took second. Again the Sox avoided disaster as Mathewson's long fly to center was run down by Speaker. Boston rallied in the second when a walk and a single by Wagner put runners on first and second with one out. But Hick Cady popped to Merkle at first, and Bedient grounded out to second. The Giants broke through in the third, when right fielder Josh Devore walked and advanced to third on ground outs to third and first. With two outs Red Murray's drive to left-center tipped off Tris Speaker's glove for a double, scoring Devore. The Sox responded with nothing in their half of the inning, with Speaker whiffing for the final out.

The Giants rallied again in the fourth, when third baseman Buck Herzog doubled into the crowd and Meyers sacrificed him to third. But Fletched popped to Gardner at third and Mathewson flied out to

Hooper in shallow right. With one out in the bottom of the fourth, Larry Gardner hit a long drive to center but was out Snodgrass-to-Doyle-to-Herzog trying to stretch it into a triple. The Sox were rescued by their defense in the fifth. Devore led off with single but was caught stealing, Cady to Wagner. Larry Doyle followed with a long drive to right, caught by Hooper as he ran into the crowd. Fred Snodgrass followed with a single to left field. But Bedient was able to induce Murray to pop up to catcher Cady. In the bottom of the fifth, Mathewson saved some energy by getting Boston on three pitches, all outfield flies, two to left and one to right.

After Bedient gave up only a walk to Chief Meyers in the top of the sixth, the Red Sox came very close to tying it in the bottom of the inning. Harry Hooper flied out to first before Steve Yerkes singled to right and Speaker walked. Duffy Lewis forced Speaker at second on a ground ball to shortstop Fletcher, with Yerkes taking third. With two out Larry Gardner, known as a clutch hitter, was at the plate. But with Lewis breaking for second, the Giants faked a throw there on a pitchout, with Mathewson cutting off Meyer's throw and picking off Yerkes at third.

In the top of the seventh, the Red Sox made their fourth error when Stahl dropped Mathewson's pop up. Matty then singled to center and was forced at second by Devore, who stole second. But Snodgrass grounded to Gardner for the third out. Finally, the Red Sox tied the game in the bottom of the inning. After Gardner flied to Snodgrass, Stahl blooped a hit to shallow left-center, and Wagner walked. As Joe warmed up, Olaf Henriksen pinch-hit for Hugh Bedient. After two quick strikes and two outside pitches, Henriksen lined a ball down the left-field line, striking the third-base bag, scoring Stahl, and sending Wagner to third. Hooper then flied out to Snodgrass in center. It was 1 to 1 as Smoky Joe Wood entered the game.

According to Boston papers Joe was welcomed by loud applause from the partisan though small Boston crowd. This time he was fast, forcing the Giants to hit to the right side. After two ground outs, to first and second, Herzog singled to right. But then Joe got Meyers to ground to Yerkes at second. The top of the eighth was behind him. But Boston also was retired easily, on three ground outs in the bottom of the inning. The Giants' Moose McCormick pinch-hit for Fletcher to lead off the ninth and flied to Harry Hooper on the first pitch. After Mathewson struck out, Devore walked. But Joe got Larry Doyle to ground to second. With one out in the bottom of the ninth, Jake Stahl hit a double to left-center. When Wagner flied to deep right, Stahl failed to move to third. But it didn't matter because Cady flied to left. The anticipated matchup between Big Six and Smoky Joe seemed to be settling in.

But Smoky Joe was very shaky in the top of the tenth. After Snodgrass grounded back to Joe, Red Murray doubled to left and Fred Merkle singled to center, knocking in the lead run and taking second on the throw from Speaker. Wood struck out Buck Herzog and, more importantly, bare-handed a grounder from Chief Meyers to prevent an insurance run. Wood's hand was so swollen by the time he reached the dugout it was impossible for him to lead off, even though he was hitting over .290 at the time. What followed remains a classic of baseball lore. Clyde Engle pinch-hit for Joe and hit a fly to left-center, where Fred Snodgrass easily ranged under the ball . . . and dropped it. Hustling, Engle made it to second. After failing to bunt, Harry Hooper reached the same goal by flying deep to center, where Snodgrass made a very difficult catch, with Engle tagging and moving to third. Yerkes walked before the second infamous play of the half inning by the Giants.

On an inside curve to the left-handed Speaker, Tris popped up between the plate and first base. By every account, including Joe's, it was an easy play for first baseman Fred Merkle. But Mathewson called for catcher Chief Meyers, who couldn't reach it.[11] Apparently Speaker then warned Christy that the pitcher would pay for that mistake. He did when Spoke drove a hit over second baseman Doyle and into right field, scoring Engle, with both runners moving up on the throw home. After an intentional walk to Duffy Lewis, Larry Gardner worked the count to 3 and 1 before hitting a fly to Josh Devore in right field. The throw was so off target that Meyers didn't make a play as Yerkes slid head first across home and Christy Mathewson threw his hands in the air in defeat. The final score was Boston Red Sox 3, the New York Giants 2. The winning pitcher, despite giving up an earned run in the tenth, was Smoky Joe Wood.[12]

In his reflections on the final game of the 1912 World Series, Joe didn't remember that, as some have asserted, Speaker tricked the Giants by imitating Mathewson's voice and calling for Meyers to make the play. Wood put the responsibility with Mathewson, who should have named Merkle. But Joe Wood recalled Spoke yelling, "That's going to cost you, Matty." In the videotape interview at the seventieth anniversary of the opening of Fenway Park, Joe summarized his role in the last game of the 1912 World Series:

> [Bedient] got into a little bit of trouble along in the seventh or eighth inning and I went in when they called me in. We got on to the tenth inning . . . and they got one run off of me. And Chief Meyers hit another ball back at me which would've scored another run, but I knocked it down and picked it up and threw him out. . . . I got to the bench and [the wrist] was all swollen up and it was lucky I had thrown him out or they would've had two runs and how many more I don't know. . . . We got in the tail of that inning and we got two runs. That's how lucky I was to get the third win out of four [decisions].[13]

The game was characterized by heroic pitching. Mathewson dominated early, striking out four in the first four innings but none later, totaling 124 pitches. Hugh Bedient threw 99 in his seven innings, Wood 34 in three. But like the series as a whole, it was decided by errors, physical (Giants 2, Red Sox 4) and mental ones. In the eight games, the Giants had outpitched (1.59 ERA to 2.92) and outhit (.270 to .220 batting average) the Red Sox. Mathewson's ERA was 0.94, yet he lost two games. Joe Wood had pitched well in two games, yet the disastrous first inning of Game Seven ballooned his ERA to 4.50. When the final numbers were crunched, 252,037 fans had attended the 1912 World Series for total receipts of $499,833.00, breaking both records. Each winner received $4,024.70, a figure Joe could recite on demand for the rest of his life.

The day after the Series ended, the celebration began at Fenway Park. First was a group photo in suits, in which Joe Wood was seated next to Tris Speaker in the first row, extreme right. Next the team, led by two mounted policemen, formed a line of motorcars, the lead one carrying Mayor Fitzgerald and Jack Stahl in the front, with Bedient, Speaker, Henriksen, and Joe Wood behind. They left at noon by Jersey Street, turned on Boylston to Massachusetts, where they headed south to Columbus Avenue. Entering the downtown from the southwest via Columbus, they continued to the park, where a band accompanied them over to Tremont Street, on which they continued to Cornhill and over to Dock Square and Faneuil Hall. As they exited the cars, Jake Stahl was presented a wreath, and the team gave loving cups to Stahl and McAleer before the entourage took the platform, where they joined Joseph Walker, the Republican candidate for governor, and the head of the city council. All seats and aisles were filled after many fans climbed through windows.

The program was led by Mayor Fitzgerald, a Royal Rooter who welcomed the chance to be associated with the victorious team. Other than calling Stahl the captain and being soundly corrected by the demonstrative crowd, Honey Fitz got things right. He announced that each player would receive a loving cup from the team and half the proceeds from the last game, played after their contract year. Both gifts met with loud approval from the crowd. Each player then gave a short response, with Joe Wood following Captain Wagner, who said he did his best and was pleased. After Mayor Fitzgerald introduced Joe as "Boston's idol as a baseball pitcher," Joe seconded the team leader, saying only, "I did all I could, and I want to thank you." After the other players as well as the mascot and the trainer were introduced and "Tessie" was sung, the mayor declared the fans free to meet their heroes. A friendly riot followed, with press tables overturned, but no one was hurt. The team picked up checks at Fenway late the next morning, October 18, after which they scattered to the countryside.

Wood turned down one thousand dollars for a vaudeville tour. He explained his decision to his father, who missed the money more than Joe, in the presence of T. H. Murnane at the Wood farm, published in the *Globe* in early February 1913. As re-created by Murnane, Smoky Joe said he bypassed the popular stage for the natural world, away from the temptations and irregularities of public life: "If I should take up this theatrical business I would naturally be running around the country and doing very little to recuperate. It would be about the same the year around, stopping at poor hotels, on trains, and meeting a lot of people. Seven months of this public life is about enough. I love to come here in the country, live the simple life, work on the farm, eat regularly, and have my good sleeping hours." Although the language sounds a bit contrived, the sentiments are believable. They are congruent with Joe's retiring personality off the baseball field and his preference for life in Shohola.[14]

Joe celebrated by hunting and fishing with his good buddy Tris Speaker, on Wood's only trip to Speaker's home after a week together at the Wood place in Pennsylvania. But before they headed to Shohola, Pennsylvania, and Hubbard, Texas, they remained in the Boston area for a while, presumably enjoying their home in Winthrop. Included in their respite was an evening at the National Theatre, on October 22, to hear the Red Sox Quartet, which included Buck O'Brien, Olaf Henriksen, and Hugh Bradley. In addition to Smoke and Spoke, in the crowd was mascot Jerry McCarthy, who climbed on stage and led the crowd in "Tessie." The press interpreted the visit as a reconciliation between Wood and O'Brien for their imagined fight on the train from New York. But Smoky Joe didn't forget Laura O'Shea in all the celebrations.[15] He made a trip to Kansas City and his fiancée before returning to Pennsylvania.[16]

When the official stats were released for the year, Joe Wood had moved to the top. Iron man Ed Walsh pitched in sixty-two games, and

Walter Johnson, carrying Washington on his back, had entered fifty. But Smoky Joe Wood was right behind, competing in forty-three and completing thirty-five of thirty-eight starts. He pitched 344 innings, almost 70 more than in 1911, facing 1,328 batters and striking out 258. He shut out the Yankees three times and every other team except Cleveland and Philadelphia at least once, totaling ten scoreless games. His ERA was 1.91. And of course, his 34-5 record, a winning percentage of .872, was tops in the AL. He had also proved himself as a hitter. In 1912 Joe batted .290, higher than Duffy Lewis, Heinie Wagner, Bill Carrigan, Hick Cady, Steve Yerkes, Les Nunamaker, Harry Hooper, and Clyde Engle. Included were thirteen doubles (a record for a pitcher), a triple, and a home run, as well as thirteen RBI and sixteen runs scored.

As 1912 came to an end, Joe Wood was no longer a wild young pitcher with potential. He was among the greatest of his generation, the equal of Johnson, Walsh, and Rube Marquard. The press dubbed him Sir Joseph, the "speed boy of the speed boys." And the stories, true and not, hit the papers: he had started as a Bloomer Girl and wanted to throw as fast as the wind, his snap ball was unique and dangerous, and Joe wasn't his real name. After his trip to Kansas City, Joe settled back in Pennsylvania to rest his arm, whose deadness at the end of the Series worried reporters.[17] The previous fall Joe had sidestepped entrapment by May Perry, who was either a college student or a call girl, neither . . . or both. That press release by Miss Perry, and Joe's swift and brief denial to his real love, apparently goaded him to take a decisive step to Laura O'Shea, to whom he was engaged. It was all good for Smoky Joe. All pain and drama seemed temporary. And he turned just twenty-three on October 25, 1912.

SIX

Playing with Pain

For Smoky Joe Wood 1913 was supposed to be the return of the conqueror. Some fans, especially those who didn't find conspiracy in Game Seven of the World Series, feared Joe's arm had been weakened by the excessive innings he threw during the 1912 season and the grueling Series. Those worries abated as 1913 arrived and Joe traveled to meet President McAleer at the Major League Convention in New York. The festivities centered at the Wolcott Hotel on Thirty-First Street, but the crucial negotiation came at Rector's restaurant in Times Square. On the basis of his fabulous record for 1912 and the saber-rattling of the Federal League, Joe got a 50 percent raise and signed on the evening of February 10. In his words, "I had to battle like hell with the directors, McAleer and the rest of them," but he finally got "$7500 for the next year." While players and officials inspected the new Ebbets Field, Joe Wood quickly returned to Pennsylvania, then went on to Kansas City for time with Laura O'Shea. From there he traveled to spring training.

Meanwhile, brother Pete attended to the construction of a house in Shohola, designed as the first home of Laura and Joe Wood.[1] The setting was down the road and across the street from his parents, on a hill fronting more than ninety acres that Joe had purchased with 1912 World Series money. Acting like a contractor, Pete handled Joe's finances, hired carpenters and plumbers, and even brought a Brunswick pool table to the remote hills. The house had, and has, a porch around the outside, facing both the road and a picturesque creek to the east. In order to pipe spring water to the site, Pete dug a trench across the road, under the brook, and up a hill toward Crystal Spring House. Not extravagant but very functional and up-to-date, the house used all four floors to advantage.

On the bottom level Pete and Joe turned the den into a billiard room. At the back was a modern hot-water furnace. The second floor, surrounded on three sides by the large porch, was made up of a reception hall, dining and living rooms, and kitchen (with a modern "Quick Time" range and aluminum utensils), all with wood floors (covered with rugs) and trim. On the third floor were the primary bedrooms and bathrooms, again with wood floors covered in rugs. Leading from those rooms was a serviceable attic, which included extra bedrooms and storage space. Outside Joe finally added a garage, where he kept what a commentator called his "high power motor car." Trying to be helpful and relishing buying things denied her, Joe's mother Becca purchased amenities, including china and linens. All the members of the Wood family then conspired to surprise Laura with the house at the wedding later that year.

In the meantime baseball awaited the return of the man famous throughout the country as Smoky Joe Wood. The skies above Hot Springs, Arkansas, looked friendlier than they had in 1912, when rain threatened nearly daily. In a major change the Red Sox scheduled regular games with the Pirates once the Buckos relocated from West Baden, Indiana, midmonth. Although the managers of both teams feared injury and exhaustion, a nine-game series was scheduled beginning on March 16. Sunday games were still not permitted in the southern town, and the trolley ran only to the Pirates' camp, though local officials promised a spur to Majestic Field by 1914. Right on schedule, on March 3, player/manager Jake Stahl (trimmed down by ten pounds) joined catchers Carrigan, Cady, and Nunamaker and young pitchers, including Hugh Bedient and George Foster, at the Springs. Joe arrived that night from Kansas City, with catcher Chet Thomas.

Eyebrows raised in Boston baseball the next day when Tris Speaker was spotted in Marlin, Texas, at the training camp of the Giants, the foe in the previous Series. Finding no harm in his friend's customary delays, Joe took advantage of excellent weather to work out on the fourth and the fifth and suffered only minor blisters from tape on his bats. On Wednesday, March 6, other regulars checked in, along with Dutch Leonard, a promising left-handed pitcher. Although easily twenty pounds overweight, Dutch resisted running in the rubber suits used to reduce.[2] An explosion rocked downtown Hot Springs on March 7, when gas ignited at the Mattar Brothers store, injuring several customers but no Red Sox. On Saturday, March 8, Joe, always active when not pitching, sprained his ankle chasing a wild throw while playing third base. The next day the main contingent arrived.

The Boston Red Sox had their first full workout, for an hour and forty-five minutes, the next day, Monday, March 10, 1913. There were fears that Joe Wood, reduced to a light workout, might have lingering effects from his ankle injury; sometimes pitchers took weeks or even months to heal from a seemingly simple twist, reporters fretted. More worry surfaced about Joe's health when he pitched for the first time, in relief of Hugh Bedient on Friday, March 14. He gave up singles to Hall, Janvrin, Engle, and Foster, plus a bases-loaded triple to Chet Thomas. However, Joe quickly eased doubts by giving up only one hit and no runs over the last four innings of the seven-inning contest, won by the Regulars 10–4. The next day when cold northerly winds blew in snow, players took mountain hikes and hot baths. But Spoke and Wood, both limping noticeably (Speaker from an ankle sprain), were confined to short walks in town. Receiving no guarantees that a Sunday game would be accepted, the Sox called off the next day's game.

The series began with two games on Monday, March 17; the Pirates beat the Red Sox Regulars 4–3 at Whittington Field, and the Red Sox Yannigans won 7–6 at Majestic.[3] Joe's first start came on Wednesday, March 19, 1913, one of the most traumatic games of his life. Joe retired the side in order in the first two innings. And he struck out two batters,

Hank Robinson and Solly Hofman, in the third. But between those Ks he faced Pittsburgh's third baseman Bobby Byrne. On a cloudy day Byrne worked the count to 3 and 2 and expected a curve ball next. Instead it was a fastball that hit the side of Bobby's head. Carried from the field Byrne remained unconscious for an hour and a half. Although Joe Wood completed that inning and another, he was visibly shaken. He regretted that pitch for the rest of his life, believing that he had shortened Byrne's career.[4] It was an easy 7–2 victory for the Sox, if not Joe Wood.

Then bad weather returned. The next day's game between the Regulars and the Yannigans was called in the first inning when torrential rains descended on the field. Boston also called off the next Red Sox-Pirates game. With little else to report during the cancellations, on Saturday the twenty-second the *Globe* updated its readers on the supposed fight between Joe and Buck O'Brien during the 1912 Series. According to Tim Murnane, Wood had considered a lawsuit against Christy Mathewson for repeating the stories in print. Joe is quoted as saying, "Mathewson is still sore over the defeat last Fall [*sic*] and is trying to annoy someone." O'Brien's words were stronger: "Mathewson has always been a knocker; he evidently takes himself seriously and should be stopped or get out of the game. He puts everything in the way of gossip, and gossip is a hard thing to tie to." Players felt Mathewson's comments especially damaging because Christy was vice president of the Players' Protective Association.[5]

After Easter Sunday the teams resumed their series; the Red Sox won 7–4 as Joe pinch-hit in the fifth inning, flying out. Bobby Byrne was back for the Pirates, but Speaker was again sidelined, with a strained ligament in his foot. Then more heavy rains returned on the twenty-fifth. After losing to the Pirates, 6–5 on the twenty-eighth, the Red Sox won 2–0 behind Bedient and Hall on Monday, March 31, giving the Sox the series 3-2-1. Joe warmed up for the last game but didn't play. On April 1 the team navigated through floodwater as high as the steps on the railway cars to reach Champaign, Illinois. The next day in the 10–0 win over the University of Illinois, Joe relieved Ray Collins; he struck out all twelve batters he faced as the infielders turned their backs, facing student soldiers parading near the field. In the final game against the Illini, on Saturday, April 5, 1913, Joe, Les Nunamaker, and Illinois alum Jake Stahl joined the college boys. Joe entered in the fifth and gave up two runs. He also doubled and homered. The Red Sox won, 11–2.

With the Cincinnati leg canceled due to flooding, the Red Sox traveled back to Boston by way of Chicago, Detroit, and Buffalo. In 1913 games against Harvard and Holy Cross were warmups in name only. On Tuesday it snowed, and it was still cold and windy for the Harvard game the next day. Meanwhile, Joe and Tris again took up residence in the seaside town of Winthrop, Massachusetts.[6] There was speculation that Hugh Bedient might start opening day of 1913 because of his impressive record against the A's. But Stahl once again named Smoky Joe. The sun came out that day, April 10, but it was still cold for the twenty thousand who watched the Red Sox begin their defense of the World Championship. There was one major change in protocol. The day before in Washington DC, President Woodrow Wilson had strolled to the pitcher's mound to throw out the ceremonial first pitch. Not to be outdone Mayor Fitzgerald donned Tristram Speaker's baseball cap and took the hill at Fenway. Honest Eddie Murphy in the left-hand batter's box and Rube Oldring on the right-hand side dutifully swung and missed as Honey Fitz lollipopped his heater to Hick Cady. Smoky Joe started Fenway's second season.

It was his worst showing since Game Seven of the 1912 World Series. Typically Wood's work was uneven in the first inning. He struck out Eddie Murphy, but after Oldring reached on a throwing error by shortstop Wagner, Eddie Collins got his first of five singles, and Frank "Home Run" Baker followed with a double off the left-center-field fence, scoring both runners. Then Smoky Joe dominated . . . for a while. He struck out another batter in the first and the side in order in the second, struck out Oldring and got Baker to hit into a double play in the third, and struck out two more in the fourth. But just when Joe seemed to be back to normal, including a strike out of Coombs to lead off the fifth, things fell apart. After Eddie Murphy singled, Joe hit Rube Oldring in the shoulder. Collins then hit another single, scoring Murphy.

Wood got Baker to force Collins, Yerkes to Wagner. But Stuffy McInnis made an infield hit over third, and Amos "Lightning" Strunk flashed a triple to right center and then stole home on the next pitch. The Red Sox got back three in the bottom of the fifth, with Joe scoring with Harry Hooper on Yerkes's double and Steve coming home on a sacrifice fly. But Joe's day was over. Wood had walked none and struck out seven, but he also gave up nine hits over five innings. His replacement, Charley Hall, quickly gave up three more runs to the A's. The Red Sox responded with four of their own off Chief Bender. But then the scoring suddenly stopped. Surprisingly, given the famous pitchers on the mound that day, Philadelphia won 10–9.

Despite his poor showing in the first game of 1913, Joe was so popular in the Boston area that the next day, April 11, 1913, James A. Gallivan, board of street commissioner, City of Boston, sent a memo to James R. McAleer, president of the Red Sox:

Dear Jim:

I am sending herewith a copy of "Practical Politics," which I spoke to you about, and which contains the story about "Joe Wood for Mayor." I told Joe last night that I would send the paper to you and that you would turn the paper over to him. He seemed anxious to read it, so will you see that he gets it after you have finished with it?

Sincerely yours,
James A. Gallivan

The document suggests that Wood run as "reform" candidate against the mayor, John F. Fitzgerald, grandfather of President John F. Kennedy. It assures McAleer, "Joe has been consulted concerning his candidacy, but thus far he is not prepared to make a decisive answer, although his friends say that he will not refuse to run."[7]

The enclosure quotes Tim Murnane, sportswriter for the *Boston Globe*, as believing that "Joe could beat Fitzgerald in every ward, with the possible exception of Ward 11." Even more euphorically, it adds, "There are those who believe that if Joe says he will run, the mayor will decide that he won't run." Most pointedly, the article confides that Manus J. Fish, superintendent of public buildings, might revoke the lease of Fenway Park in support of Mayor Fitzgerald, then asserts that Mr. Fish would be willing to change his plans as soon as Wood wins. The document summarizes, "Joe Wood has speed, and it is probable that on Patriots' Day he will be nominated formally for mayor of Boston." Despite Gallivan's words in later interviews Joe denied any involvement in or meetings about his running for mayor.[8]

While this political intrigue ran its course, on April 14, still at Fenway, Joe calmed fears about his health in a game against New York, mostly called the Yankees, pitching a complete game 2–1 victory, striking out nine and allowing only four hits. Once again the first inning was a problem. Bert Daniels, New York's right fielder, singled to right, stole second, and scored on a fielder's choice. After that Joe was nearly unhittable, retiring the side in order in the second, fourth, and sixth through ninth innings. With Boston down 1–0 in the eighth, Joe led off with a double to right. With two outs and Wood on third, Speaker was walked intentionally. With the count 3-2 and Tris running, Duffy Lewis doubled to right-center field, scoring both Wood and Speaker. It was the first Red Sox win of 1913. With Joe apparently back to 1912 form, Stahl used him four days later in relief at Philly. Wood struck out Stuffy McInnis with the bases loaded in the ninth to preserve an 8–5 win.

When Wood started again, on April 21 in Philadelphia, things seemed in sync. He pitched two innings, walking two and giving up one hit and a run. He was roughed up a bit on a close play in the second, bruising his thigh and pitching hand. But when he left the game in the next inning, with the Red Sox ahead 3–1, he appeared merely exhausted from running the bases. When Hugh Bedient couldn't hold off the A's, giving up five runs (mostly because of poor fielding by middle infielders), the Sox lost 6–4. The real damage was reported the next day. Joe left with an injured thumb, sustained while sliding into second base, and might be out for the following Washington series. At that point there was hope he would be back in three or four days. Then on the twenty-seventh of April, the team announced a more complicated situation. Joe would be out for at least two more weeks.

As May began, he was still having pain in the second joint of the thumb, which made it impossible to curve the ball. But with the Red Sox faltering (going from four and one-half to nine games back in the three weeks Wood was out), Jake Stahl gambled with Joe's future by bringing him back on May 12 in relief of Dutch Leonard against the Tigers in Detroit. It was probably too early, and Smoky Joe wasn't effective.[9] Inheriting two runners he gave up a double to Bobby Veach and a single to Del Gainer to tie the score. Then in the ninth he walked Donie Bush, and after a sacrifice and a single to Sam Crawford, Ty Cobb hit a long sacrifice fly to Lewis in left, bringing in the winning run. Wood was also erratic three days later, on May 15, in his first start since the injury. Against the Browns in St. Louis, he gave up only five hits but walked seven, indicating a loss of command. Joe struck out ten as the Red Sox won 15–4.

With Boston still eight games behind, in fifth place at 11-16, Stahl took even more chances. Even though Joe was exhibiting inconsistency, the manager sent Wood to the mound just four days later, against the White Sox, in Chicago on May 19. Joe was somewhat more settled this time and won 10–1 in a game called after eight because of darkness. Although he struck out eight, the wildness continued; he walked two, threw a wild pitch, and hit a batter. Joe pitched only two more games in May. Two days after the 10–1 victory, on May 21 in Chicago he entered in the ninth after the White Sox had rallied with six runs to make the score 10–9. With the bases loaded and two out, Joe got Babe Borton on a come-backer to preserve the win. May 30 in Washington Joe lost the morning game of a doubleheader, 4–3. In the afternoon game Harry Hooper hit the first pitch from Walter Johnson into the right-field bleachers for the only score of the game as Ray Collins four-hit the Senators. On the same field and day, Joe Wood and Walter Johnson both lost.

Smoky Joe Wood finished May 1913 with a mediocre 3-3 record. But his first assignment of June was in the Polo Grounds against the Yankees, always a welcome site and team for him. The game on June 2 was a bit of a struggle. In the second game of a doubleheader, with New York allowed to bat first, Joe gave up only three runs, though his wildness was again alarming. He walked eight and threw a wild pitch while giving up six hits and striking out nine. In his first incomplete game since opening day, he was replaced in the eighth, by Charley Hall and then Bedient. The Sox gave up three in the ninth but held on to the 8–6 win. Back in Boston the next day, Mayor Fitzgerald and Manager Stahl raised the AL pennant in center field at Fenway, and the Red Sox beat Chicago 3–2. Smoky Joe entered to much applause in the ninth and finished the game by striking out two of the four men he faced, including Ray Schalk to end it.

He was back as the starter three days later against the White Sox, in a game that would further test his vulnerable arm. The Red Sox took a lead in the first on Speaker's walk and a triple to right by Duffy Lewis, but the White Sox tied the game in the second on a Wagner error and two singles. Both teams scored in the third, with Joe walking and scoring on a sacrifice fly to center by Tris Speaker. A run by the White Sox in the fourth was answered by the Red Sox in the seventh on doubles by Cady and Hooper. By then Joe had found his groove, and he shut out Chicago through the twelfth inning. In the bottom of that inning, with two out, Speaker walked and Lewis hit a ball off the left-field wall that caromed away from Ping Bodie, allowing Speaker to slide safely home. Boston won 4–3, with Joe striking out eleven and walking one, though he made two wild pitches. His third consecutive win gave him a 6-3 record.

Playing hurt Joe once again needed significant rest before starting, on June 16, against the Browns in Fenway. Like his previous start it was a grueling twelve-inning contest. Joe was sluggish in the first, giving up a run on a wild pitch after a triple, and St. Louis got another in the fifth, on a walk, sacrifice, and single. Meanwhile, the Red Sox scored two and Joe tightened up, retiring the side in order in the sixth, seventh, and eighth innings. St. Louis almost won in the ninth. After a lead-off single, George Stovall hit a ball into the left-field corner. With Lewis's throw slowing about twenty feet from home, Joe intercepted it and relayed to Les Nunamaker, who tagged Burt Shotton to keep the game tied at two. In the twelfth with one out and Clyde Engle on third, after a walk and fielding error, Joe hit the first pitch from Walt Leverenz into right-center field. The right fielder didn't chase it, and the Sox won 3–2. Joe struck out ten, walked two, and threw the one wild pitch.

But the control issues didn't go away. In Philadelphia on June 20 Smoky Joe again struggled, walking five, but he pitched a four-hitter, struck out nine, and gave up only an unearned as the Red Sox won 6–1, Joe's fifth in a row. Just when he didn't need the frustration and pain, his final two starts of June 1913 were exhausting complete game losses at Fenway. On June 25 the Yankees gained a rare victory over Joe Wood, 5–2, on the day the Red Sox mounted the World's Championship banner. The game was tied 2–2 after seven, but errors and wildness gave the Yankees two in the eighth and one in the ninth. Joe permitted only four hits and struck out seven, but he also walked five and hit three batters (two in the ninth). On June 30 the Red Sox carried a 1–0 lead through seven innings against Washington, with Joe striking out nine batters, six of them in a row, in the first five innings. But the Senators tied the game in the eighth on Alva Williams's pinch-hit to right field. Walter Johnson entered in relief, and Joe tired in the eleventh. He gave up a lead-off walk, threw wide on a pick-off attempt, and allowed three singles for two runs. The Big Train struck out Carrigan, Hooper, and Yerkes to end the game. Washington 3, Boston 1.

Wood got a breather on the Fourth of July, in the first game of a doubleheader against Philadelphia at Fenway Park. It was an extremely sloppy game, with the Red Sox making six errors (four by shortstop

Wagner) and the Athletics four. Joe only pitched four innings, giving up seven hits and walking four. But the Red Sox scored seven runs in the fourth, including a record two doubles in one inning by Joe, who went 3 for 3 for the day. With such a big lead, he was replaced by Hugh Bedient, who finished the game, mercifully called by the umpires at the end of seven innings. According to scoring at the time, Joe won his ninth against five losses, though his complete games streak stopped at five. The score was 13–6.

After such a short outing, Stahl brought Joe back quickly. He was on the mound July 7 for the final game of the Philadelphia series, the second game of a doubleheader. Wood was shaky, giving up eight hits and walking seven. Scarier than his wildness, however, was his tumble to the ground in the second inning after bunting for a hit and colliding with A's first baseman Stuffy McInnis. But Joe recovered and scored. He had a 7–0 lead by the fourth, a shutout through the sixth, and won 8–3. Joe Wood got a strong, easy win in the second game of a doubleheader at Chicago on Saturday, July 12, 9–0, his fourth over Chicago that year. He struck out only four but walked just two and gave up four hits. The Red Sox scored early, with three runs in the first inning; Lewis and Speaker both had three hits, including two triples by Duffy and one by Tris.

On July 18, 1913, three days after Bill Carrigan replaced Jake Stahl as the manager of the Red Sox, Joe pitched the game that shaped the rest of his career.[10] The weather was good that Friday in Detroit, and the crowd was reasonably large for a weekday. Joe was pitching well, giving up only one hit through the first three innings, when he got a little wild in the bottom of the fourth and walked a couple of batters to put runners on first and third with one out. When Bobby Veach hit a swinging bunt up the third-base line, Sam Crawford was caught off third. But as Wood pivoted to throw to Gardner, he slipped on the grass (which he remembered as a bit wet) and fell on the thumb of his pitching hand, the same finger that had sidelined him earlier in the season. After rookie Vic Moseley replaced Joe, the Tigers scored three in the sixth and two in the seventh to win 5–1.

It seemed to be no big deal at the time, with Joe predicted to be out just a couple of weeks. Apparently of more consequence was the rumor in Detroit that Joe and Tris would be traded to the Tigers for Ty Cobb, a deal reportedly made over the head of President McAleer in a power move by C. H. and his son John I. Taylor. That story proved groundless as the injury to Smoky Joe's thumb became the real story. Three days later, on July 21, after x-rays showed a fracture — a subperiosteal fracture as Joe regularly recalled in later years, leaving a piece of bone chipped off the end of the thumb — the finger was put in a cast for ten days. On August 1, when the brace was removed, discoloration remained at the second joint. Joe wasn't the only Red Sox player with a health concern. Other injuries — to Wagner, Tris Speaker, Gardner, and Ray Collins — left Boston out of serious contention for the pennant.[11]

On August 29 the *Washington Post* quoted Joe as willing to sacrifice the rest of 1913 for his long-term recovery: "I would be taking a great chance if I did [come back]. My thumb is getting along nicely, and the broken bones have all healed. I am working out every day, but it is doubtful if I go into the box before next year."[12] Despite the caution in these words, Joe started rehab that year. On September 8 he pitched three scoreless innings of an exhibition game in Manchester, New Hampshire, as the Amoskeag Textile Club dedicated their field. Joe had a triple in his only at bat. He also pitched one more game, in Boston on September 17. He relieved Dutch Leonard in the last inning of a 2–0 loss to Cleveland and retired the three batters he faced, one on a strike out. He also pinch-ran for Olaf Henriksen in the seventh inning of a 10–9 loss at Philadelphia on the twenty-fourth. The next day Joe warmed up during a 5–4 win against the A's but didn't play. With Joe out and Speaker missing the final week and one-half after a benign tumor was removed from an ear, the Sox finished a distant fourth.[13]

The 1913 season was uneven for Smoky Joe Wood. He struck out more than seven and one-half batters per game and gave up three fewer hits than he had strikeouts. He also surrendered no home runs, completed twelve starts, and had a winning percentage of .688 (11-5). Though his ERA, 2.29, was the highest since his rookie year, it was the best on the Red Sox staff. But his walks per innings pitched almost doubled, and he threw one more wild pitch than in 1912, though he pitched almost two hundred fewer innings. The frequency of hit batters was up almost 60 percent. The two injuries to his thumb made his control erratic, and he had neither command of his curves nor hop on his fastball. There also was discomfort in his shoulder. Nevertheless, Joe and the Red Sox expected that he would fully recover in the off-season.

Once the season was over, Joe hung around Boston. On October 8, as he, Tris Speaker, and Bill Carrigan were preparing for an "automobile trip" to Lewiston, Maine (Carrigan's home), Joe discovered a kitchen fire in the Putnam Hotel, their sometime dormitory, at 1:00 a.m. The ensuing alarm interrupted the Bankers' Ball in the neighboring Symphony Hall. But all parties met the disturbance with curiosity and humor, not distress. As the *Globe* reported later that day, with a touch of hero worship, "After the firemen returned, Wood and Speaker gave an exhibition of dancing on the sidewalk, with a little vaudeville conversation thrown it, to the amazement of the banker's party." At the end of the month, on October 31, Joe played in a golf tournament with Clyde Engle and Secretary McRoy in Auburndale, Massachusetts, and shot 91.

More personally, Joe and Laura Teresa O'Shea were married on Saturday, December 20, 1913, in Milford, Pennsylvania.[14] The bride and her sister arrived in Port Jervis, New York, by train, on Erie no. 4, the Chicago–New York Express, at 3:39 p.m. They then "motored on to Milford." The wedding was a small, private affair, witnessed by Miss Edith O'Shea, the bride's sister from Kansas City, and Pete Wood, Joe's brother of Parkers Glen, Pennsylvania. In a local announcement Joe is noted as the son of Mr. and Mrs. John Wood and grandson of Bradner Wood, original settler in the area. Officiating was the Reverend L. B. McMickle at a 5:00 p.m. ceremony in the parsonage of Milford Methodist Church.[15] After the wedding the couple were to retire to Joe's "four-story bungalow" "after January 15, 1914." Appropriately, Joe's parents were reported as pleased. Students of baseball trivia will note that Tris Speaker gave the Woods a silver tea service.

Seemingly inconsequential was the additional notice that a scheduled reception, which one paper archaically called a "skimmerton," "headed by Dr. F. E. Gessner of Port Jervis," had to be postponed until December 27 because Joe had contracted ptomaine poisoning.[16] After the honeymoon all apparently returned to normal at the new Wood household in the Delaware River Valley. But more pain, which had nothing to do with Joe's thumb or shoulder, was waiting in the wings as 1914 began. According to the Wood family Bible, Joe's mother, Becca Stephens Wood, left John F. on "January 10, 1914" and moved with Zoë to an apartment in downtown Port Jervis, aided by Joe's brother, Pete. Following so soon after the wedding, that separation alone would have set an emotional roller coaster in motion. But just over a month later, the diagnosis of his illness after the wedding was revised. In late February the express train from New York to Cleveland on the Erie line made an unscheduled stop as physicians rushed to the Wood home.

At 2:00 a.m. on Sunday, February 22, 1914, the Dr. Gessner who had sponsored the wedding party and Dr. C. N. Skinner, both of Port Jervis, New York, assisted by a Miss Cox of Narrowsburg, New York, removed Joe Wood's appendix through a two-inch incision made while he lay on the kitchen table. In the words of Dr. Skinner, "It was a light attack of appendicitis [back in December]. But in view of Joe's wedding at that time and his desire to get away on a honeymoon trip, [Joe] did nothing about it. Results now show that the delay in the case was serious." Dr. Gessner added, "The appendix was found bound down by adhesion, and the tip in a gangrenous condition, bordering on a rupture. The intestines were inflamed, and his general condition was found so bad that an immediate operation was resorted to in order to give him relief." As Dr. Skinner clarified, "Had he waited 24 hours there is no telling what the result might have been."[17]

Telegrams in the JWA trace the exchanges between the Wood family and the Red Sox. Joe's brother, Pete, informed J. J. Lannin, president of the Red Sox, of the illness: "Joe Wood taken suddenly ill with appendicitis. Operated upon Sunday morning at 2 o'clock at his home in Parkers Glen, by Dr. F. E. Gessner of Port Jervis, New York."[18] Lannin's reply was simple and direct: "Sorry, indeed, to hear of Joe's illness and hope for speedy recovery." Manager Carrigan's initial response came in the papers. As reported in the *Boston American*, Bill responded to the successful surgery: "This is the first news of Wood I have received. If he is able to take his turn on the slab commencing June 1st I guess I must consider myself lucky. Poor Joe; I sincerely hope that he is not suffering any. He will be allowed to remain out of his uniform just as long as his doctor prescribes, but his failure to make the training camp and then pitch the opening day of the season is a great blow."

On the twenty-sixth the *Globe*, after noting that Carrigan sent flowers to the Wood home, reprinted further telegrams between team president Joseph J. Lannin and Pete Wood. Lannin: "Hope Joe is improving. Wire us occasionally conditions. Tell him not to worry. Boys will work all the harder until returns to the Red Sox." Pete: "Joe has rested comfortably for the last 24 hours. All indications for a rapid recovery. He is pleased with many messages of sympathy and encouragement. We all appreciate the sympathy expressed for Joe." On March 9, according to newspapers, Joe wrote he would like to report by March 20. With the support of President Lannin, Carrigan prepared to include Wood on the team in Hot Springs. In a March telegram, retained in jwa, the catcher and leader invited Joe and Laura to spring training, if Smoky Joe was able: "If you think you can stand the ride without injury to yourself, and promise you will do no hard work, but take it more as a vacation, come along. Bring your wife as Mr. Lannin's guest. Fix transportation yourself. See you on arrival. Answer when you leave Port Jervis for here. Bill."

Initially Dr. Gessner nixed an early return to baseball. The physician allowed daily walks of five to ten miles, games of pool, and visits to the local Elks Club. The attending doctor announced on March 10 that he wouldn't release Joe until early April, after the Red Sox had broken camp. But Smoky Joe healed quickly and was persistent, leading to a change of plans. On March 21, 1914, the pitcher and his wife boarded a train in Lackawaxen, Pennsylvania, traveled through St. Louis, and arrived at the training camp just before midnight on March 23. Though he reportedly had lost ten pounds (inspiring Ring Lardner to ask how they knew he was there), Joe Wood visited the team in his street clothes the next day.[19] On March 25 he took a light workout in his uniform, followed by the baths. No one expected him to leave with the team the next week or pitch until May 1. But Joe surprised doctors and reporters by joining the team in Nashville and working out, even throwing curve balls on April 1.[20]

Since Joe was unable to pitch at the beginning of the season, he and Laura returned early to Boston, on April 9, from Dayton, Ohio, where the team was playing an exhibition game. The couple settled into President Lannin's apartment complex, where they would be joined by Tris Speaker, player/manager Bill Carrigan, and Heinie Wagner.[21] Meanwhile, Joe followed the team during the day and diverted himself at night by joining Carrigan, Cady, Leonard, and Speaker at the Elks Lodge in Boston (located at 10 Somerset Street), where he sang and enjoyed vaudeville entertainment. Despite predictions that he wouldn't pitch until June or even July, Wood returned on May 15. Initially scheduled to start, he relieved Hugh Bedient in the ninth against the Browns. In Tim Murnane's words the next day in the *Globe*, Joe was welcomed to Fenway as a "great general returning home from a campaign." Spectators "commenced cheering, first in the bleachers back of third base, then along through to the grandstand, and around the field to the bleacherites in center field all cheering madly."

Joe didn't disappoint. Relying on his curveball he struck out the first batter and held St. Louis scoreless on one hit. In the bottom of the inning, the Sox scored twice but still fell 9–3. Despite the loss Murnane gushed: "Having Wood in a game is almost like having a tenth man, simply because he is a great fielder, a strong batsman and cool and calculating when under fire." After the game Joe sent a personal telegram to Dr. Gessner, relaying the details of the game. Gessner then released a more balanced and reassuring statement to the press, printed in the *Globe* on May 18: "It bears out what I have contended all along that 'Smoky Joe' is in excellent shape" and has "rallied in fine style after the operation." In a replay of the first game back, Joe relieved Ray Collins on May 20 in the ninth inning of a 3–0 loss to the Tigers. He again struck out one batter and this time retired the side in order. Indicative of the rest of his pitching career, Joe needed extensive rest to recover from these outings before his first start on May 27, against Cleveland at Fenway.

As in many games Smoky Joe started slowly, giving up runs in both the first and the second innings. He looked equally shaky in the third, after giving up a lead-off single. But just when it looked as if he might be unable to continue, he retired sixteen consecutive batters. Joe weakened at the end, giving up runs in both the eighth and the ninth. But manager Carrigan left him in (with Hugh Bedient in the bullpen) as Smoky Joe got Nemo Leibold to fly out to right fielder Hooper to finish the game. Boston won 5–4. Despite the struggles—he was wild early, gave up eight hits, and struck out only three—it was another complete game. Because of the weakness in his shoulder and the inability to raise his pitching arm, over the next two weeks Joe's only appearance was pinch-running, and scoring, for Hick Cady as the Red Sox lost 4–2 to the Athletics in the second game of a doubleheader on June 2 at Fenway.

After almost three weeks off, Smoky Joe Wood pitched effectively once again. In St. Louis on June 15, 1914, an overcast and cool day, Wood pitched a three-hitter against the Browns, for his fifteenth straight victory against them, dating back to early in the 1911 season. Boston's single runs in the first and the seventh were plenty. Joe struck out just four but walked only two. He was never in serious trouble and played a flawless defensive game, including five put-outs and two assists. After Joe retired the Browns in order in the ninth, with the final Boston 2, St. Louis 0, the *Globe* reported on the sixteenth that he said, "I never felt better in my life." Just as he seemed to be improving, Joe experienced his first major setback of 1914, on June 20 at Chicago in a complete game 5–2 loss. For a change Wood got through the first three innings without a significant incident. But the fourth was a disaster. He gave up three singles, a double, a triple, and a home run to Shano Collins.

But Smoky Joe could still beat the Yankees. In the second game of a doubleheader in New York on June 25, Wood entered in the eighth inning, with two runs in and runners on second and third with no outs, the Red Sox clinging to a 4–3 lead. Joe got a grounder to first, a foul to catcher Cady, and a fly to Speaker in center to end the inning without further damage. He allowed runners to reach second and third in the ninth, with one out, but Wood struck out Ed Sweeney and got Ray Caldwell on a ground ball for the last out. Afterward a reporter quipped, "They may have taken an appendix out of Joe, but they still left him his smoke." Starting two days later, on Saturday, June 27, at the Polo Grounds, Wood began his best winning streak of 1914 by beating the Yanks 5–3.[22] Joe gave up three in the second when the Yankees, taking a cue from the Giants in Game Seven of the 1912 World Series, hit four first pitches and Duffy Lewis contributed an error. After that Wood relied primarily on his curves and gave up no hits the rest of the game. Capping the Red Sox comeback was a two-out homer into the right-field bleachers by Harry Hooper. Joe struck out six and walked none.

He was even better at Washington on July 3, in the second game of a doubleheader. This time Joe pitched shutout ball for the first six innings. But with two out in the seventh, the Senators' Rip Williams singled and was doubled home by Ray Morgan. Boston tied it in the top of the eighth and then got two in the tenth when, with two out, Yerkes singled, Hick Cady doubled to center, and Joe singled to left, scoring the catcher. Wood then sent the Senators down in order to win 3–1. He struck out six and gave up only five hits in the ten innings. But the game took its toll. For the next month Joe couldn't pitch as the arm and shoulder went back on him. He just pinch-ran twice, on July 8, in the ninth inning of the second game of a doubleheader at Fenway, and two days later in the fifth inning when he replaced Rankin Johnson. Joe scored that day.

Between those two games, on July 9, 1914, due to the declining skills of Hugh Bedient and the injuries of George "Rube" Foster and Joe Wood, the Boston Red Sox made a major purchase from Baltimore of the International League. For twenty-five thousand dollars they bought the rights to journeyman catcher Ben Egan and two young pitching prospects, Ernie Shore and George Herman Ruth. Ruth, barely twenty years old, had won his last nine starts, over a two-month period, and Shore was 7-3. Two days later, on July 11, Ruth started and won at Fenway against the Cleveland Naps 4–3, showing good control but tiring in the seventh. At the plate Babe was 0 for 2. Three days later Shore also beat the Naps, 2–1, a two-hit complete game.

Within a week the Sox made another move, a trade, to give strength to the ailing pitching staff. On July 28 they moved along Ben Egan, who came up with Ruth and Shore but played no games for Boston, and pitchers Fred Coumbe and Rankin Johnson for Vean Gregg of the Cleveland Indians, who had won twenty games each of the past three years.[23] Joe's condition also factored into that addition because he was in Youngstown, Ohio, visiting Bonesetter Reese. On July 29, 1914, the day after Gregg was added, the *Globe* reported, "Joe Wood returned today from a visit to Doc Reese of Youngstown, where he was examined for a lame salary wing. The bonesetter felt of the pitcher's wrist, then his elbow, sunk his knee into Mr. Wood's shoulder, then slapped him on the back and remarked: 'Rest for four days and you will be as good as ever.'"[24] Despite such optimism within three weeks Joe's injuries had led to two dramatic moves.

On August 8 Smoky Joe Wood returned to the mound against the Tigers in Detroit. Once again he had little speed and relied on his curve ball, striking out no one, walking three, and making a wild pitch. But he gave up only six hits and just two runs, both in the second inning on a walk, sacrifice, double, and single. Joe was 2-3, with a double, run, and sacrifice as the Red Sox came back to win. When Joe tired after seven, Dutch Leonard pitched a scoreless last two innings for the 5–2 Boston win, Joe's fifth against just one loss. Again Joe needed a long time to recover before his next start. On August 19, the day after Babe Ruth returned to Providence for the Grays' playoff run, Wood took the mound against the White Sox at Fenway, in the second game of a doubleheader. Typically Wood got off to a shaky start, giving up a lead-off single to Buck Weaver and a run-scoring double to Shano Collins. But Joe then gave up nothing, scattering eight hits and five walks as a two-run single by Hooper and a two-RBI triple from Gardner won 4–1.

After relieving Ernie Shore on August 25 to pitch a scoreless last two innings in a 3–1 loss to the Indians at Fenway, on August 31 in Boston, Joe went eleven innings in the second game of a doubleheader against the Browns. His command was much better this time; he struck out fourteen while walking only two, with one wild pitch, and gave up just six hits. But an error by shortstop Everett Scott led to two runs in the eleventh. Luckily the Red Sox got the two back, on singles by Wally Rehg and Tris Speaker, before the game was called a tie. Just four days after the marathon against St. Louis, he pitched at Fenway in the second game of a doubleheader against the first-place Athletics. Joe gave up a run in the first inning, when Eddie Collins tripled and scored on a bad relay from Duffy Lewis. But the Sox responded with three in the bottom of the first and another in the third. When the A's scored two in the seventh, the Red Sox immediately countered again with two. Lewis made up for his throwing error by going 3 for 3 with a triple. Joe struck out nine, including Chick Davies with two on, to end the game, 6–3. Wood gave up eleven hits but walked none, improving his record to 7-1.

He lost for the first time since June 20 on September 7, 1914, against the Yankees in New York, in a game controversial that day and even more so two weeks later. Joe was fine through the first two innings. But during a Yankees rally in the third, with one out, Joe objected to umpire Oliver P. Chill's calling Fritz Maisel safe at home on a throw from second baseman Hal Janvrin. Wood's reaction was so unrelenting that the umpire threw him out of the game. Hugh Bedient, who replaced

Smoky Joe, threw three wild pitches, hit a batter, and walked another to give New York a 4–0 lead. New York won 7–4. Joe gave up two walks and two hits, while striking out another two in his two and one-third innings in a game called after seven for darkness. He had another rough outing on September 11 in Philadelphia. He carried a 5–1 lead into the third, but a walk, an error, a wild pitch, and a single led Carrigan to remove Joe with no outs in the third. The game was called an 8–8 tie after eight innings.

He righted the ship at Washington on September 15, when he threw a four-hitter against the Senators, winning 2–1. The only Washington run came on the speed of Clyde Milan, who in the sixth walked, stole second, and scored on an infield hit. The Sox won it in the ninth on a walk to Hoblitzel and two throwing errors. Joe struck out four, one being Rip Williams to end the game. But he again struggled with control, giving up four walks and throwing another wild pitch. He continued his winning ways five days later, on September 20, at Detroit, in the second game of a doubleheader. Once again he started slowly, giving up a run in the first on a single to Donie Bush and Ty Cobb's double past third. But Boston got three in the fourth and two more in the fifth, more than they needed to win 7–2 when the game was called for darkness. Despite the win Joe had given up nine hits, two walks, and a wild pitch that scored a run.

Before Joe Wood's next outing, he appeared on the fringe of a controversy from the league office. On September 21, 1914, American League president Ban Johnson announced a stiff fine (one hundred dollars) and a one-month suspension for any pitcher found using sandpaper to create an emery ball. The charges were filed by Connie Mack of the Athletics, focusing on Ray Keating of the Yankees but also naming Joe Wood. Although no fines or suspensions followed, the subject didn't die. On November 8 in a syndicated column umpire Billy Evans described the September 7 game when Joe exited in the third inning. According to Evans umpire Bill Dinneen said the wild pitches by Bedient were caused by doctored balls passed from Wood to his reliever.[25] According to Evans, Russell Ford developed the pitch in 1910 by tying emery paper inside his undershirt and then replacing it in a hole in the palm of his glove, where the ball was roughed for grip and a sliding effect. Keating and Wood imitated Ford.

After pinch-hitting unsuccessfully in a 10–1 loss to the Browns the previous day, Joe returned to the mound in St. Louis on September 26 for his final outing of the year. It was a remarkable game in only one way: Wood was defeated by the Browns for the first time in sixteen decisions, dating back to May 24, 1911. As usual Joe was hit early, for two runs in the first inning. Even though the Red Sox countered with four in the second, the Browns got four in their fifth. Wood struck out eight Browns, but he also gave up six hits and walked three. When the game was called after six innings, Joe lost 6–4. On October 1 President Lannin announced that Carrigan, Hooper, and Wood had signed for the following year. After issues with his contracts in previous years, Wood was described by Lannin as glad to sign, get in better shape, and lead the team to another world championship. Although there were no direct quotes from Joe, he was clearly motivated by injuries to get a 1915 deal.

Despite all the health problems, in 1914 Smoky Joe won ten games, his sixth consecutive year of double-digit wins, as the Sox finished in second to the Philadelphia Athletics, eight and one-half games behind. Despite periods of wildness, his control was better than during the previous season; his walks and wild pitches were significantly lower than in 1913. He completed eleven of his fourteen starts, and his ERA was well below 3.00, though 2.62 would be his highest with the Red Sox. However, Joe was no longer top on the Boston staff, which included ERAS of 2.51 (Ray Collins), 2.00 (Ernie Shore), 1.70 (Rube Foster), and the miniscule 0.96 (Dutch Leonard). The Sox finished second primarily because they had only two .300 hitters (Speaker at .338 and Hoblitzel at .319) and a .250 team batting average. Joe caught the batting virus, hitting only .140, which eventually lowered his lifetime batting average by more than three points.

As Joe returned to his new house, he and Laura adjusted to the separation of John F. and Rebecca. Obviously, the repeated abandonment of the family by John F., along with his quirky, independent habits, had been costly to the marriage. As Richard Wood (Joe's grandson in Juneau, Alaska) explains, further difficulties arose when Laura first came to Pennsylvania and Rebecca had a hard time relinquishing control of domestic space and rituals. Having her home so prearranged by her mother-in-law alienated Laura, the new woman in town.[26] (Laura never acclimated to family politics and country living, in later years finally remaining as much as possible in New Haven, Connecticut.) Consequently, Rebecca Stephens Wood and Zoë took up long-term residence above the main street in downtown Port Jervis, New York, about fifteen miles from the Wood homestead.

Even with these family issues, Joe hoped that routines of the farm and outdoor life would repair his arm and shoulder during the winter of 1914–15. As the end of the calendar year approached, the Red Sox were confident of the upcoming season, with no essential holdouts and the Federal League in trouble financially. Particularly intriguing was the prospect of veteran Joe Wood teaming on the mound with Babe Ruth, Vean Gregg, Rube Foster, Dutch Leonard, and Ernie Shore during the 1915 season. By January 10, as noted in the *Globe*, Joe named himself fit from hunting and fishing and had fifty pounds of pickerel to prove it. He gave a very confident statement to reporters in Port Jervis as he purchased his tickets at the Erie line window on February 27. The key to "feeling fine and fit" was "skating, skiing, fishing and hunting." The *Globe* reported that he declared himself "in better shape than [he had] ever felt." His journey to Hot Springs would be essentially the same as in 1913 and 1914 — Kansas City and then South.

Many of the players arrived in Hot Springs on Saturday, March 6, 1915, to snow and ice in the mountains. After visiting Laura's family in Kansas City, Joe and Laura arrived in Hot Springs at 10:25 p.m. on Sunday via Crawfordsville and Little Rock. Most of the concern that spring focused on injuries the previous year to Gregg and Wood.[27] Those anxieties turned out to be well founded. Before mid-March Joe was suffering from a stone bruise on his heal and a depressing lack of arm strength; he told Tim Murnane he would give $5,000 of his $7,500 salary for full recovery. At the first workout, on March 16, Joe's results were frightening to Murnane of the *Globe*: "'Smokey [*sic*] Joe' simply lobbed the ball to the plate, and made a face every time he let the ball go, as if the effort pained him." The next day the reporter was more discouraged, declaring Joe "weaker" "than the first day" and potentially "of little value to the Red Sox." Joe began 1915 on the sidelines.

Most believe that Smoky Joe Wood's most impressive feats were thirty-four wins in 1912; the defeat of Walter Johnson 1–0 on September 6, 1912; the strikeouts of Fletcher and Crandall in Game One of the 1912 Series; or a no-hitter plus two one-hitters and two two-hitters in 1911. But his most amazing pitching was during the five months beginning on May 8, 1915, in New York. That day he took the mound with a clearly injured arm. After every game the pain was so excruciating he couldn't eat with his right hand or lift his arm above his shoulder for a week. Now we know that he had a torn rotator cuff, not repairable then by exercise, medication, or surgery. But he felt responsible for the bills of his whole family and would give the Sox their money's worth. Pain was not the issue for Smoky Joe Wood.

Joe first pitched in 1915 on May 8 at the Polo Grounds against the Yankees. After New York scored ten runs in the fourth inning off Ray Collins, Carl Mays, and Ernie Shore, Joe pitched shutout baseball for the final four, giving up four hits and a walk but also striking out four. It was clear that his strained shoulder needed rest, however. So it was May 16 in Cleveland before he was able to start. Amazingly, he threw eleven scoreless innings and broke up Guy Morton's no-hitter with a one-out single in the ninth. Joe scattered ten hits and walked two while striking out four. The biggest jam was in the eighth, when he loaded the bases with one out before getting Ray Chapman to hit back to the mound, where Joe initiated the 1-2-3 double play. Carl Mays replaced Wood and won in the fourteenth, when Boston combined four hits, including doubles by Wagner and Lewis, for a 3–0 victory.

Smoky Joe Wood lost his first decision of 1915, in Chicago on May 23, 4–2. But before giving up two runs in the fourth, he extended his scoreless string to eighteen innings at the beginning of his injury-delayed year. Indicative of his hurt shoulder, he added five walks to the seven hits. But it was the base running of Eddie Collins (going first to third on a sacrifice bunt before scoring on a sacrifice fly) that brought down Joe and the Red Sox. Indicative of lost hop on his fastball, Joe struck out only two White Sox. On May 28 in Philadelphia, Joe entered a 5–5 game in the sixth and held the A's scoreless for the last four innings, winning when Duffy Lewis tripled into right-center field, knocking in Hooper and Wagner with one out in the ninth. The final score was 8–5 Sox. Joe gave up three hits and a walk while striking out two. An exhausting game followed at New York on June 1. Joe started slowly, giving up two runs in the first and another in the third. But Wood held New York scoreless for the next ten innings. Meanwhile, the Red Sox tied the game in the fourth, and in the thirteenth Tris Speaker walked, stole second, and scored on Doc Hoblitzel's single. Wood and the Sox won 4–3 as Joe gave up thirteen hits and three walks but struck out six.

Unknown to the spectators that day, the real and continuing drama was inside Joe Wood's right shoulder. But because he took so long between pitches for the pain to subside, the New York fans began ridiculing his delays, counting down as in a boxing match, believing the pauses a tactical move by a veteran. A reporter for the *Boston Globe* on June 2, 1915, captured the scene: "Without paying the slightest attention to his critics, Joe, on receiving the ball from the catcher, would walk five paces back of the mound, and squint at the L structure in the background. Then he would slowly advance to the pitcher's slab, after which he would massage the ball with his gloved hand. Then he would rub his hands on his uniform, glance at the catcher, and then pitch the ball — if he didn't throw to first." Maddening to the opposition, brilliant to Sox fans, and uplifting to his teammates, the long pauses were just painful to Joe Wood. But there was a payoff; this win was his second of nine in a row.

Joe had to wait almost a week to start again, but he was brilliant against the White Sox on June 7 at Fenway. It was an overcast, wet day, with heavy rains in the area. The field was littered with sawdust to keep the surface as dry as possible. It was also the first game umpired by ex–St. Louis Brown Bobby Wallace. The dramatic climax came in the fourth inning when Joe faced the bases loaded with two outs, after two singles and a walk. He struck out Jim Breton and then retired the side in order for the rest of game, winning a complete game shutout, 3–0. Joe walked two, hit a batter, and gave up four hits while striking out four. He also played well defensively, inspiring Murnane to declare on June 8, 1915, that Joe Wood's fielding was "the finest in the business, and it [was] doubtful if there ever was a pitcher who could field the position equal to him."

Three days later, on June 10, Joe won in relief against the Tigers at Fenway. Ernie Shore and Dutch Leonard struggled, giving Detroit a 5–4 lead in the top of the seventh. The Red Sox responded with two in the bottom of the seventh before Joe entered. He struggled, getting Cobb on a fly to right with two runners on in the eighth and putting two more on in the ninth before getting two fly outs for a 6–5 victory. According to scoring methods at the time, Joe was the winner after giving up three hits and a walk in his two innings, striking out only one. In another courageous showing he kept the Tigers at bay in the comeback by the Red Sox. On June 14 Cleveland's Joe Jackson got three hits off Smoky Joe, including a triple and a run in the fifth inning. But the rest of the Indians made only two hits and no runs, as Wood won his fifth decision in a row, 4–1. Joe had a good fastball that day and excellent command as he walked only one batter while striking out three.

On June 26 Joe won his sixth game in a row, 4–2, over New York in the second game of a doubleheader. He gave up a run in the sixth, on some shaky defense and a sacrifice fly, and another in the ninth after an infield hit and two walks, giving way to Carl Mays. But Boston used doubles by Duffy Lewis, Hick Cady, and Hoblitzel, as well as a solo home run from Joe, to win. In addition to the two hits over eight innings, Joe walked three and, a rarity, didn't strike out a batter. He got his seventh consecutive win, in relief against the Athletics on June 30 in the second game of a doubleheader. He entered in the seventh inning with Amos Strunk on third. Joe immediately gave up the tie-breaking single to Wally Schang but held Philadelphia scoreless after that as the Red Sox scored three in the seventh and another run in the eighth, to win 10–7.

Smoky Joe returned against the A's at Fenway on July 3, again in the second game, this time winning easily, going only six innings, as the Sox won 11–0. Looking stronger he was able to pitch again four days later, against Washington in Boston. He struggled a bit in this game, giving up ten hits and walking two while striking out three. But the game was over early as the Sox scored two in the first and six more in the third on five singles and triples by Joe (to right-center field) and Hooper. It moved his record to 9-1, and on the surface, it looked like Smoky Joe Wood might be back.

Just halfway through the 1915 season and after missing almost a month, it was conceivable that he could win twenty games . . . if his shoulder held up. But the first inning on July 14 at Cleveland brought back the early vulnerability. After a single, sacrifice, and walk, the runners moved with the pitch, and as Larry Gardner ran to cover third base, Jay Kirke hit in the vacated spot, scoring a run. Elmer Smith and Bill Wambsganss then singled in two more. Joe gave up no more runs as the Red Sox (despite another double from Joe) lost 3–2, ending Joe's winning streak at nine. He rebounded four days later, beating the White Sox 6–2 at Comiskey Park, following another rough first. After Boston scored two in the top of the inning on a two-out double by Duffy Lewis, Eddie Murphy doubled to lead off for Chicago, followed by a walk to Eddie Collins and singles by Jack Fournier and Shano Collins, tying the score. But Joe gave up only one more hit. He also had two singles and a sacrifice and played flawless defense. As Tim Murnane summarized in the *Globe* on the nineteenth, "Joe Wood gave a wonderful all-round performance, pitching, hitting and fielding well. He had perfect control and a lovely break." With that victory the Sox moved into first place, where they would remain the rest of the season.

Over the next week Smoky Joe relieved three times against the Browns in St. Louis. On the twenty-first Joe replaced Babe Ruth in the ninth, with Boston leading 4–2, a run in, and two out. Wood walked Doc Lavan on a disputed call before striking out two pinch hitters, Ivan Howard and Muddy Ruel, to end the game. (That day Ruth went 4 for 4, including two doubles and a long home run to right.) The next day Joe again entered in the ninth, in relief of Foster and Mays, and struck out two to preserve a 7–3 win. Joe wasn't as fortunate when he relieved Ernie Shore in the eighth on the twenty-fourth. With one out and Burt Shotton on second, he got Jimmy Austin to fly to Hooper in right, but Ivan Howard singled to tie the game at two. In the bottom of the ninth, Joe walked Tilly Walker, George Sisler reached on an error, and after a sacrifice, Browns' catcher Sam Agnew hit a sacrifice fly to Speaker. St. Louis won 3–2.

Despite his chronic shoulder problems, three days later, on July 27, Wood again started, at Fenway against Chicago. He retired the White Sox in order in six of the nine innings, giving up only an unearned run on a four-hitter and winning 3–1. Three days later, on July 30 in Boston, he permitted one hit in one and two-thirds innings in relief of Dutch Leonard but was the losing pitcher against the Tigers. He retired the side in the eighth, with two men on and one out, on flies to Tris Speaker. But in the ninth, with Boston ahead 6–5 and one out, Joe walked Ossie Vitt and threw wildly to first on a Donie Bush bunt down the third-base line, allowing the runners to advance to second and third. With Ty Cobb at bat, Joe threw inside at the knees for a wild pitch, allowing the tying run. Cobb's grounder to first scored Bush. The Tigers won 7–6.

Despite the pain in his shoulder, on August 7, 1915, against Cleveland at Fenway, Joe was so good that Tim Murnane declared in the *Globe* in the next day that he "probably never pitched a more effective game in his life." In the first game of a Saturday doubleheader, he threw a one-hitter, the only hit a slow grounder by Bill Wambsganss that shortstop

Janvrin didn't attack. Joe loaded the bases on three consecutive walks with two out in the fourth, but he then struck out Elmer Smith. On Wednesday, August 11, he won the first game of a midweek doubleheader at Fenway against the lowly Browns, 11–3, coasting after the Red Sox scored five in the top of the seventh to lead 11–1. He also singled and scored a run. Five days later, on August 16, Joe shutout the Senators 1–0, allowing only five hits. The Red Sox got just two hits, one a triple to start the game by Hooper, who scored on a sacrifice fly. But the shoulder sidelined Joe for five weeks.

Joe's final win of 1915, and as a member of the Boston Red Sox, came on September 23 at Fenway Park. In seven innings against the Naps, he gave up six hits, a walk, and a wild pitch while striking out just two. Once again his speed was missing, but he used breaking pitches and location to survive. Carl Mays finished the last two innings in the 5–4 win. Smoky Joe Wood's last start for the Sox featured two players with whom he always will be identified: Walter Johnson and Babe Ruth. On October 2, 1915, in Washington, Boston had clinched the pennant, so the play was lethargic. In the third, after Joe Judge doubled, Clyde Milan drove him in with a single. Clyde then stole second, took third on an errant throw by Sox catcher Pinch Thomas, and scored on a single by Charlie Jamieson. The Senators added another in the sixth, when Jamieson singled and scored on a double by Tom Connolly. Walter Johnson won 3–1. Joe gave up seven hits and walked two while only striking one. Ruth relieved Smoky Joe and pitched scoreless baseball.

Tim Murnane's comment on the third about Joe's condition is instructive. In the "Echoes of the Game," the reporter wrote that Wood, though "anxious for a try-out," was "far from right, having very little speed and depending on his curve and headwork. For the upcoming Series, he didn't "look good enough to take a chance on against the Phillies, unless to finish some other pitcher's game." His last game for Boston came in New York in the first game of a doubleheader on October 6, 1915. Smoky Joe was one of four pitchers (also Shore, Leonard, and Mays) used in the 2–0 victory in the first game, Boston's one hundredth win of 1915. Joe pitched the fourth, fifth, and sixth innings, giving up two hits and striking out three. He got no decision and finished the 1915 season 15-5 with an ERA of 1.49.

Initially there was speculation that because of his effectiveness that year and experience in the 1912 Series, Smoky Joe Wood might start Game One of the 1915 World Series. As he later told interviewers, Joe discussed that option with Bill Carrigan but admitted that his arm was hurting. In the Murdock tape, for example, Joe quotes himself telling Carrigan, "Bill, [I will be ready] if you need me. . . . But my arm is terrible." At other times Joe reassured his manager that he would "be in [his] corner," but he variously described the arm as "pretty darn bad," "not any good," or just plain "bad."[28] And so Joe Wood warmed up for each game but never was called upon. Later he took solace from remembering that Carrigan also didn't call on Babe Ruth to pitch. (Ruth pinch-hit in the first game and grounded out to first base with a runner on first and two out in the ninth.)

From the bullpen Smoky Joe Wood saw another remarkable World Series. After losing the first game at the Baker Bowl in Philadelphia, the Red Sox won three consecutive games 2–1. In Game Two George Foster pitched a three-hitter and had three hits himself, including a two-out single in the ninth to drive in Larry Gardner with the winning run.[29] In Game Three in Boston at Braves Field, Dutch Leonard pitched his own three-hitter; he defeated Philadelphia and Grover Cleveland Alexander 2–1 when, with two out in the ninth, Duffy Lewis singled to center, driving in Harry Hooper. In Game Four the next day at the same venue, Ernie Shore won 2–1 with Duffy Lewis making great catches in the third, seventh, and eighth innings, and driving in the winning run on a double. The final game, back in Philadelphia on the thirteenth, Boston came from behind led by Hooper, who hit two home runs, the second off Eppa Rixey in the ninth to win it 5–4.

Little hoopla accompanied the Red Sox victory in 1915. The team avoided a dinner with politicians and turned down a potentially profitable series of exhibition games with the A's in California. The Sox ownership pleaded exhaustion and neglected loved ones. For his part Smoky Joe used his winners' share of $3,780.25 to motor back to Parkers Glen in a new car, accompanied by Laura and Mrs. Gessner. By then the couple probably knew that their first child was on the way, though such intimate matters weren't released to the public in those times.

On November 26, 1915, papers reported that Joe drove Charles Wells, a lumberman from the family farm, fifteen miles to a hospital in Port Jervis after a cant hook cut the worker above his left eye. The journey was credited with saving Wells's sight. Joe's commented modestly, "It was only what one fellow would do for another." Soon afterward, on December 7, his 15-5 record was declared the best winning percentage in the AL for 1915. He also took satisfaction in his nine consecutive wins and a batting average of .259, including a triple and a home run. The next day, December 8, he declared that his arm was responding to treatment and he would be ready the next year. On December 19 Joe's 1.49 ERA was named AL best.

But by then the Red Sox management was playing hard ball. On December 14, 1915, a rumor was floated that Joe would be traded. He was to be sent to the Yankees along with Larry Gardner and Ray Collins. In return the Red Sox would get Fritz Maisel. Meanwhile, either Joe or Collins would be transferred to Cleveland, with Ray Chapman moving to Philadelphia and Frank Baker shifting from the A's to the Yankees. New York would throw in fifteen thousand dollars to get Baker.[30] Though the deal didn't materialize, Wood was clearly expendable. While insisting that Joe was expected to report for spring training, President Lannin badmouthed "fancy salaries" and players not in "form," implicating Joe on both counts. On February 21, 1916, the organization admitted that Wood was being shopped. The Red Sox offered him five thousand dollars (a one-third cut). Joe refused and awaited a trade. But it was Speaker who was sent to Cleveland.[31] With his friend gone Joe withdrew further to deal with his "mounting frustration over his impaired state."[32]

Joe was being evasive when he said in *The Glory of Their Times* that in 1916 he stayed in Shohola and "fed the chickens."[33] Wood's sabbatical year from baseball was actually irritating and painful. He worked at his home, doing the required chores and enjoying the birth of his first child, Joe Frank Wood, on May 20, 1916. He installed a trapeze in the attic of their home, where he worked out regularly to strengthen the muscles in his shoulder. Having exhausted the legal options of the medical profession, Joe sought alternative solutions. He heard that a chiropractor in New York had helped two Phillies: Tom Seaton and George Chalmers. So in the winter of 1915–16, Smoky Joe regularly took the Monday morning train from Shohola, Pennsylvania, into New York, returning on Saturday nights, to visit A. A. Crusius, who practiced illegally as a chiropractor in Times Square.[34] Crusius had him throw hard and long to specify the pain.

Also Andy Coakley, the baseball coach at Columbia, invited Wood to join the college players for winter workouts in their indoor gym.[35] At the university Joe followed Crusius's instructions, with painful results: "I'd go into a corner of the gym and throw a baseball as hard as I could. I'd do that until I just wasn't able to stand the pain anymore. And I do mean pain. After about an hour I couldn't lift my arm as high as my belt. Had to use my left hand to put my right into my coat pocket. And if I'd go to a movie in the evening I couldn't get my right arm up high enough to put it on the arm rest."[36] By the fall Joe, as he told Lawrence Ritter, "began to get restless" to return to the game. If local records are correct, Joe even played near his home place, pitching a no-hitter for Milford, Pennsylvania, against Lake Ariel, on September 3, 1916.[37]

Still the property of the Boston Red Sox, Smoky Joe Wood wasn't on the roster of the 1916 World Champions. Unwilling to accept offers by either Joe Lannin or (after October) Harry Frazee, Joe had responsibilities in Pennsylvania. Most troubling, sister Zoë contracted polio. In Joe's words, "They [Rebecca and Zoë] went downtown shopping one morning from our apartment. And they went to get into a taxi to come back home and she couldn't lift her legs." The doctors arrested the disease. But in Joe's words, "It disfigured her something terrible. Her left leg is very much smaller than the right. One hip is clear way up under her shoulder." (She would later marry and have a child.) Meanwhile, Smoky Joe was in phone contact with Tris Speaker, who believed in Joe's natural abilities and competitive spirit. And Joe wanted to prove to others, but mostly to himself, that he still could play Major League baseball.

SEVEN

Indian Outfielder and Utility Man

The story of Smoky Joe's release from the Red Sox reads like a soap opera scripted by sportswriters. The tone was set on February 11, 1916, when reporters spotted Wood at the Somerset Hotel in New York. Asked about his status with the Sox, the pitcher reacted with pique, identifying club president Lannin as "the only one who could answer that question." Persistent, a *Boston Globe* interviewer wanted to know why Joe was visiting New York. This time Wood controlled his anger and answered coyly that he wanted "to break the routine of farm life and to do a little shopping." Whether the shopping included a late Christmas present to himself—for example, a contract with the Yankees—he left to the imagination of readers.

The Red Sox response came in print eleven days later when manager Carrigan denied that Wood was being waived, then pointedly repeated the words of president Lannin that players must be "in shape for effective work" given their "fancy salaries." The subtext was clear: with the end of the Federal League, players must prove themselves healthy and worthy. On the same day, February 22, 1916, the *New York Times* specified that unless Joe Wood took a $2,500 cut in salary, the club might release him. The *Times* also leaked that other clubs had already waived on Wood, without noting any collusion by the owners.

Before the end of the month, on February 27, the *Globe* began to prepare its readers for the loss of the star pitcher. In an elegy-before-the-fact,

the paper wrote the career of the "Smoke King" as a closed book, portraying the loss as necessary because Joe Wood had averaged fewer
than twenty-five games per season. While admitting that he was "one
of the most brilliant ball players in the business," the writer qualified
his praise with the telling phrase "when in condition to perform." By
March 1 the same paper further justified the release of Wood by naming
his expensive contract and reputation as a difficult negotiator. Omitted,
of course, were his league-leading 1915 ERA and the fact that the Red
Sox wanted him to take a 33 percent cut. Before the month was out,
Christy Mathewson became a player in the rising drama. In a syndicated column on March 6, Matty suggested that the hoopla surrounding
the 1912 World Series might be contributing to the negotiations with
Wood, though on March 30 Mathewson insisted Wood was "naturally
one of the greatest players ever in the big leagues." At the end of March,
having expressed the position of Sox management, Hub papers imagined a reconciliation.

After one more bit of speculation — in mid-April that Wood was
joining the Yankees — the rumor mill temporarily fell silent, so quiet that on July 23 papers across the country declared Joe back with
Boston. The *Globe* confirmed that the pitcher would join the team for
a workout with manager Carrigan and President Lannin on July 25 in
Cleveland, where Tris Speaker made his new baseball home in center
field at League Park. Surprisingly, there was easy agreement on a pro-
rated return to his previous year's salary. But when Joe worked out in
Indians uniform, speculation spread across the city that he had been
sold to Cleveland. Once those stories were denied by all players and
managers in the drama, Smoky Joe Wood seemed to be back with the
Sox, even though Bill Carrigan wasn't particularly impressed with his
performance. Joe was even penciled in as a starter for the upcoming
series in Detroit. But as inevitable in this saga, things fell apart — once
again over money.

Within a day Melville E. Webb reported back in Boston that Wood
wanted not only his $7,500 but a guarantee for the following year,

which the Sox were unwilling to accept. Also reported was a counter-offer by Joe of $10,000 of his own money for his release, also rejected by the team, according to the *Globe*. As portrayed by the paper, Joe undermined the negotiations by grandstanding the day after the try-out when he sat in the crowd at League Park as a conspicuous hold-out. Joe had his own story to tell. After he returned to Pennsylvania the following day, July 28, he reported in local newspapers that he didn't seek a contract for the 1917 season. Instead, Wood declared he wanted to join Speaker in Cleveland. Whatever the real intentions of the team and the player, nothing was worked out. So Wood, though reserved by the Red Sox, didn't rejoin the team that had won the 1916 World Series over the Brooklyn Robins.

The last act of the Wood-to-Cleveland drama began at the base-ball meeting in mid-December 1916. On December 15 Boston papers reported discussions between Lee Fohl, the second-year manager in Cleveland, and Harry Frazee, by then president of the Red Sox. No de-tails were given, except that Frazee declined the offers. Within a week Tim Murnane added that the same meetings floated the idea of a trade of Wood, portrayed as having "a keen liking for the big city," to New York for Ray Caldwell, the sometimes ace of the Yankees who, suffer-ing from a knee injury and recurrent losing battles with alcohol, had posted a 5-12 record in 1916. When that exchange didn't materialize ei-ther, the Cleveland option seemed back on the table; the *Washington Post* reported on December 30 that President Jim Dunn of Cleveland had turned down a Wood-for-twenty-thousand-dollars cash deal. On January 10, 1917, there were rumors in Boston that Steve O'Neill, the Cleveland catcher, might be part of a Wood trade. But four days later the *New York Times* reported that Joe would stay in Boston. That's how things stayed for the next month or so.

Finally, on February 23, 1917, a deal started to develop. That day Frazee gave Dunn permission to talk to Wood, a meeting given credibility by the employment in Cleveland of Speaker and Rob McRoy, then Indians business manager. The next day that story changed. Frazee and Dunn couldn't agree, according to papers, though McRoy would travel provisionally to New York for a meeting with Wood. By then Steve O'Neill was out of the picture, but Ray Chapman was suggested as an alternative. That day, the twenty-fourth, the *Globe* once again painted Smoky Joe as unreasonable, saying McRoy would try "to persuade Joe to be a little more conservative in his demands." The paper also quoted "persons who claim[ed] to know" as "skeptical about Joe being able to stage a comeback." The grounds for a divorce between Joe and Boston were set in print.

The split came on February 24, 1917, a Saturday. At first Harry Frazee remained in Boston, holding out for twenty-five thousand dollars while Wood remained in New York. But negotiations were clearly moving when Frazee traveled on to NYC and McRoy followed to examine Joe's arm. After a five-hour meeting (mostly between McRoy and Frazee) at the Walcott Hotel in New York, the three agreed to the sale of Joe Wood from the Boston Red Sox to the Cleveland Indians for fifteen thousand dollars. The next day Lee Fohl was quoted in the Cleveland *Plain Dealer* as "tickled to death" at acquiring such a "smart" player who knew "the right way to do things." He promised a slow rehab in which Joe would coach the young pitchers. Accompanied by his wife and "nine-month-old son," called "Joe, Jr.," Wood arrived in Cleveland at 2:00 p.m. on Tuesday, February 27. McRoy, manager Fohl, and secretary Bill Blackwood escorted the threesome to the Hollenden Hotel and then League Park, where Smoky Joe Wood signed for seven thousand dollars.

Joe had a less-than-heroic view of his years in Boston. Despite the phenomenal 1912 season, Joe's time with the Red Sox was mostly, in his words to interviewers, "trouble" stemming from the reality that he "was more or less prone to be in some kind of a damn accident." Joe continued, "I only pitched about three full years all the time I was with Boston. The rest of the times I was laid out with a broken blood vessel in my ankle because the blood wouldn't dissolve, I had a broken toe, I had appendicitis." Most debilitating were the arm problems. As he explained to Paul Green, "I slipped on wet grass and broke my thumb. It was in a cast a couple of weeks, and whether I tried to pitch too soon or hurt my shoulder in the fall I'll never know, but I never was the same. There was always pain which only got worse and the hop was gone. It took a couple of weeks sometimes before I could even lift my arm."[1] Bizarre medical treatments didn't help either.

Joe's assessment of the crippling pain was typically stoic: "There wasn't anything I could do about it." He also reminded interviewers that before money got in the way, the Red Sox had supported him: "The club themselves paid the bills to send me all around the country to different doctors. Even sent me down to Bonesetter Reese . . . down in Youngstown, Ohio. People used to go from all over the country to Bonesetter Reese, claimed they'd go in on crutches and walk out without the crutches, and so on." Asked if Bonesetter did any good, Smoky Joe answered without self-pity, "No." Other doctors "painted things on your arm, and they'd map out this and that and go in there with this and over there with that, put this hot stuff on you that burned, and so on." Clear-eyed, Joe understood there were no operations because specialists "didn't know enough about it."[2]

While the Red Sox were dynastic, in the midst of winning four of seven World Series between 1912 and 1918, the Indians were shaping a better future from a roller-coaster past. Cleveland was present at the beginning of organized baseball. Their source was the Cleveland Forest Citys, a team that played the Cincinnati Red Stockings as early as June 2, 1869. Though Cleveland became a charter member of the National Association of Baseball Players in 1871, its team was out of the league the next year. The Cleveland entry into the National League (beginning in 1879) did better, lasting six years. After spending 1885 without professional baseball, the city entered a team in the American Association in 1886, which joined the National League in 1889 and, as the Spiders, played with distinction in the 1890s. The team's fortunes improved dramatically when owner Frank DeHaas Robison built League Park in 1891 and peopled it with Cy Young, Jesse Burkett, and Chief Zimmer. They played for the championship in 1892 and 1896 and won the Temple Cup over the Baltimore Orioles in 1895 with player/manager Patsy Tebeau, Young, George Cuppy, and Louis Sockalexis. But business took over. In 1899 Robison moved the best players to his St. Louis franchise. Cleveland went 20-134 and left the NL.[3]

Fortunately for Cleveland, one of its citizens, Charles Somers, the wealthy son of the very wealthy Joseph Hook Somers, was interested in Ban Johnson's scheme to develop a second Major League to compete with the National League. Somers, along with his friend Jack Kilfoyl, a clothing magnate, created a charter team in the American League for Cleveland in 1901. But Somers wasn't done. He also bankrolled a team for Boston and loaned money to Connie Mack and Charles Comiskey for franchises in Philadelphia and Milwaukee. In thanks for these founding investments, Somers was elected vice president of the AL. Back in Somers's Cleveland, League Park, with a capacity of nine thousand, became home to a team called the Bluebirds, or simply the Blues. The team played their first AL game on April 24, 1901, lost to the White Sox 8–2, and finished the year in seventh place.[4]

In 1902 the team, now called the Bronchos, complemented star Bill Bradley with newcomers Addie Joss, Elmer Flick, and Napoleon Lajoie, in whose honor they became the Naps in 1903. The next two years the team improved to fifth and then third place, with Lajoie becoming the player/manager in 1905. In 1908 the Naps finished second, and things looked better in 1910 when they acquired Joe Jackson and League Park was renovated as a steel-and-concrete structure with box seats. But their fortunes once again deteriorated, reaching the bottom in 1914, when injuries to Ray Chapman and Jackson, the decline of Lajoie, and the defection of Cy Falkenberg to the Federal League caused a last-place finish. Total attendance was only 185,000 at League Park that season. Changes were in order. On January 16, 1915, after a contest by local papers, the team name was officially changed to the Indians in honor of Louis Sockalexis, the Native American star for the NL team in the 1890s. Lajoie was sent to Philadelphia, manager Joe Birmingham was replaced by Lee Fohl, and Jackson went to Chicago midyear 1915.[5]

When the Indians still finished next to last in 1915, and attendance fell to an abysmal 160,000, the team went into receivership, and Jim Dunn (a construction boss with connections to Charles Comiskey) purchased it and League Park from the bankers who had foreclosed on Somers. The purchase price was reported as five hundred thousand dollars. Most dramatic was the acquisition of Tris Speaker on April 8, 1916. Things got better. Veterans Chick Gandil, Jack Graney, Terry Turner, and Speaker were blended with a talented group of players twenty-six or younger: Braggo Roth, Guy Morton, Bill Wambsganss, Ray Chapman, Stan Coveleski, Jim Bagby, and Steve O'Neill. They still finished sixth in 1916 but were in first in late June and raised their record to .500, at 77-77. Speaker won the batting title with a .386 average, and attendance rose to nearly half a million. The future was now much brighter for the Indians.[6]

As Joe told later interviewers, he was still "a pretty poor individual" and thus was delighted to get a second chance with the Indians. He respected Lee Fohl, a "fine man" liked by everyone, and more important for an arm-wrestler with Boston management, Wood appreciated Sunny Jim Dunn, who treated Joe "very nicely."[7] Being in Cleveland for the signing made the trip to New Orleans, the Indians' spring training site, an easy one. Smoky Joe traveled with Laura and the baby, Joe Frank, by train to Chicago; from there wife and child continued to her parents' home in Kansas City. Joe returned to Cleveland, ready the first of March to resume his career in the company of manager Fohl and four players, including two who would become friends of Wood: Stan Coveleski and Steve O'Neill. As they boarded the Big Four and then transferred to the Queen and Crescent in Cincinnati, the big news was the trading of Chick Gandil and the promotion of Lou Guisto from Portland in the Pacific Coast League.

After the usual delays the travelers arrived in a steamy Louisiana; they took the field in eighty-three-degree heat at 1:00 p.m. on Saturday, March 3. At that first practice Joe said he intended to take it easy for the first ten days and not throw curves for two weeks. That seemed especially wise when the weather at Heinemann Park dropped forty degrees as the team quietly defied laws against business on Sunday. Though Tris Speaker continued his late arrivals, Joe was pleased to see his locker next to Spoke's. While Smoky Joe waited to pitch, he played in the field. On March 5, with the weather still cool, he played catch with manager Lee Fohl, took batting practice, and went to third base. The next day, the sixth, was fifty-six degrees and windy as Joe pitched on the side to Steve O'Neill and then played shortstop. After workouts on the seventh through ninth, in which Wood played short, he wasn't in the club's first exhibition game, on Saturday, March 10, against the New Orleans Pelicans, a 1–1 tie. On the eleventh the Indians beat the Pelicans 4–1, but still neither Wood nor Speaker was in the lineup. More exciting were military drills, exhibiting patriotism while keeping the draft boards at bay; AL president Ban Johnson offered five hundred dollars to the team with the best discipline and conditioning.[8]

Finally Joe got his first action on March 15, 1917, in center field for the Yannigans in an intrasquad game. Wood batted fifth and hit a double and a triple in four at bats. The next day, a Friday, he was even better, going 2 for 4 with another triple and a home run as the Yannigans trounced the Regulars 19–4. But such success was, for the time being, a dead end. Joe had been bought by the Indians to pitch, not hit. So on the seventeenth Wood was relegated to helping the young pitchers. He extended his own workout from fifteen to twenty-five minutes two days later, but still no curves. The next day he played center for the Yannigans, batting fifth and getting a hit in four at bats, as the Regulars won 10–4. After that he endured not playing from March 21 until well into the season. At least on April 6 the National Commission reinstated him from the ineligible list for not reporting to the Red Sox in 1916. In the meantime the United States entered World War I, initiating discussion of whether baseball was an essential occupation.

Finally the 1917 season, in which Bill Wambsganss and Stan Coveleski would emerge as major players, got under way on April 18 as the Indians behind Coveleski beat the Tigers 6–4 in Detroit, despite two doubles by

Ty Cobb and a double and a home run from Bobby Veach. Joe Wood remained on the bench. As the delay extended from days into weeks, the Indians decided to meet fan expectations by giving Wood work. On May 2 he pinch-hit for Pete Allison, who was replacing Speaker, suspended for arguing with umpire George Hildebrand on April 30. Both Wood and the Indians failed, and the team lost to the White Sox 8–3 in Cleveland. The next day the injury bugaboo, which haunted his career, returned when Joe entered another game against Chicago, as a pinch runner in the ninth inning. He twisted an ankle sliding into second base. The Indians won 2–1 on Eddie Cicotte's bases-loaded walk of Ray Chapman. Luckily this time the x-rays on Joe, taken May 4, 1917, were negative.

Expectations were rising that Smoky Joe Wood would soon pitch for the Cleveland Indians. Always the showman Frazee of the Red Sox thought it would be dramatic — and profitable — to have Wood make his first start against Boston at Fenway. He ran the idea by Jim Dunn, who referred it to manager Fohl. Lee rejected it, choosing instead to pitch Smoky Joe versus the Yankees, a team that Wood had dominated with the Red Sox. Joe took the mound against New York at League Park, on May 26, 1917, the day married men were declared exempt from the draft, relieving Joe from service (though brother Pete served).[9] The preceding day the Indians had scored six runs in the ninth inning to beat the Yanks 6–5 and remain in fourth place with a 20-17 record. Hoping for more luck the Indian fans were enthusiastic at the return of the Smoky One. As described by Henry P. Edwards, the sportswriter for the *Plain Dealer*, on May 27, fifteen thousand fans "applauded him when he came out of the dugout to warm up; they applauded more vigorously when he stepped into the box in the first inning and shot over two strikes on Aragon. And they did not forget him when he went to bat at the end of each inning."

The first four innings were encouraging, with Joe leading 2–0 despite the New Yorkers making hits in every inning but the second. In the fifth the Yanks scored two runs, one unearned on an error by Lou

Guisto, to tie the game. Struggling on, Joe gave up single runs in the seventh and the eighth; he lost 4–3, with Jim Bagby relieving him in the ninth. Reporters said most hits were "scratch" and "fell just inside the foul lines," but Joe gave up eleven and walked a batter, striking out only one. Writers saw the "graceful motion" in Wood's delivery, but the "famous smoke ball was not in evidence at any stage, and his curve had no such break and no such speed as Joe was wont to flash along the American League trail." Joe was expected to start again in early June against the Red Sox. But he didn't take the mound in that series or in the following one at the Polo Grounds. Even when the team returned home on June 10 for a single game against the White Sox, he was not available.

Finally, as Cleveland opened a three-game series against Washington on June 12, 1917, a press release quoted Dr. Robert Drury of Columbus, Ohio (the physician who examined Joe in the preseason): "Wood should never have pitched more than one or two innings, and those just for the sake of practice. He has strained his arm badly and probably permanently as the result of his trying to earn his salary too early in the season." The doctor chastised Joe, declaring he had so stretched "ligaments and tissue of the shoulder" that it was "a wonder [he had] any arm left." Wood's public statement blamed his foolishness on the desire to please fans: "I realized too late that I had pitched longer than I should have, but the fans were anxious to see me, and I was equally anxious to show them what I can do." In an implied response to old salary disputes, he insisted, "I'm not going to take another cent of salary from Jack Dunn till I do pitch again." Wood also was "anxious to help [Owner Dunn] get back some of the money he spent for [Joe's] release." The Indians insisted they would keep Joe on the club and the payroll.

It was two months before the Indians returned Smoky Joe Wood to the mound. This time they used him in shorter stints. On August 8, Joe pitched the seventh and the eighth innings in relief of Jim Bagby during an 8–2 loss to the Yankees at the Polo Grounds. Joe gave up two hits and an earned run while striking out one and walking two in the first game of a doubleheader. On August 12 in Cleveland he entered in the tenth inning with two men on after Otis Lambeth had walked both batters. Wood got out of that jam and also pitched two scoreless innings in the eleventh and the twelfth. He struck out two and only gave up a hit. But the pain forced him out of the game, and the White Sox won 4–3 in the thirteenth when Joe Jackson squeezed in Swede Risberg. Once more Joe needed long rest. In the meantime Joe published an interview in *Baseball Magazine* called "Doing the Comeback Stunt." While paying lip service to his comeback, Joe redirected the discussion to the often-neglected player's point of view.

He made a shrewd argument. First he defused the impression he was being provocative by saying he had "no wish to reopen old controversies" by focusing on his "disagreement" "with Mr. Lannin over the salary question." He assumed that "the public" was not "vitally interested" "in a ballplayer's wages" and its influence on costs to the fans. But he also invited the reader to consider "the extreme brevity of his precarious calling." Furthermore, he wanted to correct "a general impression" "in a number of papers" "that [he] was of little use to the Boston club during 1915." His record, omitted by those sources, "would have spoken for itself," he said, encouraging a reexamination of those details. More personally he assured the fans that any downtime in 1915 "was as disappointing" to him "as it was to the owners." In the Series "Carrigan expected to call upon" him and had him "warming up every game," but "the three regular pitchers" didn't show "any sign of distress." It was an argument as convincing as any by lawyer John F. Wood.

Finally, on September 8, 1917, he was able to pitch the eighth inning in relief of Jim Bagby during a 2–0 loss to the White Sox in Chicago, giving up no hits and two walks while striking out one. His last outing of that season was in relief of Guy Morton, on September 15 in St. Louis. Joe gave up a run in the eighth and forced in another with a walk in the ninth. But he struck out Baby Doll Jacobson to end the game, gaining a save in the 5–4 win. Even with Joe nursing his arm most of the season, in 1917 the Indians finished with an 88-66 record, their best since 1908. The numbers for Wood were not as encouraging. Smoky Joe pitched in five games, starting just the one against the Yankees. He got a shaky save in the last game, lost his only start, had an ERA of 3.45, and gave up seventeen hits in fifteen and two-thirds innings. He walked seven while striking out only two. Offensively he had no hits in six at bats, whiffing half the time. His fastball was missing its hop, the command was uneven, and the doctor's reports were negative.

Meanwhile, Pete Wood, Joe's brother, was having an active year with the Fisk Tire semipro team. The company, located in Chicopee Falls, Massachusetts, had established a baseball team around 1915 and entered a six-team league, the centerpiece of its AAU competition. In support of athletics Fisk also built a twenty-acre recreation facility that featured track and field. The baseball squad was named the Red Tops after the trademark red tread on the white sidewall of its top-of-the-line tire. The company was gaining national attention because Norman Rockwell advertisements, focused on bicycle tires, were being featured across the nation in boys' magazines.[10] Pete joined the Fisk Red Tops in July 1917 after being released by Springfield of the Eastern League. On July 29, 1917, Pete returned the favor by beating Springfield 5–0.

The Fisk Red Tops didn't just play locally. The *Chicago Defender* on August 18, 1917, noted a game played that day at the Thirty-Ninth Street Grounds (three blocks south of Comiskey Park and the home of the Chicago American Giants of the Negro League) between Cuban stars and the Fisk Tire Company of Springfield, Massachusetts, called the "Eastern semi-pro champions." Apparently Joe was contributing to Fisk's success because, according to the article, "[The team] for three years has won the championship of Springfield and this year, with the assistance of Smokey [*sic*] Joe Wood, formerly of the Boston Americans and now of Cleveland, they went out and won the state championship. After new laurels they are out to take the national title, playing the crack teams in cities en route." Ironically, given Joe's pro beginnings, the first game that day on the South Side was between "the Bloomer Girls" and "the Manhattan Giants." Three days later Pete pitched again, against the Shaw Taxis at Garden City Park.

Soon after Pete and Joe finished their seasons and well before spring training for the 1918 season, the press was speculating that Joe wouldn't be returning as a pitcher. On November 9, 1917, the *Washington Post* declared, "Lee Fohl and Tris Speaker, who are running the Cleveland team, will try Wood in the outfield next spring. Smoky Joe is a natural hitter and a splendid all around player."[11] Three months later, on February 21, 1918, the *Hartford Courant* reported that Joe would be at first base. Maybe Joe was too busy after the birth of his second child, Steve, two days later, to take notice of such writing.[12] In later interviews he showed no knowledge of the speculations. But he was anxious to prove himself and provide for his family. There was even a report that after he had failed as a pitcher in 1917, he told Lee Fohl over the winter that "he was willing to pay his own expenses to training camp and then after he had got into condition talk over the matter of the contract." Whether he was that generous or not, Smoky Joe Wood was impatient for 1918.

When the Indians, including Steve O'Neill, Fritz Coumbe, Stan Coveleski, and Lee Fohl, left Cleveland for New Orleans on March 4, Joe Wood had already made his own way to camp. Most of the attention by reporters focused on pitcher Jim Bagby, who was holding out for a raise from his 1917 salary of three thousand dollars, but there were hints that off-season rumors about Wood might have some validity. Although Joe was pitching on the sidelines by March 7, when the complement of players arrived in camp on Saturday, March 16, Wood was stationed at first base. The next day, in the first exhibition game against the New Orleans Pelicans of the Southern Association, he was playing left field and batting fourth. He had two hits and a stolen base, and his squeeze bunt scored Ray Chapman with the winning run in the top of the fourteenth. He also hit a home run in another game against the Pelicans. Such success led the Indians to announce that Joe would be used as a pinch hitter that season.

Although newspaper accounts indicate that Wood was being tried as a position player throughout the 1918 spring training, in later years Joe told a simpler, more entertaining story. As he remembered, the shortage of quality players at the end of World War I negatively influenced the play on the field. One day when a defensively challenged player, identified as Big Ed Miller, was hit in the chest with a fly ball, traveling secretary Bill Blackwood said something like, "For God's sake, put Woody in there. He can catch that ball." Of course this incident (if true) could have encouraged the trial of Wood, which was anticipated over the winter and become an experiment that spring.[13] But as the year played out, Joe wouldn't be used just because he could catch flies. Lee Fohl and others discovered the value of Joe Wood as infielder and clutch hitter.

As spring training progressed, Joe played fitfully as a position player. After his teammates made friendly accusations that he threw them the shine ball in batting practice on March 29 (a charge he denied), he was back in center field on the thirtieth against the Pelicans, going 0 for 1 in a 1–0 victory in eleven innings, with his sacrifice of Chapman to second base setting up the winning run. Out of the lineup on the thirty-first, he played again on April 3 in an 11–7 win over Shreveport of the Texas League, going 0-4 while batting third and playing center field, where he made two put-outs and an assist. Still trying to make the team as a pitcher, he basically was absent as a position player the last two weeks of the preseason. Joe was not on the field against the New York Giants, Minor League squads, an Army team (Camp Shelby, Massachusetts, April 9), or even in Indianapolis (on April 15 as the Indians defeated Nap Lajoie's A Indians, 5–0).

Joe Wood was also absent from the Indians' lineups for the first week of the 1918 season, against the Tigers, the Browns, and the initial contest in Detroit. He entered on Thursday, April 25, against the Tigers as a late replacement for Eddie Onslow (in one of the two games he played that year) and got a hit in his only time at bat while playing left field. Joe got his first start of the 1918 season in Detroit on April 27, batting sixth and again playing left field in a 3–2 win. Wood doubled in the eleventh inning but was out trying to stretch his hit into a triple. The moderate success got him playing time against the White Sox when the Indians returned to League Park. Joe played in consecutive games, April 29–May 1, batting seventh and defending in left field. He had four put-outs and an assist in the second game, throwing out Joe Jackson at the plate on an attempted sacrifice fly. That day Wood also went 1 for 3, including a double and a walk, in a 13–3 loss to the White Sox. But in the three games he hit only 1 for 10.

Over the next ten days Joe showed signs of brilliance at bat and in the outfield. On May 2 he started in left field at St. Louis, again batting seventh, and went 2 for 4, doubling in the seventh over left fielder "Sheriff" Smith and scoring the winning run when Jim Bagby singled. In the same game Joe also played well in center when Speaker had to leave with ptomaine poisoning. In the sixth inning, when Braggo Roth misjudged a Ray Demmitt drive to right-center with runners on second and third, Joe took over and made the play. In the eighth Wood caught a liner in front of the wall and threw out Jack Tobin at the plate after reaching Fritz Maisel's twisting fly to short left. Such plays inspired the *Plain Dealer* the following day to revisit Joe's storied past and praise his recent excellence: "Once an idol of the mound, where he hurled no-hit games, won a pennant and a world's series, Joe, as an outfielder, today sparkled as brilliantly as Tris Speaker. He caught 'em in center, he snatched 'em in left, he threw out a runner trying to score from second base on a base hit and he scored the run which beat the Browns."[14]

But it was his hitting that kept him in left field and batting seventh. The next day, May 3, Joe hit two more doubles, knocking in three (including two in the sixth with two out) in a 5–4 win against the Browns in St. Louis. He also hit doubles on the fourth and the sixth in losses to the Browns in St. Louis and the White Sox in Chicago. He followed with three singles in four at bats the next day in a 7–1 win over Chicago. With hits on the eighth in Chicago and the ninth in Detroit, he helped put Cleveland in first place. He added a squeeze bunt in the third inning on May 10, scoring Rippy Williams, in an 8–2 win over

Washington. From May 2 to May 10, Joe batted 11 for 35 (.314), with five doubles and a sacrifice fly, good for five RBI and three runs.

Then his defense got shaky. The game that put him in jeopardy was the 1–0 loss suffered to Walter Johnson and the Senators at Washington on May 11. Joe again played left and batted seventh, going 1 for 4. And he threw out Johnson at home on a fly by Howie Shanks in the eighth. But he also struck out twice and made two errors on foul flies, in the third and fourth innings. Though the game was won cleanly by Johnson's lead-off triple in the sixth followed by Shanks's two-out single to center, the press speculated that Joe's inconsistent fielding would bench him. In fact Jack Graney became the lead-off hitter for the next five games. At least Joe's timely hitting received good reviews. In the *Washington Post* on May 14, 1918, J. V. Fitzgerald compared Wood with the Nationals' Sam Rice and the Giants' Cy Seymour. In an aside Fitzgerald predicted a similar shift for Walter Johnson and Babe Ruth, called by Fitzgerald "a natural as well as mighty clouter," playing "first base when" not "pitching . . . because of his slugging propensities."

Joe played first base on May 16 when John "Shotgun" Peters misfired in his only game as an Indians catcher, making four errors in the first inning of a 6–5 loss to Philly. Inserted when Rippy Williams moved from first base to catcher, Wood went 1 for 2, scored a run, and made seven put-outs and an assist. But he also made an error in the ninth, which combined with a miscue by Ray Chapman to allow the winning run. Luckily for Joe Wood, Graney strained his throwing arm on May 18, 1918, against the A's in Philadelphia. Joe replaced Jack in the bottom of the fifth, playing left field, batting leadoff, and going 1 for 1 in a 3–2 win. When Joe went just 1 for 10 in the next two games, on May 21 Fohl moved him down to sixth in the order. Wood responded with a 3 for 4 day, including a bases-loaded single in the third (scoring Speaker and Roth) as the Indians defeated the Red Sox at Fenway. The *Cleveland Plain Dealer* on the twenty-second declared, "Joe Wood carried off the real batting honors with a sacrifice, two singles and a double, scoring one run and driving in two others," moving his batting average to .319.

On the twenty-third he again went 1 for 3 but couldn't corral Amos Strunk's Texas Leaguer, which bounced off Joe's glove for the only hit off Guy Morton in the Indians' 1–0 victory at Fenway.

Joe Wood's place in the Cleveland outfield was solidified the next day, May 24, at the Polo Grounds in his most memorable game as a position player. He wasn't the only hero as Stan Coveleski followed up thirteen- and twelve-inning games in his previous two starts with a complete game over nineteen innings (it took three hours and forty-eight minutes), winning 3–2. But Joe starred both at the plate and in the field. Batting sixth Wood hit a lead-off homerun in the seventh, which scraped the top of the left-field wall, just eluding the reach of Ping Bodie, to put the Indians ahead 2–1. With one out in the ninth, he caught Elmer Miller's drive one-handed while leaping against the left-field fence. With no outs in the twelfth, Joe fumbled Miller's single but recovered to throw Elmer out at second. In the nineteenth, after Wamby grounded out to second, Smoky Joe hit a no-doubter deep into the left-field bleachers off George Mogridge's curve, with the pitcher calling him "everything in the book" as he rounded the bases. At ninety, Joe recalled, "The first thrill I got was a home run that tied the score. Next one I got a fly ball that probably would've scored a run and beaten us. . . . I hit another [home] run that won the ball game. And that was that."[15]

A revised interpretation of his achievements as a player quickly followed. An article in the *New York Times* on May 25 declared: "[Wood is] as fine a piece of outfielding bric-a-brac as there is in the game right now. He moves around here and there in left field and is in just the place where the ball is hit. As graceful as an infielder and as dangerous with his bat as any of them." It was a theme embraced in a poem simply called "Smoky Joe," retained in the JWA:

> When you pranced upon the hill,
> Smoky Joe,
> You could hypnotize the pill,

Smoky Joe,

So each batsman whiffed the air,

Wrenched his muscles, tore his hair,

Trying to slam it "over there,"

Smoky Joe.

Now you're shining out at left,

Smoky Joe,

With a style that's neat and deft,

Smoky Joe.

If you keep the pace you've set

You will be a Speaker yet,

That's an easy money bet,

Smoky Joe.[16]

The poetry may not be resonant, but the intent is clear. Cleveland fans were being encouraged to imagine Joe's pitching mastery reborn as an outfielder in the league of Tris Speaker.

Between May 25 and 27 the Indians lost three consecutive games to the Yankees at the Polo Grounds; Joe batted only 2-10, but with a double and a triple. The next day, in addition to walking, Wood hit another homer off Allan Russell, the victim of his first home run on the twenty-fourth. With Cleveland behind 2–0 in the seventh, this home run (into the right-field stands) came with Roth on base. Two batters later Steve O'Neill hit another homer, and the Indians won 3–2. Still in left field for the four games back in Cleveland during the last days of May, Joe was 4 for 13, with a couple of walks, runs, and sacrifices. June 1 found Joe at first, where he went 1-4 with two runs scored. The next day Braggo Roth was suspended for "insubordination," not being in shape, or fighting with manager Fohl (depending on the newspaper report), and Wood shifted to right, moving up to fifth in the order. But the change didn't sit well; over the next two days, he was 0-7. When Roth returned on the fourth, and Joe was moved to sixth and left field, he responded with 2 for 3.

That is where he stayed for almost all the games remaining in June, playing well in the field and showing flashes of brilliance at the plate, especially in the second half of the month. On June 7 he was 3 for 4, with a double, a run, and a stolen base, in a 14–7 win over Boston in Cleveland. Still at home on the thirteenth and fourteenth, he went 5 for 8 in the contests (including another double), beginning a twelve-game hitting streak. From June 13 through the first game of the doubleheader on the twenty-fifth, he was 18 for 46, a .391 average. Included were four doubles, six runs, five R B I, and a stolen base. Even when Joe tailed off in late June, going only 3 for 18, he batted .259 for the month, good enough to establish him in left field.

Joe could still be adventurous on defense; he made throwing errors at League Field on both July 1 and 2, against the Tigers and then the Browns. But his hitting could be explosive. In those same two contests he had a two-run single in a 4–1 win and then went 3 for 4, hitting a double and scoring the winning run in the eighth. In doubleheader wins on the Fourth of July against the Browns in Cleveland, Joe was 1 for 3 in both games, with a run in the first contest and two R B I in the second. On July 6 Joe Wood, batting sixth and playing left field, went 2 for 4, including a double down the left-field line, after which he scored. But he also made an error. Meanwhile, second baseman Bill Wambsganss received orders to report to Camp Zachary Taylor in Louisville on July 25. To prepare for his loss, the Indians began experimenting with Joe at second, beginning with an exhibition game in Newport, Rhode Island, on July 7, lost to the Naval Reserve Sailors 3–2. Joe was 0-4 while batting sixth.

On July 8 Joe was back in left field in the first game of a doubleheader at Fenway, 1–4 while batting sixth. But Joe was basically hitless for the next week, going 0 for 14 against the Red Sox and the Yankees while playing the corner positions in the outfield and first base. Then, just when it looked as if he were flagging under the rigors of regular play, on July 14 he began an amazing run. That day, playing left and batting sixth, he went 2 for 4, bunting for an R B I hit. The next day Joe had four hits, including an RBI single and a home run into the left-field bleachers leading off the eighth in a 5–3 win at the Polo Grounds. It was his fourth homer in the Polo Grounds that year. At Washington the following day, Joe added two singles, a walk, a sacrifice, and a hit-by-pitch against Walter Johnson. On July 17 he also singled in the first inning at Washington, scoring Wamby, before flying out to Wildfire Schulte, the first out made by Joe Wood in twelve at bats. For the remaining games in Washington and the Philadelphia series, Joe was 3 for 13, playing left and batting sixth; he contributed a bases-loaded double in the second game against the A's on the twentieth of July.

The next day the long, last home stand of the 1918 season began with a doubleheader against those same Athletics, in which Joe played both left and right fields, batting 2 for 7, with a double high off the right-field screen in the fourth inning of the second game. As the wartime initiatives brought the remainder of the 1918 schedule under scrutiny, the Indians didn't play again until the twenty-sixth, when they began their concluding games at League Field — eighteen with the Yankees, A's, Red Sox, Senators, and White Sox. Wood continued to hit well at home, going 19 for 63, just over .300. He tripled in back-to-back games with the Yankees on the twenty-sixth (going 3 for 5) and the twenty-seventh and knocked in the only Indians runs with a two-out hit in a 2–2 tie with the Yanks on the twenty-eighth. Against Philadelphia Wood had an RBI in both ends of a doubleheader on July 30 and the next day scored three runs and drove in one as the Indians won over the Athletics 10–1. Against the Red Sox Joe had 2 for 4, including a double, on August 3, and 3 for3, with two stolen bases and an RBI in the second game on the fourth. His triple to deep left field led to the only run in the bottom of the tenth as Cleveland beat the Senators in ten innings on August 6. Against the White Sox in the second game of a doubleheader on the eleventh, he was 2 for 4, including an RBI single as the Indians scored four in the ninth to beat the Sox 6–5.

During this home stand Joe also played second base, replacing Bill Wambsganss, who had joined the armed forces that July 25. Although

Joe hit well batting fifth in the order, he didn't flourish at second. He was flawless in the first start, on the twenty-sixth against the Yankees, making five assists and two put-outs. But in his second game at second base, on July 27, he booted a grounder by the Yankees' lead-off hitter Good Time Bill Lamar, which led to a run. With one out in the second, he made a bad throw on a ball hit by Hank Thormahlen, who also scored. The next day against the Yankees Joe dropped a throw on a sacrifice bunt in a game suspended after ten innings because of rain. Even in a washed-out game the next day, July 29, against the Athletics, Joe made two errors on a ball hit by Philadelphia's Charlie Jamieson, leading to two runs. On July 30 in a doubleheader against the A's, he played both games at second, handling ten put-outs and six assists without a miscue. But on the last day of July, in a 10–1 win against Philly at League Park, he made an error in the sixth, though it wasn't costly.

As the final month began in that shortened season, Joe played better second base. In the first three games he turned a double play and handled twenty-two chances flawlessly. Unfortunately, in the doubleheader on August 4 against the Red Sox, slipperiness returned as he made an error in each game, in only five chances. In the following five games with the Washington Senators beginning August 6, Joe made eight assists and three put-outs in the first game and no errors for the series. In the final home games, against the White Sox, beginning on August 10, Joe also played second without incident in games one and three. But in the first game of the doubleheader on August 11, Joe made two errors, one that led to a White Sox run. The next day Lee Fohl tried thirty-seven-year-old Cotton Top Turner at second and Joe back in right, where he played well and singled; the Indians won 11–2. This change became long-term when Braggo Roth was suspended for the rest of 1918. Although insubordination was also rumored, on August 14 the *Plain Dealer* officially reported, "Roth has not been keeping in condition" "when Cleveland had a chance to win the pennant."

The prescription was obvious. The Indians would improve defensively with Joe in right field, Turner at second, and Joe "Doc" Evans playing third. The payoff came immediately as the Indians beat the Yankees 7–2 on August 14 at the Polo Grounds in the first game of Cleveland's long final road trip. Neither Turner nor Wood made an error, and Turner had four hits, including two doubles and a triple. Joe, hitting cleanup, walked and hit a homer into the right-field stands leading off the fifth. The *New York Times* on the fifteenth declared, "The most persistent home run swatter who visits these parts is Joe Wood; even more so than Babe Ruth. Wood rarely lets a day go by without making a home run at the Harlem lot." In Cleveland the *Plain Dealer* that day praised his defense: "In the sixth inning he reached up on the wall to take Hyatt's drive. In the seventh, he made a running catch of Lamar's liner, while to wind up the game, he made a one-hand running catch of Lamar's drive to right center with his back to the plate when he made the capture. Never waiting for the applause which the fans were willing to give him he kept on going for the club house."

After going 1 for 4 the next day, August 15, in a 3–2 loss to the Yankees, Joe followed with another monster game. As the Indians revenged the previous day's loss by winning easily 12–4, Wood, again playing right and batting fourth, singled to center in the second, doubled to left scoring Chapman in the fourth, and then stole home. He also singled to center in the seventh and to left in the eighth, scoring both Graney and Speaker. In the next series in Boston, Joe batted fourth in all three games, walking three times and going 3 for 10, with two RBI, a run scored, and a double against the left-field scoreboard in Fenway. Equally useful were his utility skills; he played first base in game one, right in the middle contest, and second base in game three. On August 21 he began a game at second against the Senators in Washington. But when Jack Graney hurt his arm on a throw in the second, Joe switched to left, made no errors, and batted 2 for 4 in a 5–3 win. The next day, August 22, he was listed among the top five batters in the AL.

Except for manning center for Speaker on August 27 and 28 when Spoke was suspended for arguing a play at the plate, Joe played left and batted fourth for the remainder of the season. He played in ten of the last eleven games, recording a strong last contest of the 1918 year, with 2 for 5 and three RBI in the September 1 victory in Chicago over the White Sox. But he tailed off some over the last two weeks, batting 9 for 38 (.237). Even with this short slide, his final .296 average placed him tenth in the AL in that war-shortened year. After a slow start he entered 119 of Cleveland's 127 games: 95 in the outfield, 19 at second base, 4 at first, and 1 as a pinch hitter. His five home runs tied him with Harry Heilmann for fifth in the league. His twenty-two doubles were seventh. Better yet his sixty-six RBI tied him with Babe Ruth for third place, and his slugging average was .403. He also stole eight bases, including a straight steal of home, without being caught.

As Joe explained in later years, the keys to his success were simple. First he choked up: "I made up my mind I'd have to hit a little better. So instead of getting on the end of the bat, I slid up on the bat six or eight inches, where I had a better feel of it, better balance." And then he used a bat with a thick handle, like Joe Jackson's, so contact inside, close to his hands, might still get bloop hits. But it was his power that got the attention of sportswriters. Fred Lieb wrote, "If Ruth and Wood each played seventy-seven games a year on the Polo Grounds they should have a great carnival to decide who is the leading home run hitter in America." His success against the Yankees was also noted, one commentator recording that of the six homers by Indians in Polo Grounds in 1918, five were hit by "Woodie." The piece claims that Wood hit .347 against the Yankees, including three doubles, three triples, and the five home runs.[17]

Joe's achievement as an everyday player contributed to a very tight American League race. Though the Indians finally lost to Boston by two and one-half games, Joe was part of the pennant talk. Indicative was an article by Hugh Fullerton in the *Atlanta Constitution* on August 26, 1918, imagining that year's World Series. It was assumed that the Cubs would take the NL flag, as they did. In a potential match-up between the Cubs and the Indians, Fullerton liked the Indians outfield, including Joe Wood's "steady improvement in the fielding end of the game." The writer also saw Joe playing first base in Series games. That same paper on January 5, 1919, reminded its readers of Joe as an "aggressive, not rowdy," and "intelligent" pitcher for the Red Sox. Most memorable was a day at the Polo Grounds during the 1912 Series when Smoky Joe Wood "won by cool calculating craft. He deliberately took his time, wasted what seemed to be precious moments hitching his belt, acted as though he were pitching in batting practice and soon had everyone wild. . . . He then proceeded to win almost as he wished." For Cleveland, the writer continued, Wood fielded more effectively than Graney and played second when needed. And he was just twenty-eight.

As Joe Wood journeyed to Cleveland for the trip to New Orleans on March 10, 1919, he joined a large group that included manager Fohl, pitchers Stan Coveleski, Jim Bagby, Fritz Coumbe, and George Uhle, and catcher Steve O'Neill. Significant that year was the return of Elmer Smith, the left-hand-hitting outfielder who had started his career with Cleveland as a twenty-one-year-old in 1914. He was traded to Washington in 1916, bought back by the Indians (for four thousand dollars) in 1917, and then served in World War I, missing the 1918 season. Joe would still be used at various positions, but he would platoon in right field with the rejuvenated Smith, Joe batting against left-handers and Elmer versus righties. In Joe's words he became a "switch around" player.

Even though the season was shortened to 140 games and rosters were trimmed to twenty-one players because of financial concerns in the wake of World War I, the Indians added veteran clutch-hitter Larry Gardner, backup catcher Les Nunamaker, and Charlie Jamieson, a rising star. The focus was on whether Jack Graney's left-arm problems, aggravated the previous year when he slid back into a base, would allow him to play left field effectively. But Indian fans were reassured that Graney had visited Bonesetter Reese, who declared Jack fully healthy for 1919. Instead it was Joe Wood who was injured. When (as in 1918) he arrived early at the De Soto Hotel to work with the pitchers and catchers, the ring finger on his left hand had been smashed while he was loading railroad ties back in Pennsylvania. Doctors had to remove the fingernail, with the pain so bad that Joe had trouble sleeping. As a result he spent much of the early camp tutoring young hurler George Uhle, simplifying his windup and refining his pick-off move.

On March 14 Joe was still in street clothes, with fear he would be out of action at least another week. Because Tris Speaker was typically casual about arriving for training, Wood temporarily bunked with twenty-year-old rookie Uhle. But Joe's regular ways didn't tame George's chaotic life. The youngster awakened at 6:00 a.m. on Sunday, March 16, needing a cigarette. He lit up and lay back in his bed. Awakened by the smoke from the burning bedclothes, Uhle started pounding the flames, scattering some hot ashes onto Joe's bed. Luckily no one was hurt. When the second squad joined the camp on the eighteenth, Wood got into shape by shagging flies. Not wanting to fall behind in workouts, he tried hitting while holding the injured finger away from the bat. But the unnatural angle between bat and hand caused a blister on his palm. He had to skip the first exhibition game, against the New Orleans Pelicans, on Sunday, March 23, which the local team won 14–10.

Because the Indians pitching staff was thin that year, competitive games were played only on Sundays to protect their arms. On Sunday, April 6, Joe got his first game, playing right field and batting fourth, then moving to center when Elmer Smith entered. Wood was 0 for 3 in the 4–1 win. Joe played in one more game, batting third and going 0 for 3 in a 3–0 loss to the Pelicans. But the inflammation in his hand made him questionable for the first series of the regular season in Detroit. Meanwhile, influenza, deadly across the United States the previous year, struck Jack Graney just as he arrived at camp. (Graney's debilitation reminded manager Fohl that flu on the Indians team early in the 1918 season contributed to using Joe as a position player.) There was equally serious sickness back in Pennsylvania. Joe's father, John F. Wood, had pneumonia, and both Laura and Zoë, Joe's wife and sister, had contracted the flu. John F. and Zoë recovered, but in less than a week Laura was worse. And she was almost five months pregnant, with twins. With such a dangerous situation for her and the unborn children, on April 10 Joe stopped sending worried telegrams and set off for Parkers Glen.

While Joe was back home, reporters remained high on him as an outfielder. Indicative was Hugh Fullerton, who in an article published in the *Atlanta Constitution* looked both backward and to a bright future. While analyzing the upcoming season, he wrote, "Wood has developed into a remarkable outfielder and is improving all the time." He gave much of the credit to Joe's friendship with and tutoring by Tris Speaker: "Coached by Speaker, [Joe Wood] has grown out of the filler-in stage and become almost as great as an outfielder as he was a pitcher." Certainly Wood had demonstrated his prowess at the plate. But Fullerton warned fans, "The idea that he is in only to hit is a mistake." Joe could "field and throw far above the average of outfielders" and had the unique ability to play "batters with the knowledge gained by long experience as a pitcher."[18]

While Wood was in Woodtown, the team broke camp; they played Tulane University (and won 14–1) on the way to Evansville, where they were scheduled to play exhibition games with the Milwaukee Brewers, managed by ex–White Sox skipper Pants Rowland. When Laura was in full recovery, Joe wired on April 15 that he would arrive in Indiana for the final exhibition game. He did so, as a replacement for Elmer Smith, batting fourth and playing right as the Indians won 4–3. Smith went 1 for 3, with a double, and Joe was hitless in his one time at bat. The team traveled by train from Evansville to Detroit for the opening day against the Tigers. No surprise, Elmer Smith was declared the opening-day right fielder, batting fourth. Between a bum finger, insufficient conditioning, family problems, and the emergence of powerful, left-handed-hitting Smith, Joe Wood had to wait his turn.

By the end of May it was clear that in 1919 Joe Wood had a revised role in the Cleveland outfield. He did not play in sixteen of the first twenty-nine games. He was a pinch hitter (0 for 3) in three others, and in two he played without batting. In that stretch he only had three hits and as many sacrifices as safeties. Without regular play his batting average dipped to just over .100 (3 for 26). Finally, after not starting in the first three games against the Browns, he batted fourth and played right field on April 30 in St. Louis, hitting his only double of the first two months, sacrificing, and reaching as a hit batsman. Despite this success Joe only pinch-hit in the following two games and then didn't play in five consecutive games. Batting fourth and playing right field on May 10 and 11, he was 0 for 8 and then didn't play for three more games in a row. He was 1 for 2 on May 18, plus a sacrifice, walk, and run (singling and scoring in the seventh), which gave Cleveland a 4–3 win over the Yankees at League Park. The only other noteworthy events of May were the four walks he received on the twenty-sixth as the Indians beat Babe Ruth and the Yankees 12–7 and his entry into center in the ninth on May 31 after Speaker was ejected for fighting with Chick Gandil, spiked as Tris slid back to first base.

Once June arrived, Joe started to produce. After Ban Johnson suspended both Speaker and Gandil for their altercation, Elmer Smith played center in the game on June 1 as Wood stayed in right, batting sixth. Joe was only 0 for 2, but he had two walks, his strong suit early in 1919, and the Indians beat the White Sox 5–3. The next day, back in Cleveland against the Browns, Wood and Smith switched outfield positions, and Joe went 2 for 4, with a triple and two runs, as the Indians won 6–3. He also made an error. Most memorable was a play in the fourth inning. With the bases loaded and no one out, Browns shortstop Wally Gerber flied to Wood, who threw home. As George Sisler scored, Indians shortstop Ray Chapman cut off the throw, trapping two runners, Baby Doll Jacobson and Yale Yeastman Sloan, off base. Chappy threw to Larry Gardner, who tagged one runner for the second out. Larry then relayed the ball to Wambsganss, who got the final player in a run down. Gardner handled the ball once more before Wamby made the out. It wasn't as famous as the one Wambsganss would make in the 1920 World Series. It was your regular 8-6-5-4-5-4 triple play, if you are scoring at home.

Playing regularly, whether in right or in center, helped Joe at the plate. On June 3 and 5 he replaced Speaker in three more games, making no errors and going 2 for 9 with four walks, four runs, and two stolen bases as the Indians split a doubleheader with the Browns and lost to Philadelphia, 10–6. After Tris returned on June 7, 1919, Joe was mostly absent from the lineup. In the nine games played between the seventh and the sixteenth, Wood was inserted in only two. On the eleventh, he was 0 for 3 batting fourth and playing right field, but again he walked (and scored) and had an assist. On the fourteenth, also in right field and batting fourth, he was 2 for 4 with a sacrifice fly in the third inning, scoring Jack Graney, as the Indians defeated Boston in thirteen innings. On June 17 Joe pitched for the only time that year. In the first game of a doubleheader at Fenway, he relieved Tom Phillips in the ninth inning, with one out and runners on second and third, retiring the last two batters to preserve a 4–3 win by the Indians and gaining Wood a save. In the second game Joe returned to right field and batted fourth, going 0 for 2 with a walk and a sacrifice.

The next two days were typical of the platooning used by the Indians that year. On the eighteenth Joe started in right and batted fourth, singling to center and scoring Speaker in the first inning. Then Elmer Smith replaced him, going 2 for 4, as the Indians won easily 13–3 over the Yankees in the Polo Grounds and moved into a tie with the White Sox for first place. The next day at the same venue, Wood replaced Smith and sacrificed in his only at bat as the Indians won 4–3. But two days later, on June 21, Joe made a crucial error when he dropped Truck Hannah's pop fly in short right, scoring Wally Pipp with the Yankee's first run. Although Joe was 1 for 4 batting fourth, the Yanks won 2–1. During the remaining nine games in June, Wood didn't play in five. He pinch-hit unsuccessfully twice (in the ninth innings on the twenty-second and the twenty-fifth). On the twenty-fourth he was 1-4 in Comiskey Park, singling sharply to left in the first with two outs and two strikes, plating Jack Graney as Cleveland defeated the White Sox 2–0. On the twenty-eighth he tripled in three at bats as the Indians lost to the Tigers 3–1 in Detroit.

July began with the Indians stopping a six-game losing streak by beating the White Sox at Comiskey Park, 14–9. Joe batted fourth and played right field; his only hit in four times at bat was a single to center in the first with the bases loaded, knocking in Graney and Wamby, after which Joe also scored. More significantly Jack Graney pulled a muscle legging out a triple and was lost for nearly two weeks. For the next twelve games, Wood replaced Graney in left and batted fourth. With more regular play his batting improved, 12 for 51 with eight walks. His best offensive production was on July 10 in a doubleheader against the Yankees at League Park. In game one he was 1 for 4 but failed to get the squeeze down in the ninth, leaving Wamby out to dry, as the Indians lost 1–0. He made an error in game two but was 2 for 4 (four RBI) with a double to left and a run as Cleveland won 7–3.

With Graney back in the lineup, Joe Wood played on the fourteenth against Washington, batting fourth and in right field. He was 0 for 5 as Cleveland won 7–1. After another day off Wood played consecutive games against the Red Sox in Cleveland on the sixteenth and the seventeenth. In the first game in four at-bats he had a single to right field, scoring Chapman in the eighth, and in the second he made two of the four Indian hits and scored two of their four runs. With Joe in right and batting fourth, Cleveland won both games. He did not play in the infamous game against Boston at League Field on July 17, when Lee Fohl brought in a pitcher inactive for two months to face Babe Ruth, who hit a grand slam as the Yankees scored five in the ninth to win 8–7. The next day Fohl resigned, and Tris Speaker became manager of the Cleveland Indians.[19] That change didn't increase Joe's playing time; he only played in one game out of the next nine. On July 25 he replaced Speaker, injured diving for a line drive by Ty Cobb in the eighth inning. Joe was 1 for 2 the rest of the game, won by Detroit 11–5. After Joe went 0 for 5 on the twenty-ninth batting fourth, Speaker moved him down to sixth on the thirtieth, where he went 1 for 3, with a walk and the only Cleveland run as the Indians lost to the A's in Philly 2–1.[20]

Joe didn't play in thirteen of Cleveland's twenty-six games in August. But that month he finally started adjusting to part-time play, hitting 8 for 23, nearly .350. With the emergence of Joe Harris at first base (after recovering from an auto accident in France while returning from World War I, Harris hit .375 in sixty-two games during 1919), Wood was shifted to seventh in the order. Typical of his Cleveland years, two of his three best games that month were against Boston. He was 2 for 4, including a double on August 7 in Fenway, and he was 2 for 3, with two runs scored and four RBI, against the Sox in Cleveland on the twenty-second. In between on August 12 at the Polo Grounds, he saved a 2–1 victory by snaring Del Pratt's drive near the right-field bullpen to end the game. Two days later, on August 14, 1919, Joe wasn't in the lineup. The Woods' twins, Robert and Virginia, were born that day back in Pennsylvania.

After two more days to get the twins and Laura as comfortable as possible, Joe was 1 for 2 against the Yankees in Cleveland on the seventeenth. Over the next week he hit .500 (4 for 8), playing irregularly. At League Park versus the A's on the twenty-fifth (the day after Ray Caldwell was struck by lighting and continued to win a complete game 2–1), Joe had a double and a triple, a run and a sacrifice, as the Indians won 12–0 in the middle of an 8-of-9 win streak between August 22 and 31. Remarkably, the team played all twenty-four of its final games — the whole month of September — on the road. In the opening series against the Browns, in which the teams won two games apiece, Joe only started in the second game of the doubleheader on the first. For the series he was hitless in five times at bat.

Finally, Joe Wood started to show some power in the next series against the White Sox. Between September 5 and 7, he was 3 for 7 with a double, a triple, and a home run, deep into right-center field at Comiskey Park (some scorers recorded the last a triple and error because the umpire initially called Wood out before the catcher dropped the ball). Out of the action for the next seven games, Joe didn't play on the tenth when Slim Caldwell no-hit the Yankees at the Polo Grounds, 3–0. He had doubles on the nineteenth and in the second game of a doubleheader the next day, both at Washington. The twenty-first he walked pinch-hitting for Smith in the five-run ninth of an 8–4 win against the Senators, the tenth straight for the Indians. The White Sox clinched, however, on the twenty-fourth as the Indians lost to the Tigers 4–1 in Detroit (Dutch Leonard had won the day before he and Wood bet on a game, described in the chapters 9 and 10); Joe got three of the Indians' six hits, including a double. He only played again in the last game of the year, batting 1 for 4 and making an error as the Indians lost to the Browns, 8–5.

The Indians did well against the mighty White Sox in 1919, finishing only three and one-half games behind. After the season Joe Wood picked up some extra cash on October 12 by playing in a benefit All-Star Game in Springfield, Massachusetts, 180 miles from Shohola, Pennsylvania. Joining Wood were Chick Shorten, Nick Altrock, Joe Dugan, George Burns, and Rube Marquard, as well as Joe Wilhoit, who that year hit in sixty-nine consecutive games with Wichita of the Western League before joining the Red Sox. Meanwhile, some Chicago White Sox were throwing the Series against the Cincinnati Reds. In interviews Joe claimed no direct knowledge. But he heard suspicions through Tris Speaker. Implicitly admitting that Spoke considered betting on that Series, Joe recalled, "There was a whole lot of hoopla . . . about a fix and so on. . . . Speaker . . . told me, in a letter or on the telephone, I don't know which, that there wouldn't be any money placed on the games. The word was out. There was something wrong."

Initially bought and paid to pitch for the Indians, Joe made a courageous effort. But his arm couldn't take the strain. So he switched to the outfield, where his speed, intelligence, and drive paid off in 1918, when he became a top-ten player in the American League. Before the year was out, World War I required that he fill in at second base, as well as play some first and center. The next year he was asked by two managers, Lee Fohl and Tris Speaker, to share right with World War veteran Elmer Smith, who (like many Cleveland players) became Joe's friend. Initially limited play lowered his batting average and power. But Smoky Joe Wood rationalized that baseball was his only occupation. For this choice he would gain more glory in his remaining years in Cleveland and Major League baseball.

EIGHT

Glory Revisited

As in previous years Joe Wood planned to leave with the first group, primarily pitchers and catchers, from Cleveland for their 1920 spring training camp in New Orleans. He was to join Stan Coveleski, Ray Caldwell, George Uhle, Tom Phillips, and others, who were scheduled to arrive in Louisiana early, by February 29 of that leap year. Joe had good stories from the off-season to share, including the one about prospect Bob Clark getting lost in the Pennsylvania woods on a hunting trip with Wood, Coveleski, and O'Neill. But at the last minute Joe was detained by "illness in his family," no small matter since four small children were home. Wood was able to leave with the second group, on March 2, 1920, including Bill Wambsganss, Doc Johnston, and newcomers Frank Grabfelder and Otto Neu (in his unsuccessful attempt to play more than one game in the Majors). Smoky Joe's primary role in the spring, as in 1919, would be to coach up the young players.[1] Uhle was his project the previous year. This year he would mentor sandlotter George Cykowski.

From the beginning of spring training, Joe and Elmer Smith also competed for the right-field job. In the first exhibition game they played to a draw. Both of them went 2 for 2 with a triple and a walk. Smith also had a double in the 11–6 win over the New Orleans Pelicans. The injury jinx almost got Joe again on Tuesday, March 9. While he was hitting fungoes in batting practice, Dick Niehaus lost control of his bat and hit Joe in the chest. After a few scary moments, Wood was able to resume. Otherwise it was a relatively uneventful March at the De Soto Hotel. Steve O'Neill and Joe Harris were holding out, and Jack Graney got another dose of flu. But there were no major injuries. The *Atlanta Constitution* on March 18 speculated that Joe might return to pitching. But likely the writer misinterpreted Joe's time on the mound with young pitchers. Speaker considered Joe a power-hitting outfielder. Besides, the pitching corps was deeper for 1920 than it had been in 1919.

Indicative of what was to come, on March 21, in a 5–0 win over the Pelicans, Joe did not play. On March 23 Wood played center field for the Regulars, going 2 for 3 with a sacrifice in an 8–7 six-inning victory over the Yannigans. He also played center again, batting third, for the right-handers against the left-handers on the twenty-sixth, hitless in three at bats. By then it was clear that Elmer Smith would start on opening day since the scheduled pitcher for the St. Louis Browns, Allan Sothoron, was a righty. As training camp neared its close, Joe got hot and made five hits, two of them doubles, between April 1 and 4 in two intrasquad games and one with the Pelicans. But his late rush didn't change the plan. In the final game in New Orleans, on April 7, he only replaced Smith, going 0 for 1, and didn't play at Memphis on April 9 or against Louisville on the eleventh. When the Indians opened the fiftieth season of League Field on the fourteenth against the Browns, Coveleski pitched a five-hit shutout, 5–0, and Elmer Smith played right, batted cleanup, and got two hits while scoring a run.

During the championship season Joe Wood platooned with Elmer Smith in right field, for the most part hitting fourth when he played. But his playing time was reduced even from 1919 levels; he played in eleven fewer games and had fifty-five fewer at bats. Indicative, in April and May he didn't play in nineteen of the thirty-seven games. As in 1919 he started very slowly, at one point hitting only 2 for 31. But he finished the period with a respectable 11 for 49 by hitting .500 (9-18) between May 16 and the first of June. At the same time he contributed with walks (eight), stolen bases (three), sacrifices (four), and runs (ten), as well as a hit batsman, while often sharing cleanup and right field with Elmer Smith in games. Typical of his career his best offense came at the Polo Grounds; on May 16, for example, he was 1 for 2 plus a run, stolen base, sacrifice, and walk, after replacing Smith. June was more of the same, with Wood not playing in fourteen of twenty-eight games and only serving as a runner in two others. He used seven walks to get five runs, but he was still under .250, hitting 7 for 29. His only multi-hit game came on June 11, against the A's at League Field, when he was 2 for 2, including a double, a run, three RBI, and two walks.

His best games of July, and the whole year, were on July 17, in a doubleheader in which the Indians won both games 5–2 at Fenway, Joe's other (besides the Polo Grounds) favorite place to hit. In game one he replaced Smith and was 1-2 (with a sacrifice), hitting a home run in the seventh inning (his only one that year) that bounced into the stands in center field. He also threw out Sad Sam Jones at the plate from deep right field. In the following game he was 3 for 3, with two doubles, a sacrifice, and three RBI. His single to left in the first scored two, and his double, following Speaker's double, scored another in the fifth. For the month Joe had a slightly better average, 11 for 42, playing in eighteen of thirty-three games but pinch-running in only two of those games and replacing Speaker and Smith defensively at the end of two others.

In one of the most dramatic months in the history of baseball, August 1920, Joe Wood played very little. In the first fourteen games, with the Indians in the midst of a pennant race, Joe didn't play in the outfield. He ran for Steve O'Neill in the seventh inning of a game against the Yankees at League Field on the ninth, lost by Cleveland 6–3. But before that token appearance he took the mound again. Very attentive observers might have seen him warming up in an 8–5 loss to the Senators at League Park on August 1, but he didn't enter that game. On August 4, in the same series, he pitched in the eighth. Except for the two-thirds inning he pitched in 1919, it was his first action on the mound since 1917. And it wasn't pretty. Wood gave up four hits and two walks, for five earned runs, in that inning. Though he struck out a batter and retired the Senators in order in the ninth, Joe couldn't locate his curve and gave up opposite field hits off his fastball. Washington won 11–3.[2]

Whether driven by sentiment or strategy, Tris Speaker found enough in this shaky outing to tell reporters that Joe Wood was being groomed for the postseason if the Indians made the World Series. In an article titled "Wood Rounding into Form," published in the *New York Times* on August 13, 1920, the Cleveland manager was quoted as saying, "I am counting on Smoky Joe as a relief pitcher to help us out." Tris continued, "Wood has shown that he has plenty of stuff, and I feel sure his arm will stand the strain. At first I was doubtful whether he would be able to show any of his old-time speed and sharp-breaking curve, but he still has both, and I expect him to turn in several good games for us before the season is over. He will be a big help in saving a game now and then." But it was never to be. August 4, 1920, at League Park in Cleveland, Joe Wood pitched his last game in the Major Leagues.

Maybe because his arm needed a lot of rest after that game, Joe Wood didn't play again for two weeks, except for one pinch-running opportunity. So he was on the bench on August 16, 1920. The Cleveland team was staying at the Ansonia Hotel, on the Upper West Side, Broadway at Seventy-Third, just west of Central Park. The hotel, opened in 1904, was enormous, sporting more than twelve hundred rooms, a spa, an indoor swimming pool, and many restaurants. More darkly, the previous World Series reputedly was fixed there, and Babe Ruth kept rendezvous with various women at the Ansonia after he joined the Yankees that year. It was overcast, with hints of rain, that day when the Indians played the Yankees at the Polo Grounds. For a Monday there was a large crowd (about twenty-three thousand), which included Ray Chapman's brother-in-law, Daniel Daly. With right-hand submariner Carl Mays on the mound for New York, at the end of the fourth the Indians held a comfortable 3–0 lead. The first batter in the fifth was Chapman, with Speaker on deck. Some reported that Chapman leaned into the first pitch; others asserted he froze. In any case he made no move to avoid the ball, which hit him on the left temple.[3]

As Mays retrieved the ball in fair territory and threw to Wally Pipp at first (in case the ball hit the bat), Speaker ran to the plate, and umpire Tommy Connolly, sensing the severity of the situation, called for a doctor. Quickly the Yankees' physician and Dr. Joseph Cascio of St. Lawrence Hospital rushed to the field, where Chapman slumped at the plate, with blood oozing from his left ear. They put ice on his head, and in a few minutes he was able to stand, to applause from the fans. Two players, identified by Mike Sowell as Jack Graney and "another Cleveland player" (Joe, however, claimed that these players were himself and Les Nunamaker), began to escort Ray to the clubhouse in center. But before he made it to second base, he started to fall and was caught by his supporters. Smoky Joe didn't believe Chappy was seriously hurt, though he "never looked at him, to tell the truth." Taken by ambulance to St. Lawrence Hospital, Ray fell into a coma and showed signs of paralysis. Just after midnight, at 12:29 a.m., doctors removed a piece of his skull one-and-a-half inches square to extricate bone fragments and relieve pressure. But Chapman died at 4:40 a.m. on August 17, 1919.[4]

Joe believed that Mays had marked Chapman for the beanball, threw to first without concern for the fallen player, and yelled at the umpire to call Chapman out. For years Wood repeated those accusations. But eventually Joe found no value in such talk, calling it not "nice" to repeat the rumor that Mays had targeted Chapman. He noted that Mays was "very disliked" but was "a damn good pitcher" who shouldn't have been banned from Cleveland for the rest of 1919. Joe even allowed that Chapman might have crowded the plate. More typical of Wood, decidedly loyal to his friends, he often repeated that Chappy was "wonderful," "one of the finest," and a "very high-type fellow." On the other hand, he didn't accept that the team played burdened by grief or used Chapman's death as incentive to win. Wood said they were professionals who knew their jobs.[5]

After Joe, with Graney or Nunamaker, helped Chapman from the Polo Grounds, he continued his aid of the Chapman family. He accompanied the body when it was taken from the undertaker James F. McGowan, at 153rd Street and Amsterdam Avenue, to Grand Central Station. Joe then joined Mrs. Chapman (who was pregnant), her father, her cousin Jane McMahon, and Tris Speaker as the body was placed on a Lake Shore Limited train at 6:30 p.m. for the solemn trip to Cleveland. Of course, the next day's game was canceled as arrangements were made for the funeral, which would include the Indians players, and the burial.[6] Meanwhile, the Indians continued the series against the Yankees. Without a manager they lost 4–3 on the eighteenth when New York scored two runs in the bottom of the ninth and then won the next day 3–2 behind Ray Caldwell and a home run from Elmer Smith, despite Babe Ruth's forty-third homer for the Yankees. Afterward the players boarded a train to Cleveland for the Chapman funeral.

Initially the service was scheduled for St. Philomena's Church in East Cleveland. But the anticipated turnout was so great the service was relocated to St. John's Cathedral downtown. The city hall and courthouse flags were flown at half-staff. A high mass was offered on Friday, August 20, at 10:00 a.m., with thirty-six priests attending and the sermon delivered by the Reverend Dr. William A. Scullen, chancellor the Cleveland diocese. There were 20,600 "flowers from a fan" purchased in honor of Chapman. Initially, Wood and Steve O'Neill (a Catholic) were to join Speaker and Tom Rafferty as pallbearers. But there were complications. Mike Sowell claims that Speaker was thrown into emotional exhaustion by the tragedy. Charles Alexander contends that Tris had a virus. Bill Felber believes there was a fight between Speaker and Catholic players. For whatever reason Speaker was unavailable, and Joe Wood, with O'Neill and five others, served in the Chapman funeral.[7]

When Speaker's illness continued, Smoky Joe Wood became interim manager. With Joe as their leader, Cleveland lost back-to-back shutouts to the Red Sox (12–0 and 4–0) on August 21. Despite Joe's denials grief may have been an issue. Certainly the players were rushed to make the games, arriving in Fenway at 1:30 for the 2:00 start. In the process they quickly fell one and a half games behind the White Sox.[8] Joe did not play in the first of those games, but in the second he was in center after substituting for Graney (Jamieson, batting fourth, switched from center field to left field), hitting first and going 0-2. The next day Wood and George Burns got away from the stress over Chapman's death and the pennant race by traveling to Camp Devens (northwest of Boston), where they served as umpires in a game won by the home team against Fort Ethan Allen, 15–5. The following day the Indians played another doubleheader, which they split with the Red Sox, Joe 0 for 6 (three K's). That made him 0 for August because he didn't play again until September 1 in Washington.

Soon there were organized attempts to remove Carl Mays from baseball for his beaning of Ray Chapman. That was a long-term project. More immediately, within five days of Chapman's funeral, Indians players tried to instigate a boycott of Mays in the Yankees' upcoming series against the Philadelphia Athletics. Wood confirmed to the press that letters had been sent to AL teams, an action Joe clearly supported, as did most teams, except the White Sox and the A's. Things got more complicated when Tris Speaker distanced himself from the letters and the banning of Mays. After meeting with Ban Johnson, president of the American League, and Connie Mack, the manager of the A's, Speaker said he would not participate in such actions and that Indians players would be reprimanded for moves against the Yankees pitcher. With lack of support from the top, the movement lost steam, and Smoky Joe started softening his stance out of loyalty to Speaker and the lay of the political land.

As the Chapman tragedy lost some of its sting, Joe was again absent from the Indians' lineup, not playing in any games from September 3 to 21, which included the team's crucial return to first place on the sixteenth. Possibly Speaker was trying to build up Smoky Joe's arm strength for the stretch drive and the World Series. But when the tight race between the White Sox and the Indians entered its last week, Joe returned to the outfield. He responded well. He got a pinch hit for Harry Lunte in the eighth inning of a loss to Chicago at League Field on the twenty-third, the day after the White Sox players were formally charged with fixing the 1919 Series. In the last two games against the Browns, Wood was 1 for 3 and 3 for 4, scoring three runs and driving in two, as Eddie Cicotte admitted throwing the previous championship. Joe was even better in the clinching game at Detroit on October 2, 1920. He played right field and batted sixth in the 10–1 victory, Jim Bagby's thirty-first win.[9] After singling to center in the second, Joe had three consecutive walks and scored in the seventh. Joe then tripled leading off in the eighth and scored again.[10]

Despite only playing part-time down the stretch, the stress of the pennant race in 1920 inspired Joe to a quote often repeated: "I slept a real sleep last night for the first time in many a night. When I wasn't lying awake thinking and planning and fighting over the next day's ball game in that furious pennant drive, I was dreaming restless dreams about it."[11] After a double, a hit by the pitcher, and a run as a replacement for Speaker in center in the final loss, 6–5 to the Tigers on October 3, Joe Wood finished the 1920 season 8 for 11, with a double, a triple, and six runs, raising his batting average for the year above .270. The Indians returned to Union Station just before midnight on Sunday the third as the American League champions, the third pennant for Joe Wood as an active player and the first for Cleveland in the American League.

Despite his experience and hot finish for the year, Joe's work for 1920 fell under the shadow of Elmer Smith offensively. As the *New York Times* explained on October 1, in its preview of the World Series, "Last year Smith gave way to Wood every time a left hander appeared on the hill, but this season Smith has had plenty of opportunity against the southpaws." Joe had a slugging average almost as high as 1918 (.401 to .403), and because of his selectivity, his on-base percentage approached .400, at .390. While Smith's on-base percentage was almost identical at .391, he batted nearly fifty points higher than Wood, at .316, while achieving a career-high slugging percentage of .520. The short porch in right field at League Park, only 290 feet to the wall, was an especially attractive target for a left-handed power hitter like Elmer Smith. On the other hand, Joe excelled on defense, making one error while Smith made seven.

Normally the first game of the 1920 World Series would've been played in Cleveland. But Jim Dunn, the Indians' owner, wanted to add seats to his park, which required a few days to complete. So the opener was shifted to Ebbets Field in Brooklyn. There was the usual concern over the weather. At 9:00 the night before Game One, a major rainstorm threatened the opening. But the day of the game, Tuesday, October 5, it was clear and in the upper sixties, though with a stiff, cold north wind. There was also the ongoing Black Sox scandal, which at one point even threatened to halt that year's championship.[12] Though writers called for righteous play between Brooklyn and Cleveland, they also noted that odds first favored the Indians at 6 to 4. A good human interest story was Doc Johnston at first base for the Indians, while his brother Jimmy played third for Brooklyn. New York mayor John Hylan (a resident of Brooklyn) would throw out the first ball with Cy Young in the stands. It was a best-five-of-nine series.

The Indians arrived by train early that morning, put up in the Hotel Pennsylvania, and reached the field by noon for a game moved up from 2:30 to 2:00. The official attendance that first day was listed as 23,573. To inspire his players and incite the fans, Tris Speaker had the Indians take the field at 12:45 in new blue uniforms, with black armbands on their left sleeves in memory of Ray Chapman. It was overcast, with the threat of rain, as the game began, but the sun was out by the fourth inning. On the mound for the Indians was Stan Coveleski, the spitballer who looked to Damon Runyon as if he were eating an apple when he moistened the ball. The best news for Joe Wood was that Wilbert Robinson, the manager of Brooklyn, had chosen left-hander Rube Marquard to start the game for the Robins. That meant that despite the high batting averages of his fellow outfielders, Joe Wood, who eight years before pitched the opening game of the 1912 World Series for the Boston Red Sox, would be starting in right field for the Cleveland Indians. He also would bat sixth in support of Coveleski.

Joe was equal to the task. In a tricky wind he retrieved Ivy Olson's fly for the first out in the bottom of the first, went to the right-field wall to catch a smash by Hy Myers for the second out in the bottom of the second, and defended flawlessly in two other chances. At the plate in the second inning, he scored the second Indian run. After walking, Wood moved to third on a wind-assisted single by Joe Sewell to right field and then scored on Steve O'Neill's first double, just inside the line over third base. In the fourth, with one out, Wood hit the first pitch for a double, a one-hopper high off the wall in left-center field, six inches from being a home run. Then, one out later, he scored the third and final run for Cleveland when Steve O'Neill once again doubled, this time to the right-field fence. Joe struck out in the sixth. His day ended when Doc Johnston batted for him in the ninth. The Indians won 3–1 behind Stan Coveleski. Typical of games those days, it lasted less than one hour and forty-five minutes.

The weather was better the next day, but following the "switch around" pattern, Joe didn't play in Game Two, on Wednesday, October 6, which Brooklyn won 3–0 with Burleigh Grimes beating Jim Bagby. Wood almost entered that game; he prepared to pinch-hit for Harry Lunte, with Les Nunamaker on first base and two outs in the ninth. But Charlie Jamieson flied out to left field to end the game. Wood reentered the series the next day, Thursday, October 7, when lefty Sherrod Smith pitched for Brooklyn. As in Game One, Joe played right and batted sixth. While the weather and Steve O'Neill's hitting (2 for 3) were once again excellent, Joe's luck wasn't as hot. In the second inning he hit a drive inside the right-field line, caught just off the ground by Tom Griffith as he crossed into foul territory, robbing Wood of a triple. Joe struck out on a 3-2 count leading off the fifth, though (as Hugh Fullerton reported in the *Atlanta Constitution*) the pitch on 3 and 1 was high and probably inside as well. In the seventh Wood grounded out to second for the third out, leaving him 0 for 3. The Robins won again, this time 2–1 on a three-hitter by Smith.

The silver lining for Cleveland was Duster Mails, who, replacing Ray

Caldwell in the first with one out and two runs in, went the next six and two-thirds without giving up a run, a foreshadowing of Mails's return in Game Six. After a traveling day the series switched to Cleveland, where the Indians players checked into the Hollenden Hotel. On Saturday, October 9, 1920, Cleveland finally got its chance to host a World Series game at League Park. It was an unusually hot day for northern Ohio in October, with a high sun, no clouds, and almost no wind. Men donned shirt sleeves, and women were constantly fanning themselves. Despite the heat 25,734 fans crowded into the park. Outside the stadium kids climbed surrounding poles, and other lucky spectators positioned themselves strategically at windows in adjacent buildings.

Joe once again was not a starter, and his replacement, Elmer Smith, hit a single to center, driving in Wambsganss in the first. But in the third for Brooklyn Marquard, on release after his arrest for ticket tampering, replaced Al Mamaux, who had himself relieved Leon Cadore. With two on and none out, George Burns pinch-hit for Elmer Smith and drove in two runners with a single. Knowing that Burns would have to play first base if he remained in the game, Speaker sent in Wood to bat for first baseman Doc Johnston. Joe lined out to center field and then remained in the game to bat sixth and play right field, with Burns moving to first. In the fifth Joe grounded out to short for the third out. He came to bat in the seventh, with two on and nobody out. But after a passed ball, Jack Graney pinch-hit for Joe, grounding into a fielder's choice. Cleveland evened the Series at two each as Stan Coveleski got his second victory, using only eighty-six pitches, in a five-hit, 5–1 win.

The next day, Sunday, October 10, was a battle of right-handers, Burleigh Grimes for Brooklyn and Jim Bagby for the Indians. Because of this matchup, Elmer Smith returned to right field and his customary cleanup position. It was an easy victory for the Indians in a game of firsts. Smith went 3 for 4, but more memorably, he hit the first grand slam in the modern World Series over the right-field screen in the first inning with no outs. Even when Clarence Mitchell, a left-hander, replaced Grimes in the fourth inning, Smith stayed in the game to continue his assault on the right-field fence. With one out in the fourth, Bagby also homered, into the new stands in center field, the first time a pitcher hit a home run. In the fifth, after Pete Kilduff led off for Brooklyn with a single to left-center, Otto Miller followed with another hit, to center. Then, miraculously, with the count 1 and 1 and runners moving, Clarence Mitchell (a good-hitting pitcher who batted left handed) smashed a line drive. It was caught by Bill Wambsganss, the second baseman, who reached to his right, recovered, stepped on second base, and then turned to tag Miller (frozen in his tracks) for the only unassisted triple play in a World Series. Cleveland won 8–1 to lead the Series three games to two.

The night before Game Six, the shadow of the previous World Series lightened a bit with a prank. When Les Nunamaker found sixteen dollar bills under his pillow, he immediately panicked. Afraid the money would be misunderstood as a bribe (à la 1919), the Indians catcher reported the incident to Ban Johnson. In his haste Nunamaker failed to notice that the dollars were Confederate.[13] Though Joe had done little offensively since Game One, Speaker stayed with him. Since Game Six was given to left-handers, Smith for Brooklyn and Mails for Cleveland, Joe returned to right field and batted sixth. In his first at bat on Monday, October 11, Wood rewarded Speaker's faith by singling past the third baseman with one on and one out in the second. But he was stranded at second base. Wood made the last out in the fourth on a high fly to right and then in the seventh drove a ball so deep to center that Joe was almost to second by the time Hy Myers made the catch. Joe also made two put-outs and played errorless right in support of Duster Mails's 1–0, three-hit win. The game was won in the sixth. With two outs Speaker singled to left, and first baseman George Burns doubled high off the left-center fence. Played before 27,194, the game gave the Indians a commanding 4–2 lead in the 1920 Series.

Showers were forecast for that night, but clearing was expected for Game Seven, the next day, Tuesday, October 12. Back in Boston there was a rumor (fueled by sentiment, Joe's one relief outing, and Speaker's hints that he might use Wood) that Joe would pitch for the Indians. It was sweet for the press and fans to think so, but Stan Coveleski was ready and had won two games for the Indians. The Indians also wanted the 1920 Series to end in Cleveland. In a sense the celebration began the night before when Wamby and Elmer Smith were presented diamond-studded medals for their play in Game Five and the players gave diamond cuff links to Dunn and an antique watch to Tris Speaker. The next day Coveleski was again sharp, giving up just five hits as the Indians won 3–0, with Speaker tripling in a run in the fifth and Jamieson doubling in Coveleski in the seventh. The final out, a force out of Big Ed Konetchy from shortstop Joe Sewell to second baseman Bill Wambsganss, ended the game and the Series at 3:57 p.m. On the seventy-fifth birthday of Tris Speaker's mother, the Cleveland Indians became the champions, in front of 27,525 fans.[14] To win Speaker had used just nine players, leaving Wood, and his .200 batting average in four games, on the bench.

Joe Wood must have had mixed feelings about the victory. Always happy for change in his pocket, he was pleased to receive $3,986.33 for the Series, a figure the players and management shared with the widow of Ray Chapman. Although Stan Coveleski was by then a good friend and fellow hunter in the Pennsylvania hills, Wood could only watch from the sidelines as Covey became the first pitcher since Smoky Joe in 1912 to win three games in a World Series.[15] But the final words should be Joe's. Typically, Wood was plainspoken. For all their success the Indians "couldn't hold a candle" to the 1920 White Sox, who were unmotivated, sensing (as Cicotte told Wood) that Chicago dare not win as investigations hung over them. Besides, the Sox were crippled by the end-of-the-season suspensions. During the Series itself Joe was as surprised as anyone at the triple play by Wambsganss. The key to the Indians' success, Joe believed, was the great pitching of Stan Coveleski, Jim Bagby, and Walter Mails.

The city and the team arranged for a celebration on the evening of October 13, 1920, at Wade Park in East Cleveland. There were fireworks, much singing, and even a motion picture taken of the event. Things began serenely enough, with a band playing while the attendees sang "The Long, Long Trail," followed by Howard Reese (adorned with brightly colored feathers on his hat) dancing and singing "He Rambled." Although many of the players were scattered throughout the crowd, when Coveleski, Mails, and Johnston arrived, the band played "Hail, Hail, the Gang's All Here," topped by the team singing baseball's new anthem, "Take Me Out to the Ball Game." Harper Garcia Smyth led the crowd in "America" and "Till We Meet Again" before the mayor congratulated the team, mentioned the "manly spirit" of Ray Chapman, and finally deferred to Smyth, who introduced each player using a megaphone. But since the crowd was restless and the firecrackers continued, hearing was becoming difficult.

What happened next is not clear. Apparently the fans broke through the rope designed to keep them fifty feet from the platform. In the process the revelers also broke some chairs in the area. To get the intruders to settle, Mrs. Carl W. Kettleman, Tris Speaker, Joe Wood, and Wheeler Johnson placated them with the song "Watching the World Go By." But when Johnson, Coveleski, and Dunn reached from the stage to shake hands, a second surge led to chaos. As Mike Sowell has noted, "Hundreds of people were crushed against the platform, and chairs were trampled to splinters. The players grabbed their loved ones and fled for safety, while the mayor and other officials shouted for the crowd to disperse. As the people in the rear continued to push forward, those trapped in the middle of the mob lifted their babies above their heads and passed them forward to the stand in an effort to get them out of danger. On the edge of the crowd, several people were knocked into the adjoining lagoon and brook." Though police inspector Graul later insisted that no one was pushed into the pool, Smyth implored, "Show you are good fans. Go on home," which they did.[16]

On October 14 the team gathered for a farewell meeting at League Park. Joe and Stan Coveleski, also from Pennsylvania, were the first players to leave, by automobile. But they didn't exit without plans for a longer celebration. As the *New York Times* explained the next day, "A number of Indians arranged a hunting trip for deer in Pennsylvania in December. The party will include Joe Wood, Stanley Coveleskie [*sic*], Steve O'Neill, Bill Wambsganss, George Burns, Jack Graney and Trainer Percy Smallwood." Significant in their absence would be Tris Speaker and Les Nunamaker, who were off for fishing in Canada and the Gulf of Mexico. While Tris and Les traveled north and south, the Pennsylvania group camped at a cabin on an acre of land just a few miles southwest of Shohola in an area called Lord's Valley, which Joe had purchased in November 1919. They would name it Indian Camp to commemorate the 1920 championship.[17]

Such hunting trips inspired Joe Wood as a marksman, one of his many natural talents. He acquired two favorite guns, both now in the possession of Joe's grandson David Wood of Milford, Pennsylvania. One is a SAKO bolt-action from Marlin Fire Arms in New Haven. But his most prized weapon was a 35-gauge pump-action Remington, 1912 vintage. On that gun remain the twenty notches where the pitcher-turned-outfielder recorded his deer kills. Even more conspicuous is a following *X* for the one bear Smoky Joe also bagged. When his big game days joined his playing days in the past, Joe had liked to stand sentinel on the back porch of the family home and shoot groundhogs with a .22. Finally, though, as he recorded in later conversations, killing lost its appeal. In his later years he would sit for hours on porches at Woodtown and Westville, just watching and waving. First a timid soul, uncertain how to respond if a deer ran in his direction, then the fun-loving sportsman with his baseball buddies, Joe finally became a spectator of his neighbors and passersby.

As many newspapers reported, the Indians planned to stand pat for the 1921 season. The pitching looked solid, especially with the emergence of Duster Mails in the World Series. Despite some criticism and second-guessing, Tris also wisely stuck with Joe Sewell, who would hit over .300 the next year and begin steady improvement as a shortstop. Larry Gardner had one more .300 year in him as well, again rightly

judged by the manager. Speaker was particularly happy with the outfield, where he had a stable of quality players who allowed strategic
changes late in games. Wood, Graney, Smith, and Jamieson were the
cards he wanted to play. As a platoon player Joe could play quality defense at both corners and center field when Speaker was hurt. And in
1921 his hitting would rise to excellence that neither he nor Spoke could
have predicted.

Some changes were on tap. Spring training was moved from New
Orleans to Gardner Field in Dallas, Texas, where the team trained near
the White Sox (Fort Worth) and not far from the Reds (Cisco) and
even the Giants (San Antonio). The team stayed at the Jefferson Hotel
and took a trolley to the park. On March 11 the Indians enticed Riggs
Stephenson from the University of Alabama to help at second base.
From the beginning Stephenson hit Major League pitching; that year
he batted .330. But his defensive weaknesses, especially with throwing, limited his playing time for Speaker.[18] George Uhle, Joe's protégé
in the spring of 1919, would be called upon more than in the previous
year, with 1921 serving as a springboard for three twenty-win seasons
with the Indians. The shift of training site also encouraged the players
to trade in the horses on New Orleans betting tracks for rodeo ones in
Texas, Speaker's home state. But all these changes were relatively small.

When the first train, usually peopled by pitchers and catchers, arrived in Dallas at 2:00 p.m. on February 28, Joe was not aboard, representing the end of his mound work and the confidence in the Indians
staff for 1921. Wood instead journeyed south with friends Elmer Smith,
Joe Evans, Charlie Jamieson, and Jack Graney. Some players were slow
to arrive. Larry Gardner took his time but insisted he wasn't holding
out, just conserving his energy. Mails, on the other hand, was just late.
Not encouraging for Joe's chances as an everyday player was speculation that Elmer Smith, a pull hitter, could challenge Babe Ruth if Elmer
learned to hit to the opposite field (especially on the road). While many
players used rubber suits to lose weight, player-centered Tris Speaker
also allowed basketball and handball games. In the first, on March 16,

Joe played on the victorious Yannigans (7–5), batting fifth (going 2 for 4) and manning right field and center when Speaker retired late in the game. The next day he and Tris traveled more than fifty miles each way, to Teague, Texas, to aid a local team.

In the first game with the New York Giants on Sunday, March 20, Elmer Smith started, but Joe replaced Elmer in right field and scored the winning run in a 3–2 victory. Wood walked, took second on a fielder's choice, and advanced to third on a wild pitch. On a 1 and 1 count, Chet Thomas lined a hit to shallow left, with Wood sliding in safely on a close play at the plate. As solid as the outfield looked, there were lingering questions in the press about Joe Sewell's defensive abilities at shortstop, following his six errors in the seven games of the 1920 World Series, but Speaker stuck with the youngster (who would be elected into the Hall of Fame in 1977). Meanwhile, Joe was becoming the backup to Elmer Smith and, when necessary, Tris Speaker. Wood went 0-3 batting fourth and playing center field for the Yannigans on Friday, March 25. Two days later he replaced Smith in left field, batting fourth and going 3-4 with a double in a 17–7 win over the Cincinnati Reds. As April approached and the team broke camp, Joe played sporadically; he went 2-4 with a double in a win over the San Antonio Bears.

Joe was 0-4 in a loss to Galveston while batting fourth and playing right field, but then he didn't play much during the rest of the spring. He had one at bat in two games against Mobile and was absent in two with the Chattanooga Lookouts. Finally, on April 11, playing right field and batting fourth, he went 0-1 in the 2–0 win against the Indianapolis Hoosiers. As the season started, Joe was once again (as in 1919 and 1920) the second choice in most games because of the predominance of right-handed pitchers. He didn't play in the first game, on April 13, lost to the Browns 4–2, or the home opener, April 21, won over St. Louis, 4–3. But he had a better start than in 1919 or 1920. By the time the team arrived in Cleveland for its first home game, Joe was 3 for 9, with two doubles. He added 2 for 4 with a run in the opening series, and in his first start, on the twentieth, he had a double in Detroit, with the Indians losing 9–6.

Before opening day at League Park that year, a victory party was held in Cleveland on April 21. As biographer Charles Alexander has noted, at that celebration Tris Speaker received a number of gifts, including a new car, some fancy horse-riding gear, and an Airedale puppy. Tris gave the dog to Joe, who presented it to his children. Named "Spoke," the animal remained in the family for thirteen years and later developed a taste for woodchucks on their Pennsylvania farm.[19] That night the team was feted at the Hanna Theatre by Joe E. Brown and his "Jim, Jam, Jems" review.[20] When Joe returned to action, in back-to-back games in Cleveland against the Browns and the Tigers on April 24 and 25, he was 4 for 7, with a double and a run. On the twenty-eighth, still in Cleveland, he batted cleanup and went 4 for 6, with a double and three runs scored as the Indians beat the Tigers 10–4. Even though he was 0-4 in the last game of April, for the month Wood was 11 for 27 (.407) with four doubles.

More adept at part-time play than in the previous two years, in May Joe entered only seven of twenty-seven games and yet batted .381 (8 for 21), including a double and a triple. He had more two-hit days: at home on May 8 (versus the White Sox) and on the thirteenth (against the Senators) and then in St. Louis on the twenty-eighth. He also had a single and two RBI on May 11 in a 14–1 win over the Nationals. Between April 20 and May 13, he had at least an RBI in nine consecutive games, for a total of fourteen. June was almost a mirror image of May. Because of Speaker's preference for left-hander Elmer Smith against righties and Smith's continuing success (especially as a power hitter), Joe played in only nine of the twenty-six games that month. But he hit even better than in May, .429 (9 for 21), with two more doubles. He had hits in seven of those nine games, often going 1 for 1 (on the third, sixth, and twenty-eighth) or 1 for 2 (on the twenty-sixth and the thirtieth). The highlight was a game at Dunn Field on June 29 against Detroit in which Wood was 3 for 3, including a double, a run, four RBI, and a sacrifice, as the Indians beat the Tigers 9–6.

Joe Wood flirted with .400 throughout the tight July pennant race.

On July 4 against Chicago in Cleveland, in the first game of a double-header he was 1 for 1 and drove in a run before being replaced by Smith in a 6–4 win. Joe was 1-2 in the nightcap before Elmer entered, as the Indians came from behind to win 11–10. That gave Joe a .437 average. After a down period, on July 17 Wood was 3 for 3, doubling in Speaker and then scoring himself in the first, the only runs by Cleveland as they lost to the Nationals 13–2. That brought his average back to .400. On July 26 at Fenway, Shriners Day (Nunamaker, Gardner, Wood, Speaker, and Burns were Shriners), in the eighth Smoky Joe (batting fourth) hit the first pitch from Herb Pennock over the clock in left field (with Wamby on second), his first homer of 1921. That tied it 2–2 before the Indians scored six in the tenth to win 8–2 over the Red Sox, weakened because Shano Collins and Nemo Leibold were testifying at the Black Sox trial. Three days later in Fenway, still batting fourth, Smoky Joe went 2 for 3 with a walk and led off a three-run rally in the fourth with a single to center field. The Indians won 3–0. He also caused a stir when he was spotted warming up in the bullpen during the ninth inning. He ended July hitting .389.

Joe returned to batting excellence in August, hitting .440 (11 for 25), including two doubles, a triple, and two home runs, even though he didn't play in sixteen of the twenty-seven games. He had consecutive two-hit games against the Senators in Washington on August 5 and 6 (including a triple and raising his average to .398) before getting only one official at bat (he walked five times) in the next nine games. Meanwhile, August 17, 1921, was the anniversary of the death of Ray Chapman. Each fan entering League Park for the doubleheader was given a rose to honor the fallen shortstop. Also in attendance was Chapman's father. Chappy's wife was still too grief-stricken to attend. The first game began on a frightening note, as Charlie Jamieson, the first hitter for Cleveland in the bottom of the first, hit a sharp drive towards right field. It struck Philadelphia first baseman Jimmy Walker on the right temple, just above his ear.

Walker, knocked unconscious for a full minute, was treated on the spot by the Indians reserve outfielder Joe Evans, who had completed his medical training at the University of Mississippi in the off-season. Evans feared a skull fracture and sent Walker immediately to Lakeview Hospital. While the players and the crowd dealt with the eerie echo of Chapman's injury, the game continued. At the beginning of the Indians' half of the fifth inning (the same in which Chapman fell), Bill Wambsganss took the first pitch, called a ball by home-plate umpire Billy Evans, who then asked for time to initiate a minute's silence for Chappy. Joe Wood joined the other Indians in leaving their dugout, removing their caps, and bowing their heads. After the tribute Evans called, "Play ball," and the game resumed; it was won easily by Cleveland 15–8. Joe substituted late for Elmer Smith, batting fourth and playing right field, going 1 for 1 and scoring a run (raising his average back to .400). Before the game ended, Joe Evans reported that Walker would recover from his concussion and there was no skull fracture. Rains washed out the second game.[21]

Smoky Joe Wood continued his effective work for the rest of August. He had another two-hit game (with a double and a run, raising his average to .404) against Boston in Cleveland on the twentieth, the day before Commissioner Landis banned the Black Sox players. Wood also had a power surge at the end of the month. On the twenty-eighth at Dunn Field, he helped Stan Coveleski defeat the Washington Nationals 3–2 by going 3 for 4 and knocking in all the Indians' runs (his average back to .402). Batting fourth Wood hit a double to center in the first (scoring Wamby and Spoke) to tie the game at two and then homered to left field leading off the sixth for the game winner. Three days later in the second game of a doubleheader at Detroit, he hit another home run in a 7–3 loss to the Tigers and ended August hitting exactly .400.

Joe Wood started September of the 1921 season by going 5 for 10 in the last three games of the series with the Tigers, hitting two doubles, scoring two runs, and making seven put-outs in the game on the second. His average was .405 on September 3. But Elmer Smith, who returned to right field on the fourth, was even hotter. While Joe returned to the bench, Smith was 8 for 12, with two doubles and four homers. Finally, Joe's average slipped below .400 on September 7 as the difficult part began in the Indians camp, for two reasons. Starting on the tenth, the rest of the season was played on the road. One day later Tris Speaker twisted his right knee when he tripped over first base in St. Louis. Joe picked up the slack, playing center and right fields. He had three hits against the A's on both the thirteenth (a triple, his fourth home run, three runs, and four RBI, raising his average to. 399) and the fifteenth (a double, four RBI, a stolen base, and a sacrifice), and three more against the Senators on the seventeenth (returning his average to .394). More crucially, his triple on the sixteenth (the day Goose Goslin debuted for the Senators) knocked in O'Neill and Jamieson in the eighth for the only runs as Cleveland shut out Washington and moved into first place.

Back in Fenway on September 22, Joe batted third and played center; he hit a double to the left-field fence, drove in two runners, and made a difficult catch in left center on a drive by Nemo Leibold as Cleveland won in twelve innings, 9–8. Two days later in New York, he helped George Uhle win a crucial game against the Yankees. After striking out on an 0-2 count with the bases loaded in the third, Joe (batting fourth and back in right after Speaker's return) redeemed himself with a triple to right in the sixth, scoring on a sacrifice by Larry Gardner in a three-run sixth, with the Indians winning 9–0. Unfortunately, as Wood sat out, the Yankees won the final two games, even with Speaker in the Indians lineup. When Cleveland lost two of the first three games to the White Sox at Chicago, the Yankees clinched the pennant on October 1. Despite hitting .308 as team, the Indians lost six of their last eight games, three of them to the Yankees. Cleveland finished four and one-half games behind.

Although Joe stumbled to the finishing line, hitting 1 for 10 against the White Sox and 2 for 18 in the last two series, 1921 was an impressive year. Flying under the radar Joe Wood had some very strong offensive games, with power reminiscent of 1918. While Joe's tandem Elmer Smith had another good year, including sixteen home runs in

129 games (versus twelve in the same number of games in 1920) and a .290 average, quietly Joe had established amazing numbers. He played in a mere sixty-six games but hit .366, four points higher than Tris Speaker. Better yet, in only 194 at bats, he had sixty RBI, an RBI:at bat ratio second only to Babe Ruth (who had fifty-nine home runs and 171 RBI, his career high). Between April 20 and May 13 Smoky Joe had at least one RBI in nine consecutive games. His slugging average, .562, was the best on the team, and his on-base percentage (.438) was only .001 behind Speaker. He also played well in the outfield, covering center in twelve games and making just three errors all season.

A rumor was floating around baseball circles in the off-season that Tris Speaker was burned out managing and might give way to Joe Wood.[22] But Spoke's resolve returned in 1922, as did most of the 1921 team. The Indians made just one major trade before the 1922 season. To get first baseman Stuffy McInnis from the Red Sox, they gave up their own first baseman George Burns, the rights to Joe Harris, and Elmer Smith, the hero of the 1920 World Series who regularly shared right field with Joe Wood. When Speaker made no move to fill the void, Joe became a regular for the first time since 1918.[23] Of course, Jack Graney and Charlie Jamieson were still with the club as left-handed hitters; Graney would be out of the Major Leagues by the end of the season, while Jamieson would bat over .320 in 1922 and stay an Indian for another decade. But they were used primarily in left field. Right belonged to Joe Wood.

During 1922 spring training in Dallas, Texas, the weather didn't co-operate. As in 1921 March was wet and cold. At least Joe had new stories of his hunting expeditions from Indian Camp, which that winter included Stan Coveleski's brother Harry and triumphs as an ice fisherman. Joe again traveled with the first squad, leaving earlier than ever, at midnight on Tuesday, February 21. But this time no one misunderstood. There would be no comeback as a pitcher, as he explained to the press the next day. Wood was there early only to coach the youngsters. As the sessions began in early March, his star pupils became Vasco Barton and George Keidel. With the retirement of Chet "Pinch" Thomas,

Wood and Les Nunamaker mentored the Yannigans, beginning with initial workouts against the Dallas Marines. In the first inning of one game, Joe twisted his ankle sliding into third, but he played the complete game, impressing reporters with his passion and dedication at age thirty-two.

Once the intrasquad games began, Joe eased into play, pinch-hitting in the fifth, and last, inning for pitcher Barton of the Regulars, who lost to the Yannigans 4–0. He also was 0-1 with a run in the 10–3 loss to the Reds on the nineteenth. Back at practice he almost got bit by the injury bug yet again. First a groundskeeper's son hit Joe in the head with a bat, leaving a large knot. Then pitcher Carl Guess, who would play for the Corsicana Gumbo Busters of the Class D Texas-Oklahoma League that year, hit Joe in the cheekbone while Guess warmed with Riggs Stephenson. But Wood quickly healed from both mishaps. Back on the field on March 22, Joe went 2 for 3 (including a home run) as the Indians defeated the Kansas City Blues 10–3. The next day he tripled against the same team in an eleven-inning 9–9 tie, though he made a crucial error. On the twenty-fourth, versus the Dallas Marines, he was 2 for 4 in a 12–7 win.

Always helpful Joe continued his work with the young Cleveland players. The *Cleveland Press* noted, for example, that he was working with Jim Lindsey, a prospect from Louisiana, on his windup as well as helping Pat McNulty, from Cleveland, chase down deep flies in the outfield. Joe played in games between the Regulars and the Yannigans on both the twenty-seventh and the twenty-ninth but got only a sacrifice fly. As they started north, the Indians played in Oklahoma City, Kansas City, and Des Moines.[24] In Marshalltown, Iowa (the home of Indians president Dunn), Joe was the only offense for the Regulars, who were defeated 5–2 by the Yannigans. Wood got his side's one hit off Guy Morton and then homered off Nelson Pott with a man on in the ninth. On the basis of such performances, Ross Tenney of the *Press* declared on April 10, 1922, that Joe Wood was "pounding the pill as hard as Elmer Smith did." Things looked good for Cleveland's opener on the twelfth against the Tigers (Cobb was out with a sprained ankle) in the newly renamed Dunn Field. It was cloudy and cold that Wednesday as Smoky Joe Wood batted seventh and played right.

Joe started his last season as a Major League baseball player 2 for 4, including a double and a run as the Indians easily defeated the Tigers 7–4. Stuffy McInnis, their new first baseman, was just a home run short of the cycle as Guy Morton pitched a complete game. Joe was equally impressive the next day when he was 2 for 3, with a walk, another double, and two runs scored as the Tribe won 8–3. Although he went 0 for 3 on the fifteenth, Joe was hit by a pitch and scored a run in the Indians' third consecutive win, 11–4, behind Jim Bagby. Once again McInnis had three hits. The next day Joe was 0-3 as the Indians beat the Browns 3–0 to take over first place by themselves. This time Duster Mails looked like he might return to 1920 form as he pitched a complete game shutout. Two days later, in the second game of the series with the Browns, won by Cleveland 17–2 behind Uhle, Wood went 2 for 3, with a walk and a double, and scored two runs. Speaker had four hits, including two doubles, and both Nunamaker and McInnis three apiece (all doubles).

The Indians opened the 1922 season at Dunn Field by winning their first five games. But then they cooled off the rest of April, winning only one game after May 20 and finishing 7-8. Joe, who regularly batted seventh and played right field, hit .333 (19 for 57) for April, with five doubles. In the last two games of the series in Detroit (April 22 and 23), he was 5 for 7, and the next day back in Cleveland against the White Sox, he went 2 for 5, including a lead-off single and the winning run in the tenth inning. Joe also was 3 for 4, with three runs, in a 6–5 loss to the Browns in St. Louis on the twenty-ninth.

The next month Joe ran cold and hot. He was hitless in twelve of the twenty-nine games that month. But he had four hits, three of them doubles, and two runs scored on May 7 in a 10–7 loss to the Browns in Cleveland. On the twenty-ninth, again at Dunn Field, he was 3 for 4 as the Indians beat the White Sox 8–5. In May Joe also had six two-hit games, including a double and a triple on May 27 in Detroit. For May

Joe Wood was 28 for 108, a mediocre .259. He also managed a game. When Speaker came down with a bad cold on May 24, Joe replaced his friend as manager despite dealing with a two-week cold himself. In Joe's one game as interim, he was 0-2, and the Indians lost 6-2.

In June the seesaw rose and fell even more dramatically. In the first two games, on the first and the second, Joe was 4 for 6 with a couple of sacrifices, in games won by the Indians over the Tigers in Cleveland. The Indians were still at home on the eleventh (the day Jim Dunn, who had died of heart failure on the ninth, was buried in Marshalltown, Iowa) when they defeated the Athletics 9–8. Wood was 4 for 4, with two runs scored, a double, and a home run. He also completed a double play on a throw to Steve O'Neill. But in other games before midmonth, he was 4 for 29.

After Joe did not play in five consecutive games in the middle of June, a rumor in Cleveland newspapers said that the Indians were try-ing to recover Elmer Smith, in part because of Wood's diminished pro-duction. But beginning on June 21, 1922, changes rendered such dis-cussion pointless. On June 21, 1922, 550 miles away from Cleveland, in New Haven, Connecticut, John T. Blossom was appointed the athlet-ic director at Yale. Although it would take another three months for that move to affect Wood, on the field that day Joe got his second wind, batting fourth, walking, doubling, and driving in a run. For the rest of June, he was 15 for 32, a blistering .469, including three-hit games on the twenty-third and the twenty-sixth and 4 for 4, with a double and a home run, on June 30.

July was streaky, for both the Cleveland Indians and Joe Wood. Over the first eight games of the month, the team lost six. In those contests Joe was just 7 for 27, despite getting four hits (two in each game), with a double, a stolen base, a sacrifice, and three runs, in a doublehead-er against the Tigers in Detroit on the fourth. Beginning on July 8 the Indians won twelve games in a row on the road. After the first game, in which he was hitless in three at bats, Joe hit in the other eleven games. Batting fourth he had three three-hit games. At the Polo Grounds on the ninth he was 3 for 6, scoring the tying run in the ninth (on a hit by McInnis) as the Indians beat the Yankees 9–7 in thirteen innings. At Fenway on the twelfth, he was 3 for 4, with a hit batsman, three runs scored, and two RBI. Joe was also 3 for 4 on the twenty-second at Washington. Smoky Joe had a two-hit game (a double and a home run) on the seventeenth at Philly. His hit streak reached seventeen games before he went 0 for 4 on the twenty-seventh. For those games he was 25 for 68 (.368), with thirteen runs scored, five doubles, and the two home runs. He also finished the month 4 for 8, with a double, two triples, a stolen base, a sacrifice, and a walk.

As August got under way, some reporters felt that Joe was wearing down from the regular play of 1922. Hugh Fullerton wrote on August 7, 1922, in the *Chicago Tribune* that Jamieson was rising for the Indians but Wood was "slowing down considerably, which, of course, [was] to be expected." Ironically, that day Wood was in the middle of five consecutive two-hit games, in which he batted 10 for 19, with two doubles and a triple. Flourishing after Speaker moved him back to sixth in the order on August 6, Joe had a 3 for 4 game, including a double and a home run, in the first game of a doubleheader at Philadelphia on the fifteenth. On August 18 he tripled in a run and scored in the sixth, then singled two innings later, scoring again. Back in the Polo Grounds on August 23, Wood went 2 for 4 (including a triple to right-center) and had two RBI in the four-run first that led the Indians over the Yankees 4–1. The next day Joe was 2 for 4, with a home run and two RBI, and caught a Ruth drive against the wall in right, doubling Dugan off first. August 26 the *Boston Globe* declared, "'Smoky Joe' Wood is playing great ball.... He is an artist of the first rank." For the month Joe Wood batted .301, with five doubles, three triples, and two home runs.

He slumped a bit at the end of August, going only two for his last fifteen at bats. That ineffectiveness continued into September, his last month in Major League baseball. Joe was hitless in five of Cleveland's first six games that month, leading to a mere 12 for 55 (.218). There were, however, last moments of glory. He had three hits, including a double, on September 2 against the White Sox at Dunn Field in a 2–0 win, and he had two more in St. Louis on the sixth. On September 9 in Chicago he hit a home run, the last of his career, leading off the second inning in a 3–2 victory. With the pennant lost, on September 17 manager Speaker started inserting rookies. That day and the next Joe was only a defensive replacement in center in the first game and a pinch hitter (0 for 1) in the second. Following were six consecutive games he did not play (including, sadly, his last series in Fenway Park). On September 23 at Dunn Field against the Yankees, he was 1-3, with two runs and a double.

The next day there was a dramatic ending to Smoky Joe Wood's career. On September 24, 1922, a Sunday, Dunn Field was filled almost to capacity, with more than twenty thousand attending. The reasons were clear. Even though the Indians were out of the chase, they had a chance to spoil things for the Yankees. And Babe Ruth was in the house. It was a good day for the Indians, as George Uhle beat Bob Shawkey 3–0. Joe started in left field, batting sixth. With the game scoreless in the seventh, Joe was 1 for 2 and scheduled to bat fifth if the Indians rallied. When Wamby went out to start the inning, it looked like Joe would have to wait.

But Homer Summa tripled and Larry Gardner walked. With Wood on deck, Joe Sewell hit a sacrifice fly to right, giving Cleveland the lead as Gardner moved to second. Joe then singled to left, scoring Gardner. With Stuffy McInnis up, the Indians executed the hit and run, with Wood racing to third. Right fielder Babe Ruth bobbled the ball, let it roll five feet away, panicked, and threw to second base. Sensing Ruth's bad decision, Tris Speaker, coaching at third, waved Joe home, where he slid in just ahead of the throw from second baseman Aaron Ward. In his last play Wood stole a run as the Yankees endured another defeat at the hands and feet of Smoky Joe.

The Indians won their last two games against the Tigers at Cleveland, earning fourth place (78-76) at the conclusion of 1922. But by then Joe Wood had left for home, early and permanently. Suddenly, after two seasons in which his hitting skyrocketed in Cleveland, Joe Wood exited the baseball stage. One report, by Francis J. Powers, theorized that after "the departure of Elmer Smith," fans, angry at the performance of the team and nostalgic for Smith, "had given Wood a hard time." Sensitive to such razzing, Joe found that "life at Parker's Glen with Mrs. Wood and the children [held] much allurement." Good copy. But Joe's recollection is more accurate: "Jack Blossom lived in Cleveland [where he had an auto business]" and "was a Yale grad [he played short and captained the 1913–14 baseball teams], and they had just taken him on as a new athletic director. Jack Blossom happened to know Speaker" and "asked him who would be a good man to take over here." Tris mentioned Wood. [25] Joe "was interviewed by this fellow and that fellow and old Yale ballplayers and so on. And finally they decided to take over" his contract to coach freshmen and assist Bernie Tommers.

The announcement came on November 7 that Joe would coach at Yale and assume his duties after the Christmas holidays. Joe was consistent with his explanations. For example, in an interview with Mark Alvarez, published posthumously in 1987, Joe recalled, "When I went to Cleveland in '17, our older son was a year old. I was there [with the Indians] for six years, and I probably could have stayed four or five years longer in the big leagues. But I used to come off a trip and the babies, they didn't know who I was. That kind of worked on me a little. So I came to Yale and took this position where I could be home and be with the family."[26] Joe certainly enjoyed family life with Laura and their bright, active children. But Smoky Joe was also attracted to the security of regular, long-term employment. And Wood was a willful man whose comeback was fueled by a desire to prove himself to just one person: Howard Ellsworth Wood. As he told Lawrence Ritter, "I was satisfied. I figured I'd proved something to myself."[27] Since there was no Hall of Fame, he also couldn't imagine a batting title or more World Series heroics earning him baseball immortality.

Even as he prepared for life after the Majors, Smoky Joe Wood could take satisfaction in his very productive last year. Playing regularly in 1922, as he had in 1918, Joe put up equally impressive numbers. He played 141 games in the outfield, and pinch-hit another time. His 150 hits in 505 at bats gave him a .297 batting average. More impressive were the ninety-two RBI, a record of sorts.[28] The only falling off was in at bats/strikeouts (from 11.4 to 8) and defensive skills. He made a career-high eleven errors in the outfield, a major drop-off from previous years. And his totals for the Cleveland years remained impressive. In his five seasons he played in 460 games and had 1,450 at bats, scoring 202 runs, with a .298 batting average. He had an RBI every 5.3 at bats and slugged as high as .562. Despite Wood's part-time play in 1919–21, only Speaker, Wambsganss, Steve O'Neill, and Larry Gardner played in more games for the Indians between 1918 and 1922.[29]

Smoky Joe Wood came to the Cleveland Indians hoping to resurrect his pitching career. But his shoulder was permanently injured. Joe was flexible and resilient. A natural athlete, he became a useful utility player and outstanding defensive outfielder. Using a thicker bat and choking up for better contact gave him power and a reputation for clutch hitting. As he admitted in 1982, calling his fall from the pinnacle of 1912 frustrating was "putting it mildly." Joe explained, "All my dreams had been shattered, but I decided to prove I was a ballplayer and I made it with Cleveland, who bought me from Boston"[30] With the Indians he didn't just survive. He flourished, especially in 1918, 1921, and 1922. In the process his story, as told by writers like F. C. Lane and Grantland Rice, transcended baseball. For them Smoky Joe Wood's life became a study in courage in the face of unwanted, undeserved challenges. Even Tris Speaker could do no better.

17. Joe and Tris Speaker fishing on Lake
Whitney, Texas, after the 1912 World Series.
Courtesy of Joe Wood Archives and Rob Wood.

18. Joe on the family farm with his
father, John F. Wood, and his sister,
Zoë. Courtesy of Joe Wood Archives
and Rob Wood.

19. The house that Smoky Joe built for his wife, Laura O'Shea Wood, in 1913, with the help of his brother, Harley Cortwright "Pete" Wood. Photo by author.

20. Many of the 1915 Boston Red Sox, a team including some of the most famous and infamous players of all time: Smoky Joe, Babe Ruth, Tris Speaker, Dutch Leonard, and Carl Mays. Courtesy of Joe Wood Archives and Rob Wood.

21. Joe with James C. Dunn, president of the Cleveland Indians, considered by Smoky Joe "the brightest man who was ever owner of a baseball club." Courtesy of Joe Wood Archives and Rob Wood.

22. The draft registration of Howard Ellsworth Wood,
"Base Ball Player," for World War I. He was exempted as
married with a child. Courtesy of National Archives and
Records Administration, Atlanta GA.

23. (*Above*) This swing, improved by choking up on a thick-handled bat, made Joe a clutch hitter for the Cleveland Indians. Courtesy of National Baseball Hall of Fame Library Cooperstown, New York.

24. (*Opposite top*) Cleveland Indian Championship picture, 1920, with Ray Chapman's image inserted in upper left corner. Courtesy of Joe Wood Archives and Rob Wood.

25. (*Opposite bottom*) Joe, his friends, including cook Cubby at Indian Camp, Lord's Valley, Pennsylvania, during the 1920s. Courtesy of Joe Wood Archives and Rob Wood.

CLEVELAND AMERICAN LEAGUE BASE BALL CLUB
CHAMPIONS 1920

26. Joe, Laura, and their children pose
for a family picture in Cleveland, 1922.
Courtesy of David Wood.

NINE

The Yale Years

After attending the fall practice in 1922, Smoky Joe Wood's first official duty for Yale was more social than athletic. On January 25, 1923, he attended a banquet held by George Weiss, owner of the New Haven team in the Eastern League, honoring Wild Bill Donovan for winning both the league championship and a postseason game with Baltimore of the International League in 1922. The celebration at the Hotel Taft in New Haven included sportswriters Grantland Rice, Damon Runyon, Hugh Fullerton, and Fred Lieb. Among the invited players were Frankie Frisch, Stuffy McInnis, Ed Walsh, Hugh Jennings, Kid Gleason, Chief Bender, and Rabbit Maranville. Joe Dugan and Babe Ruth represented the Yankees. In addition to Coach Tommers and athletic director Jack Blossom, present were president of the NL John Heydler, Harry Frazee, and Clark Griffith, and the man who would soon have Joe Wood's reputation in his hands, commissioner of baseball Judge Kenesaw Landis. Joe was a featured guest.

Within three weeks Joe sat high in his new "big Nash" as he rode to his first official day at Yale, February 11, 1923. The next day pitchers and catchers reported. Within six weeks, on March 24, 1923, twenty-two players traveled south for games against Oglethorpe, Mercer, Auburn, Alabama Polytechnic Institute, and the University of Georgia. But the most memorable game that spring was back at Yale Field, on April 12, 1923. That day Lou Gehrig was scheduled to pitch for Columbia, but at the last minute Coach Andy Coakley put Lou on first, where he played flawlessly and, batting third, got two hits, a double, and a run. Yale won 4–3.[1] While leading the freshmen to an 11-0 record by the end of May, Wood helped Coach Tommers develop a solid pitching staff. Meanwhile, on May 1, 1923, rumors surfaced that Joe would replace Tommers at the end of the season. The change became official on June 25, when Bernie became athletic director at Milford School. Two days later Yale defeated Princeton 5–1 at Yankee Stadium, in front of eight thousand fans, to win the Big Three Baseball Championship (Harvard, Princeton, and Yale) as Ray "Ducky" Pond pitched a four-hitter over the Tigers. It was the second consecutive title for Yale.[2]

By the time Joe called his first fall practice, for October 22, 1923, he appointed as freshman coach Clyde Engle, utility player in the American and Federal Leagues, known primarily for hitting the ball dropped by Snodgrass in the 1912 World Series. After retiring from the Cleveland Indians in 1916, Engle had been baseball coach and athletic director at the University of Vermont from 1919 to 1922. Wood and Engle called the batteries together the next spring on February 11, 1924. In March Clyde Milan, speedy outfielder for the Washington Senators until 1922, joined the practices and impressed with his still-considerable skills. Joe Wood's biggest challenge was the loss of pitcher Bill Holabird, a sensation on the 1923 freshman team who didn't return to school. Without depth on the mound, Joe relied heavily on Pond, who was effective when he had control. When Joe had to resort to other pitchers, the team was vulnerable.

Wood's approach was fatherly and methodical. He wrote out detailed strategies in a notebook, using examples from his Major League career to inspire his players. Joe's playbook, kept by his son Bob, offers hints of Wood's style. For the first significant game coached by Joe, won by Yale 4–2 over Fordham, he noted, "Pond 5 Eno 4," naming the pitchers and their innings. He proudly listed the results of key competitions, as when Yale beat Harvard. More personally, Coach Wood encouraged players to "not be afraid of making mistakes or errors as lack of confidence is a ballplayers [*sic*] worst enemy. Confidence is easily half the battle." After reminding the players to back up, hit the cut off, and reposition themselves with each hitter, Joe considered "error[s] of omission" and "mechanical errors" unavoidable. His comments were not "individual criticism" but to benefit "the whole club." But he cautioned, "If one keeps making same mistakes[,] then he lays himself open to criticism or to be taken out of game."

Yale started off well, with Ducky Pond pitching a four-hitter over Columbia and a three-hitter against Catholic University on the southern tour. But Joe had to rush home for a sad ceremony. Sunday, April 20, 1924, was the Bill Donovan Memorial game in New Haven. Donovan had been killed in a train wreck as he traveled to Chicago for the winter baseball meetings. To benefit Donovan's family, the Philadelphia Athletics played a New Haven team before representatives of the Eastern League teams and both Major Leagues, as well as Commissioner Landis. During the game a monument to Donovan was unveiled in center field. Afterward Joe, sportswriter and football innovator Walter Camp, and ex-congressman Tom Reilly were named overseers of the memorial fund.

For the rest of Joe Wood's first year, the team was uneven. They lost two early games to Penn but on April 29 upset powerful Georgia, with Henry Scott pitching a 4–3 victory. And with Ray Pond on the mound, they won 2–1 against Dartmouth and beat Georgetown 1–0 in ten innings. Unfortunately, the bats went cold as Joe began his first Big Three Championship; the Bulldogs were shutout twice by the Princeton Tigers (1–0 and 7–0). But they beat Harvard twice: 3–2 and 8–7 by scoring four in the eighth and two in the ninth. Yale was 15-15, with the Big Three finishing in a three-way tie.

At the conclusion of the 1924 season, the young Wood family retreated to Shohola, Pennsylvania, and Woodtown, with its twin lakes, massive trees, hills, and ubiquitous rhododendrons. While growing up the Wood children became friends with the Hinkles (often flying kites with Donald and Harley), a prominent family that included Ed Hinkle, an early developer who unsuccessfully tried to recruit Joe in real estate.[3] As the children grew older, the Woods chummed with the Durham family, regular vacationers from Greencastle, Indiana. In the railroad town of Port Jervis, New York, they often dined at Flo-Jean's, a popular restaurant overlooking the Delaware River, and visited Rebecca and Zoë in their apartment.[4] Back in New Haven expectations were very high for the 1925 baseball season, especially with the return of pitcher Bill Holabird, undefeated as a freshman in 1923.

But that spring was nearly disastrous. Ducky Pond was wild in losses to Fordham and Catholic University. Only Holabird kept the ship afloat, pitching a five-hitter over William and Mary and a two-hitter against NYU. After the team beat West Virginia, Amherst, Brown, and Columbia, Smoky Joe was given a three-year extension to his contract on May 17, 1925. But Yale lost important games to Cornell, Syracuse, and Colgate. Then, May 30, 1925, began one of the most dramatic finishes in Joe's Yale years. That day the Blue rallied with two runs in the ninth to beat Princeton at New Haven, 7–6, before Princeton evened the series, winning 5–2. Then in consecutive games the Elis won easily over Harvard, 25–15 and 18–4. The rubber game against Princeton on June 20 was at the Polo Grounds. Yale led off 6–2 before Princeton scored three in the bottom of the eighth. Yale responded with three in the ninth before Princeton second baseman Cooper hit a grand slam to tie it. Yale won 10–9 in the tenth, when Pond hit a sacrifice fly, scoring Widdy Neal, who had tripled. Joe noted dryly, "Won Championship."

By early 1926 Smoky Joe had settled into coaching baseball, enjoying his young children, and making regular trips between the Shohola farm, which Joe preferred, and the New Haven environs, Laura's favorite. Despite the complications of raising four children, including twins, Joe had gained the peace he sought when he left Cleveland and the Major Leagues. A minor inconvenience arose when Joe contracted chicken pox as the first full practice was called on March 1, 1926. Unfortunately his illness was a sign of many health issues that year. During the preseason, captain Dan Lindley got appendicitis and Holabird got "the grippe," fancy French for the flu. First baseman William Kline severely sprained an ankle during the southern tour, and shortstop Wayland Vaughan dislocated his shoulder.[5]

In what would soon be revealed as a fortuitous addition, Dean Frederick Jones and Burnside Winslow from Yale's Baseball Committee joined the spring tour. After easy victories over Georgetown and Navy, Joe's team played irregular baseball the rest of April. Once they stumbled into May, the Elis enjoyed one of the best runs of Wood's coaching career. They capped wins over Brown, Columbia, Catholic, and Boston University with Holabird's one-hitter to beat Cornell 4–1 and a victory over Holy Cross for the first time in four years, 6–5. By June Joe Wood's team, with only one regular batting below .300, was considered Yale's best since World War I. In the Big Three competition, the Blue beat Princeton twice, 8–6 and 8–7, by scoring two in the ninth. With Princeton eliminated, on June 22 Yale led Harvard 6–1 after five. But the visitors scored six in the sixth and another in the eighth to upset Yale 8–7. In the return match Yale collapsed and lost 13–5. Despite allowing Harvard to win its first Big Three Championship since 1921, the 1926 Yale baseball team finished 20-10.

Just days after the 1926 season, Smoky Joe Wood learned of another drama brewing far west of New Haven, Connecticut.[6] It began earlier that year with charges by a one-time teammate in Boston who had purchased his first motorcycle with a loan of two hundred dollars from Wood: Hubert Benjamin "Dutch" Leonard. Leonard told AL president Ban Johnson that Joe had conspired with Tris Speaker and Ty Cobb to bet on and fix a game late in the 1919 season. In late spring of 1926, Johnson traveled to Cleveland to inform Speaker, and Cobb learned the allegations from Tigers star outfielder Harry Heilmann. Joe Wood remained out of the loop. He heard of Leonard's accusations by phone from Speaker, who called in late June or early July. For the rest of the summer, there was calm, probably ensured by a payment from Johnson and Frank Navin, Tigers owner, of twenty thousand dollars for the evidence . . . and Dutch Leonard's silence.

With a well-financed Leonard in California, everything remained steady state until September 9, 1926, when Johnson shared this history with the AL club presidents, who informed Commissioner Landis. Beginning the next day Landis telegrammed and phoned Leonard to arrange a meeting in either Chicago or Los Angeles. But Dutch had excuses. First it was business and then his wife's supposed illness. After the 1926 Major League season ended but before Speaker and Cobb made a hunting trip to Jackson Hole, Wyoming, Johnson met with Cobb and Speaker, asking them to resign and accept banishment from the league. The arm-wrestling between Landis and Johnson intensified when the commissioner finally got his interview with Leonard, in Sanger, California, on October 29, 1926.

Leonard reported that after a game (which he pitched and won) on September 24, 1919 (just days before the infamous Series between Chicago and Cincinnati), he had met with Speaker, Wood, and Cobb under the grandstands in Detroit. According to Leonard, Cobb agreed to put up $2,000, Leonard $1,500, and Wood and Speaker each $1,000 for a bet that the Tigers would win the next day against the Indians. Dutch said that they wagered because Speaker assured the group of a Detroit victory. According to Leonard, Speaker said he would pitch himself, if necessary. Besides the profit from the bet, a Tigers victory would increase the chances that Detroit would win third-place money. (Cleveland had clinched second place.) Cobb suggested a Detroit gatekeeper, called Fred West (actually Fred Grasser, who had boxed as Kid West) as the person to place the money, which would be routed through Joe Wood.

On November 3, 1926, after returning from the hunting trip, Ty Cobb submitted his resignation to the Tigers organization as required by Ban Johnson. Thus Ty's twenty-one years with the Detroit Tigers abruptly ended. That was no surprise since Cobb was known for his impatience, anger, even violence. As Charles Alexander has summarized, "A sixth-place finish, slumping attendance at Navin Field in the second half of the season, an antagonistic relationship with the club president, and reports of widespread discontent among the players all added up to a strong case against Cobb's continuing for a seventh year as the Tigers' manager."[7] Meanwhile, Kenesaw Mountain Landis was taking over the inquiry from Ban Johnson. On the eighteenth of November, Leonard was notified of a meeting with Landis and the others, scheduled for 11:00 a.m., Monday, November 29. Leonard again refused. Finally, on November 27, as Landis, Speaker, and Cobb met at the commissioner's office, Joe was included in the process via telephone.

On November 29 Spoke also resigned, ostensibly to rest and end his career on a high note. That action was more surprising than Cobb's quitting since Speaker was popular, respected, and led the Indians of 1926 to within three games of the Ruth and Gehrig Yankees. On December 15 the league left the matter to Landis. By then Joe was on his way to Chicago. Once the winter baseball meetings had ended, the commissioner wired Leonard on the seventeenth to set up another meeting. Dutch refused yet again, in a phone conversation with Landis's secretary, Leslie O'Connor. So Commissioner Landis decided to meet anyway — with West and the others — on December 20. The meeting took place at 2:00 p.m. at Landis's office in the People's Bank Building, 122 South Michigan Street. By then Joe had been in the Windy City for almost a week, meeting with Tris, Ty, and lawyers. Strengthened by their legal rights, the three declared Leonard's absence prejudicial and gave the impression that proceedings had become a whitewash.

The primary material evidence was two letters to Leonard. One was from Ty Cobb, dated October 23, 1919, referencing "our business proposition" in which Cobb's side offered $2,000 "to put into it" while "the other side quoted . . . $1,400," though the money was gathered too late. In Ty's words, "When we finally secured that much it was about two o'clock and they refused to deal with us, as they had men in Chicago to take the matter up with and they had no time, so we completely fell down and of course we felt badly about it." He added, "Everything was open to Wood and he can tell you about it when we get together." The other letter was from Joe, posted from Cleveland, only dated "Friday," and noting an enclosed check for $1,630. The letter began: "The only bet West could get up was $600 against $420 (10 to 7)," then added, "Cobb did not get up a cent. He told us that and I believe[d] him." Joe claimed, "We won the $420. I gave West $30, leaving $390, or $130 for each of us."[8]

The formal questioning took place on December 20, 1926, once again in Landis's office. In his testimony Joe admitted to meeting with Leonard at the ballpark and placing a bet with West at the Cadillac Hotel, as well as receiving the winnings at the train station. He claimed some money was his, neither Speaker nor Cobb had bet anything, and these actions were unknown to Speaker, on or off the field. Joe also supported Cobb's testimony, remembering Cobb's inquiry as "none of his [Ty's] business" and therefore deserving of Joe's "anonymous answer." Mysteriously, Wood said an unidentified "friend" "from Cleveland" was the third party. Joe also declared that there was no meeting the next spring between him and Leonard (when Dutch claimed to have reexamined Joe about Cobb's bets). Joe suggested that Leonard's charges were motivated by Dutch's being "very bitter against Mr. Cobb because he let [Leonard] go to the Coast League." Later, when Landis and O'Connor quizzed Joe about the "Cleveland" person, Ty interrupted and diverted the discussion away from the topic. (See analysis of this testimony in light of the Ritter and Murdock tapes, in chapter 10).

The information and testimony were released to the press the next day, December 21, 1926, as requested by Cobb and Speaker, effectively trumping any previous actions by Ban Johnson. Most of it, edited to focus on Leonard's charges, appeared in newspapers around the country. The next night, December 22, Joe left Chicago by train for New Haven. On the afternoon of the twenty-third, he met for two hours with Harold F. Woodcock, business manager of the Athletic Association, and Burnside Winslow, chairman of the Yale Baseball Advisory Committee, the man who had accompanied Joe on the spring baseball trip. The chairman of the Board of Athletic Control was also alerted. Afterward Yale announced that no decision would be made until early January.

Local papers defended Wood for his stand against gambling in college athletics but also suggested that Clyde Engle would replace Joe if a change was warranted. Meanwhile, Joe returned to Cleveland on the twenty-ninth, where he and Speaker employed high-powered attorneys William A. Boyd and Edward L. Burke. He also met with Cobb and Ty's attorney, James O. Murfin. With the strategy set, Joe returned to New Haven just after the first.[9]

On January 4, 1927, the Yale Athletic Board of Control met in the trophy room of the gymnasium from 8:00 p.m. until after midnight. The university tried to appear casual, noting that many cases were under consideration and Joe wasn't required to appear. The next day Professor Nettleton, chairman of the board, made the announcement: "No action has been taken or is now contemplated by the board of control of the Yale University Athletic Association to alter its existing relations with Joe Wood. During his terms of service at Yale he has confirmed in character and conduct the definite endorsements which led to his appointment as athletic coach. The board of control possesses no evidence which, in its judgment, discredits the honesty and integrity of his past record." Joe didn't elaborate for the press. Soon papers announced that Yale freshman players would report on February 22, 1927, the varsity infielders and outfielders on March 1, regular rituals of the ivied institution.[10]

This episode didn't hurt Smoky Joe Wood at Yale. On Saturday, January 8, 1927, the following letter appeared in the local paper:

> We always had a leaning toward Yale and this leaning hasn't been straightened back any by the action of the Yale athletic officials in standing by Joe Wood, former major leaguer accused of betting on a game by "Dutch" Leonard. It seems that Old Eli has taken the view that, if Wood did do what Leonard says he did, it wasn't so terribly terrible and that, anyway, they don't believe it and that Joe, since becoming a coach at Yale, has been a fine gentleman, a successful coach and a wonderful influence on the young athletes over whom he has had supervision.[11]

Crucially, Joe gained support from alumni, who fell in line with the athletic department and Yale authorities. Early in 1927 the *Yale Alumni Weekly* declared the decision "eminently reasonable," "sportsmanlike," and "fair to Mr. Wood" since charges were "sensational" versions of an "old scandal." The *Weekly* said the judgment gave "much relief among Yale men."

Landis was nearly ready to act on the Leonard charges. On January 24, 1927, he called a meeting at the Blackstone Hotel in Chicago with AL team presidents to receive additional material claimed by Ban Johnson. When they found nothing new, Johnson, apparently caught in a bluff and nearly prostrate from stress, took a leave of absence from the presidency of the league. Frank Navin was appointed acting AL president. Three days later Landis gave a brief statement on the accusations: "These players have not been, nor are they now, found guilty of fixing a ball game. By no decent system of justice could such a finding be made." Conspicuous in its absence was any reference to betting on baseball, the focus of most of the hearing.[12] In clear opposition to Ban Johnson's decree, Landis judged the players could remain in the AL, with clubs other than Cleveland and Detroit. Though the verdict ignored Wood, behind the scenes Landis offered to help Joe with any problems at Yale.[13]

Joe looked to the 1927 baseball season for a return to normalcy. With thirteen players back from 1926, Yale fielded a very competitive team. But even on the April tour, the Leonard affair wouldn't disappear. In a show of support for Joe, Tris Speaker appeared at the game against Georgetown on April 11, sitting on the Yale bench the day before his 1927 team, the Washington Senators, opened at home against the Red Sox. After a shaky start in which the Yale won two and lost three, Joe returned to Connecticut and more scandal-tinged drama. The Leonard episode gave special meaning to an exhibition game in New Haven on April 24, 1927, between All-Stars of the Eastern League team (which included Clyde Milan) and Connie Mack's Philadelphia A's. Before the game a clock was presented to Mack and a rifle to the new member of the A's, Ty Cobb. The crowd gave a loud ovation when Ty came to bat in the first. Among those cheering for Ty was Joe Wood, from his front-row box seat. Cobb reached on a base hit, but the Eastern Leaguers won, 3–2.

Things finally settled for Joe when the 1927 Yale baseball season began in earnest. When Bill Holabird or sophomore R. A. Sawyer pitched well, Yale was strong, beating Penn, Columbia, Cornell, Catholic University, and Cornell. But when the bats went cold, the Bulldogs were shut-out by Georgetown (3–0) and Holy Cross (7–0). June began wonderfully when Sawyer threw a one-hitter against Princeton, in a 4–0 win on June 4. Yale followed with another win over the Tigers, 4–3, on the eighteenth. But Harvard defeated Yale on June 21 and 22, 10–6 and 6–5 (when Harvard's captain, Izzy Zarakov, hit a two-run homer with two out in the bottom of ninth), to take the Big Three once again. Yale finished 18-14. After all the drama off the field that year, Joe hurried into the 1928 season, hoping for a renewal. Following their eastern trip with the usual suspects, the team was a disappointing 2-3, and star Bruce Caldwell had a broken hand. When they returned to Yale Field, sporting a new steel and concrete grandstand that covered half the twelve thousand seats, and continued losing, Joe made major shifts in the lineup.

By May 16, when the sons of Eli beat Williams 3–2, they enjoyed a nine-game winning streak. After Yale beat Princeton 8–3 on June 2, the team seemed poised to take back the Big Three title from Harvard. (With such recent success on June 14 the contracts of both Wood and Engle were renewed for another three years.) On June 16 at Princeton, Yale took the Tigers 10–1, with Caldwell getting a single, a double, and two triples. The Bulldogs also took the first game against Harvard, 3–2, and the next day at Soldiers Field in Boston took a 4–1 lead in the ninth. But two walks, a wild pitch, and a passed ball opened the door to four Harvard runs. In the decider at Cambridge, Massachusetts, Harvard won 2–1 in thirteen innings, scoring on a bases-loaded error. That day Bruce Caldwell signed with ex-umpire Billy Evans and Joe's old team the Cleveland Indians, who beat out the Yankees for his services.[14] Despite a slow start the Yale baseball team improved to 20–13 in 1928.[15]

As the Depression became real, Joe took a cut in salary from $7,500 to $5,000. But that was enough income to support his simple life, including his off-season time in the Shohola area, where the Twin Lakes had become popular. Camp Shawnee was a summer place for boys, and the Watson Boarding House was famous as the retreat of Lionel and Ethel Barrymore. Some homes were connected to the Wood family. George Stark, a cousin to the Wood children and the son of an early leader of the Salvation Army, resided there. After Aunt Beck from the Wood clan married a Bradford, she, her husband, and their daughter ran a boarding home called the Bradford House. Joe retained Indian Camp for his reunions as the hunting season opened each December. Clyde Engle joined what Joe identified as the core "members of that gang: Steve O'Neill, Ed Klepfer, Bill Wambsganss, Elmer Smith, and Stan Coveleski."[16] Smoky Joe also established a hunting club on the home place, where local men pursued deer and raccoons.

Unlike the previous couple of years, the "Woodmen" of 1929 got off to a fast start, sweeping all games in their eastern trip. Glowing with such victories Yale announced on April 11 it would join Pennsylvania, Princeton, Columbia, Cornell, and Dartmouth in creating the Eastern Intercollegiate Baseball League. After losing to Dartmouth, the team followed with wins over Penn, Columbia, and Providence, but Joe's team couldn't win against top opponents like Holy Cross and Cornell. The season once again came down to the Big Three. After splitting games with Princeton, Yale beat Harvard easily 16–1 and 6–4. In the deciding game at the Polo Grounds, Princeton won 10–4 despite Fay Vincent's double and triple and a homer by catcher Johnny Hoben. Yale finished 17-10.

Excellence in Yale baseball continued in the new decade. In 1930, the year Yale joined the Eastern Intercollegiate Baseball League (EIBL), Albie Booth became the shortstop and Fay Vincent rose to greatness at first.[17] For Joe the most irritating change required coaches to sit in the stands during games, to encourage independence and leadership among the players.[18] In the first EIBL game at Yale Field, on April 12,

1930, Joe faced his 1912 World Series adversary, Jeff Tesreau, as the Blue beat Dartmouth 4–3. Early in the season Yale had enough pitching to seize first place in the conference by winning over Penn 8–3 behind three hits from Vincent and the pitching of Roswell "Hoppy" Rudd. But Yale lost the rematch 10–2. The rest of May the Bulldogs won over Columbia, Cornell, Colgate, and Syracuse before losing to Georgetown, 10–9. In June Yale lost two 1–0 games, to Providence and Brown, as Dartmouth won the first EIBL championship. But the Big Three competition remained. In 1930 Yale and Harvard split their games, with no playoff between those teams. There was one with Princeton. After Yale beat Princeton 11–7 in New Haven and lost at Princeton for the first time since 1925, a tie-breaker was played at the Polo Grounds on June 21, 1930. Yale won 10–9 in eleven innings, on a bad-hop single through shortstop. With that victory Yale finished 1930 14-13.

Still fit at forty Smoky Joe Wood returned to Boston Braves Field on September 8, 1930, in support of a local children's hospital and needy ex-players. Over twenty-two thousand fans watched a team of All-Stars from the Boston NL and AL teams play against stars from other teams. The Boston side included the famous outfield from the Red Sox — Harry Hooper, Duffy Lewis, and Tris Speaker — as well as Cy Young, Jimmy Collins, and Larry Gardner. Their captain was Bill Carrigan. The opposition included the Philadelphia one-hundred-thousand-dollar infield of Eddie Collins, Home Run Baker, Stuffy McInnis, and Jack Barry, as well as Johnny Evers, Honus Wagner, Jack Coombs, Ed Walsh, Chief Bender, Jeff Tesreau, and Ty Cobb. Their captain was Fred Mitchell. Joe was 0 for 1 and pitched two innings, giving up three hits. He also played center as Boston won 8–4.[19]

Joe was also enjoying many reunions with ex–Major Leaguers coaching for teams played by Yale. Jack Slattery, with Washington when he opposed Joe in 1909, was at Harvard during 1923. Bill Clarke, who had played at Baltimore, Boston, and New York of the NL and Washington in the AL just before Wood got to Boston, coached Princeton until 1927 (he returned there in 1934). Jeff Tesreau, of course, coached Dartmouth throughout Joe's tenure at Yale. Similarly, Jack Barry of the famous A's infield returned to coach the Holy Cross Crusaders against the Bulldogs. Wood's ex-teammate Larry Gardner went back to Vermont as the baseball coach in 1929, where he would remain until Joe left Yale. Most immediately, Harry Hooper coached Princeton for the 1931–32 seasons (with Tris Speaker joining in the 1931 conditioning program).[20] And Andy Coakley, who had played in the AL before Joe and in the Majors until 1911, was at Columbia.

In 1931 Yale again was quick out of the gate. Led by cleanup hitter and captain Fay Vincent and Albie Booth, shifted to the outfield at the beginning of the season, the Bulldogs defeated Virginia twice, Columbia, and Dartmouth to remain undefeated. But their early lead in the EIBL disappeared on April 18, when they lost to Columbia, 7–6 in eleven innings. Things started slipping away on April 25, when the league-leading Penn Quakers won 3–2. Yale stayed in the league race by defeating Cornell and the Princeton Tigers. But at the Princeton graduation, Yale got only three hits and lost 3–1. The Blue then defeated Harvard 7–3 at New Haven on June 16, but Harvard scored three runs in the ninth to win 4–3 the next day in Cambridge. With that upset Penn won the EIBL. But on June 20 at Yankee Stadium, Yale defeated Princeton 13–6 by scoring seven runs in the eighth. Yale then took the Big Three by beating Harvard 4–3 in ten innings, ending 1931 with a 15-9 record.

Before the 1932 baseball season, Yale experienced major gains and losses. Expectations were raised when Johnny Broaca, star of the 1931 freshman team, became eligible for the varsity. But tragedy also struck over the summer when the appointed captain Ed Warren lost his left arm in a boating accident on Racquette Lake in New York. Also Albie Booth continued his visits to a Wallingford sanatorium for treatment of a lung infection that shortened his captaincy of Yale basketball. Even with these subtractions Yale was expected to contend in the Eastern League and win more "gold baseballs" as Big Three champ. Encouraging was an opening 8–3 win over Springfield, with Broaca pitching four hitless innings and striking out seven of fourteen batters. In the EIBL opener

Johnny also defeated Columbia 10–6 while striking out a league record thirteen. Nine days later Broaca again beat the Lions, 2–1, retiring the first ten and last eight and striking out ten in a four-hitter.

But Yale suffered triple losses on April 23. Penn beat them 8–0 in Philadelphia, Broaca left the game with a sore arm in the first, and the Bulldogs fell from first place in the EIBL. They regained the lead on April 30 at Yale Field by winning 4–3 over Penn in ten. On May 3 Yale easily beat Wesleyan 15–2. But the best story was in right field, where Joe played captain Ed Warren, who singled, scored a run, and drove in one while making two errorless plays in the outfield . . . with only a right arm. After Yale split a doubleheader with Dartmouth, they tied Princeton, both 4–2 in the EIBL. Then Booth returned in the second week of May, and Yale hit stride, beating Cornell twice and previously unbeaten Providence. With both the Big Three competition and the EIBL title at stake, on June 11 at Yale Field Johnny Broaca pitched all twelve innings in a 5–4 win over Princeton. A week later Yale won 6–3 at Princeton for Joe and Yale's first EIBL title. It looked as if Yale would sweep the championships when they beat Harvard 4–2, with Albie Booth hitting a grand slam. But Harvard won the final two games as Yale finished 17–11.

In response to the Depression, Yale reduced the cost of tickets, drafted plans to eliminate the central training table, and dropped the spring tour. But more difficult than the financial crisis was Johnny Broaca. He was as negative on the 1933 year as he had been positive in 1932.[21] The team opened the season without Broaca, suspended for missing practice. Although Joe at first declared Johnny wouldn't join the team on the New York trip, the coach later accepted that his star had been unavoidably detained at his home in Lawrence, Massachusetts. Broaca responded by throwing a four-hitter in a 1–0 loss to Columbia. Three days later ex–Harvard star Charlie Devens of the New York Americans no-hit Yale in a New Haven exhibition, won by the Yanks 6–0.[22] That day Joe's youngest son, Bob, stood mesmerized while watching Lou Gehrig though the batting cage. Afterward the Iron Horse kidded him, "What's the matter? Don't Yale bat boys talk?" For years Bob cherished his picture standing sheepishly next to Gehrig, wearing Lou's glove. (Bob remembered selling a Gehrig-signed ball and the picture for nine thousand dollars.)[23]

Riding Broaca and the seesaw, Joe's team beat Dartmouth, lost to Penn, and gave Columbia their first league loss, 3–1. When the Bulldogs won the Penn rematch 7–6, they climbed back into the EIBL race. But Yale's next game, lost 8–0 to New Haven semipro team the Chevies (named for a local car dealer coowned by Albie Booth), changed the history of Yale baseball. That day Johnny Broaca refused to take the mound. The next day Joe banished him from the team, without comment. Broaca enjoyed giving his side. which was reported in the May 4, 1933, *New York Times*: "Last Friday I pitched a hard game against Columbia, and when Wood called upon me to pitch yesterday I recalled the advice given me [not to pitch more than once per week]. He said to me, 'You're through.' Very regretfully, I left the squad, for I wished to obey every order given me by captain or coach. I have no criticism of Coach Wood, but I do not see how I could have acted differently." Actually Broaca wanted to be paid, like the Chevies.

The Yale team responded well to the loss of Broaca, beating Dartmouth and Colgate, then shutting out Cornell 2–0 and 1–0 in a New Haven doubleheader. They had a chance to repeat as EIBL champs if they could sweep Princeton and Harvard.[24] But Yale failed in the first game; Princeton won 10–7 by scoring five runs in the ninth. (Meanwhile Broaca took solace from his imagined mistreatment from Coach Wood by signing with the Yankees on June 2.)[25] With George Parker five-hitting Princeton to win 6–0, Yale evened that series before beating Harvard 5–3 and 4–2, finishing one-half game behind Columbia in the EIBL. When Yale lost the playoff to Princeton 5–2, the Blue finished 17-12.

In another economy move, in 1934 the playoff game in the Big Three was discontinued. In response to the various retrenchments, Coach Wood focused his season on pitcher and captain George Parker and conference games. Yale opened well, beating Dartmouth 9–3. But they were blasted by Fordham 14–3 at Yale Field, and then Parker lost twice, to Penn 1–0 and in relief to the NYU Violets 4–3. There was a final thrill when a 4–3 win over Penn in eleven innings brought Yale within a half game of league-leading Cornell. But in May Yale lost games to Brown, Dartmouth, and twice to both Cornell and Columbia, dropping precipitously in the EIBL. In the traditional rivalries Yale beat Princeton 3–1 (on a three-hitter from Parker) and 14–5, before falling to Harvard 3–2. Even after Bernie Rankin shut out Harvard 2–0, Yale finished 5-7 in the EIBL and 8-13 overall, Joe's first losing season.

There was sadness off the field as well. That summer, on July 18, 1934, Laura's father died in Kansas City. While wife and husband mourned the loss of Mr. O'Shea, there was renewed hope with Yale baseball. The freshman team had dominated in 1934 with Larry Kelley playing first and Walter Klimczak third. Another prospect was closer to home. All the Wood children were natural athletes, including Virginia, who became a talented golfer. Predictably, the boys were gifted in baseball. In addition to competition at school, they played regularly at Donovan Field in West Haven and at Lighthouse Point in East Haven for city teams. They also joined colonial and industrial leagues, playing for teams like the Hillcrests and Story's Dairy. By 1934 the oldest, Joe Frank Wood, was leading the way, indicated by his two-hitter for Hillhouse High in a 13–0 win over Yale's junior varsity on May 4. He would later play at Yale.[26]

Joe was impatient to rebuild Yale baseball. He called the pitchers and catchers together on January 21, claiming "a whole new team" and a pitching staff focused on control. There were concerns. Johnny Broaca was irretrievably lost, already playing his second season with the New York Yankees. Larry Kelley was a question mark since being dismissed from the basketball team for throwing his jersey at Coach Elmer Ripley. But on February 16, 1935, permission was granted for a baseball trip to Japan, like Harvard's the previous year. Then another seesaw season began. Yale opened 1935 with an easy 16–4 win over Trinity, with Klimczak and Kelley the offensive stars and Louis Walker giving up just three hits and no runs over five innings. But they lost the EIBL opening games to Penn, 4–3 and 1–0, before bouncing back by beating Penn 7–6, rallying from a 6–2 deficit in the seventh.

The bumpy road returned when Yale lost to Dartmouth, split a doubleheader with Columbia, and lost to Cornell. They reversed things again by handing Dartmouth their first loss on May 15, behind Klimczak's five hits, including the game winner in the bottom of ninth, and Larry Kelley's home run. Continuing the pattern, a loss to Cornell was followed by wins against Brown and Cornell. True to form, poor pitching led to losses against Fordham (7–2) and the Holy Cross (14–4), but then Ted Horton pitched a two-hit shutout of Princeton 6–0 in a rain-shortened game, with Kelley going 2 for 2. As the season drew to a close, Joe's team suffered losses to Princeton 8–7, when the Tigers scored five runs in the ninth, and Harvard, 4–2 in thirteen innings. In a final reversal Yale easily took Harvard twice, 9–2 and on Regatta Day, 6–2 behind Ted Horton's five-hitter, to finish 12-12.

In the midst of this roller-coaster ride was an entertaining and resourceful game between Yale's regulars and a "picked" team, played on June 11. All three Wood boys joined Albie Booth, Bruce Caldwell, Ducky Pond, and others as the opposition. With Bob playing first, Steve third and right field, and Joe pitching, the Woods went a combined 3 for 7, including a triple and three RBI by Steve and a stolen base and three runs by Bob. The Yale players won 13–9, with Johnny Dugan, Larry Kelley, and Walter Klimczak all homering. Kelley was only a single short of hitting for the cycle. The proceeds supported the Yale baseball team's trip to Japan. Using the profits of the game, as well as substantial funds from Japan (particularly Waseda University), fifteen Yale players set out a month later, on July 11, 1935.

On Monday, July 15, the team, escorted by faculty member Dr. Andrew Barr Jr. was welcomed to San Francisco by Yale alums. The next day they sailed for Honolulu, where they played local and service teams and finished 3-4 over sixteen days. After leaving Hawaii on August 6, they arrived on August 15 in Yokohama and traveled on to Tokyo. While in

Japan Yale faced Waseda, Keio, Meiji, and Kwansei Universities, as well as teams from Tokyo and Osaka; the team finished 4-6-1. One player, whose rich father paid his son's bills (including gambling debts, as long as the boy didn't drink), became homesick and returned from Honolulu, to Joe's relief.

Naive about foreign places, Joe sounded like the Ugly American: "They used human excrement for fertilizer over there. And you'd get out in the street and get behind them in an automobile, it was just murder." The noise disrupted his routine: "In the morning they'd wake you up by coming down the streets in those wooden shoes." He expected better engineering: "Everything was this [flimsy] bamboo stuff," and the Japanese drove "on the wrong side of the street." A typical U.S tourist, Joe at least "got a bunch of beautiful silk shirts, robes, handkerchiefs, and underwear, all monogrammed" and delivered "in an hour."

Always conscious of money, Joe remembered that Yale paid for the chaperone and the travel to San Francisco. After that Japan handled everything, including the time in Honolulu. The food was "beautiful" on the boat, and the team "taxied up to the Imperial Hotel in Tokyo" where they stayed "most of the time." "When we left there, we went up to Kyoto, played a couple of games there. Took a boat and made another stop at Yokohama on the way home," he recalled. Some critics were unhappy that the foreigners won most games. But Joe felt the results inevitable at prestigious schools like Yale, Harvard, or Princeton. If the United States wanted to win, they should have taken, he said, teams from Holy Cross, Fordham, Boston College, or Providence. After the brutalities of World War II, Joe wondered if Yale baseball had been the pawn of Japanese propaganda. All the picture-taking was suspicious.[27]

The Yale team returned to San Francisco on September 25. Three of the players — Larry Kelley, Tommy Curtin, and Bernard Rankin — immediately flew to New Haven because they were late for football practice. Another player, Richard Cummins, was even later since his parents forbade his flying. He took the train. While in Los Angeles Joe predicted that the Cubs, who reminded him of the 1914 Boston Braves, would win the 1935 World Series. As Cubs fans know, on October 7 Joe was proved wrong. Back in New Haven Joe watched the Hopkins Prep footballers lose 18–7 to the Yale 150-pound team. Playing left end and kicking the extra point for the losers was Joe Frank Wood. On the baseball field, with Klimczak and Kelley at third and first and senior Tommy Curtin as captain, things looked promising. Curtin joined the batteries on January 18, 1936, with the first indoor workout on February 3. But Tommy didn't play for Yale that year.

Nineteen thirty-six was a year of unmet expectations. On February 7 Curtin came down with what appeared to be influenza. When he didn't recover, he was put in St. Luke's Hospital in his hometown of Pittsfield, Massachusetts. The diagnosis was leucopenia, chronically low white-blood-cell count. He was hemorrhaging and required blood transfusions, given by a circle of supporters, from his brother to friends and classmates. Meanwhile, on March 5, Yale announced that the eastern trip would be resumed, beginning on March 28, including games against universities, the Quantico Marines, and Norfolk of the Piedmont League, and the launching of the aircraft carrier *Yorktown* on April 4. But in less than a week that trip was canceled. After nine blood transfusions Curtin was still listed as critical. Anxiety filled the gymnasium as the Yale baseball team practiced outdoors for the first time on March 16, 1936.

On April 6 their captain and second baseman had his fourteenth transfusion. Two days later Yale made seven errors and lost to Springfield College 8–2. That day Curtin had his sixteenth transfusion. After beating Wesleyan (3–1) behind the pitching of Ted Horton and Bernie Rankin and Williams 6–5 in ten innings, Yale split a doubleheader versus Penn in Philly, with Larry Kelley hitting a homer and a double (four RBI) in the victorious second game, 11–2. Off the field Curtin was reported somewhat improved as he received his nineteenth transfusion on the twenty-first. The next day Yale won 4–2 over Providence, with Lou Walker pitching a five-hitter and Kelley getting three hits, including a double and two RBI. After losing to Dartmouth 3–1, the team responded with a 14–7 whipping of Columbia in New York on April 29.

Three days later captain Tommy Curtin died, after twenty-one trans-fusions, on Saturday, May 2, 1936. He was twenty-two. The doctors remained baffled, taking comfort in xenophobia by saying he may have contracted a disease in Japan. Influenza was also mentioned. But they really didn't know. Curtin was an exemplary student athlete, regularly on the dean's list. In addition to playing baseball, he was a basketball and football star, playing receiver and place kicker. The day he died Yale lost to Dartmouth 9–3 in Hanover, New Hampshire. Before the game there was a thirty-second silence honoring Curtin. The funeral was held in Tommy's hometown, Pittsfield, Massachusetts, at Sacred Heart Church. Among those serving as pallbearers were teammates Larry Kelley and Bernie Rankin. In attendance were baseball coaches Wood and Engle. Tommy was buried in St. Joseph's Cemetery.

The Yale baseball team struggled the rest of the 1936 season, but there were bright moments. On May 16 they defeated Cornell 4–1 at Yale Field, with Ted Horton hitting a two-run home run and Lou Walker (uncle of President George Herbert Walker Bush) pitching a five-hitter. And on June 3 they handed Holy Cross their second loss of the season, 4–2. But Yale then lost key games to Brown and Princeton and was no-hit by Japanese pitcher Wakahara of Waseda University on June 8, followed by another loss to Brown, 5–3 in ten innings. Playing spoiler Yale beat Princeton 13–6, with Kelley using a single, a double, and a home run for four RBI, and then Harvard twice, dropping the Crimson into a tie with Dartmouth in the EIBL. But Yale lost 3–0 to Harvard on Regatta Day, lowering their record to 11-13, Wood's second losing season. At least on December 1, 1936, Larry Kelley won the second trophy given by the Downtown Athletic Club, the first time it was called the Heisman Trophy.

There was one more significant loss in the Wood family before Joe could return to baseball in 1937. On January 12, 1937, Laura's mother died in Kansas City, less than three years after her husband. Once again there was little time for grief as the batteries reported in mid-January, with the first practice on Monday, February 1. Meanwhile, a circus atmosphere surrounded captain Kelley, who was starring in basketball and repeatedly turning down offers to play professional baseball and basketball. Early on, Yale showed its potential by defeating Columbia 17–2 (with Kelley driving in four on three hits and sophomore Eddie Collins Jr. going 5 for 5) and St. John's, 4–2, on Monroe Jubitz's four-hitter. After victories over Penn and Brown, Yale lost to Columbia, 4–3, despite nine Lion errors, three by shortstop Sid Luckman.[28]

Yale stayed in the race by taking a doubleheader from Cornell, 3–1 and 3–0, with Jubitz throwing a one-hitter in the second game. But a Yale loss at Hanover, New Hampshire, 3–1, gave Dartmouth essentially a two-game lead in the EIBL. After the Blue also lost to Holy Cross, Yale slipped to third place. But Yale bounced back by beating first-place Dartmouth 10–3 at Derby Day on May 22. The turnaround was complete on June 9, when Yale beat Fordham 6–4. The next day Harvard beat Dartmouth twice, opening the door for Yale.

The Bulldogs responded by beating Princeton 9–2, behind Horton's pitching and Larry Kelley's 3-4, including a double and a home run. Yale kept the EIBL lead by beating Princeton again, 13–4, as Klimczak got five RBI on a double and a three-run home run. On June 22 the Elis won Joe Wood's second EIBL title by beating Harvard 7–6 in fifteen innings. The next day Harvard beat Yale, 10–7, but at the Regatta Yale won easily, 13–3, with Eddie Collins Jr. hitting three singles, a double, and a homer and Larry Kelley (in his finale) making three hits, including a double and a triple.[29] The 1937 team was Joe Wood's best, 21-7.

Larry Kelley refused to turn pro, in either football or baseball, reportedly turning down five thousand dollars from the St. Louis Cardinals and their vice president Branch Rickey to play baseball and become an executive with the team. Kelley instead took a summer European tour, a job at his alma mater Peddie School, and graduate work at Princeton. When the final EIBL records were released, Yale had the best fielding average, and Eddie Collins Jr. hit .396 as a sophomore. On the Fourth of July Ted Horton signed with the Toronto Maple Leafs of the International League, where he played ten games before leaving baseball. Later that summer Walt Klimczak also signed with the Maple Leafs, though he only played one game that year.[30] On October 1 Joe presented the Malcolm Farmer Awards to Horton for service and Eddie Collins Jr. as most valuable. Track star George Weed received the first Thomas F. Curtin Jr. Award on November 25, for excellence in scholarship and athletics.

Meanwhile, the Wood children enjoyed many sports. The Yale swimming coach took them to the pool, and they played golf in New Haven and Port Jervis, where Joe had a lifetime membership after helping rebuild a burned clubhouse.[31] Joe liked beer, always enjoying a bottle or two after golf, but he always preached moderation to his children, important in Shohola since Art Rohman was open on Sundays and, as Bob Wood explained, "no one bucked Art."[32] In New Haven they lived in a Westville stucco house that they had rented since 1936, northwest of New Haven and not far from the Yale Golf Course. In 1938 they bought a permanent home across the street, at 90 Marvel Road, from an employee of the chamber of commerce relocating to Dayton, Ohio. The security they found there helped ameliorate the loss of Joe's mother, Rebecca, on April 14, 1938. Despite her long estrangement from John F., Becca was buried in the Wood cemetery near Shohola.

At least Joe had Yale baseball. With the team weakened by the losses of Horton, Kelley, and Klimczak, Joe repositioned Eddie Collins Jr. from second base to center field, giving speed and stability to the outfield for the 1938 season. With this new lineup Yale won early games over Columbia and Penn while losing to Cornell. Pitcher Moe Jubitz and catcher Paul Wargo led the way.[33] A loss to Brown was redeemed by victories over Dartmouth and Columbia, with Collins and right fielder Greg Doonan both having four hits. But then came a losing streak to Army, Cornell, Dartmouth, and Princeton, 2–1 when the Tigers scored two in the ninth with two outs. At least Yale finished strong in 1938. They won the rematch with Princeton on June 18, 5–2, and then upset Harvard 5–0 on June 21, as Jubitz pitched a four-hitter. After Harvard won the next day, 6–3, Yale won the final game, on June 24 in New

London, Connecticut, 7–6. With his father present Eddie Collins Jr. was made captain.

Eddie, also a halfback in football, hit .366 in 1938, playing both the outfield and the infield. With Joe's coaching the team was again top in EIBL fielding, but the hitting was next to last. The best Yale could do that year was .500, at 13-13, though the team could claim the remnants of the Big Three championship. In the off-season the university announced on December 5, 1938, that the team would resume a southern trip (dropped in 1935) for 1939, playing Navy, Richmond, and the Georgetown Hoyas. On December 23, wrestler Herbert Pickett won the second Thomas Curtin Scholarship. Before the 1939 season, media noted that Eddie Collins Jr. was endorsing a drive to conquer infantile paralysis. Interestingly, Joe's sister Zoë was not mentioned, though Yale was a leader in polio research.

The Achilles heel of the 1939 team, weak hitting, was exposed immediately. On April 7, 1939, Yale was no-hit by University of Richmond sophomore Ned Butcher. The next day Joe Frank Wood, often called Joe Jr., pitched his first varsity game for Yale, at the University of Virginia. He took a 4–3 lead into the eighth, but faltered and lost 8–4, though he had three hits. The pattern was repeated on April 10 at Georgetown; leading 4–2 after five, the Bulldogs gave up three in the eighth and lost 6–4, with Joe Wood losing in relief. Back home Moe Jubitz won two four-hitters, against a New Haven team (including Walt Klimczak, who played that year in the Can-Am and International Leagues) and Cornell. But then the Bulldogs lost to Brown, Dartmouth, twice to Penn, and Holy Cross.

Finally Yale showed life in mid-May. On the tenth Joe Frank won his first game, a five-hitter against Brown, 8–2, walking six but striking out nine. After losing to Cornell the Elis beat the Columbia Lions twice, 8–7 (with Joe pitching a complete game) and 18–11 (with Harry Holt getting five hits, Collins three, and Joe Wood hitting a home run). On May 27, 1939, the day freshman Ted Harrison struck out twenty against Harvard, the varsity defeated Tufts 4–2 on Jubitz's five-hitter. But the only significant win the rest of the year came on June 3, when

Yale beat Princeton 3–2, with Joe Frank driving in the winning run in the ninth. They lost the rematch to the Tigers and, worse yet, three games to Harvard: 3–0, 8–1, and finally 5–4 (with Joe Wood taking the loss). Yale finished 1939 a disappointing 11-20.

After making the first team in the EIBL, that summer Eddie Collins Jr. signed with the Philadelphia Athletics and played his first game on July 4 in Philly against the Red Sox. Smoky Joe had his own thrill on a Major League baseball field a week later. Just short of his fiftieth birthday, Joe Wood returned to Fenway Park for an All-Stars Game between the American and the National League sponsored by the Veterans of Foreign Wars. It began at 3:00 p.m. on Wednesday, July 12, 1939. Most impressive was the famous Red Sox outfield of Lewis, Speaker, and Hooper, and the one-hundred-thousand-dollar infield from the Athletics: McInnis, Collins, Barry, and Baker. Noteworthy pitchers included Cy Young, Walter Johnson, Wood, Herb Pennock, and Chief Bender. The score was the same as a similar game in 1930, 8–4, but this time the NL won, with stars like Frankie Frisch, Johnny Evers, Honus Wagner, and Red Murray. Pitching for them were Grover Cleveland Alexander and Charley "Red" Nichols. A highlight of the game was Joe's home run over the left-field wall in the eighth inning off Chippie Gaw.

Not all the news was happy in the off-season between 1939 and 1940. On December 26, 1939, Clyde Engle died of a heart attack in a Boston hotel room. On the evening of January 24, 1940, Joe appointed another ex-teammate, Steve Yerkes, to replace Engle as freshmen coach. The 1940 season would depend on a deep pitching staff that included Joe Frank Wood, Ted Harrison (who lost only one freshman game in 1939), Dick Ames, Al Stevens, and Eric Franzen. After bad weather through mid-April, Yale got wins over Trinity and Williams. But they lost to Brown on the twenty-fourth, 3–2 in ten innings, despite fifteen strikeouts from Ames and 2-5 by Joe Jr. at shortstop. With Harrison pitching a four-hitter and striking out thirteen, on April 27 Yale won its first league game, beating Penn 3–2, followed by wins over Brown and Dartmouth, as Harrison struck out eleven.

After Yale losses to Columbia and Holy Cross, brothers Joe and Steve Wood faced each other, on May 9, 1940, when Colgate traveled to Yale. The Bulldogs won 5–4 in ten innings. Steve played well, going 2-3 with a home run and two RBI while holding Yale scoreless through six innings. Big brother Joe also had two hits and two RBI, pitching a complete-game victory. Two days later Yale beat Penn 10–4 behind Ted Harrison's four-hitter and fourteen strikeouts, giving the Sons of Eli a 3-and-1 record in league play. Yale kept hope when Harrison pitched a three-hitter, striking out twelve, to beat Columbia 1–0. But in Ithaca, New York, on the eighteenth, Cornell took two games from Yale: 2–1 (in 10 innings) and 2–0. After beating the Amherst Sabrinas 5–4 (saved by Joe Wood) and losing to the Holy Cross Crusaders, 5–3, on May 25 (the day Cornell won the EIBL title), Yale easily defeated Princeton, 11–1, on Harrison's four-hitter.

Joe Frank Wood's greatest game as a Yale Bulldog came on May 30, 1940, when he no-hit Wesleyan, 11–1. Joe struck out eight, walked none, and faced only thirty batters. The only run came in the ninth, on a wild pitch after an error. Joe also had two doubles and three RBI. Yale beat Fordham 4–1 on June 1 behind Harrison's five-hitter and Joe's two hits, a run, an RBI, and a stolen base. But then Yale lost two crucial games, to Princeton (2–0) and Dartmouth (2–1). Yale won over Harvard 8–7 in twelve innings, with Joe Wood winning in relief. But they lost to the same team twice by the score of 4–3, on the nineteenth in Cambridge and the twenty-first in New London, Connecticut, with Joe striking out thirteen in the loss. Yale finished the season 16-11, with Ted Harrison posting a 1.08 ERA and a record eighty-five strikeouts. Joe Frank Wood was elected captain for 1941.

After the Yale baseball season ended, Joe and Laura took their family, in two Chrysler Imperials, on a final tour of the places that had shaped their lives. The trip wasn't the first choice of the children. Joe Frank didn't want to leave his friends, and Bob had to forgo his second year as pitcher and first baseman for Plattsburgh of the Northern League.[34] The Woods first visited Laura's relatives in Kansas City. In

Hutchinson, Kansas, they played golf at Prairie Dunes and were introduced at a game between the Hutchinson Pirates and St. Joseph Saints
of the Class C Western Association. In Ness City the Wood sons joined
the local team against Larned, Dodge City, and Hays.[35] The Woods survived a night-time rainstorm along the Million Dollar Highway from
Durango to Ouray, Colorado. There they stayed at the old Beaumont
Hotel and visited Bird Mine, with Joe's only regret seeing "so few people [he] knew."[36] Continuing west, they joined brother Pete for golf in
LA (see chapter 10).

Nineteen forty-one was a transitional year. Jeff Sawyer (Yale '29)
followed Steve Yerkes as Joe's freshman baseball coach. Steve and Bob
Wood (both still at Colgate) took service exams before the baseball season, though Pearl Harbor was still eight months away. At Yale, with the
spring trip abandoned, Joe Frank started the season by losing to Vermont
on April 8, 4–2, though he had two hits, a run, and an RBI. Joe gave up
four runs over six innings against the Penn Quakers on the sixteenth;
Ted Harrison lost in relief. Yale then beat Tufts, 3–0, and Columbia, with
Joe getting three hits, including a triple. But the most celebrated game
of the year came on April 21, 1941, at Yale Field before 2,500 people as
Joe hit and pitched effectively against his brothers and Colgate.

Yale scored two in the first and three in the second, leading until
Colgate tied the game in the top of the seventh, 5–5. But Yale scored
five in the bottom of the inning and added another in the eighth to win
11–5. The oldest son gave up ten hits and struck out nine, walking only
one. For Colgate Bob (called Bobby) batted sixth and went 1-4 while
playing first base. Steve, who gave up six walks and eleven hits, was 1
for 3 batting eighth. He left in the seventh. Both Joe and Bob had an
RBI. Smoky Joe reflected, "I had hoped all three would have a big day,
but Steve can take it." On whether his sons were big league material,
their father replied in the *Hartford Courant* and the *Washington Post*
on April 22, "They've got to be a little bit better than they are now, but
I think they all have a chance." The best player? Joe responded, "Well,
you'll have to ask somebody else. I'm afraid I don't know."

For the next five weeks Yale played well but lost key conference games. Joe Jr. continued his hot hitting (two hits, two RBI, and the winning run) as Dick Ames won over Brown (4–3), and Yale took the Eastern League lead on April 26 by beating Penn 4–1, with Joe raising his average to .429. On April 30 Yale ended Holy Cross's twenty-game winning streak, 3–2 in ten innings, with Joe pitching a five-hitter and driving in the winning run. Between conference losses to Cornell and Dartmouth, Joe threw a five-hit, 2–1 win over Rutgers, striking out twelve and knocking in the winning run in the eleventh. After wins against Wesleyan (with Joe hitting a three-run home run) and Georgetown (Joe's win), on May 17 (the day Steve was elected Colgate captain), Yale beat Cornell 8–6, with Joe getting two hits (hitting .320). After wins over Trinity, Army, Dartmouth, Columbia, and Fordham, Yale had seven straight.

But in June Yale couldn't get past Princeton as Joe Frank Wood slumped at the plate. On June 7 the Bulldogs lost to the Tigers 5–4 in twelve innings. Princeton also won the return match, 5–3. In both games Joe was 0 for 3 as Princeton won its first Eastern League title. Yale took out the losses on Harvard. First Joe Wood, in his last time on the mound for Yale, struck out nine of the first twelve batters, and thirteen overall, in a 1–0, two-hit win on Yale's commencement day. Yale repeated the win on June 19, besting Harvard 3–1 behind Harrison. Despite the disappointing 7-5 record in the EIBL and the loss of the title to Princeton, 1941 was the second best winning record (to the 1937 team) during Joe's tenure, 17-7.

After graduating from Yale in June, Joe Frank Wood was pursued by the Athletics and the Cubs. But after being recruited by Nemo Leibold, he was signed by future Hall of Famer Herb Pennock, who had pitched with Smoky Joe in 1915 and in 1941 directed the Red Sox farm system. Mixing love and baseball, Joe Frank Wood married Harriet E. Rice, of Marlboro, Massachusetts, on July 12. Five days later he was named to the second team EIBL as an outfielder.[37] His 1.80 ERA was also second in the league. That same day, July 17, he pitched a seven-inning five-hitter over the Hartford Senators, 4–0, in his first game for Scranton of the Class A Eastern League. More impressively, in Scranton on August 7, 1941, with his parents in the stands, he threw a no-hitter against the Albany Senators, retiring the first eleven batters, striking out five, and facing twenty-nine. The only player to reach second was future Hall of Famer Ralph Kiner, also in his first pro season, who also grounded out to end the game. Later Joe pitched a one-hitter over Elmira, 7–0, his fourth shutout.

World War II initiated more changes in the life of Joe Wood. On July 15, 1941, three days after the marriage of Joe Frank Wood and Harriet Rice, son Bob, not yet a graduate of Colgate, entered the service as a draftee (the draft was instituted in November 1940). By then in love with Harriet's sister Connie, Bob commuted regularly between the Rice home in Marlborough, Massachusetts, and Fort Devens, about twenty miles away, where he worked at the Recruit Reception Center and played basketball and baseball. In August Steve joined Bob at Fort Devens, where the two young men assisted with physical exams for re-cruits. But by Bob's own admission, they "mostly played ball." When the Japanese bombed Pearl Harbor on December 7, the United States immediately joined the Allies, and Steve was shipped overseas to the Pacific arena. Bob remained at Fort Devens for two and one-half years.

And then the unthinkable happened: Smoky Joe Wood was fired by Yale University. Rumors the previous year had suggested that de-clining attendance might cost Joe his job. But when the change came, gate receipts weren't the issue. On March 19, 1942, the *New York Herald Tribune* described the dismissal of Wood, varsity tennis coach William Hinchliff, and Ben Thomson, golf coach and pro at the Yale Golf Course, as "a war-time economy move," claiming that Hinchliff would receive a pension while Wood and Thomson would be "terminated without compensation." The Associated Press, quoting Yale athletic director Ogden D. Miller, said the action was part "of a retrenchment program begun by the Yale Athletic Association soon after the war was declared." Included was a brief quote from Wood, indicating his disappointment: "I have nothing to say; I have no plans." He was to vacate his position by June 30. It was also reported that Jeff Sawyer, former Eli pitcher and freshman coach, would take over baseball operations.[38]

In the New Haven paper, athletic director Miller explained that the dismissals resulted from "the University's responsibility to stress sports on a group basis as training for special combat service, and because of the economic exigencies occasioned by war conditions." The alumni quickly pitched in. Stanley J. Keyes Jr., of New York, wrote Miller, claiming, "All of us [alums]" are owed "a lot of explanation as to why 'Smoky Joe' Wood was let out and more important why no pension? If ever there was an institution in Yale athletics it was Joe Wood." The response, dated March 25, 1942, regretted that sportswriters inaccurately released "financial details of a man's employment," which should be "the private concern of himself and his employer." Miller then revealed Joe was to "receive half salary for the next two years without his services being required." The decision "was based on the circumstances which war times have put before us," requiring deemphasis of sports "not equipped to carry effectively the type of physical training program" required by the armed services. Also influencing the decision, Miller added, were shrinking enrollments and financial retrenchment.[39]

As spring arrived in 1942, Joe Frank was with Louisville, a Red Sox affiliate in the American Association. With the war taking his talent, Smoky Joe found little solace in the season. The baseball team was only as good as its one star, Ted Harrison. After losing big to Penn (16–2) and Columbia (12–2), the team won games behind Harrison against Penn, 4–1, and Cornell, 2–1. Ted also threw a six-hitter over Columbia, 2–1. But they couldn't win without Harrison on the mound, except on May 23. In a surprise move Jack Neville pitched and beat Fordham, which had lost only two games, 2–1. Playing left Harrison drove in the winning run. In Joe's last weeks at Yale, the team lost to Harvard, 5–3 in fourteen innings, before Harrison won the rematch 3–1, in ten innings on a four-hitter (Harvard gave Joe a pen and pencil after the game). Two days later the Bulldogs lost Wood's last home game to Princeton in eleven innings, 2–1. With Harrison preparing for service, Yale also lost Joe's last game, 12–8, against Princeton, on June 13, 1942.[40] The Elis finished sixth in the EIBL, with a 4-6 record, and 6-12-1 overall, Joe's fourth losing season in nineteen years. Smoky Joe's teams were 285-230-1, winning eight Big Three championships and the EIBL in 1932 and 1937.[41]

After all those games Joe came to understand why so few Yale baseball players made it to the Majors (twelve before he arrived and four from his years). At Yale, as at Harvard and Princeton, "the classic boy . . . has something bigger in mind . . . than to go into professional ball." On the other hand, many students were desperate to share in the new national pastime. In Joe's words, "Many boys came out for the ball team and had no more chance than the man in the moon to make the ball club. . . . That's where I got my ulcer." "These boys would rather come out and make an athletic team than . . . graduate Phi Beta Kappa. . . . The toughest job we had was to cut those boys." For Coach Wood too often the gifted players were short on desire, while the motivated ones lacked talent.[42]

By the end the Yale years had become a web of public persona and private feelings. Smoky Joe was an effective leader and baseball strategist whose players cherished their days on the Yale field. He also received strong public support from alums during crises. The result was a positive reputation, reflected in the words of Geoff Zonder, then sports archivist at Yale, on a July 25, 1999, videotape: Joe was "more like a father to the kids," and consequently "people who played for him just loved him." He worked the way "Yale wanted its coaches to be" and thus was "singled out on many occasions as somebody to represent the university." On the other hand, the distance between his skills and those of his charges was troubling. And Joe's identification with the underdog didn't stop at the doors to the halls of ivy. Fay Vincent Jr. feels (like his father) that Wood resented privileged players' lack of passion and Yale's emphasis on football.[43] At times Joe "mailed in" the coaching.[44]

The last words on Yale should be Joe's. He admitted it was a "whole lot easier to do it yourself than to show others how to do it," but he felt qualified because he had played all positions, even catcher in high school. From the outset Joe had been honest with the school: "When I came to Yale, I knew nothing about coaching. I knew I was a natural ballplayer, and I would just sit down and figure it out myself. . . . And that's what I told them." Joe remained confident in his methods as "just a basic part of the game," believing that "if they did it that way, it worked." Finally, in Joe's judgment and matter-of-fact style, "I sure as hell did my best. The best that I knew how. If that wasn't good enough, well, then it wasn't."

TEN

Final Innings

After Yale Smoky Joe Wood remained at his Westville home, keeping a low profile. But he was a legend with neighbors like the Bergin twins, John and Tom, who lived at 50 Marvel Road. John pitched at Amherst and played in the area Industrial League. Tom, a catcher, went to Princeton. The twins were intimidated by Joe, having heard stories from their father, who saw Joe pitch for the Red Sox. They respected Joe's privacy while considering him remarkably handsome, a sharp contrast with his "unobtrusive" and "humble" ways. It took a lot of courage for Tom to approach Joe, sitting silently on the front porch at number 90. In the presence of such celebrity, young Bergin hesitantly extended his hand, mumbling, "I would just like to shake the hand of Smoky Joe Wood." Joe responded with modesty, but the star quality remained. Tom's lasting impression was of Joe at Yale, throwing slow, tantalizing knuckleballs, while the young catcher imagined "only God could throw them like that."[1]

As World War II heated up, Joe and Laura were anxious for their two sons in the service, even when they were stateside or at mostly safe stations, like those in New Zealand. They distracted themselves from worry over Steve and Bob by following the Minor League career of the oldest boy, Joe Frank Wood. During the summer of 1942, Joe Jr., twenty-six, moved from Class A Scranton, the home of his no-hitter, into AA ball at Louisville of the American Association. With the Colonels he posted a decent 3.74 ERA but a disappointing 4-10 record. He also batted a miserable .070. At least in 1943 Joe Jr. was closer to home, back with Scranton of the Class A Eastern League. Once again under the tutelage of ex–Major Leaguer Nemo Leibold, Joe Jr. regained his stride. He pitched shutouts against Albany on June 13 and the Utica Braves on August 1. On September 6, the day Scranton clinched the Eastern League pennant, Joe pitched four and one-third innings, getting no decision. Though in 1943 he only hit a buck-20 and had just a 7 and 7 record (with three shutouts), his ERA dipped to 2.69.

Joe Jr. wasn't the only Wood on the field that summer. Smoky Joe returned for baseball in Boston, though not as a featured guest. On July 12, 1943, for Mayor Tobin's Annual Field Day, the main Fenway attraction was a hitting contest between Babe Ruth, then retired, and the new sensation, Ted Williams, a Navy cadet awaiting training. The competition fizzled as Babe caromed a ball off his arch and hit only two grounders, two short flies, and three fouls. He whiffed three times. Williams, who had hit three home runs deep into the right-field stands before Ruth took his turn, won in a walk. Ruth managed the All-Star Service team, which included Williams (a three-run home run) and Dom DiMaggio (a two-run triple), to a 9–8 win over the Boston Braves. The Babe also flied out to right as a pinch hitter. Afterward Smoky Joe joined old-time players (including Fred Parent, Jack Barry, Duffy Lewis, Eddie Collins, and Casey Stengel) for dinner at the Kenmore Hotel.

Nineteen forty-four ushered in more transitions in the Wood family. On Sunday, February 27, 1944, Joe's father—the brilliant, willful, and eccentric John F. Wood—died at the home of Joe's sister, Zoë, Mrs. Walter J. Theimer, in Rio, New York (about twenty-five miles from Woodtown). He was eighty-nine.[2] Within a month there were more-positive doings. On March 11 the *Chicago Tribune* announced that "young Joe Wood" would be joining the Red Sox that summer. The *Christian Science Monitor* was even more complete, printing a cartoon explaining that during the 1943 season Joe Frank had been working at a defense plant in New Haven while pitching on Sundays for Scranton.

Meanwhile, on March 18, 1944, the youngest son, Robert K. Wood., married Constance Rice, the sister of Joe Frank's wife, Harriet.

There was more joy in the Wood family when Joe Jr. made the Red Sox squad for indoor workouts at Tufts College and then on March 25 joined manager Joe Cronin and the other players for advanced spring training in Baltimore. After a foolish April 1 exhibition game against the Coast Guard team in which he faced nine batters, giving up five walks and four hits (including a triple and home run), Joe was more effective two days later, permitting just a run in three innings, and again on April 9 against Brooklyn, allowing just one run over four innings, though it was the one that gave the Dodgers a 3–2 win in twelve innings.

The reward was Joe Frank Wood's Major League debut at Fenway Park on Monday, May 1, 1944, against Washington. He gave up just a run in three innings of relief as Boston lost 11–4. Not quite as good on May 5 at Yankee Stadium, in two innings of relief he permitted three hits, two walks, and two runs while striking out two. Finally, Joe Jr. started, at Fenway Park on May 14, in the first game of a doubleheader loss to Detroit, which dropped the Sox into the AL cellar. Wood pitched four and two-thirds, striking out three and walking one, but also giving up eight hits as the Sox lost 6–1. On May 21 he was sent to Louisville. In nine and two-thirds innings in the Majors, Joe Jr. totaled thirteen hits, seven earned runs, five strikeouts, and three walks. He was 0-1 with a 6.52 ERA.

After not pitching better at Louisville, 3-3 with an ERA of 5.16 in twelve games, on July 31 he was traded by the Red Sox, along with pitcher Lou Lucier and utility man Johnny Lazor, to the San Diego Padres of the AA Pacific Coast League for Rex Cecil. The slide stopped there. Though he struggled with control, Joe Frank pitched a five-hitter in his first game, a 10–1 win in San Diego on August 11, followed by a 3–1 win on August 16 over the Solons in Sacramento. With Joe's success the Red Sox picked up his option on August 31, and he remained in San Diego that season, pitching well. For the abbreviated season with the Padres, Joe Jr. posted a 5-4 record with a 2.51 ERA in ten games. And he finally hit better, at .241.

Before Joe Frank completed his roller-coaster 1944 season, Joe and Laura decided three houses (Joe had inherited the home place) were more than enough. So they sold Indian Camp. It was an easy sale since the McConnell family, from whom they had purchased the acre and cabin in 1919, had a buyer. On August 2, 1944, a deed was registered that "Joseph Wood and Laura T. Wood, his wife, of 90 Marvel Road, New Haven, Connecticut" had exchanged their acre of land to Mathew J. McConnell of Blooming Grove, Pike County, Pennsylvania, in "good and valuable consideration and five ($5.00) Dollars, in hand paid."[3] Implied was another advantage; Joe and Laura would no longer be shelling out seventy-five dollars a year for two weeks of hunting on the surrounding one thousand acres. Moving into their midfifties, the couple had started downsizing.

On March 20, 1945, Joe Frank reported for Red Sox spring training in Pleasantville, New York. Four days later he pitched three good innings with the Regulars as they defeated the Yannigans, 3–2. He was even better on the twenty-seventh, when Joe combined with Joe Bowman to one-hit the Yannigans 8–0 in a six-inning practice game. But the bubble burst on March 30, when he started against Joe McCarthy's Yankees in Atlantic City, New Jersey. In his four innings Joe gave up seven runs on eight hits and four walks. He wasn't any better in a return against the Yankees on April 6. In two innings of relief, he walked four and gave up six hits and six runs. On the evening of April 17, 1945, Joe Wood Jr. was released to Sacramento of the Pacific Coast League. By May 24 he was 2-2 with the Solons before the Wood curse, arm problems, set in. But there was encouraging news back East for the Woods.

On June 30, 1945, George "Specs" Toporcer, director of Minor League operations for the Red Sox, announced that Steve Wood, Smoky Joe's second son, had signed with Boston. Just weeks before the atomic bomb ended the war, Steve was discharged after three years of duty. Although officially assigned to Louisville in the AA American Association, he was immediately optioned to Scranton's A team of the Eastern League, where Joe Frank had started. In Steve's debut in Scranton, Pennsylvania, on July 10, 1945, for the Miners against the Hartford Bees, he gave up only one hit, a triple to the first batter he faced, and no runs in five innings. He walked no one and struck out five in a 7–0 loss. With Smoky Joe and Laura traveling over to see the team play from time to time, Steve posted a 3.66 ERA. He held opponents under a hit per inning but lacked command, giving up four and one-half walks for each nine innings. He also hit only .133.

Meanwhile, in California Joe Frank Wood battled chronic arm problems, later diagnosed as a rotator cuff injury. As he struggled with control, he became hittable. For example, he won a game on July 25 in Sacramento, easily beating his old team, the San Diego Padres, 23–6. But all the runs were earned as Joe gave up fourteen hits and walked four. Similarly, on August 2 at Doubleday Park in Sacramento, he allowed thirteen hits while striking out only three in a 4–1 loss to the LA Angels. Joe Frank finished the year 9-14 with a high ERA, 5.22. But recognizing Joe Jr.'s revived hitting (.287 for the Solons), Bob Feller used him against Satchel Paige's Kansas City Royals at Wrigley Field in LA on October 26, 1945. Feller's Pacific Coast All-Stars won 3–2, with Joe playing center, tripling in a run, and scoring in the tenth. (The Royals' second baseman was Jackie Robinson.)[4]

The 1946 baseball season was the beginning of the end for the Wood boys in organized baseball. Steve moved down to Class B, with the Providence Chiefs of the New England League, and posted an 11-6 record with a 4.86 ERA in twenty games. In April 1946 brother Joe hurled a 4–0 seven-hitter over seven innings for the Sacramento Solons against the Oakland Oaks. But it was his only win of the year, while posting a 1-3 record. By then Joe and Laura were in California. On June 12, 1946, they were among the 6,500 fans attending a game between the Hollywood Stars and the San Diego Padres, noted in the *Los Angeles Times* as "Smokey [*sic*] Joe Wood, famed Red Sox twirler of yesteryear, whose son is now pitching for Sacramento." But two weeks later the same paper noted that the Solons had released two pitchers, "Jim McCarthy and Joe Wood, Jr., the latter the son of famed Smoky Joe."

Not one to give up easily, thirty-year-old Joe Frank signed with the Fresno Cardinals of the Class C California League. But in twelve games he was 3-7 with a 6.04 ERA.

That wasn't the end for the Wood family in Los Angeles, however. Crucial to Joe and Laura's security in their golden years, they moved there in support of a golf enterprise. Already situated in the state was Pete, Joe's older brother, who had moved West in the midthirties with Spalding Sporting Goods. In 1947 Joe Frank was off to Oklahoma, where he played his final twenty games as a pro in the Class D Sooner League, with the Seminole Oilers and the Ada Herefords, for a combined 3-4 record and 5.54 ERA. By then Pete had leased property at 11030 Wilshire Boulevard, near the intersection of Sepulveda, where Smoky Joe and Laura joined Pete and his wife, Stella. The darkening nights had limited evening activities during World War II. But reelectrification made possible night practice of the newly popular sport, golf. The *Los Angeles Times* reported on April 13, 1947, "Joe has pulled himself out of retirement in Pennsylvania to come out here and help his brother, Harley (Pete) Wood, in the business of showing folks how to drive golf balls."

It was an especially happy period for Joe and Laura, whose children were grown and starting their families. Laura, more the city-lover than Joe, was energized by the Hollywood scene; she liked meeting the movie stars. While he never realized his fantasy of playing with Bob Hope and Bing Crosby, Joe met a few old friends (Fred Snodgrass dropped in one day) and sometimes gave golf lessons, often making one thousand dollars on a weekend.[5] As Joe explained, "I staked [Pete] to getting into a business out in California. He had rented a piece of property from the government, put in a driving range there, a golf driving range. I went out with him after the war, opened up the business again for nights, which had been closed down during the war on account of the lights, you know. I made more money in those seven years than I'd made working twenty years [at Yale]."[6] New friends also helped Joe make shrewd investments, one of which "went sky high."[7] The golf business eventually ran its course; the *Times* reported on October 21, 1953, "Chet

Beer is taking over the Westshire Golf Fairways at 11030 Wilshire from Pete Wood." By the end of the year, Joe and Laura had returned East.[8]

Waiting on the corner as they turned onto Marvel Road was Gary Whitney, son of Virginia Wood Whitney, born on Joe's sixtieth birthday, during the California sojourn. Accompanying Joe Wood back from Los Angeles was also a new legal name. While West, Howard Ellsworth Wood decided to become Joe Wood . . . for real. And so he completed the process. The document, called an affidavit of identification, reads

> We, the undersigned, are brother and
> sister of Howard Ellsworth Wood, who
> has used the name of "Joe" Wood most
> of his life, and who was a famous
> American League pitcher known as
> "Smokey Joe" Wood.
> Due to the fact that the birth records
> in Kansas City, Mo., call for the name,
> Howard Ellsworth Wood, we wish to verify
> the fact that Howard Ellsworth and "Joe"
> Wood are one and the same person.

It is signed by both "Zoë Wood Theimer" (notarized on June 9, 1947) and "Harley C. Wood" (notarized on May 26, 1947).

By the time Joe and Laura returned to New Haven, many changes had occurred in their children's lives. Bob returned to Colgate for his degree in sociology with a minor in psychology, though an arm injury kept him from playing baseball. He entered the medical equipment business before enrolling at Yale in the midfifties for a master's in public health.[9] He and Connie eventually had three children: Robert, Jeffrey, and Durinda. Bob's twin sister, Virginia, married Clarence Whitney, a high school classmate, who became a real estate agent and eventually ran for mayor of New Haven. After living in the Marvel Road home while Joe and Laura were in California, they and their three children settled not far away. Joe Frank and Harriet returned to Shohola and

had four children: David, Carol, Richard, and Jonathan. They moved
into the house that Joe and Pete built in 1913, where the oldest son took
up mink ranching (like Bobby Doerr) in 1947.[10] Steve, named by Bob
"a wine, women, and song" guy, also married. He and Maree lived in
her hometown, Milford, Massachusetts, where he worked in a diaper
factory.[11] They had four children: Celine, Marilyn, Elaine, and Larry.

Even though he avoided the spotlight, Joe kept periodic contact
with baseball. Bob remembered joining his father and Tris Speaker
(considered "a second father" by Bob) in the mid-1950s, just after Ted
Williams's second stint in the service. Entering the Red Sox training
room, the three visitors discovered Ted in the whirlpool taking thera-
py for a sprained ankle. Always the student of hitting, Williams jumped
from the hot tub and quizzed Smoky Joe and Spoke about how they
gripped their bats. As Joe reported later to Mark Alvarez, in 1956 Pete,
Joe's brother, traveled from California so they could attend the World
Series. Consequently, Joe Wood was in the stands when Don Larsen
pitched his perfect game.[12] But he also enjoyed Pennsylvania, where
he attended an old-timers reunion at the Frederick Suydam estate in
White Mills, Pennsylvania, and in 1956–57 helped coach Welcome Lake
in the Delaware Valley League.

Because Joe preferred the quiet, unhurried ways of the country, his
grandchildren, especially the children of Joe Frank Wood, have fond
memories of their granddad in Shohola. David Wood remembers playing cribbage with Joe at the renovated old homestead after school. Most
vivid for David is an old baseball, almost black, that sat on a bookcase
in the living room. Joe told his grandson that it was from the 1912 World
Series, darkened by licorice Joe chewed and spit on the ball for a better
grip. (Over the years David wondered what happened to that ball, but
no one in the family ever knew.) Laura was mostly close by the house;
everyone was aware that she preferred the stimulations of New Haven.
Whether in the city or Woodtown, the aging couple enjoyed porches,
where they sat quietly, always waving at passers-by so they wouldn't be
considered stuck-up.

Richard Wood, David's brother, described a typical day with Smoky Joe Wood in the 1950s:

> When we would go to town (Milford or Port Jervis) to do errands, he would teach my younger brother Jonathan, who was about four years old, the names of people who lived at certain houses along the way. We would pass the motel and that was old Bill Bossler with new Bill Bossler, nearby. Upon entering Milford, just past Apple Valley, he would turn left and pull through the funeral home and look at the list of names to see who had died. Then on to Port Jervis for golf, groceries, etc. He would stop at the bananas stand just off of the singing bridge (Delaware River). Sometimes he would go to the dairy, nearby, to buy milk and bring back the empties. Coming back through Milford, he would stop at the news stand (Lloyd's), just past the main intersection, and get a newspaper.[13]

Always gracious he would stand when women entered a room, and he was fond of his *New York Times* crosswords.

But Smoky Joe also loved to drive his Chryslers ("Cadillac, hell, Chrysler's the car for me"), particularly when he could travel for a bargain and some refreshment to boot. As Richard remembers,

> After being back home for a couple hours, he might drive to Shohola to buy eggs from one of the farmers, usually one near the sharp turn that then plunges down to Bee Hollow. Instead of heading down into Bee Hollow, he would turn left and there was a farm nearby on Knealing Road (off Twin Lakes Road) that sold eggs. I don't know why he bothered to buy directly from the farmer, maybe they were cheaper or fresher, or maybe he liked to help out the farmers. Then on to Shohola and Rohman's to bring back the case of empty beer bottles and get a new case of Horlacher's or Kaier's beer.[14]

But Joe never abandoned baseball; he installed an antenna that reached above the hills so that he could follow baseball on television as well as the radio.

Not all the news in rural Pennsylvania during the 1950s was happy, however. In late 1958 Joe and Laura joined Tris Speaker and his wife, as well as Rocky Colavito and others, for a reunion at Grossinger's, just thirty miles to the east and north of Shohola. But Spoke was ill and carried a breathing device, what Joe described to Ritter as a gas atomizer, when they played golf. Afterward, Speaker visited the Wood home for the last time. As Richard Wood remembered, the Grey Eagle was dressed very "courtly," probably in a suit, as he and Joe prepared for a walk over the Wood property, accompanied, everyone assumed, by Richard. But a friend visited that day and took Richard back home with him, leaving the walk to Richard's sister. Within weeks, on December 8, 1958, Speaker died of a heart attack while fishing at Lake Whitney, Texas. The next year, recognizing that the family couldn't afford it and "couldn't get help in those parts," Joe sold the home he had built and ninety-seven acres, to New York attorney David Mosteller, reportedly for fifteen thousand dollars.[15]

Even with that money, Joe's tightness became more pronounced in the 1960s. As Richard remembered, though his grandfather "had a lot of stocks, like his Kroger stock, and didn't need to be thrifty," Joe and Laura "would cut coupons, shop the sales, make a shopping list and visit two or three grocery stores to get the sale items at each." One day this need "to save a couple of dollars" got ridiculous: "They used to shop at an outlet store, over in New Jersey, that sold pallets of marked-down groceries. I liked those flavored apple sauces that were the fad at the time, and they got me a bunch of jars [that] said 'Be sure to visit the New York World's Fair.' This was in 1967, three years after the fair." Even when Joe served ice cream, he carefully opened the carton at the seams and cut off an inch for each person.[16] Such parsimony led Richard to consider gambling by Joe "paradoxical." It must've been "the money and Tris' influence." Otherwise, Joe's careful ways would have prevailed.[17]

Smoky Joe also valued orderliness as he aged. He made his morning coffee the night before (pouring it into a jar in the sink), kept a bowl of sliced cucumbers in vinegar in the fridge, and bought antacids by the big box, popping them into his mouth each day. When the grand-children visited in summer, they threw baseballs and golf balls around the lot while Joe apparently sat passively on the porch. But still pos-sessing great eye sight and not wanting confusion or lost objects, Joe would direct the youngsters to the balls. When in New Haven, or when the television reception got better in Shohola, he and Laura routine-ly watched the *Lawrence Welk Show* or a baseball game, especially if her favorite, Rocky Colavito, was playing. Joe's reading included the *Sporting News*, bought by Bob, until Joe "only read obituaries." As he sat watching or reading, Joe would sit with his right shoulder lowered and his arm hanging down, relieving the pressure where it was bone against bone.

With adequate finances for his modest life, Joe Wood indulged in golf. He wasn't your usual golfer, though. As his grandson Richard Wood re-membered, "He was all business. Would hustle between shots. No lolly-gagging. People would let him play through. I guess since he did it al-most every day, it was exercise for him, not leisure. Never saw him ride a golf cart. He always walked and pulled his own bag."[18] He did follow one trend, especially among golfers who didn't want to waste money on tees. On par threes Joe would smack his iron into the ground and place his ball on the smile-shaped divot; he always meticulously re-placed the injured ground after his shot. Smoky Joe didn't make a hole in one until he was nearly sixty years old. Then he made another in a week and four in his lifetime. As athletic as he was, Joe played golf well into his eighties.

During the 1960s the Red Sox took a renewed interest in the team's past, celebrating Fenway and initiating old-timers' games. In this spir-it, at the invitation of Thomas E. Yawkey, Joe, Laura, and other fami-ly members on April 20, 1962, attended the fiftieth anniversary of the opening of the park. Others in attendance were pitchers Ray Collins and Hugh Bedient, catcher Bill Carrigan, infielders Steve Yerkes and Larry Gardner, and outfielders Harry Hooper, Duffy Lewis, and Olaf Henriksen. The players received red electric clocks, which Joe bragged got five years' service on their batteries. Richard remembered, however, that Joe was allergic to dog and pony shows. After the game (which the Red Sox lost), the players (many in wheelchairs) were assembled for a crush of autograph seekers. Once Joe identified the setup, despite his seventy-two years, he jumped over multiple rows of chairs to escape, leaving the infirm players to sign the hats and balls. Ironically, the Yankees were even more welcoming of Smoky Joe, especially when Mike Burke was their president in the late 1960s and early 1970s. Among Joe's cherished possessions were a silver tray and a transistor radio from the Yanks.

Joe Wood's life gained a new relevance for baseball history beginning in October 1963. On the fifteenth of that month, and two years later, on October 1, 1965, Joe was interviewed by Lawrence Ritter for the seminal published interviews called *The Glory of Their Times*. As edited, rearranged, and sometimes rewritten by Ritter, the printed interview is charming. It captures Joe's directness, sense of the historical moment, and personal observations, inside and outside baseball. Not surprisingly, its need for confidentiality and a readable narrative make the published version the most innocuous. More revealing, and incriminating, is an audiotape, edited but much more complete than the written interview, which Ritter sold commercially in 1998. Joe's words are also retained in a typo-marred, forty-four-page transcript and in the unedited tapes in the Ritter papers at the Hesburgh Libraries, Notre Dame University. Equally revealing are Joe's words to Eugene Murdock at Joe's home in New Haven, Connecticut, on April 19, 1975 (in the Cleveland Public Library).

Some provocative, knotty issues concerning the Cobb-Speaker scandal are raised in the Ritter and Murdock tapes. For example, Joe Wood's description of himself to Murdock as merely a "banker," not a bettor, contradicts his testimony before Landis. Despite historical assumptions that the Cobb-Speaker scandal was the single focus of the Johnson-Landis investigations, Wood suggests that the inquiries included betting during the 1920 World Series. In his words, "In the 1920 World Series there was a dispute over some betting" in which the participants bet on their own team: "There was a bet placed on a ball game, but it was not against our club, it was *on* our club, see. And for that reason, it should have absolved all of us, see." Joe notes, "I don't think the letter [noting that bet] was ever made public."

There is also the suggestion that the White Sox of 1920 were not playing to win. He mentions a conversation with Eddie Cicotte at the Winton Hotel in Cleveland, near the end of the season, in which Cicotte told Joe that "the White Sox didn't dare win, see." Also the Tigers were willing to take it easy on the Indians to ensure a Cleveland championship: "Well, a few of the fellows from the Detroit club let it be known that they weren't going to beat their heads off to beat us, see." Even more suggestively, Joe referred to more "dirt" not revealed to Landis or in the Cobb biography. Some was so volatile that Joe didn't even discuss it with brother Pete.[19]

So what can be made of these statements, which Smoky Joe assumed would be confidential, excised, and finally lost to history? In addition to Leonard's accusations about the September 1919 game, Ban Johnson was given material on bets made prior to and/or during the 1920 World Series. In that instance Joe Wood probably bet, on the Indians. Furthermore, Joe's admission to Ritter that Leonard's accusations were "true" implies that Speaker and Cobb wagered on the 1919 game. Wood's words to Murdock indicate that he didn't put up money in that instance and thus had lied in the Landis hearings. Leonard also suspected that Cobb had stiffed the pitcher in other bets, the implied subject of Dutch's anger to Damon Runyon: "I have evidence to show that baseball is a game only for suckers to bet on. They don't get a chance unless they are in on the know. Baseball is a trust of the worst sort. It is a closed corporation."[20]

The interviews also help explain some of the oddities in the hearing itself.[21] Landis shaped the conversations to emphasize his effectiveness as commissioner. For example, at the end of Cobb's testimony, Landis asked, "Have you in mind now anything of that sort [teams lying down at the end of the season] during the last five or six years?" Cobb responded right on cue, "No. No." Later, during discussion of "hippo-droming," Landis encouraged Speaker to say such "going through the motions" had not existed in the "last few years." Equally remarkably, Landis let the players tag-team attacks on Dutch. First Joe suggested that Leonard was "very bitter against Mr. Cobb because he let [Leonard] go to the Coast League." He speculated, "I guess he was also bitter against Mr. Speaker because he didn't claim [Leonard]." Cobb then asserted: "I cannot imagine a human being with any sort of honor or ideals having the splean [*sic*] that Leonard has upon me," and called Leonard "very keen for money" like he "received . . . for his letters." Speaker added his "reputation" for having visited "other clubs and . . . players and told his troubles to them and criticized his own team."

Landis's passivity transformed the proceedings into a staged performance. When Joe said that his betting partner was from Cleveland, describing him as "a man who has never been in baseball, connected with baseball in any way and I don't — I won't mention his name," the Judge didn't pursue the matter. Later when Landis and Secretary O'Connor returned to the subject, Commissioner Landis didn't protest as Cobb cut off the questioning, rescuing Joe by assuming Landis's role as inquisitor, turning the discussion to playing fielders in unfamiliar positions, Leonard's lack of character, and the accuser's absence before the accused (the last of many justifications for the resignations of Cobb and Speaker).[22]

In such a theater of public opinion, Landis the lawyer became incredibly slipshod with the evidence. He let stand Cobb's explanation that he was only following Wood's "giving [him] the wrong information and a fictitious amount" and Joe's subsequent justification of his "anonymous reply" as okay for an affair that was none of Ty's business. The commissioner also let slide Joe's claim that he "never had any conversation with Speaker about a bet on this ball game" over the following six years. Equally unnoted by Landis was Wood's contrived addition that he asked Cobb "if he had bet anything on this ball game and he said no" and insistence that he didn't meet Leonard the next spring. More generally Landis allowed a focus "primarily on gambling" when "whether or not the game had been fixed was an even more pressing question."[23]

In addition to being a phenomenal pitcher for Boston from 1908 to 1915 and a celebrated outfielder in Cleveland until 1922, Smoky Joe was an extremely loyal person. As he said in the Ritter tapes, "My religion is to help anybody needs my help, do a favor for anybody wants a favor." The purest object of his loyalty was Tris Speaker, whom Hugh Fullerton identified as a father figure for Smoky Joe: "Wood admired Speaker above all things, and Spoke was a sort of father to the youngster, who would do almost anything Speaker suggested."[24] In Wood's words, "Speaker and me . . . we'd do anything for one another"; "I'd have gone to hell for [Tris] and he'd have gone to hell for me." The tapes suggest that Joe Wood "took the fall" for Speaker (and Cobb) while collaborating with Landis to stop the bleeding from baseball scandals between 1920 and 1927. Such service to friends and the national pastime was not lost on others.[25] Even Dutch was sympathetic to Wood's sacrifices.[26] As Joe reported to Ritter, "[Leonard] made the crack that he didn't mind what he was doing to Cobb and Speaker. But he hated to hurt Woody."[27]

As the sixties rolled into the seventies, the new bridge over the Hudson made travel in Joe Wood's Chryslers easier and faster between New Haven and Shohola. Even so, as the couple grew older, Laura tended to stay in Connecticut, where there was better television reception for her soap operas and Virginia and Clarence could help with chores on Marvel Road. Joe could hear games broadcast by Mel Allen or Curt Gowdy everywhere, so he spent increasing time in Pennsylvania. He maintained regular contact with ex-teammates still in the region, like Duffy Lewis (with the Red Sox) and Larry Gardner (at the University of Vermont). After the publication of *The Glory of Their Times*, Lawrence Ritter encouraged communication among interviewees at reunions sponsored by the author. Although Joe pulled for the Red Sox, he hardly ever attended games even though he had passes across the Major Leagues. He rarely visited Cooperstown, though once Frank "Home Run" Baker "happened to be there." The two former players "went through the buildings." Joe exchanged Christmas cards with "Wamby," "Smitty," "Covey," George Uhle, and George Burns.

Inspired by the election of Joe's friends and teammates Stan Coveleski (1969) and Harry Hooper (1971) to the Hall of Fame, Wood's supporters, especially his son Bob, joined forces to resurrect Joe's candidacy. Nineteen seventy-one was especially encouraging because the Veterans Committee voted in seven players that year, including Rube Marquard, Joe's teammate at Kansas City Jake Beckley, and Hooper. Harry's descendants had staged a successful campaign for his election, a process this group would try to replicate, beginning in 1973. Equally significant, Hooper and Dave Bancroft (another inductee) had batting averages lower than Joe's. Since the main obstacle seemed to be Joe's not playing ten years at one position, it was also a boost to Wood advocates to see Ross Youngs, who had played only nine complete seasons, elected in 1972.

There were about sixty original supporters, including most crucially Frank Williams, a statistician from Bridgeport, Connecticut, and a regular visitor to the Wood home; Richard Thompson, from Bridgeport, Massachusetts; and Doug Roberts, an attorney from Syracuse, New York, who approached news organizations like the *New York Times*.[28] Inspired to pursue Joe's case when his wife gave him a history of the World Series, Roberts focused on the Veterans Committee, believing the two-position issue prejudicial. Using a brochure describing Joe's record, the group amassed more than four thousand signatures, including those of celebrities Rob Reiner, Billy Crystal, Susan Sarandon, Tim Robbins, and Karl Malden. Among the letters they eventually collected is one from George Bush Sr. (when he was vice president), naming "mother's brothers Herbie, John and Lewis" [Walker] as having played for Joe. Eventually they garnered support from Democrat Tip O'Neill, as well as baseball experts Lawrence Ritter and Barry Halper. They even found a few old-timers to testify to Smoky Joe's record, personality, and legend. Mobilizing their argument quickly, they were able to petition the Veterans Committee for the first time in 1973–74.[29]

But they were fighting an uphill battle with the history of the Hall of Fame balloting. When his record and reputation were still well known, Smoky Joe ran a respectable race. In the second election, in 1937, Joe received thirteen votes, 6.5 percent of those cast. The next year he slipped to six votes, only 2.3 percent. As his playing days began to slide back in time, the baseball writers gave Joe only two votes in 1939 and one in 1942. Then, the Old Timers Committee in 1945 voted in Wood contemporaries Roger Bresnahan, Hugh Jennings, and Wilbert Robinson. And in 1946 Rube Waddell and Ed Walsh joined the double play combination of Joe Tinker, Johnny Evers, and Frank Chance in the hall. In the spirit of this renewal, Joe received his most votes — twenty-nine, or 18 percent — in 1947, when Mickey Cochrane, Frankie Frisch, Lefty Grove, and Carl Hubbell were inducted. That year Wood received more votes than future inductees Rube Marquard, Jimmie Foxx, Joe Cronin, Al Simmons, Gabby Hartnett, Joe McCarthy, and Eppa Rixey.

In 1948 he also received more support than Harry Hooper, Hack Wilson, Home Run Baker, Stan Coveleski, and Joe Medwick. But the writers only gave him five votes, a mere 4.1 percent. Herb Pennock was elected that year. Then Joe sunk to no votes in 1949 (Mordecai Brown's and Kid Nichols's year), followed by only one vote in 1950 and five in 1951. After that, even with the creation of the Veterans Committee in 1953, Smoky Joe Wood became less familiar to voters, as his contemporaries were elected into Baseball's Hall of Fame. He supported many of these former stars, for example, Chief Bender and Bobby Wallace in 1953. But he felt both choices in 1955 were poor. He thought that Ray Schalk was not qualified and that Frank Baker was not as worthy as Larry Gardner. In 1963 Joe essentially gave up on the process with the election of Eppa Rixey, barely a .500 pitcher, recognized primarily for his longevity (twenty-one years) and wins by a left-hander (266). Better in Joe's mind were the elections of friend Coveleski in 1969 and

Hooper in 1971.[30] (Before Wood's death Addie Joss was added to the list, in 1978.)[31]

Grandsons Gary Whitney and Richard Wood share the perception that as Joe grew older, he continued to live an orderly, neat lifestyle. He carried new, crisp bills in his wallet, all folded on the same side and in the same direction. The place settings in his kitchen were set out carefully each night, with the cups turned upside down. Every day he carried the World Series watch, made famous in Roger Angell's essay "The Web of the Game." When in Shohola, Pennsylvania, Joe would place that watch, barely one-quarter-inch thick, on a red Formica table on the left just inside the door, along with another watch (from his mother), binoculars, and a shotgun. For inquisitive relatives he would retrieve from a dark closet a baseball signed by Babe Ruth. He kept his Imperials immaculate, warming their engines as part of his morning ritual, which included putting out the empty milk bottles and picking up the paper. Always keeping lists of needed food, he would head regularly to Port Jervis on weekdays for a round of golf, usually played alone. Then he would treat himself to ice cream.

Joe remained a no-nonsense person. "Very old school" and "strong-willed," according to Gary Whitney, Joe once a week would walk down to the creek below the old family house and bathe in its cold water, using a big flat rock as a soap dish. Fastidious with clothes, he dressed well, even for yard work, which often included using a two-handled scythe, swung in a circular motion. Despite changing times he still stood up when women entered a room and took off his hat in their presence outdoors. In clear opposition to rumors that in the 1920s Smoky Joe was a militant Protestant, Gary and other relatives testify that Joe never went to church and had declared he would make up his own mind. To Gary Joe always commanded respect, not because he was an old ballplayer but because he was a "man's man," with a "tremendous physicality." In Gary's view the aging Joe Wood remained a Scorpio, a passionate man who "didn't take crap from people."[32]

The Dudas, Bob and Pauline, who lived directly across the street from

Joe in New Haven, enjoyed telling two revealing stories about Joe's later years. George Fitzgerald and his wife also lived on Marvel Road. Mrs. Fitzgerald was the minister at the Episcopal church on the corner, at number 112, where children loved to play baseball in the yard. But there was continual fear that when the ball got away and rolled down to the Wood home, Joe might retrieve it and, even as an old man, throw it back to the children with intimidating speed. The other story is more personal for Bob Duda, who had a habit of putting his leaves in the street. Joe, always fastidious and often crusty, one day shouted across Marvel Road that his neighbor shouldn't clutter the street that way. Bob responded that Mr. Wood should find something better to do than criticize his neighbors. Once they calmed down, the two became friends and would sit and talk for hours on Joe's small front porch.[33]

But the quiet and order couldn't protect Smoky Joe Wood from a series of losses during the 1970s. First his brother Harley died in Los Angeles in July 1971. That left only Zoë and Joe of the immediate Wood family. Of the four children Steve had always been the most worrisome, the one most dismissive of his father's advice about moderation. As Bob recalled, Steve was very pleasant most of the time, but when intoxicated, he became antagonistic and "thought he could conquer the world." After Steve and Maree separated, he moved to Florida, where he befriended ex–Major League pitcher Joe Dobson and followed the Red Sox in spring training. But he also ignored warnings about his heart, gained weight, and continued smoking and drinking. On January 9, 1975, after another hard night out, Steve got out of bed and, in Bob's words, "just toppled over."[34] He was fifty-six. His obituary noted he was captain of the Colgate baseball team, served with the Yale Medical Unit in New Zealand, and pitched against Ted Williams in the service. Steve was buried in the family cemetery.

Three years later Smoky Joe had his first major health issue . . . at eighty-eight. In May 1978 he had prepared for a day trip to Pennsylvania. Even the car was packed. But at the last minute Joe noticed something high on the house that might be causing a leak. Not wanting to leave anything undone, he got a ladder and climbed to repair the problem. But the ladder broke, sending Joe to the ground. The impact broke his clavicle and ribs and punctured a lung. He couldn't breathe very well, but he was conscious when taken to the hospital. Then he developed pneumonia. His two sons, Joe Frank and Bob, divided the care into twelve-hour shifts, but their father got worse, slipping into delirium, at times trying to take off his clothes. The doctors put Joe in pulmonary intensive care. Finally, after days of concern for his life, Joe responded. Once he returned home, his fans and neighbors redoubled their belief in his strength and resilience.[35]

And then it was his wife Laura's turn. Because there was only six months difference in their ages, their birthdays were celebrated together by immediate family, on or near the birthday of Bob and Virginia, August 14. That year, 1979, the family would honor the ninetieth birthdays of both Laura and Joe on August 12. Because of the special occasion, Ruth Meranda, a cousin from Utah, and Zoë, Joe's younger sister, were to attend as well. In the final days before the party, Laura and Joe seemed in good health. Bob even drove to Pennsylvania to help with the final preparations. But before things could be put in order, word came that Laura was in trouble, with her heart. At first she was stable and resting at home in New Haven. Then on August 2 she suddenly fell on the bedroom floor and, in Bob's words, just "went out," as had her son Steve four years earlier. The death certificate notes that Laura Theresa O'Shea Wood died at St. Raphael's Hospital at 10:15 p.m. of ventricular fibrillation forty minutes after an aortic aneurysm. She was eighty-nine. Her body was cremated at Evergreen Crematory under direction of Hawley W. Lincoln Funeral Home, New Haven, on August 6.

Joe Wood's ninetieth birthday, on October 25, 1979, drew the attention of many dignitaries and friends. In the political world, he received best wishes from Presidents Gerald Ford and Jimmy Carter.[36] Closer to home Joe also heard from Tip O'Neill. Within the baseball community Commissioner Bowie Kuhn and Lee MacPhail, president of the American League, sent congratulations, as did Haywood C. Sullivan, vice president and general manager of the Red Sox. More personally, he heard from Joe Sewell, writing from Tuscaloosa, Alabama, his old hunting partner Stan Coveleski, Elmer Smith (the man with whom he shared right field in Cleveland), and Luke Sewell. The last of these ex-players even credited Joe with teaching him to catch a knuckleball during Luke's rookie year and Joe's next-to-last, 1921.

Most resonant of his reputation in baseball and around New Haven, Connecticut, is a letter dated July 18, 1979 (just two weeks before Laura died), from the "Office of the President" at Yale. It is addressed to "Mr. and Mrs. Joe Wood" at "Twin Lakes" in "Shohola, Pennsylvania":

Dear Mr. and Mrs. Wood:

I write to offer the greetings of all of us at Yale University upon this extraordinarily happy occasion. As a former neighbor in Westville, may I note the pride I take in that association and salute the contribution you both have made to our community. As President of the University where Mr. Wood served for almost two score years, with great distinction, may I thank him for setting an example as a teacher and coach seldom equaled and never surpassed. And so one who has ever been, and always will be, unalterably faithful to the Boston Red Sox, may I send a fervent admirer's regards to the greatest pitcher Boston ever had, and one of the greatest pitchers to grace the grandest game of all. With warmest best wishes to you both, and to your family,

Respectfully yours,
A. Bartlett Giamatti[37]

It is a dignified, formal letter, driven by Yale's desire to repair some political damage from the university's release of Joe in 1942. It has the charming public voice used with such facility by Bart Giamatti. But Bart can't repress the worshipful boy in himself, a "fervent" fan "unalterably faithful to the Boston Red Sox" and "the grandest game." Such sentiments would overwhelm Giamatti five years later at the Wood home.

Following his ninetieth birthday a number of interviews were conducted with Smoky Joe Wood. A couple were designed for publication. Most were motivated by curiosity about specific players and incidents from one of the oldest living ex–Major Leaguers. The most personally revealing is one Joe gave to his grandson Richard Wood, which focuses on family history. But most essential to understanding the emotional life of Smoky Joe Wood is a discussion with Lee Goodwin in December 1980. During this conversation Joe's memory was beginning to fog, and he often had a hard time hearing the questions. But his answers were direct, clear, and more revealing than he likely realized. In that conversation more than any other, Joe decided, in his words, to "just tell my own experiences and the way I feel about it. That's all."

For example, he said that he "never worked" as an adult. "[I] worked more when I was a kid than I did when I was a man." That's because baseball was never a chore; "[I] had fun playing something that I'd have played for nothing, if I could've afforded it," which separated him from the modern players, he believed, who are all about the money. Consequently, leaving home wasn't difficult for him: "No, Lord, no. . . . I wanted to play baseball." And his parents? They were "tickled to death as long as I was making the money. . . . It all went there." With his father often absent and his mother preoccupied with many tasks, the young Joe had freedom: "I used to slip in one door from my mother and out the other one. [She] wasn't aware of where I was all the time. I was never old enough to be told anything, as a kid, before I was out and gone." He "certainly" enjoyed being a father, but the credit went to Laura, who "did all of it [in the beginning and] did a great job." He never pushed his boys too hard to play baseball.

They also discussed one of Joe's favorite topics: money. Goodwin wanted to know if making money with the Red Sox changed his lifestyle. Joe's answer is surprising, indicating that many others grew dependent on him: "No. I have been tied down all my life putting out my money for somebody else. I took care of my brother for a while, but I got back everything with interest. And then my mother and sister, and father, and then as our family come along, I had to dish out here and there for the family. In the meanwhile I made a few investments that turned into something." But Joe had "no idea of getting rich." In his words, "Money is just as good to me as what it will buy, so I wouldn't give a nickel for millions. As long as I have enough to get along on my even keel, the same way I am used to living, that's all I care about."

Most fascinating are his words on his injury. The pain was "right in the joint" but "wasn't anything that was constant. Just when you get in a certain position." More than the pain, the loss of strength was debilitating; the arm "just wouldn't do it, that's all." Curiously, though, "The few throws that I had to make from the outfield it didn't seem to bother me." But he didn't feel cheated; it "was just a pain in the neck.... I never talked so very much about it. I had it. That was all there was to it, and our salaries were so low and we wanted to hold on to the job so that we could keep the checks coming in." In fact he felt guilty "when you can't do it and you know you can't do it and still they are paying you." He felt "pretty lucky" that Dunn, Fohl, and Speaker "stayed with" Joe for a long time "trying to get" him back on the field. The comeback wasn't magical; "I didn't do any exercises.... I was a natural ballplayer." His improved hitting was simple, too; "instead of getting on the end of the bat, I got slid up on the bat six or eight inches ... where I had a better feel of it and a better balance."

Equally instructive are his feelings. Of his fall from the heights, Joe advised, "You have to laugh those things off, that's all. Some of the kids used to wait after the ball games outside, after we had our showers and were dressed, were going out to get in the car to go home. They'd say, 'There goes Smoky Joe Wood, smokeless now.'" According to Joe you do "all the work" "to get the arm so you can throw the ball, always hoping." But when "it wouldn't," you must "take it as it comes, that's all." Not able to "do anything else," Smoky Joe felt "lucky" that he "was able to follow through and to go and make a living out of it." Truthfully, he said, "If I would've had a few more brains, I wouldn't have been throwing the ball all the time." But in his day there were no "finishing up pitchers." "Nowadays ... they have a bullpen just for that."

Charmingly, in the Goodwin interview Joe debunked all kinds of myths, personal and national. Making him into superhuman hero was silly because he just had a gift: "I could do anything in the sporting line: golf, pool, billiards . . . ice skating, track, run races, hop, skip and jump. All those things. . . . Just natural." Major changes when he came from little places like Ness City and Ouray to The Hub? In Joe's mind there was no story there either. He felt no deep problems adjusting: "I liked it everyplace. . . . I didn't think too much about the cities and towns and so on. I just was out there playing ball. That's all I thought of, all I ate and drank and everything else. Baseball." To assertions that the Old West was unique, Joe responded, "Oh, I don't know. They were people out there." Sure, "It was the wild west. That was all there was to it. They had cowboys and so on." But he was drawn to absurdities: "They have more cowboys now than they had then. Make-believe cowboys. Get them on a horse, they'd fall off."

At ninety-one Smoky Joe Wood still had a lot to say about baseball. He assured Goodwin, "The whole idea of pitching is to have a wind up . . . in a position where your body helps your arm." The high leg kick is "wrong, unnatural," though it "takes the concentration from the hitter." Luis Tiant, who "doesn't have enough to knock your hat off if he hit you right in the eye. But he turns around, and they don't know where the hell the ball is, or from where it's coming." It is most natural, Joe believed, to pitch "what people call three-quarters." Doing so Joe relied on his fastball and "never had a change of pace" [but] "had a very good curve ball." Smoky Joe Wood emphasized location, especially with the best hitters: "It wasn't exactly what you had. It was where you put it." In his day pitchers were "high inside and low outside," but they have "been low now for about twenty-five or thirty years [1950s to 1980]." He theorized that low pitches and night lights forced catchers into deeper crouches to see the ball better.

Because of Joe's tendency to be more revealing in his final years, Lee Goodwin heard some amazing clarifications. When Goodwin asked about players of color, Joe's response was initially observational. He said "colored players" tended to go into boxing and football more than baseball, adding somewhat defensively, "I'm not saying they aren't good athletes, but they go for big money." Sensing his response was not well informed, he added defensively, "I didn't live in the small towns where there were any colored people." When asked whether Joe played in exhibitions against blacks (when, for example, Smoky Joe Williams demonstrated his dominating talent), Joe responded, "No." Did it feel good to be famous? "Naturally, naturally," but it really didn't affect him, he believed. Finally, unlike later players, "[I] never tried to offend people. . . . I found out that's the best thing to do . . . over the years."

In this tape Smoky Joe Wood's observations about aging are brilliant. Had he learned to enjoy getting old? Joe: "No, sir. . . . If I could swing a golf club, I'd sure be out playing." Given his acceptance, had he found the process interesting? Joe: "No. I don't see anything interesting about it." "But I get up in the morning, and I don't have a bit of trouble putting in the time all day long, right around here, without even going out of the house. Of course, when the weather eases off a little, I'll get back out there and do some walking and so on." He was "a little bit scared of this bronchial thing;" he had "taken a shot" but noted, . . . "Any little trouble settles in those lungs and that's it." Joe saw the connection with smoking. "I hadn't quit smoking when I came back from California [in] '53. But . . . here in Connecticut they give you free x-rays for your chest. . . . And . . . the report was positive. . . . So that's when I stopped. . . . Dr. Wilson said it was chronic bronchitis," verging on emphysema. Crucial for Joe was avoiding just "sitting around here waiting to die."

He was obviously lonely, telling Goodwin, "Virginia . . . and her husband [fill] the void in my life since losing my wife. Nobody will ever take her place." Recognizing the hard times ahead, the children had taken action. Clarence and Virginia had moved in with him, and Bob sought medical aid. Though Joe had some loss, his hearing remained acceptable, and his operation for cataracts was successful. But in the spring of 1981 he had to quit driving and gave his last Chrysler (with its "autopilot" as Joe called the cruise control) to son Bob.[38] For his age Joe's general health was good, though he would sit silently on his porch for hours. On the other hand, the mental issues were a worry. So the children took him to a geriatric specialist at Yale, Leo Cooney. Even as he showed signs of dementia in his nineties, Smoky Joe remained at home with minimal care. When a neighbor boy joined the Little League, Joe found the strength to watch him play. The youngster was ecstatic, and the family was pleased to see Joe in the community.

By the early 1980s the Red Sox organization was vigorously supporting old-timers games and former stars. In this spirit Smoky Joe Wood was invited to opening day at Fenway in 1982, April 12, where he was captured in a video. Joe was nattily dressed, in a blue plaid shirt setting off the requisite bow tie, deep red. He fitfully straightened his glasses, as if to clarify things, using his left hand. His right was nearly immobile. At the ballpark he donned a tan trench coat and a felt hat, with a dark blue sport coat added to the blue shirt and red tie. Though disabled Joe used his right hand when he shook hands with Tony LaRussa, manager of the Chicago White Sox, as son Bob looked on proudly. Asked if he was going to throw a curve or fastball, Smoky Joe quipped, "Tell them it's going to be a roller." Joe threw left-handed and laughed afterward as Red Sox catcher Rich Gedman returned the ball. In an interview that day, Joe was loyal to his best friend, declaring, "Speaker was the greatest of all of them. I never in my life have seen a better outfielder than Tris Speaker." "If [DiMaggio and Mays] could play as well as Speaker, they could never surpass him."[39]

As the final years turned into the final months, Joe did his best to keep his cherished routines. People would occasionally visit him on the porch in New Haven, and Bob would take him to Pennsylvania whenever health and time would permit. But aging was making some rituals difficult. The last time Carl Vogt saw Smoky Joe he was "badly crippled and walked with crutches" as he entered the post office in Shohola.[40] To the very end Joe shared his opinions about baseball. Among recent pitchers he liked Juan Marichal and could identify with Jim Palmer's courageous return from arm problems. Among position players he liked the intensity and hustle of Pete Rose. And though no one was better than Tris Speaker, Smoky Joe Wood had to admit that THE CATCH by Willie Mays was the best he saw. Politically the union was a good way for players to make more money, but Joe also wanted the costs for fans reduced. And with expansion "colored fellas" improved teams otherwise weakened.

Joe Wood's final appearance at Fenway Park was on May 27, 1984, when he threw out the first ball at the second Red Sox old-timers' game. As former Red Sox players were introduced on the field by Ken Coleman, Smoky Joe waited in the passenger's side of a golf cart in right field. Dressed in a gray suit, white shirt, blue sox, a black bow tie, and stylish brown shoes, the former pitcher wore a present-day Red Sox cap and large brown mitten-type gloves on his hands, for circulation problems near his thumbs. He fidgeted with the glove on his left hand, apparently trying to get a tighter fit, as the announcer called Wood a great *left-handed* pitcher.[41] As the cart began its procession down the first-base line, Joe removed his cap, probably just a reflex action because playing to the fans was not his style. The driver paraded Joe to the playing field as the television inserted a medium shot of him as a young player, underwritten with *1908–1915*, his years as a Red Sox player.

As the cart progressed inside first base, the greatest speed-ball pitcher in Red Sox history got a major ovation. With Joe looking generally in the direction of the fans behind the dugout, the announcer authorized the moment: "A deserved hand for a great gentleman." With his picture on the scoreboard behind him, Joe nodded faintly and briefly doffed his hat in his left hand, then replaced it as the cart stopped in front of the stands. For the first time he looked directly at the crowd and asked directions from the driver as he prepared the ceremonial pitch to Gedman, number 10. Joe took the ball in his left hand, the right one remaining limp in his lap, and waited patiently for his cue. Though Gedman was no more than twenty feet from the cart, Joe's wrong-handed toss only made it halfway. Rich scooped up the baseball and returned it to the sensation of 1912, patting Joe behind his right shoulder as the announcer requested, "A hand for Smoky Joe Wood." As he was driven from Fenway for the last time, Joe managed a half-hearted smile, gripping the ball randomly across the seams with his left hand.

That fall Richard Lee, mayor of New Haven from 1954 to 1970 and a longtime friend of the Wood family (a high school classmate of Joe Frank), successfully pursued an honorary doctorate for Joe Wood. Although Lee worked primarily through Yale secretary John Wilkinson, President Bart Giamatti, who knew Wood's achievements through Bart's father, looked forward to meeting Smoky Joe. For many years the Giamattis had lived in Westville, a short walk from 90 Marvel Road, but by his own admission, Bart "never had the nerve to visit [his] hero." During the ceremony Joe sat in a wheelchair in an off-white shirt, plaid suit, and deep red tie. He had a hearing aid in his left ear, and his mouth was open as if he were studying Giamatti's words. But Joe was looking past the president, over the certificate, and into space. Obviously nervous as he performed his duties, Giamatti then hooded Joe and read the proclamation granting Coach Wood a Doctor of Humane Letters. On the formal document Bart's name was signed as "Angelo Bartlett Giamatti, PhD LLD."

Although suffering from advanced Alzheimer's disease, Joe Wood sensed the drama of the moment. According to grandson David Wood, he repeatedly glanced at the picture of his wife, even mumbling his affectionate name for her, Peg. Joe's son Bob repeatedly asked Joe to take his hand down from his face, where he was trying to cover tears. When Giamatti said that Joe allowed Yale to honor itself by honoring him, Bob added, "He's had a lot of great things happen. But this is hitting him the hardest that I've ever seen." When Bart expressed concern — "We don't want it to be an unhappy time" — Bob assured Yale's president that Joe was happy and encouraged his father, "Hang in there, Dad. You're doing great"; the emotions are "okay" and "all right." Bob explained to a reporter that his father was "very appreciative" but "a little apprehensive" as the first ballplayer to receive a Yale honorary doctorate.[42] It was,

Bob added, Joe's greatest honor since the first game of the 1912 World Series.

With Joe's health clearly in decline, during the early weeks of 1985 the family faced a tough decision. He was increasingly disoriented in space and time, often crying out in the night for his wife. It was obvious that he needed more care than Virginia and other caretakers could give. Sadly, everyone, including Joe in his more lucid moments, knew that (in Bob's words) "he shouldn't have been alive." So they moved him to a nursing facility in the area. But Smoky Joe couldn't understand what was happening to him, why he was being taken from his home. Overtaken by fear he didn't make the transition very well. It brought out the fighter in Joe Wood, who became a difficult patient. Even though the move was the best action, it was not a pleasant end. Smoky Joe Wood died on July 27, 1985, at Soundview Convalescent Home in West Haven, Connecticut.

When the end came, Clarence and Virginia were close by. Appropriate to his dedication to his father, son Bob was attending a sports memorabilia show in New Hampshire. The attending physician, Leo Cooney, is now head of geriatrics at Yale. As a loyal Red Sox fan, Dr. Cooney felt privileged to attend to Smoky Joe. And, yes, during the end-of-life care, he checked. In his best professional opinion, it was a rotor cuff injury that had sidelined Joe Wood seventy-five years earlier. The official cause of death, most common for patients who finally refuse to eat, was "dehydration." As the wire service noted, arrangements were made by Hawley Lincoln Memorial Funeral Home, at 493 Whitney Avenue in New Haven. The next day Lou Brock, Enos Slaughter, Arky Vaughn, and Hoyt Wilhelm were inducted into the Baseball Hall of Fame at Cooperstown.

The funeral was delayed until September, when a joint service was held in Shohola, Pennsylvania, for Joe, Laura, and Joe's sister, Zoë Theimer, who had died in 1984. It was a small, private service at the family cemetery. Though it didn't include representatives from the baseball community, quite a few people attended. A tent and chairs were set up at

the gravesite, and a microphone system used. Rob Wood, the older son
of Bob Wood, gave the eulogy. Laura and Joe were, by law, cremated
and their ashes interred. The tombstones are simple. Hers reads

LAURA O'SHEA
wife of
JOE WOOD
May 4, 1890–Aug. 2, 1979

Befitting his close-to-the-earth life, his marker makes no heroic claims,
settles no scores, in or outside baseball. It is

JOE WOOD
Oct. 25, 1889–July 27, 1985

ELEVEN

Legend and Legacy

"It's funny how some things stand out and others fade away."

—JOE WOOD, in Honig, "Joe Wood"

The legend of Smoky Joe Wood begins with the records he established during his fourteen years of Major League baseball. The SABR book for 2007 lists him eighth all-time in overall winning percentage among pitchers with at least one hundred wins, fifth among right-handers. His 1912 season (34-5 for .872) is fourth in winning percentage. The sixteen consecutive wins that same year are now fifth in the American League, but he remains tied for first in consecutive wins in a single season in the AL. Because he pitched just under the required 1,500 innings (he was fewer than 65 short), his hits per nine-inning game is omitted from the SABR book, but his average would otherwise place him in the top ten. Joe Wood's lifetime ERA of 2.03 is third all-time (if the 1,500 inning minimum is waived). His thirty-four wins in 1912 remain ninth in the modern era, his 1915 ERA of 1.49 is in the top thirty, and his ten shutouts in 1912 is tenth. Wood also still holds the second highest percentage of starts that were shutouts.[1]

On the offensive side Joe Wood hit .283 overall (Hall of Famer Harry Hooper, for comparison, hit .281), including .298 as a position player. His .296 average in the first year off the mound was tenth in the American League. He bettered that production with his .366 in 1921 (Joe had fewer than 200 at bats and thus isn't included in the official statistics), and he had 92 RBI in 1922, both top ten in the league. According to statistics established by Richard J. Thompson, Joe Wood was a significant force as a clutch hitter as well; as a position player he had a better RBI:at-bat ratio than Tris Speaker, Nap Lajoie, and Shoeless Joe Jackson, and was only slightly below that of Ty Cobb. In the modern era only Ruth and Wood have three hundred innings pitched in one season and five hundred at bats in another. They also were the only players to start a World Series game at both pitcher and outfield.[2]

These impressive statistics are only magnified by Joe Wood's reputation in his time. During the early twentieth century, Smoky Joe Wood's fame was comparable to that of Cy Young, Ty Cobb, Christy Mathewson, Tris Speaker, and Walter Johnson. Especially remarkable are the words of his peers. Most famous is the statement of Johnson, which still resonates nearly one hundred years later: "Can I throw harder than Joe Wood? Listen, my friend, there's no man alive that throws harder than Smoky Joe Wood."[3] Equally noteworthy is Napoleon Lajoie's summary of Joe's skills in October 1912: "The swiftest pitcher I've ever faced. . . . It is not exaggerating it a bit when I say that at times I have been unable to see Wood's fastball as it sped over the plate. . . . He perfected his curve ball so that it's about the quickest breaking ball I've ever tried to hit."[4] Similarly, Harry Hooper recalled, "I think the thing I remember best about 1912 . . . was the pitching of Smoky Joe Wood. . . . I've seen a lot of great pitching in my lifetime, but never anything to compare with him in 1912."[5] Most perceptive, though, was Charley Hall, who noted in 1911: "Show me anything athletically that involved working with the hands and body and ask me who I'd single out as the best, I'd say without hesitation that I'd pit Joe Wood against the world. He was the most natural and talented of them all."[6]

It wasn't just the best players who recognized Joe's greatness. Clark Griffith, the leader of the Washington Senators in 1912, declared that Joe Wood "equaled by only one man now pitching — Walter Johnson" and predicted Wood might "win three games in the first four days of the contests."[7] (It took a couple of extra days.) Before radio brought baseball to the smaller places in the United States, newspapers alone described the game, primarily for fans in the major cities. To many scribes working for those papers, men who reported the game with close scrutiny in metropolitan areas like New York, Boston, Chicago, Philadelphia, Washington, and St. Louis, Joe Wood represented the game's highest ideals, best abilities. Most influential was T. H. Murnane, dean of Boston sportswriters, who noted, "Joe Wood, now in his twenty-third year, is said by experts to be the best of all the pitchers."[8]

Once the arm troubles forced Wood to pursue a second career primarily as an outfielder, the legend of Smoky Joe Wood shifted to his courage in the face of diminished skills and celebrity. In 1917 Damon Runyon established the elegiac tone in his reminder that "in 1912 . . . [Smoky Joe Wood] rose to the pinnacle of pitching greatnesss."[9] Once no hope remained for Wood's return as a pitcher, his resilience became the subject of reflections. The key article was by F. C. Lane in *Baseball Magazine* in October 1921, which judged Wood's career "more striking, more uncommon, truly more remarkable" than that of Tris Speaker. Joe surpassed Tris, according to Lane, because the ex-pitcher "determined to fight against those hard circumstances which had so abruptly terminated his career" and "against all seemingly insurmountable handicaps he made good."[10] Even more precise was Grantland Rice a year later: "Two qualities . . . carried [Joe Wood] through—brains and courage."[11] For those writers Wood's reemergence was the story of human courage in the face of life's inevitable pain and loss.

But the mythmaking surrounding Smoky Joe Wood has not always been accurate. *Babe Ruth and the American Dream* reiterates many misconceptions, describing Joe as "a matinee-idol type from Colorado, always perfectly turned out, tall and slim, with slicked-down hair and piercing eyes." In the company of Speaker ("tough, muscular Texas roughneck," "hard drinker and compulsive gambler"), the two are imagined as "dashing, abrasive, quick-tempered products of the last frontier . . . bad men to cross and good men to have as friends." Asked to comment

Wood said it sounded good but the only fact was that "he and Speaker were good friends." The exaggeration continues today in, for example, *First Fall Classic*, where Smoky Joe Wood is identified with Protestantism and the Wild West, as well as the Confederacy, teetotaling, and "hard thoughts and old ideas." Neither religious nor a cowboy, Joe lived almost exclusively in northern states and loved his beer. When truth and legend have conflicted, it is often easy to print a false Smoky Joe.[12]

But one truth has been undervalued in the story of Smoky Joe. He was a poster boy for playing baseball for itself, not for fame or money. A continuing appeal of Joe Wood is his passion for the game. He is most convincing when he claims, "I would've played baseball if I never got paid for it."[13] As tempting as it is to relegate such sentiments to a simpler, sweeter age of innocence, Smoky Joe Wood actually endured his share of poverty and disappointment. Nevertheless, Joe abandoned himself to his gifts, without limits or timetable. Such a commitment came with risks and danger. He gained fame at twenty-one but also tore his rotator cuff before there was a remedy. But he had few regrets. To Lawrence Ritter Joe confided, "I used to love to be in there. I don't know of anything that I'd rather have done. . . . I would have played ball for nothing if I could've afforded it."[14] Other times Joe declared, "Baseball is all I ever wanted. I could eat, sleep, and dream baseball."[15]

His passion for the game informs another legacy, his interviews with Ritter and Murdock and others lovingly preserved by his son Bob. In these tapes for the most part Joe was a reticent and self-effacing talker. But when encouraged to feel safe, he was disarmingly direct and revealing. The result is a rare intimate record, an often brutally honest man speaking with strong conviction—and charming humor—about the game and its legends. From Joe we learn that Cy Young was a "two-fisted drinker" who liked his Cascade Whiskey and Rube Waddell liked to blow into his beer so he could study the expanding head on the brew.[16] Eddie Cicotte considered himself a jokester, but his jokes weren't funny, and his "slick, smooth" style wasn't successful with the women. According to Joe Wood the most effective way to pitch Joe Jackson was to "duck." At the plate when you missed a pitch from Walter Johnson, you didn't know whether you had swung over or under the ball. Only Eddie Ainsmith, a catcher with the Senators, tipped a pitch for Joe.

He was just as straightforward about the conditions, on and off the field, of Deadball Era baseball. When he broke in with Boston in 1908, most of the unmarried players lived in Putnam's Hotel, where food was delivered via dumbwaiters, with little partying in the rooms. The teams traveled at night in special Pullman cars, which were often too warm. But the sleepers were comfortable. Typically, the players would board the train at 10:00 or 11:00 p.m. and wake up the following morning in the next town, except for St. Louis, which was a two-day ride. Most of the time they ate in the hotels, and going to movies was a common diversion. Some reporters (for example, Tim Murnane, Paul Shannon, and Herman Nickerson) would ride with the players. Certain unnamed scribes would "ride" the players, though Joe felt he was treated "average." Because there were no coaches, players themselves analyzed the games, when not playing cards.

Other details in the interviews add color to the games. Duffy's Cliff, in Joe's view, was "six or eight feet high" but less than a forty-five-degree angle from the rest of the field. One of his most pleasant memories was from 1922, when he hit a 420-foot home run over that wall, and the net, out of Fenway Park. The pitchers of his time, he said, unintentionally threw a version of the slider, but they "weren't smart enough to pin it down." As Joe Wood observed, it wasn't just the screwball, called the fade away or outshoot, that was key to the success of Christy Mathewson. Big Six was the only player who could control the high curve effectively. In Joe's day the spitball was "just another pitch"; "if it hadn't been for the shine ball, the mud ball, and so on, and the emery ball, they never would've outlawed the spitball. They had to outlaw every ball so as to keep you from going to your mouth."

Most captivating are his personally revealing reminiscences. He had a good curve ball, which he "thumbed" to get movement, but his most confidence was in the fast ball with the snap and hop: "I was so fast I just loved to pop 'em through there." He only used the curve, on average, six or eight times a game, "just enough to let 'em know" he "had it." The strongest offensive team of his era was the Detroit Tigers. Obviously Cobb was a force. But Sam Crawford gave Wood even more trouble; he "wasn't a race horse. He was a power hitter and could hit" Joe "like the devil." The player who gave the most trouble was relatively obscure, with a lifetime batting average of barely .240, Pete Compton, who played for the St. Louis Browns from 1911 to 1913.[17] Smoky Joe admitted to being nervous before he pitched a no-hitter against the Browns, but then the game started and "bingo. It was all over." Most poignant is his reflection that he should have cared better for his arm; "I didn't think my arm would ever leave me. But it did."

Of the interesting options for Smoky Joe off the field, pool was the most potentially lucrative. Charlie Peterson, the champion trick-shot artist, offered Joe ten thousand dollars to represent St. Louis in a three-cushion league. Similarly, Benny Allen, when he was champion with Johnny Kling in Kansas City, asked Joe to compete in the city's pool championship. But Joe never wanted to be a shark. He enjoyed the game best as relaxation between friends. In a billiard room run by the gambler Jack Doyle in New York, Joe first took seriously a nickname like Smoky Joe. Doyle explained the advantages of having an attractive tag, marketable to the press and fans. Joe took that advice into consideration when Paul Shannon first called him Smoky Joe. Though Joe rarely used it himself, even in autographs, and his wife, Laura, didn't like it, that advice encouraged Joe to be more flexible about the moniker.

Essential are his impressions of the 1912 World Series. Most students of baseball know that Wood struck out Crandall and Fletcher to end the first game of the Series, with the tying and winning runs on second and third. But as Wood reveals in these tapes, he worried that the Giants would pinch-hit an obscure player, then on the Giant's bench, Beals Becker. In Joe's first year in professional baseball, 1907, when he was in Hutchinson and Becker at Wichita, Beals had hit Joe mercilessly. But McGraw instead sent Becker in to pinch-run and preserved Wood's fondest memory. On the same series he says that Snodgrass shouldn't have been the goat of the last game. More crucial was the dropped foul fly. Aware of Hooper's impression that Wood was so nervous he was unapproachable during the 1912 Series, Joe insisted that he was never jittery because he was "only twenty-two years old" and oblivious to the gravity of the moment. It "didn't bother me," he said.

Understandably Joe Wood's reflections on famous players centered on Tris Speaker, his teammate and roommate in Boston and Cleveland, manager with the Indians, and longtime friend. Joe correctly remembered Tris was called up before Joe but sent back down to Little Rock when Wood arrived in August 1908. Of course, Tris's nickname, Spoke, was a play on his family name, but given their friendship, Joe surprisingly didn't learn where or when Speaker acquired the name. It was true, in Joe's opinion, that Speaker was the greatest outfielder ever, and yes, he played at times twenty-five or thirty feet behind second base. Those skills were developed, Joe remembered, by Cy Young hitting balls over Speaker's head for hours at a time during the 1908 season. And Tris would drink with Cy, even some mornings, in order to hang out with the great pitcher.

For Joe Wood, Tris Speaker was unobjectionable, in character, skill, and intelligence: "He was a grand person. There was no getting away from it. He was wonderful. He could do everything in baseball [pounds table to emphasize his words]. He could hit and field and run and throw . . . and steal bases . . . and he knew what he was doing every minute." Unlike many other stars Speaker was able to translate his abilities for less gifted players. His more democratic approach made him an inspirational manager; in Joe's words, Tris was "wonderful. Everybody played for him, loved him." Then, casting his cold eye on life and death, Joe Wood added, "Cigarettes killed him . . . absolutely. He used to hang down in the runway, on a bench going down the tunnel into the club house, hang down in there and watch the ballgame and smoke his cigarettes every inning." Despite this one weakness Tris Speaker was the greatest outfielder. Only Willie Mays approached him in ability.

Ty Cobb simply was the "greatest baseball player that ever lived," according to all the old-timers. Joe didn't fear Cobb, he remembered, but he'd "pitch and pray" because "whatever you'd throw up [Ty] hit." And he was a terror on the bases. When Wood came up in 1908, pitchers were already knowing "damn well he was going to go" and then saying, "I'll get him the next time." Indicative of Cobb's domination was the story of Cy Morgan, pitcher for the Red Sox, who brushed back Cobb during the 1909 season. Infuriated, when he reached third base, Ty yelled at Morgan, "Get in there, you son of a bitch, I'm coming all the way." Intimidated by Ty Cobb the pitcher was unable to tag him after a passed ball and the next day was traded to the A's for cowardice, Joe explained. "Cobb always told me and other fellows he played against, 'All you got to do is give me room to get in there and it'll be all right, but if you don't give me room, I'll cut my way in.' Fair enough," for Joe.[18] "When the average ballplayer would be thinking what they were going to do, Cobb would be doing it. . . . [He] could beat you alone."

Joe was humored by Ty's obsession with money, particularly the stock market and the wires running into his hotel room so that the Peach could follow his fortunes. Cobb had a fatal flaw as a manager. As Joe explained to Lawrence Ritter, "Ty Cobb was the greatest ballplayer that ever lived. And he figured that other ballplayers should do things as well as he did. And they couldn't do it. For that reason he was a bad manager."[19] On a sadder note Joe remembered seeing Cobb in the late 1950s at Cooperstown, near the end of Ty's life. They had, in Joe's words, "quite a little talk" initiated by Cobb's saying he that was doing "no good." Later it was obvious to Joe that cancer had invaded baseball's greatest player, and Ty knew it. Whether such a delicate time inspired discussion about Leonard's accusations, Joe didn't say. In the face of death, Cobb's and later Wood's own, Joe was loyal. As Joe summarized, "Ty Cobb had very, very few friends," but "Ty was . . . one of my very best friends."

Shoeless Joe Jackson was the most natural baseball player ever, according to Joe Wood. His style was distinctive: "Joe Jackson would stand up there and he'd swing from his tail and practically throw himself down.

But he'd get two strikes on him and he'd choke up a little on the bat." Wood felt that Jackson's lack of intelligence forced him to the sidelines in social situations; Shoeless Joe became a bystander because he "didn't know enough to get into anything." Jackson's illiteracy was a handicap, indicated by the oft-repeated story that Joe Jackson would wait for his roommate to visit the dining room. Then Jackson would pretend to read the menu until the other player would order. Shoeless Joe would follow the other's request with "Give me the same" or "That sounds good. I'll have that too," covering his inability to read. Joe felt Shoeless Joe Jackson followed the real conspirators during the 1919 Series.

If Shoeless Joe Jackson was the greatest natural hitter, Walter Johnson was the most natural, and the greatest, pitcher. In Joe's memory Johnson was "massive-looking" and yet a "perfect gentleman," "a grand person." Walter would have set every record if he had played with a team as talented as the Boston Red Sox. Equally imposing was Ed Walsh, the only other Major League pitcher besides Johnson to pitch in his regular rotation, finish as many as three games, and then pick up his normal place in the order. Joe wasn't sure if Walsh originated the spitter, "but he was the first real star with the spitball. He was a great big broozer and a swell looking fella." Then Joe added a couple of qualifiers. Walsh "never was a pitcher" until he got the spitter and was elected to the Hall of Fame though he only pitched seven complete seasons.

A lot has been written about an angry exchange between young Babe Ruth and Joe Wood over an unretrieved loose ball when both played for the Red Sox.[20] There is no reason to doubt that story or others that Wood and Speaker made racial slurs at the Babe. But Joe Wood had a complex view of Babe Ruth. Admitting that players (including Joe) called him the Big Baboon, Wood understood that rookie Ruth was "just a great big boy," a "wild youngster" from reform school who "never sat down and counted his calories." Wood, who liked to dress well and practiced moderation, was repelled by Ruth's personal habits, especially his lack of table manners. But Joe always credited Ruth's skills, primarily as a hitter and a fielder, noting the Babe had trouble pitching deep into games and thus didn't pitch in the 1915 Series, with the Red Sox using only Leonard, Foster, and Shore.[21]

Taken together Joe's comments on The Babe add up to a character analysis. Smoky Joe found significance in Ruth's inexperience, calling him a "big kid" to Murdock and a "big hick" to Ritter. Joe added that the Babe "just didn't know what it was all about" because "he had been in this home for years." But the reform school was merely formative, not pathological. There was "no harm in the Babe," Joe maintained, even in his sexual appetite. Women were "the biggest thing on his mind," but that was "no more so than the rest of the gang" who chased skirts. Crucially, "he was no dumbbell at any time." According to Smoky Joe Ruth's behavior resulted from the rough background at the "industrial school" followed by a sudden release from such a controlled environment. That is why sexually charged Babe Ruth, Joe said, was ready to "go after a snake if someone would hold it for him."

As one would expect, Joe Wood's memories of Hal Chase focused on Chase's gambling. Most repeated is the story of Hal's attempts to get Walter Johnson involved in craps at the Addie Joss Benefit Game, which Joe considered an early form of the All-Star Game. Johnson never joined in, according to Wood. But as a card game developed, Joe, who was seated to the right of Chase, lost about forty or fifty dollars, no small sum in 1911. Apparently sympathetic to Joe's plight, Hal told him not to cut the stack, after which Joe received winning pairs and recouped some of his money. Joe's summary: Hal Chase "could handle" his cards. More than the shady dealing, Wood had issues with Chase's individualistic play. As Joe remembered, Prince Hal would throw to first without caring whether the pitcher could cover. But Joe didn't speculate on whether Chase fixed games.

Joe Wood gave interesting observations on other legends of baseball history. Since Cy Young was leaving Boston when Joe came up as an eighteen-year-old, he "didn't know Cy well enough. Didn't hobnob with him. Speaker did." Eddie Collins, just out of college (Columbia University), also wasn't familiar to Wood. But Joe felt there was "nothing too good or too nice to say about Eddie Collins—the whole family"; he was considered a "great person and very heady man" and hit Wood well. Joe repeated the understanding "that Yawkey wouldn't have gone to Boston except for Eddie Collins going with him." Addie Joss was "was just finishing" when Joe rose to the Majors. But people told him Joss "was a grand person." Joe considered George Sisler a great player, noting that George started as a pitcher, though he was a first baseman when Wood first saw him in 1915. Joe also knew Gehrig during Lou's Columbia year and regularly hosted him at Yale in exhibition games at the end of spring training.

When pressed, Joe Wood named his all-time team. At first base he would have played either Lou Gehrig or Hal Chase. The rest of the infield came easily: Eddie Collins at second, Honus Wagner the shortstop, and Pie Traynor at third. The outfielders would be Ty Cobb, Tris Speaker, and Babe Ruth. The best pitchers, according to Joe Wood, were Walter Johnson, Lefty Grove, Chief Bender, Christy Mathewson, and Mordecai "Three-Finger" Brown. He would have chosen either Bill Dickey or Mickey Cochrane as his catcher. The best defensive outfielder would be Speaker followed by Willie Mays; Joe omitted Cobb because Ty was "not so great an outfielder." Then Joe stopped the speculation, fearing that he had "probably said too much already."

The interviews also contain intriguing takes on baseball history. For example, when asked about the best Red Sox pitchers of his era, Joe said that Hugh Bedient had a great "slow ball," Ray Collins's only effective pitch was his palm ball, Charley Hall was "pretty good," and Ernie Shore showed excellence from the moment he entered the Majors. Wood took some credit for the success of George "Rube" Foster, who followed Joe's advice to hold his fastball between the seams. In Cleveland Jim Bagby had a "pretty good" screwball, and Joe's friend Stan Coveleski used an "off the cuff" spitball. Rube Marquard "was after the almighty dollar," in Joe's judgment. Jake Stahl was a "great big bruiser who graduated from the University of Illinois" and "went into a bank with his father-in-law. That was what you did at the time" to supplement your baseball income. Germany Schaefer, who stole from second back to first and opened an umbrella to encourage an ump to call a game, was the most entertaining. In baseball, as in everything, Joe observed, there are "grand people in there and shysters."

As he explained in the Ritter audiotape, Joe Wood's first indication of the Black Sox scandal came in late 1920 when Eddie Cicotte told Wood at the Winton Hotel in Cleveland that the White Sox didn't dare win again. Once the story was out, most of Joe's information came through the papers, but when pushed, Joe finally declared, "Chick Gandil was the ring leader in that whole thing. He always was a louse. Everybody knew he was a louse." Cicotte "was on the same order, only not so openly," with the "sailor ball . . . the only thing that made Cicotte a great pitcher." Joe had more compassion for Joe Jackson, "pitiful" because he "couldn't read nor write" and "somebody said something, he'd follow them, probably." Happy Felsch had the same disability, Joe felt. The question for Joe was Buck Weaver: "The only way that I can figure Weaver was connected was that they mentioned it to him and he wouldn't recall it." But when asked whether Landis's punishment fit the crime, Joe exited the discussion, asserting, it was "none of my business."[22]

Joe Wood had strong feelings about management, off and on the field. He applauded Jim Dunn, the owner of the Cleveland Indians, who gave him a second chance and paid good money for Wood as a pitcher and position player. In Joe's estimation, "there was the brightest man who was ever owner of a baseball club — Jim Dunn. . . . [He] paid what you signed for and more, too, if you earned it. Jim Dunn was a great man." On the other hand, in case anyone would disagree, Harry Frazee was more into his Broadway plays than the Red Sox. And Joe joined others in considering Connie Mack and Charles Comiskey cheapskates, reiterating that Big Ed Walsh "never got a cent more than three thousand dollars a year." Joe Wood was certain that Comiskey's tightness contributed to the temptations of the White Sox during the 1919 Series. Joe claimed to have been tossed from only one game for arguing balls and strikes. Surprisingly, he considered umpiring improved since his day, when many were "homers," shaping calls for the home crowd. More specifically, Billy Evans was "about the best umpire in the league," but Bill Klem was a "hard head."

Joe was good with financial details. When he signed with the Red Sox in 1908, the team wanted him to report for less than the $2,400 base salary, so he went home until Boston upped the ante. According to Joe the average salary for a rookie in 1908 was $400 per month, though the best players were able to negotiate a percentage of their contracts, sometimes as high as $20,000–$50,000 Like today there were major financial discrepancies among players. The theme of Joe's negotiations after the 1912 year was clear: "If you had a pretty big year, you wouldn't get any tremendous raise like you get nowadays, but you'd get a pretty good raise . . . if you battled hard enough." Off the field he received $1,000 for ghostwritten articles, and for the Regal shoes advertisement run for the 1912 World Series, he "just signed for something they wrote" and was paid in shoes, about five pairs. His 1915 salary was close to the 1913 figure.

Smoky Joe Wood also offered his perspective on the changes in the game since the Deadball Era. The game was essentially the same, though today's players are deeper in both the infield and the outfield because of the livelier ball. Also, Joe maintained, "We had to catch the ball. Now the glove catches the ball," allowing more backhanded traps. Since his playing days the most obvious modifications were the new glove, as used by Bill Dickey, which allowed the catcher to use one hand, and the tighter yarn, which made the ball travel farther.[23] He felt the skills remained about the same, but with expansion "not as many topnotch ballplayers as [they] had because you've got so many more leagues." Though he "never gave it a thought" that blacks were excluded, after moving to Yale, he "saw several Negro teams. Good ballplayers, too, believe me."[24] On strikes he felt that the players should get what they deserve, but Joe also believed that "ridiculous" salaries might "ruin the game." Fiscally conservative, he thought players and owners both should be less greedy to "cut down on the expenses of the people going to the games." Joe supported the DH; it helps old-timers after their legs go.

Most instructive is Joe's revisionist history for the Veterans Committee. For example, Clyde Milan of the Washington Senators was the best lead-off hitter of the time, with blazing speed. He should be in the Hall of Fame, according to Joe Wood. Even more egregious is the omission of Larry Gardner, Wood's teammate at both Boston and Cleveland. Joe "wouldn't trade [Larry Gardner] for a half dozen Frank Bakers. And he never once has been mentioned for the Hall of Fame." Gardner was one of "the damnedest clutch hitter that ever was," even better than Speaker when the game was on the line. On the other hand, Eppa Rixey, who twice lost more than twenty games and barely won as many as he lost, should not be in the hall. Joe agreed with Rixey, who reportedly said that the Hall of Fame had scraped the bottom of the barrel when he was inducted.[25] Finally Joe opposed renewed efforts on his behalf: "If I wasn't good enough to go in when I was in my prime, I'm certainly not good enough to go in now."

Smoky Joe suggested a few other topics for consideration. Another great player of his time who never got enough consideration for the Hall of Fame was Ken Williams of the St. Louis Browns, who hit .324 or better in five consecutive seasons, had a lifetime batting average of .319, and outslugged Babe Ruth with thirty-nine home runs in 1922. In addition to being remembered for his emery ball, Russ Ford may have introduced the slider. Despite having left field in Fenway dedicated to him, Duffy Lewis was not a great outfielder, though he was a good hitter, even with a hitch in his swing. On the other hand, Harry Hooper possessed a "fine, accurate arm" but was not a consistent hitter. After Walter Johnson the best pitchers in the AL were Eddie Plank (left-hander) and Chief Bender (right-hander), both of the Athletics. For fans of trivia Harry Hooper had hay fever, but only in California, and Joe helped Harry find a job at Princeton because Yale didn't pay enough. In passing Joe Wood noted that Tiger Ed Killian was always tough on the Red Sox.

For his talent, love of the game, and ties to baseball's Deadball Era, Smoky Joe Wood is remembered where he played and lived. On October 25, 1977, Pike County, Pennsylvania, commissioners James R. Duffy Jr.,

H. James Crellin, and Warner M. DePuy declared that date "Smokey [*sic*] Joe Wood Day" "to honor Mr. Wood as a former great baseball player, baseball coach, and a leader in [their] community for many years." Each year on that day—Joe's birthday—the city of Milford leads that celebration. Included is a trip up the road to Shohola and a few hours of drinking at Rohman's, where Joe and Babe Ruth used to drink (though not together).[26] Shortly after the old Wood homestead burned in 1991, Schocopee Road TR 407, just to the west of Woodtown, was renamed Smokey Joe Road.[27] More personally, Durinda, Joe's granddaughter, placed a baseball on his grave (in a glass and plastic container) with a thankful inscription after the Sox won the 2004 World Series.[28] In May 2007 the baseball park in downtown Ouray, Colorado, where Joe first played organized baseball, was named in his honor.

The life of Smoky Joe Wood has been celebrated in many ways, from the sentimental to the legendary. L. L. Bean asked Joe's son Bob for boots from Joe's hunting trips to be placed next to those of Babe Ruth and Ted Williams in their museum at the company's original home. According to recollections in the Wood family, a bank in San Francisco (probably the old Crocker Bank bought out by Wells Fargo in 1986) had a Smoky Joe uniform from the 1912 World Series. Another was given to the actor Joe E. Brown. There is also a third on display at the Hall of Fame. In Keene, New Hampshire, there is a [Joe] Wood Street in a cluster of roads named after famous baseball players; it is just west of Wagner, Cobb, and Hooper Streets. In 1943 Joe was given membership in the Kansas Hall of Fame. On March 21, 1948, he was elected to the Red Sox All-Time Team.[29]

Because of his work at Yale, the state's rabid support of the Red Sox, and Joe's residence in New Haven for more than sixty years, he was given the Gold Key Award in 1967 by the Connecticut Sports Writers Alliance (emblematic of the Connecticut Hall of Fame), on January 30, 1967. Previous recipients included Connie Mack, George Weiss, Ed Walsh, and Joe Cronin. Attending were baseball representatives Mickey Mantle, Yankees general manager Lee MacPhail and manager Ralph Houk, as well as Dick Williams of the Red Sox and Bob Scheffing of the Mets. Joe was granted the Connecticut High School Coaches Association Hall of Fame Award (1980), the Greater New Haven Diamond Club Hall of Fame Award (its first inductee, also in 1980), and the Doctor of Humane Letters from Yale in 1985.

Other awards were given to Joe Wood posthumously. On January 13, 1986, Joe was honored by the NCAA at its eightieth annual convention. The memorial award was presented "for his faithful service to his institution and higher education, his valuable contributions to intercollegiate athletics, and his wholesome influence upon the lives of young men." In 1995 he was inducted into the Colorado Hall of Fame, the Wayne County, Pennsylvania, Hall of Fame, and the Red Sox Hall of Fame.[30] In the last ceremony, on November 1 at the Sheraton Hotel in Boston, Joe was among the initial members in the team's hall. He joined Dom DiMaggio, Johnny Pesky, Jim Rice, Frank Malzone, Tony Conigliaro, and Mrs. Jean Yawkey. Sportscasters Ken Coleman and Curt Gowdy presented the award to son Bob Wood. More than ten years after his death, on October 18, 1996, Joe Wood was inducted into the Pennsylvania Baseball Sports Hall of Fame.

The name of Smoky Joe Wood is indelible in the history of baseball. In their 1981 book *The 100 Greatest Baseball Players of All Time*, Lawrence Ritter and Donald Honig coined the phrase "Smoky Joe Wood Syndrome," meaning when "a player of truly exceptional talent" has his "career curtailed by injury or illness" and yet "should be considered an all-time great despite his relatively short career."[31] A few years later, in 1990, others joined Ritter in telecasting a film based on the Ritter interviews. That movie, titled *The Glory of Their Times*, appeared on the Discovery Channel and remains available in DVD and blu-ray format. Joe, as a central figure in the 1912 World Series, is given significant time in Ken Burn's film study *Baseball* (1994).[32] More recently Joe Wood returned to sports headlines in 2007 as Rick Ankiel made his comeback as an outfielder after pitching successfully, but erratically, in his younger years. Writers and SABR members named the most famous precedents as Babe Ruth and Joe Wood.[33] In 2011 MLB-TV's *Prime Nine* named Joe's 1912 season the greatest "lightning in a bottle" year.

The legend of Smoky Joe Wood is also deeply ingrained in baseball literature. Most interpreters name Ring Lardner's *You Know Me Al* a primary text in the evolution of baseball stories from reporting and dime novels, limited by adolescent concerns and moral dicta, to first-rate fiction. Lardner's novel explores a darker side, using first-person narrative to suggest the confusion and braggadocio of a young, borderline Major League pitcher. In letters to his friend Al, Jack Keefe of the Chicago White Sox asserts that his skills are underappreciated — by other players, his managers, and even women he desires. Along the way, in one of his brief stints in the Majors, Jack brags, "The Boston bunch couldn't of hit me with a shovel and we beat them two to nothing. I worked against Wood at that. They call him Smoky Joe and they say he has got a lot of speed."[34] To inflate his value, the narrator claims superiority to the best: Smoky Joe Wood.

Equally intriguing is the possible influence of Smoky Joe Wood on Zane Grey. Grey most certainly knew of Wood, who was his neighbor in eastern Pennsylvania. The Wood family farm is less than twelve miles from Lackawaxen, Pennsylvania, where Grey had a home starting in 1905. Local legend says that the writer fished with Wood's brother. And the timing is right. Zane Grey published baseball books from the year after Wood joined the Red Sox until the end of his pitching career (1909–15). Even a character in the first book, *The Shortstop*, was named Hutchinson, the Kansas town where Joe played the year before the story was published. But that novel relies on Grey's own experiences and the do-it-for-a-good-woman formula. More suggestive of Wood's life is Grey's short story "The Knocker," originally published in August 1910. It describes a Kansas City woman's choice between two players, one talented but a knocker (bad-mouths his teammates) and a kinder, struggling second baseman. That could be Laura O'Shea's preference for Joe over Chick Brandon two years earlier.

The next year, 1911, was the first great year of Joe Wood's celebrity.

He won twenty-three games that year and starred in the Addie Joss Benefit Game. That was also the year Grey published the novel *The Young Pitcher*. While *The Shortstop* focuses on baseball in small towns and movement from cities to healthier western life, *The Young Pitcher* is a psychological study of resilience in the face of failure. According to the coach, Worry Arthurs, "All the victory was not in winning the game. It was left for his boys to try in the face of certain defeat, to try with all their hearts, to try with unquenchable spirit. It was the spirit that counted, not the result." Again the Wood influences are moot. But the main character, Ken Ward, is an infielder turned pitcher features a fastball with an "upward jump," which Wood claimed only he and Walter Johnson could achieve. Like Joe, Ken escapes jams by employing a snap of his wrist, giving him extra speed and a hop on the ball.[35] That sounds like the Joe Wood delivery.[36]

Other Smoky Joe references are more definite. Although it isn't always a happy thing to be associated with Ty Cobb, Joe and Ty are linked in a short story by Arthur (Bugs) Baer, called "The Crambury Tiger," published in *Colliers* magazine on July 11, 1942. It is a fictional account of the substitute team fielded by the Tigers on May 18, 1919, after Cobb was banned for attacking a fan and his teammates protested by refusing to play the following game. The story belongs to a used replacement player, describing how Cobb's stolen jersey inspires success, in baseball and sexual conquests, for substitutes. At one point the narrator describes a meeting between Ty and his teammates: "The White Sox were playing the Red Sox in Boston, so Ty wired Harry Lord of the Chicagos and Smokey Joe Wood of the Bostons asking if they would join a protective association of players with short tempers. That was thirty years ago and Lord and Wood are still giving the matter their serious consideration."[37] Joe's angry outbursts on the mound and protection of Cobb from Leonard's accusations clearly fueled Baer's imagination.

In a more popular vein, comic books kept the legend of Smoky Joe Wood alive after World War II. In August 1949 *All-Time Sports Comics* ran a feature titled "Smokey Joe" with the teasing caption: "This is the incredible yarn of a never-say-die kid whose baseball career hung by a hair—or pardon us—we really mean a *wig* full of hairs!!" Joe wears bib overhauls and has red hair and freckles. He dons a cowboy hat, chews hay, and proves his skills by throwing a rock through a knothole, hitting a cow, and angering his father. But the scouts dismiss him as a "hayseed." Noting in the sports pages that the "Kansas Bloomer Girls" need a pitcher, Joe buys a wig, names himself "Sadie," and leads the team on "a spectacular winning streak against the toughest major league opposition in exhibition games all over the country," including a no-hitter. Finally, the Red Sox promise him a contract, with the stipulation, "If you were a man." Removing the wig, he declares, "Joe Wood is the name . . . but you can just call me 'Smokey [*sic*].'" Thus, "the immortal Smoky Joe Wood" joined the "Red Sox in 1908!"[38]

But the comics were far from the end of the line. As Lawrence Ritter notes in *The Glory of Their Times*, Joe was respected, and feared, by Chicago writer James T. Farrell.[39] Farrell's *My Baseball Diary* (1957) begins by asserting, "Smoky Joe Wood, who belongs in the Hall of Fame, won 34 and lost 5 [in 1912]," then drifts back to youthful anxiety: "In memory, it seems as though he hurled all those games against [the] Chicago [White Sox]." Joe "would stand out there on the mound in his red-trimmed gray uniform, hitch up his pants and throw. To this day, I have a recollection of a strange sensation as if my head had emptied while he fired the ball in the shadowy park." Farrell's adult side knows that "perhaps Walter Johnson was faster than Wood. Perhaps Grove and Feller were. But . . . if there was a better pitcher than Wood in baseball . . . the difference was merely academic." Nevertheless, the terrified boy lives in the man: "No pitcher ever depressed a little boy in the stands more than Joe Wood did me. Why did the Boston manager, Jake Stahl, have to pitch him against the White Sox?"[40]

A second major text of baseball literature, besides *You Know Me Al*, is the poetic reminiscence by Roger Angell, "The Web of the Game," published in the *New Yorker* in July 1981. It describes a "mid-May" Yale Field afternoon at an NCAA regional tournament game between Yale and St. John's. The star pitchers would become famous Major Leaguers: Ron Darling and Frank Viola. For Angell the game becomes a blend of past and present: "I almost felt myself at some dreamlike double-header involving the then and the now — the semi-anonymous strong young men waging their close, marvelous game on the sunlit green field before us while bygone players and heroes of baseball history — long gone now, most of them — replayed their vivid, famous inning for me in the words and recollections of my companion."[41]

That companion is Smoky Joe Wood, who repeatedly fingers the memento, a gift from "a manufacturer." It is inscribed

> Presented to Joe Wood
> By his friend A. E. Smith
> in appreciation of his splendid
> pitching which brought the
> WORLD'S CHAMPIONSHIP
> to Boston in 1912.

The "web," baseball across generations, is represented by Joe and the watch, emblems of a living past. The story ends with Angell's faith that "somebody will probably tell Ron Darling that Smokey [*sic*] Joe Wood was at the game that afternoon and saw him pitch eleven scoreless no-hit innings against St. John's, and someday — perhaps years from now, when he, too, may possibly be a celebrated major-league strikeout artist — it may occur to him that his heartbreaking 0–1 loss in May 1981 and Walter Johnson's 0–1 loss at Fenway Park [to Smoky Joe] are now woven together into the fabric of baseball."[42]

Another major achievement of baseball fiction is Eric Rolfe Greenberg's *The Celebrant* (1983). The novel describes an adolescent Jewish boy's worship of Christy Mathewson. The climax of the novel is the 1912 World Series, in which even Christy's celebrant admits "the arm of arms belonged to Smokey [*sic*] Joe Wood. Mathewson at his finest never won so many games while losing so few as Wood did that year, and McGinnity in his prime was never so powerful." He records the end of Game One: "In the tumultuous moment Joe Wood showed enormous courage. He struck out Fletcher on three pitches, and on a full count he struck out Crandall. It choked the screaming mob, and it won the game for Boston." In a later conversation between Wilbert Robinson and John McGraw, the Giants skipper argues, "Boston was good enough when they beat us, but, hell, Robbie, when you played them Speaker was gone, Yerkes, Stahl, Cady, Joe Wood. We had to face Smokey [*sic*] Joe." In a novel focused on "Matty . . . the master," "Smokey [*sic*] Joe Wood" is among the elite "demigods we create and celebrate."[43]

But Lardner, Angell, and Greenberg didn't exhaust the legend of Smoky Joe Wood. Even today Joe fascinates creative writers. He appears in *Murder at Fenway Park*, by Troy Soos, pitching against the fictional baseball player/detective Mickey Rawlings. In his first at bat, Mickey, "quickly discovered why Joe Wood was called 'Smoky': he threw the ball so fast that the only thing visible was the smoke that seemed to trail behind it. I used to think this an exaggeration by the sportswriters, but the blur of the speeding ball really made it look like it had a tail of steam." Also described is the September 6, 1912, duel between Smoky Joe and Walter Johnson. And Joe reappears in a subsequent Mickey Rawlings story by Soos, *Hanging Curve*, as a right fielder for the Cleveland Indians in 1922. This time Joe hits a grounder to third baseman Rawlings, who misplays the ball into two errors, with Joe ending up on second base.[44]

Smoky Joe is not so positive a character in J. S. Winter's mystery *Murder on Mount Monadnock*, in which he joins Franklin Roosevelt, Mark Twain, Amy Lowell, Willa Cather, Jack Johnson, Robert Frost, and Lillie Langtry at the Halfway House Hotel on the New Hampshire mountain. Creative license shifts Joe's World Series heroism to 1908 and his arm troubles to 1910. The Cleveland years also disappear, though he is correctly named a "college baseball coach" during the Depression. While rehabilitating his arm Joe becomes one of many lovers of Langtry's daughter Marie and a prime suspect in her murder. Despite having a wife in Kansas, Joe carries on "a little arrangement for a while" with such "an attractive and willin' woman." Joe explains flippantly, "A little recreation was just what the doctor ordered." He also fought with his lover the night of her death, but he didn't kill her. "Red Baron" von Richtofen did it. Guiltless dalliance was enough.[45]

Smoky Joe Wood is twice the subject of noted poet, New Englander, and Red Sox fan Donald Hall. Joe appears in the "Ninth Inning," from *The Museum of Clear Ideas*.[46] Woven into images of mutability are the poet's memories of being a youthful fan of the Tigers and sharing with his mother a recent Red Sox victory over the Yankees. To create a feeling of isolation and loss, Hall imagines a transaction between a baseball player and an equally skilled poet: "My dog and I drive five miles every / morning to get the newspaper. How / else do I find out when the Sox trade / Smoky Joe Wood for Elizabeth Bishop?" In the essay collection *Here at Eagle Pond*, Hall remembers the comfort he found in the words of his grandfather, a farmer and baseball fan: "When we paused for breath in the hayfield, my grandfather's clear storytelling voice would bring Smokey [*sic*] Joe Wood together with Johnny Pesky, Cy Young and Tris Speaker together with Mel Parnell, eternal teammates on the showy all-star team of a farmer's daydreams."[47]

While less obvious than his legacy in literature, Smoky Joe Wood lives in the movies as well. Some writers argue for a link between the novel *You Know Me Al* and the baseball movies made from Ring Lardner stories in the 1930s. Specifically, *Elmer the Great* is said to be based on the 1912 World Series, implicitly connecting the movie with Joe.[48] But that film is more Lardner's revision of the 1919 World Series, which left the writer embittered about baseball. In *Elmer* the title character, Elmer Kane, played by Joe E. Brown, has an appetite like Babe Ruth and is pursued by the Cubs as the next Ruth. He hits sixty-seven home runs. But he also postures and preens, stupidly falling in with the manipulative city girl and gangsters. The dramatic issues are whether he will return to his hometown girl or accept five thousand dollars from the mob over a gambling debt. Unlike in 1919 Elmer secretly bets the bribe money on the Cubs and hits an inside-the-park grand slam home run to win the game 4–3 in the bottom of the ninth. If only the Black Sox had been so Hollywood.

Smoky Joe Wood in Depression Era movies has less to do with Ring Lardner than the star of *Elmer the Great*, Joe E. Brown, a friend of Joe.[49] The key movie for the Brown-Wood connection came a year before *Elmer the Great* (released in 1933).[50] It was called *Fireman, Save My Child* (1932).[51] Half the screenplay relies on the legend of Rube Waddell; the hero's attraction to fire engines interferes with his baseball. But the protagonist is a right-handed pitcher discovered in Kansas playing for a team called the "Rosies" (Wood played for the Bloomer Girls). And his name is Smoky Joe (Grant), who insists on holding the ball with the seams (as Wood always did) and loves to ride horses (another Wood pastime). His hometown girl also sticks with him despite his apparent engagement to a city girl. Like Laura O'Shea she declares, "Congratulations on your engagement, Joe." In a variation on the 1912 Series, he hits a game-winning homer, though he is tempted to chase a fire engine when caught between third and home. *Fireman, Save My Child* echoes the lives of two baseball legends: Rube Waddell and Smoky Joe Wood.

Then there is *Field of Dreams*, a 1989 film, written and directed by Phil Alden Robinson, and based on the novel *Shoeless Joe*, by W. P. Kinsella.[52] Joe Wood doesn't appear in the Kinsella story. But Phil Robinson is a friend of Joe's granddaughter Durinda Wood, a costume designer in Hollywood. Well aware of Durinda's grandfather, the director wanted to "give a shout out to Durinda."[53] The magical moment, emotionally and figuratively, arrives when the ghosts of famous players from the Deadball Era are conjured from the corn field. Joe Jackson declares to Ray, Annie, Terence Mann, and Archie Graham, "You wouldn't believe how many guys wanted to play here . . . had to beat them off with a stick," and adds, "Hey, that's Smoky Joe Wood, and Mel Ott, and Gil Hodges." After Shoeless Joe, Smoky Joe is the first player in the baseball heaven of *Field of Dreams*.

The sense of the uncanny pictured in *Field of Dreams* is echoed in the legend of Smoky Joe Wood. In Shohola, Pennsylvania, locals believe "in the ghostly veil of moonlit nights, the shadows of the Babe, Lou Gehrig and Smokey [*sic*] Joe Wood can be seen once again tossing the ball around along Smokey [*sic*] Joe Road." Red Sox fans remember that on October 17, 2004, Bob Wood, Joe's son, threw the first pitch at game four of the American League Championship Series in Fenway Park, which began the comeback to the first Red Sox Championship since 1918 and broke the Curse of the Bambino. Those fans today relive Joe's magic in the serial "Smokey Joe and the Time Bandits" when time-traveler Ryan O'Malley meets Joe in 1912 as a "handsome young star" made "reclusive" by too many grating questions "relating to his personal life than his pitching."[54] Red Sox Nation is also aware of the irony that since 1999 the Hall of Fame has an inductee named both "Cyclone" and "Smoky": Joe Williams, premier pitcher in the Negro Leagues, not Joe Wood. Nevertheless, Boston baseball fans still speak his name with reverence. He was Joe Wood. And he threw smoke. For them there was, and is, only one Smoky Joe Wood.

This was the man, trailing his unique baseball history, who left the usually loquacious president of Yale and eventual commissioner of baseball, A. Bartlett Giamatti, speechless on January 3, 1985. The two Barts—the worshipful boy and the man in love with brilliance—were dumbfounded in the presence of this complex man. Despite little formal education, Smoky Joe respected intelligence and became quite emotional as "Doctor Wood." He cherished traditional values, but he was driven by an intense passion for baseball, winning baseball. In his last years Joe recognized the differences reflected in culture and race. But he remained steadfast, even stubborn, about family, self-reliance, and his Chryslers. He practiced self-control and preached moderation. But he was always ready to fight—for respect, security, and life itself—even when his extremes alienated others. Like few others Smoky Joe Wood was "the natural" athlete. But his greatest legacy is not his physical skills. It is his loyalty and courage in the face of adversity. In those qualities he outperformed his more-famous friends Tris Speaker and Ty Cobb.

27. Joe as the Yale baseball coach.
Courtesy of Joe Wood Archives
and Rob Wood.

Formal picture on board Tatsuta Maru, San Francisco to Hawaii, July 1935.

Barr (Faculty), Joe Wood (Coach) Brown '35 (MGR)
ummins '36, Dillingham '35, Klinczak '37, Klein '35, Cooke '36, Rankin '36, Blake '37, Dugan '35, Ships Purser,
elley '37, Carhart '37, Horton '37, Woodlock '35, (Capt), Capt. of Tatsuta Maru, Curtin '36, Bosworth '36, Walker '36

28. (*Above*) The Yale baseball team aboard the ship to Japan, July 1935. Courtesy of Joe Wood Archives and Rob Wood.

29. (*Opposite top*) Joe's New Haven home from the mid-1930s until his death: 90 Marvel Road. Photo by author.

30. (*Opposite bottom*) Joe with Cy Young, Lefty Grove, and Walter Johnson, at a Boston Old-Timers Game, July 12, 1939. Joe pitched, played first, and hit a home run. Courtesy of Joe Wood Archives, Rob Wood, and Boston Public Library, Leslie Jones Collection.

31. Joe and his sons at Yale versus Colgate, Yale Field, April 21, 1941. Courtesy of Joe Wood Archives and Associated Press.

32. Smoky Joe Wood and the Grey Eagle, Tris Speaker, on their last journey together, at Grossinger's in late 1958. Photo by Ted Howard. Courtesy of Joe Wood Archives, Rob Wood, and Les Howard.

33. Joe's favorite place in his later years, the front porch of 90 Marvel Road. Courtesy of Associated Press.

34. Joe throwing out the first pitch at opening day of Fenway's seventieth year, April 12, 1982. Courtesy of Associated Press.

35. (*Above*) Joe's last pitch at Fenway Park, May 27, 1984. Courtesy of Joe Wood Archives and Rob Wood.

36. (*Opposite top*) Joe being presented Doctor of Humane Letters by Bart Giamatti, January 3, 1985. Courtesy of Joe Wood Archives and Associated Press.

37. (*Opposite bottom*) Smoky Joe Wood's honorary doctorate from Yale University. Courtesy of Joe Wood Archives and Rob Wood.

33. Joe's favorite place in his later years, the front porch of 90 Marvel Road. Courtesy of Associated Press.

34. Joe throwing out the first pitch at opening day of Fenway's seventieth year, April 12, 1982. Courtesy of Associated Press.

35. (*Above*) Joe's last pitch at Fenway Park, May 27, 1984. Courtesy of Joe Wood Archives and Rob Wood.

36. (*Opposite top*) Joe being presented Doctor of Humane Letters by Bart Giamatti, January 3, 1985. Courtesy of Joe Wood Archives and Associated Press.

37. (*Opposite bottom*) Smoky Joe Wood's honorary doctorate from Yale University. Courtesy of Joe Wood Archives and Rob Wood.

PRAESES ET SOCII
UNIVERSITÁTIS YÁLENSIS

IN NOVO PORTU IN RE PUBLICA CONNECTICUTENSI
OMNIBUS AD QUOS HAE LITTERAE PERVENERINT SALUTEM
NOS PRAESES ET SOCII HUIUS UNIVERSITATIS

JOE WOOD

HONORE ACADEMICO SUMMO IAM ADORNANDO AD GRADUM TITULUMQUE
LITTERARUM HUMANIORUM DOCTORIS
ADMISIMUS EIQUE CONCESSIMUS
OMNIA IURA PRIVILEGIA INSIGNIA AD HUNC HONOREM SPECTANTIA
IN CUIUS REI TESTIMONIUM
HIS LITTERIS UNIVERSITATIS SIGILLO IMPRESSIS SUBSCRIPSIMUS

SCRIBA ACADEMICUS   PRAESES UNIVERSITATIS

DATAE a.d. VI ID. DEC. MCMLXXXIV

38. Joe as an old man, still a Boston
Red Sox fan. Courtesy of Joe Wood
and Rob Wood.

39. The Wood family cemetery
near Shohola, Pennsylvania.
Photo by author.

40. Joe's watch featured in Roger Angell's
"The Web of the Game." Courtesy of
Hunt Auctions.

41. The centennial of Smoky Joe's first
Red Sox game, Fenway Park, August 17,
2008. Photos by Edra Garrett.

Epilogue

Fenway Park, August 17, 2008

Joe Wood's first Major League game was Monday, August 24, 1908, in Boston, at the Huntington Avenue Grounds. One hundred years later, on August 24, 2008, the Sox were scheduled to play the Blue Jays in Toronto. So the team decided to recognize the centennial by inviting twenty members of the Wood family to Fenway Park on Sunday, August 17, 2008, for a day game, also against the Blue Jays. The Friday game was washed out, and under drizzle the Blue Jays won on Saturday, 4–1, with Roy Halladay beating Paul Byrd in his first start for the Red Sox.

For attendees there was some good news in the bad weather and loss to Toronto. The rain out pushed back the pitching assignments, moving Josh Beckett, the Red Sox ace, from Saturday to Sunday. In a move reminiscent of the 1912 World Series, when Joe Wood was held back from Game Six in New York, the Fenway faithful would see their best pitcher throw at home with an extra day's rest. And the weatherman cooperated. It was warm, in the mideighties, with just a few lonely clouds here and there. As in Game Seven in 1912, the park was filled to overflow.

The Wood family members and their guests, totaling twenty-four, met at Gate D, at the corner of Yawkey and Van Ness, at 11:00 a.m., two and one-half hours before the game. They were escorted through that gate, down the concrete corridor, into elevators, and up to the fourth floor dining area at the front of Fenway. Lunch had the feel of a reunion.

Most of the Woods were from nearby towns in Connecticut or New Hampshire. But Rob, Bob Wood's older son, and his wife, Lucy, had traveled from Spoutwood, their organic farm above Baltimore. Durinda, the daughter of Bob and Connie, had flown in from LA. And a surprise guest was Monty Wood, Rob's son, reunited with his father after a three-year separation. The scene was convivial.

Naturally, the conversations drifted back to Smoky Joe Wood, most often called "Granddad." Jonathan Wood, son of Joe Frank, Joe and Laura's oldest child, remembered his grandfather as a "very humble" man who loved children and baseball, though he felt no need to relive his past. Jonathan remembered the eighty-foot tower Joe built in Shohola, hoping for better reception of televised games. Joe also traveled out of the valley with neighbors, especially if the Yankees and the Red Sox were playing. He supported the team performing closer to Joe's standards. Jonathan found his grandparents disciplined, hardworking people who loved family life and kept an orderly, clean, modest household that felt warm and gracious.

Steve Wood Jr., son of Joe and Laura's second child, had many of the same impressions as Jonathan but added that Joe could be stern and, even in later life, deeply competitive. Once, while Steve was riding with Joe, Smoky chased another driver through the hills of eastern Pennsylvania, declaring, "I'll show this guy a thing or two" because he had gotten close to Joe's rear bumper. Like other descendants Steve remembered his grandfather's love of ice cream, often really ice milk because Smoky watched his diet so closely. Joe kept careful tabs on his grandchildren as they played catch, with Granddaddy remaining on the porch and not participating in their games. More personally Steve recalled the fiftieth reunion of the 1912 team and getting a ball signed by all the players. Later that summer when he and his friends ran out of balls, Steve ran home for the Fenway one, which sadly ended at the bottom of a brook. Grandmother was a "sweetheart," quieter than Joe.

Mike Cousins is the grandson of Joe's daughter, Virginia Wood Whitney. He was fourteen at the old-timers game in 1984, when he sat with the family near the dugout and was impressed that John Tudor welcomed advice from his grandfather Smoky Joe on how to throw a curve ball. Mike still cherishes a poster he received that day, signed by many greats, including Ted Williams. More personally he was present when Joe received the honorary doctorate from Yale. As impressive as that day was, Mike was surprised to see his granddad, always very strong, cry so openly. Seeing such a tough man so emotional had left Mike with an indelible image twenty-four years later.

Rob, Bob and Connie's oldest child, has sensitive memories of Joe Wood and his legacy. He was eleven when he visited Yankee Stadium for an old-timers game, where he met Bobby Doerr and Joe DiMaggio. Even more impressive was his visit with his father and grandfather to the hotel room of Ty Cobb, where Ty was ill and in his bathrobe. The respect between Ty and Joe was "palpable," Rob remembers, which added to his impression of his granddad as a "mountain of a man." Like Jonathan, Rob sensed Joe's love of children, especially when Monty accompanied Rob to Pennsylvania. Rob remembered Joe as a lover of ice cream and a natty dresser, typically sporting a bow tie and a pocket watch. Responsible for the funeral service honoring his grandparents, Rob read from Psalm 23, a favorite of Laura, and chose the poem "Lord of the Dance," expressing the simultaneous living and observing of one's life, which Rob felt energized Smoky Joe.

Similarly reflective was Durinda Rice Wood, Rob's sister, who said she returns less to her grandfather's glory years than to the time when he couldn't pitch any longer. She likes to remember that Joe "soldiered on," picking himself up and making something else of his situation. For her Joe Wood has been a continual inspiration as a person who played for the love of baseball and was resilient in the face of the loss of his abilities and fame. The theme of courage, described by sportswriters during the Cleveland years, is something Rindy "thinks about" in her "own life a lot."

Once the invitees had enjoyed their lunch at the tables spread across the room, they took a few minutes to walk outside the glass partitions and absorb the stunning view of Fenway Park from above home plate. Then, around 12:45, representatives of the family were escorted down to the playing field, where they lined up around the inside of the re- taining wall. Attending the group was Drew Thurlow, a great-nephew by marriage (through the Rice family) of Joe Wood. Born in 1979, just six years before Joe's death, Drew never met Smoky but believes that Joe's history contributed to Drew's being one of four (from more than five hundred) applicants chosen for a job with the Red Sox. Drew fond- ly recalls Joe's youthful success against Christy Mathewson and Walter Johnson and his 92 RBI in his last year with the Indians. He credits Joe with making it possible for Drew to jump on the pile in 2004 as the curse evaporated.

Before the singing of the national anthems of Canada and the United States, Drew, Red Sox president Larry Luchino, and a couple of mascots escorted Bob Wood and his twin sister, Virginia Wood Whitney, the last surviving children of Joe and Laura, to an area just behind home plate. While the two stood proudly, images of Smoky Joe, including his famous duel with Walter Johnson on September 6, 1912, flashed on the screen in center field. Accompanying the pictures was the announcer's description of Joe Wood's accomplishments with the Sox and his en- shrinement in the Boston Red Sox Hall of Fame. Following the cere- mony President Luchino greeted all the Wood family.

The game was a letdown because the Jays' Shaun Marcum easily out- pitched Josh Beckett in a laugher, 15–4. The only redeeming moments for Red Sox fans were a towering home run just inside the left-field line by Dustin Pedroia (for the second consecutive night) that landed in the expensive seats atop the Green Monster and Jonathan Papelbon's strikeouts of two of the last three Toronto batters. There were also a couple of moments both nostalgic and spooky. Like Joe Wood in the ninth inning of Game One of the 1912 Series, Beckett had runners on second and third with one out in the first inning. Unlike Joe, who struck out the next two, Josh hit a batter, and Toronto followed with hits off the Monster and to all fields, scoring six runs, the same as the Giants scored off Joe in the first inning of Game Seven in 1912. Thus the most famous and infamous moments of Smoky Joe's postseason career were replicated in the top of the first at Fenway on August 17, 2008.

After the game the Wood family and their guests returned to the field for pictures, taken mostly in the Red Sox dugout and in front of the Green Monster. Especially engaging were the young girls, Smoky Joe's great-grandchildren, who posed as if snagging line drives off the scoreboard. But everyone wanted his or her picture with the famous left-field wall as the background. Because Virginia, like her twin brother, had just turned eighty-nine, she immediately escaped the oppressive heat for her home in Wallingford, Connecticut. Left to oversee all the shenanigans on the field, while reading an article on his father, was patriarch Bob Wood, who sat in the third row of loge seats between home plate and the Sox dugout. He was greeted by each person, relative or not, as he or she left the field.

Since this day the most monumental event in the family was the loss of Bob on the last day of May 2009, at age eighty-nine. He loved people and wanted them to be happy in his presence. He was very caring toward his wife, Connie, even when a stroke made their lives difficult. In the words of his son Jeff, Bob was "extremely kind and fiercely loyal to his family." He wanted to make all around him relaxed and welcome. He certainly was gracious to me and my wife on a number of occasions. More than anything else on the long road to the publication of this book, I will remember his generosity to me, courage in facing emphysema, and trust with Smoky Joe materials, some quite valuable. He repeatedly said, "If it is my time, it has been a good life," and he looked forward to being placed in the Wood cemetery "along with the rest of the crew." Wherever he is, I hope he finds a Red Sox game and a cold Bud Light. Rest in peace, my good friend.

One last note. During the writing of this book, I have been asked repeatedly if I am related to Smoky Joe Wood. My standard reply has been, "No, but I am working on it." In fact I have spent a lot of time tracing his ancestry and mine. I even had DNA testing, to compare my chemistry with that of Richard Wood, Joe's grandson. Alas, Smoky Joe and I are not closely related. But just as I was finishing the book, Linda Gass helped me find two truths. Joe and I are related by marriage: both of our relatives married into the Middaugh family, so Joe and I are something like fifth cousins twice removed. And my great-great-grandfather, Elijah Wood, was a steersman who transported lumber on the Lackwaxen River above Woodtown. So while Joe and I are not close kin, our ancestors may have met while logging down rivers between northeastern Pennsylvania and western New York. I believe so.

Notes

Introduction

1. This document was held by Joe's last surviving son, Bob Wood. Bob's materials, including pictures, news clippings, audio- and videotapes, and family memorabilia, are designated in this book as the Joe Wood Archives, abbreviated JWA. Undocumented sources throughout *Smoky Joe Wood: The Biography of a Baseball Legend*, including audio- and videotapes that capture Joe's appearance and voice, are from the JWA.

1. John F. and Howard E.

1. Corning, *Concise History of Orange County*, and Leslie, *Battle of Minisink*. See also Booth, "Short History of Orange County."

2. Orange County was home to other famous Americans: Hector St. John de Crevecoeur wrote *Letters from an American Farmer* there; Noah Webster had a school in Goshen; politicians George Clinton, DeWitt Clinton, and William H. Seward hailed from there; writer Stephen Crane lived in Port Jervis; and D. W. Griffith, the pioneer filmmaker, shot some of the first "Westerns" around Cuddebackville, New York, between 1906 and 1915.

3. Recently the gravestone of Jonathan Wood was found in a pasture near Greenville, New York. See Leek, "Gravestones Back in Right Place," 1.

4. For the history of Shohola, see http://shohola.org/ and links to the railroad.

5. See Mathews's *History of Wayne, Pike and Monroe Counties*.

6. This document courtesy of David Wood, Joe's grandson from Milford, Pennsylvania.

7. Pembleton et al., *Ness County History*, 5; and Hall, *Requiem II*, 476. The family Bible notes that Samuel C. Wood was born on February 5, 1823, married Victoria Helms on January 10, 1860, adopted John E. Williams-Wood, and "died 40 minutes past 2 a.m., March 29th, 1883." He owned the Bible when he died. John Williams later gave it to John F. Wood.

8. Ritter, "Joe Wood," 155. According to local records, he also bought "Lots No. 1 and 2 in Block No. 16 of the original town of Ness City ks, from Ross Calhoun on February 13, 1880."

9. Pembleton et al., *Ness County History*, 16. Significant for the conflicts described later in the chapter, Ness City's first school superseded one located two miles eastward where George S. Redd had been the teacher. In 1881–82 a new school was built on land given by Ross Calhoun, and John F. handed the schooling over to a Mr. Burdick.

10. Pembleton et al., *Ness County History*, 3.

11. Pembleton et al., *Ness County History*, 60. By this time John F. had money issues, as Joe noted to Lee Goodwin: "One time . . . he owned a whole big part of State of Kansas, practically owned a whole little town there [Ness City]. . . . He was worth a lot of money. He lost it all on speculating on land out there."

12. Levi B. Wood, John F.'s older brother, who had traveled to Ness City in February 1887, mysteriously disappeared there in 1889, the year of Joe's birth. Whatever the reason for his absence, Levi survived to later die in 1921 in Breckenridge, Texas.

13. See Ward, "Joseph Wood, Esq., Pitcher," 50–51.

14. Joe remembered these clowns being part of the Barnum and Bailey Circus. But the most publicized visit to Chicago by that group was two years later, in 1895.

15. See, for example, CuChullaine O'Reilly, "Anything Goes—America's First Great Endurance Race," at http//www.thelongriders guild.com/chadron.htm; http://www.wyomingtalesandtrails.com/douglasdoc.html; and Robert Cantwell, "The Great 1,000-Mile Race from Chadron to Chicago, *Sports Illustrated*, September 2, 1962, at http://sportsillustrated.cnn. com/vault/article/magazine/.../index.htm.

16. Hurricane Diane, on August 22, 1955, extensively damaged roads, dams, homes, and camps in the area, washing away the small community of Parkers Glen.

17. Quoted in Swint, "Don't Forget 'Smoky' Joe Wood," par. 4.

18. Doc Barker, born Charles D. Barker, was a veterinarian, violin player, and rancher who became a sheriff in Colorado for twenty years before moving to Fairview, Utah, near Provo.

19. Benjamin E. Smith, "Colorado," Historical Maps of Colorado, http://alabamamaps.ua.edu.

20. Scher, "Case for Ouray's Smoky Joe Wood," 10. David Wood had been a successful freighter since the early 1880s, carrying supplies from the railroad's end up to the mines and returning with ore. But his fortunes declined throughout the 1890s, following the bank panics of 1892–93 and completion of the railroad to Ouray. The final step down came when a fire destroyed his Dallas ranch in 1897. He responded quickly, but the rebuild was ramshackle. See F. Wood and D. Wood, *I Hauled These Mountains in Here*, 314–15, 326.

21. Ritter, "Joe Wood," 154. A debunker, Joe reminded Ritter that the movies incorrectly showed horses pulling stagecoaches (which Joe also called "buses") at full speed. In Ouray he never saw any horse "off trot."

22. Jorgensen, "Smoky Joe Wood," 9. For a useful, quick summary of Ouray's history, see http://www.ouraycolorado.com/History.

23. Scher, "Case for Smoky Joe," 10. Like David Wood, John Ashenfelter freighted in the early 1880s, carting explosives from the powder house at the foot of Box Canyon up to the mines. By the time the Woods arrived, Ashenfelter had expanded into fruit ranching, employing thirty men and women. See Gregory, *History of Ouray*, 1:111–15.

24. Jorgensen, "Smoky Joe Wood," 8–9.

25. Scher, "Case for Smoky Joe," 10.

26. Jorgensen, "Smoky Joe Wood," 9.

27. Jorgensen, "Smoky Joe Wood," 9; and Ritter, "Joe Wood," 155.

28. Jorgensen, "Smoky Joe Wood," 8.

29. Things got worse for labor. On December 4, 1903, martial law was declared in Idaho Springs, where two weeks later, the National Guard suspended the Bill of Rights. The next year Governor Peabody, who had refused troops to protect laborers, built a fort above Imogene Pass (from Ouray to Telluride), cutting off communication between workers in the two counties.

30. Moss and Foster, *Home Run in the Rockies*, 81.

31. Moss and Foster, *Home Run in the Rockies*, 81.

32. Moss and Foster, *Home Run in the Rockies*, 82.

33. Moss and Foster, *Home Run in the Rockies*, 83.

34. Moss and Foster, *Home Run in the Rockies*, 84.

35. Moss and Foster, *Home Run in the Rockies*, 85.

36. Moss and Foster, *Home Run in the Rockies*, 85–86.

37. Moss and Foster, *Home Run in the Rockies*, 86.

38. Moss and Foster, *Home Run in the Rockies*, 88.

39. Moss and Foster, *Home Run in the Rockies*, 89–90.

40. Moss and Foster, *Home Run in the Rockies*, 92. While Joe was traveling on a southern tour back from Redondo Beach, California, in 1911, the second team played preseason games in Denver. The next year Dutch Leonard, who would accuse Wood, Speaker, and Cobb of fixing a game in 1919, played as a twenty-year-old in Denver. Although World War I took a toll on Colorado baseball, in 1912 there were still seventy-four semipro teams in the state. See Moss and Foster, *Home Run in the Rockies*, 94–96.

41. Moss and Foster, *Home Run in the Rockies*, 87.

42. D. Smith, "Nothing but Baseball on His Mind," 77.

43. Riess, *Touching Base*, names the creed "fair play, gentlemanly virtue, self-reliance, middle-class decorum, community pride, and rural traditions" (222–24).

44. Ritter, "Joe Wood," 155.

45. D. Smith, "Nothing but Baseball," 78.

46. D. Smith, "Nothing but Baseball," 79.

47. See D. Smith, "Nothing but Baseball," 80.

48. D. Smith, "Nothing but Baseball," 80; Scher, "Case for Smoky Joe," 10; and Richard Wood audiotape, JWA.

49. Scher, "Case for Smoky Joe," 10. The Walshes were not the only famous residents. John F.'s partner and organizer of the Ouray ball team, John T. Barnett, became Colorado attorney general in 1909–10 as a Democrat. And, as Joe noted, "My brother went to school with Lee Knous, who later was governor of Colorado," 1947–1950 (Scher, "Case for Smoky Joe," 11).

50. Article in *Ouray County (CO) Herald*, July 19, 1940, Ouray County Historical Society.

2. Bloomer Girl and Minor Leaguer

1. Ritter, "Joe Wood," 155; JWA.

2. Swint, "Don't Forget 'Smoky' Joe Wood," par. 5.

3. Gregorich, "Blues, Bloomers, and Bobbies," 32–37. See Berlage, *Women in Baseball*, 34–44; Gregorich, *Women at Play*, 1–12; and Browne, *Girls of Summer*, 16. Though these teams faded as softball ascended in the mid-1930s, the Bloomer tradition revived in the All-American Girls Professional Baseball League, the subject of the film *A League of Their Own*.

4. Ritter, "Joe Wood," 157. See also Douskey, "Smoky Joe Wood's Last Interview," 69. An article on February 25, 1917, in the *Cleveland Plain Dealer* lists two other pitchers, Jack Warhop and Claude Hendrix, as rumored to have played for Bloomer Girls teams. The amount of money paid to Wood has been variously reported, figures including ten dollars a week and expenses, twenty dollars a week, and thirty-five dollars. Joe often said that he was paid twenty dollars and a ticket home.

5. Thanks to Deb Shattuck for the reference to Joe Wood as possibly being named Lucy Totton. See Green, "Joe Wood," 7–8.

6. Clarence Holmes graduated from the Kansas School of Pharmacy in 1907. Rather than pursue baseball, he passed the state exam, married Daisy Hollenbeck of Cedar Rapids, Iowa, and established Holmes Drug store in Great Bend, Kansas, just sixty-five miles east of Ness City. See also Douskey, "Smoky Joe Wood's Last Interview," 69.

7. JWA. See Douskey, "Smoky Joe Wood's Last Interview," 69.

8. Some sources name Ducky Holmes as a KU baseball coach. But Mills Ebright coached for the 1907 season, posting a record of 8-12 in his only year.

9. In following years Belden Hill often visited Red Sox spring training in Hot Springs, where Joe enjoyed reminding Belden that he gave away Wood to Hutchinson.

10. Ritter, "Joe Wood," 158. See Green, "Joe Wood," 8.

11. Swint, "History of Baseball in Hutchinson, Kansas," http://funvalleysports.com/history_baseball.shtml, par. 2–4.

12. Swint, "History of Baseball in Hutchinson," http://funvalleysports.com/history_baseball.shtml, par. 5.

13. The grounds lie between two railroad tracks to the north and east of the

Greenbush Seed Co., a block south of Avenue A, in a field that holds a small loading dock.

14. Swint, "Don't Forget 'Smoky' Joe Wood," par. 6, and "Baseball in Hutchinson," par. 6–7. As Joe judged, the only other significant player from Hutchinson in 1907–8 was infielder Ivy Olson, who went on to play fourteen years, primarily with Cleveland in the AL and Brooklyn in the NL. By 1909 the Salt Packers were reduced to the Kansas State League. The town entered a team in the Western League in 1917–18, which produced pitcher Hall of Famer Jesse "Pops" Haines. But World War I took its toll on Hutchinson baseball. See Swint, "History of Baseball in Hutchinson," http://funvalleysports.com/history/history_baseball.shtml., par. 11.

15. On March 26, 1907, the *News* wrote that "Doc" Andrews had been in professional baseball for fourteen years, first as a pitcher at Rockford of the Western Association in 1894. He managed in Tacoma, Washington, followed by Portland, Oregon (1903), Sioux City and Nashville (1904), St. Joseph (1905), and Topeka (1906).

16. Files of Joe Wood, National Baseball Hall of Fame, Cooperstown NY.

17. Earle Fleharty's 28-10 record in 1907 got him a promotion to Birmingham of the Class A Southern Association, where he was 5-5 in 1908, but he never got higher than AA.

18. Joe's brother, Pete, may have had connections to the Hutchinson Salt Packers. An article in the JWA mentions that his play with them jeopardized his eligibility for football at KU. He played in Johnny Kling's Indoor League, at the Kansas City Athletic Club, on Tuesday nights in the winter of 1908. Joe's year at Hutchinson inspired Silas Porter, a member of Supreme Court of Kansas, to invite Pete to apply for the job of assistant reporter, which paid about one thousand dollars. Instead Pete continued at KU.

19. Montford Montgomery Cross, thirty-eight, was in his first coaching job after fifteen years in the Major Leagues, from 1902 to 1907 with the powerful A's. A shortstop, he was known for his range and speed. Connie Mack considered him a clutch hitter. Cross managed for part of the next season in Kansas City and finished coaching in the Minors in 1913 with the Bridgeport (Connecticut) team of the Class B Eastern Association before umpiring in the 1914 Federal League. See Macht, *Connie Mack*, 282–83; and Wiggins, *Federal League of Base Ball Clubs*, 105–7.

20. L. Johnson, "Baseball in Kansas City," 2–3; and www.baseball-reference.com.

21. "Ball Parks of Kansas City," 12–22; and www.baseball-reference.com.

22. George "Jerry" Upp, a left-hander, pitched for the Columbus Senators in 1908 and 1909, the year he played three weeks in September with the Cleveland Naps, winning two games and posting a 1.69 ERA. He was out of baseball after the 1910 season.

23. Chester Milton Brandom, like Wood from Kansas and himself only twenty-one years old at the time, pitched well in limited innings in 1908 and 1909 for the Pittsburgh Pirates. He also played one season, 1915, in the Federal League with the Newark Peppers.

24. The Kansas City Blues Association Park was located in the square between Olive Street and Prospect Avenue, Nineteenth and Twentieth Streets southeast of the downtown area, not far from the current Negro League Baseball Museum. Although the field was reshaped when the railroad cut through in 1923, it remains as Blues Park. If, as Joe Wood describes, he met Laura O'Shea after a baseball game, they probably would've walked up a hill, across Brooklyn Street near the future site of Muehleback Field and Municipal Stadium, turned west, crossing what is now Highway 71. It would've been about one and one-half miles to her home, one block east of Troost, at 2641 Forest Avenue.

25. Joe remembered Beckley as a "great big hulk who could smash the ball," though by then no longer agile defensively, and off the field "a card from the start."

26. Hall of Fame pitcher Addie Joss also reportedly recommended that Charley Somers buy Wood from Kansas City, highlighting Joe's fastball (JWA). Joss, who hurt his arm on June 3 against the Tigers, may have returned to Toledo and seen Joe pitch in this series. See Longert, *Addie Joss*, 93.

27. Green, "Joe Wood — Still Waiting for Cooperstown," 34. See Douskey, "Smoky Joe Wood's Last Interview," 69; Green, "Joe Wood," 10.

28. JWA.

3. Rookie and More

1. See, for example, Stout and Johnson, *Red Sox Century*, 1–70; Ryan, *When Boston Won the World Series*, 15, 19, 49, 74, 75, 177; Stout, *Impossible Dreams*, xi–45; and Whalen, *When the Red Sox Ruled*, 8–24.

2. Founded in the late 1890s, the Rooters followed the fortunes of the Boston team, particularly Irishmen like King Kelly, Bill Dinneen, and Jimmy Collins. When the American League came to town in 1901, Michael "Nuf Ced" McGreevey and friends shifted their allegiance from the NL Beaneaters to the AL franchise. In 1908 the Red Sox were still supported by the Royal Rooters, whose home remained McGreevey's Third Base Bar.

3. John I. Taylor wanted the name to recall the powerful Boston Red Stockings of the 1870s and 1880s. That team, an 1871 transplant of the first professional team, the Cincinnati Red Stockings, won four consecutive National Association championships, from 1872 to 1875, as the Boston Red Stockings under Harry Wright. Later they joined the NL and quickly became champs, in 1877 and 1878, 1891–93, and 1897 and 1898. Since 1883 they were the Beaneaters, freeing Red Stockings (shortened to Red Sox) for use by Taylor and the Americans.

4. Joe Wood held his fastball along and between the two seams. He stood almost straight up, with his left leg close to the rubber as the right leg cocked in a subtle twisting as he faced the batter. As he started his delivery, he rocked back gently on his left leg, the initial power coming from his hard lean onto his right leg. His legs got even more contorted as he turned three-quarters away from batter and raised

right-hand-in-glove behind his head. When his left leg reached toward home plate, the back (right) leg trailed behind, putting all the strain on the arm, which whipped across his body as his right leg bent to the outside before landing. His signature was the snap of his wrist as he released the ball, which gave the hop. As Elmer Colcord testified (JWA) that "snap ball" was imitated by young boys throughout the Boston area. See, for example, "Wood's Strong Wrist Great Aid in Pitching."

5. Douskey, "Smoky Joe Wood's Last Interview," 70; Green, "Joe Wood," 12.

6. *Cleveland Plain Dealer*, March 14, 1917. An article in the *New York World-Telegram*, March 1944, retells Bill Carrigan's story that he "had a way of making his catcher's glove explode like a shot when the ball landed. This fascinated Wood, and when Carrigan sensed this juvenile eccentricity, he used it as means of eliminating the young pitcher's wildness." In tapes Joe refuted this contention. With typical aggressive humor Wood said Carrigan "tried" to catch Joe, "but the ball was bouncing back . . . most of the time." Joe preferred Hick Cady; he needed "a catcher that had good arm because" Joe "couldn't hold a man on first base."

7. Alexander, *Spoke*, 23.

8. See Duren, *Boiling Out at the Springs*.

9. A cause of the Red Sox swoon of 1910 was a weak infield. Despite excellence from outfielders Speaker, Lewis, and Hooper, Boston ranked next to last in fielding.

10. Elizabeth Middaugh Wood, Joe's paternal grandmother, established the cemetery in which many members of the Wood family are buried. During the Civil War she refused to allow her oldest son, James (a brother of John F.), to enlist. While putting up hay at the Bradford Place nearby, he was injured and developed "white swelling," tuberculosis of bones and joints, which led to his death in less than a year. His mother chose to bury him where the sun would strike first in the morning, surrounding it with stones from the Kilgour Quarry. Thus the Wood cemetery near Shohola, Pennsylvania.

11. Charles Alexander, in *Spoke* (32–33), explains that Redondo Beach was the winter home of John I. Taylor, making the training convenient for the owner. But a long, complicated return was costly (twenty thousand dollars) and exhausting.

12. In a JWA article, Tim Murnane is quoted as saying Joe Wood was generally "not superstitious, but he will sit up all night rather than sleep in any but berth No. 9 on a Pullman sleeper."

13. Nowlin, *Great Red Sox Spring Training Tour*, 148.

14. Nowlin, *Great Red Sox Spring Training Tour*, 150.

15. Markson, "Day for Addie Joss."

16. The 1911 Red Sox were on both ends, being no-hit on August 27 by Big Ed Walsh of the White Sox by the same score, 5–0.

17. For playing in this series, Joe received a watch fob with a diamond. See Alvarez, "Interview with Smokey Joe Wood," 55. For Joe's eventual use of that diamond, see chapter 10.

18. New York papers recorded Joe's mastery, as in "Manhattan vs. Smoky Joe," which ends

> Wood pitched again—O bitter phrase—
> O blighting echo of the days
> Sadder than any New York cop
> O "could you slip me a five, old top?"
> Aye, in each dreary Harlem flat
> Sadder than "Baker at the bat"
> O death; where is thy sting?
> O grave! Where is thy serpent's kiss?
> O Baker, Bender, Coombs and Plank,
> You look like money in the bank,
> Compared to this last scratch of pen,
> "Wood pitched again." (JWA)

19. JWA.

4. The 1912 Regular Season

1. Ryan, "Holy Smoky," E1.

2. As described later, 1912 was the first year for Fenway Park. But other significant baseball parks were constructed before World War I. Navin Field in Detroit, which became Briggs Stadium (1938) and Tiger Stadium (1961), also opened in April 1912. A year later came Ebbets Field in Brooklyn. In 1914 Weeghman Park, later Wrigley Field, was opened in the Federal League.

3. Evangelist Billy Sunday, an ex–Major League baseball player, built a tentlike tabernacle over the grounds from 1914 to 1916. The site was purchased by Northeastern University in 1934.

4. Stout and Johnson, *Red Sox Century*, 70–79; Stout, *Fenway 1912*, 81–119; and R. Johnson, *Field of Our Fathers*, 1–2.

5. *Hartford Courant*, April 10, 1912.

6. In JWA two different locations are given for their home. One is 196 Circuit Road in the Cottage Park area of Winthrop. Also listed is 71 Revere. Since Wood and Speaker returned to the community the next year, they may have lived at both places. Pictures in papers of them playing the piano, washing dishes, and hanging out with neighborhood kids were staged according to Joe.

7. In tapes Joe made clear his preference for Forest "Hick" Cady over Carrigan. A rookie in 1912, Cady (according to Wood) was asked by Joe, "How would you like to catch me?" Hick's response was "Oh, my God," fearing Joe was confused. Wood considered Cady a "very fine boy," well liked by other players. More to the point, Cady was "good sized fellow" with a "pretty good arm." Though Joe never knew how Hick

got the nickname, he was a hard worker, and though he had a problem with drinking, Cady's wife was always there to support him.

8. Johnson entered that game in relief of Long Tom Hughes, who had put two runners on in the seventh. After striking out a batter, Walter moved both runners into scoring position with a wild pitch. Then Pete Compton, Joe Wood's nemesis, hit a single into left center field, scoring both runners. Today we would consider the runners the responsibility of Hughes, but in 1912 they were charged to Johnson, the pitcher who allowed them to score. The decision was argued even then. See an article by umpire Billy Evans, in the *New York Times*, November 10, 1912, s4.

9. Previously Joe had a variety of nicknames, including "Bullet Joe Wood" and the inevitable "Woody," sometimes spelled "Woodie." The *Globe* only reluctantly used the *Post*'s "Smoky," waiting until Wood's streak ended, and even then spelling it "Smokey." Other national papers, like the *New York Times* and the *Atlanta Constitution*, didn't put "Smoky Joe" into play until the World Series. Joe Wood and Hall of Famer Smoky Joe Williams from the Negro Leagues were both called "Cyclone" and "Smok(e)y." Most likely the influence went from Wood to Williams since, as John B. Holway says in his chapbook *Smokey Joe and the Cannonball*, African American oral history places the naming of Williams in October 1917.

10. See Ryan, "Holy Smoky," E1.

11. Joe's tugging at his pants became part of Boston legend, indicated by a poem in JWA. It notes the habits of Buck Weaver, Harry Lord, Kid Gleason, and Jimmy Callahan, then declares them

> outclassed when once you've seen
> Joe Wood pull up his pants.
> No crisis finds him unprepared—no odds
> how fierce the fight;
> He merely grabs his trousers top and
> yanks it out of sight;
> When he's in danger of a rout it seems to
> give him heart
> To seize his garments one by one and pull
> the things apart.
> I hope the Red Sox win the flag—I'm
> rooting might and main—
> And Joe will help 'em do it, if his trousers
> stand the strain.
> Some secret mascot's in that act—'twas
> done for years by Chance—
> But Frank looks like an amateur
> When Joe pulls up his pants.

12. Once again we have Joe's own words, on the seventieth anniversary of opening of Fenway Park: "Clark Griffith saw a chance to have a big crowd so he suggested that the manager of our club, who was Jake Stahl, who talked to me when I had at that time about, I don't know how many, consecutive games, eleven, twelve, thirteen, something like that [thirteen] to give Walter a chance to defend his record of sixteen straight. He asked me about it, and it was okay with me. So they accepted it and they had the first and only big crowd was swarming around on the field. And our benches were right up on the line, along with the spectators, and it was only a few feet from the foul line. And even that day in order to warm up they had to put the crowd back so I could have an opportunity to warm up. I happened to win the game." See also Green, "Joe Wood—Still Waiting for Cooperstown," 36.

13. *Boston Globe*, September 7, 1912.

14. From p. 14 of transcript, courtesy of Roger Abrams.

15. In tapes Joe clarified that Krug was still on the skin of the infield, not even in the outfield grass, when the ball "hit him in the belly." He said that Heinie Wagner was being rested for the World Series, maybe also scouting the Giants. Wood remembered that three runners scored when just two crossed the plate and the miscue near the end of the game when, in fact, it was only in the third inning. But Joe didn't hold a grudge. Marty's son later reported to the Wood family that after the game Joe offered to take Marty out for dinner and beer, telling Marty to "forget about it."

16. One of the stories passed down in the O'Shea family, and from them to the Woods, is that Laura's predecessors, her father and grandfather, had once given directions to Jesse James. Her father was a house painter but also dabbled in making violins.

17. From the collection of Jim Swint.

18. JWA.

5. The 1912 World Series

1. Stout, *Fenway 1912*, 215–17.

2. Vaccaro, *First Fall Classic*, 40.

3. Vaccaro, *First Fall Classic*, 32–33, 41; Stout, *Fenway 1912*, 237–38.

4. Ritter, "Harry Hooper," 149.

5. Doc Crandall was a pitcher, but he also played second and first that year, hitting .313.

6. Scher, "Case for Ouray's Smoky Joe Wood," 12. See Ryan, "Holy Smoky," E1.

7. In publications on the 1912 World Series, Joe's brother was commonly called Paul, not Pete, a mistake passed down over the years. As relatives have verified, Pete was never called Paul.

8. Murnane, "It Is the Simple Life," SM4. The story of a fight between Wood and Buck O'Brien led to a rumor that O'Brien would be traded to the White Sox in December of that year. It didn't happen then. But on July 2, 1913, he was traded to the White Sox for five thousand dollars. His Major League career ended after six unsuccessful games for Chicago and a 0-2 record. See Honig, "Joe Wood," 176.

9. Because it was a conflict relocated in the United States from Europe, especially Ireland, the tension between Catholics and Protestants was present on most Major League teams, as it was in the country as a whole. See Hartley, *Christy Mathewson*, 52, for a discussion of Sam Mertes, a Mason, whose position on the Giants was opposed by Irish Catholics in Upper Manhattan. See also the *Sporting News*, July 21, 1906.

10. See Hartley, *Christy Mathewson*, 98: "It was later said that Joe Wood, expecting himself to pitch, had bet a large sum on the Sox to win the next game." Mike Vaccaro (without documentation) asserts that Joe's brother bet one thousand dollars; see *First Fall Classic*, 176–77.

11. Joe claimed that his brother caught a ball from the final game of the 1912 Series, but it wasn't the one that dropped between Merkle and Meyers. It went into the grandstands.

12. It is commonly believed that Speaker gave the ball to his mother immediately after the game. Wood said he couldn't confirm that happened, though he did say Mrs. Speaker was there.

13. JWA.

14. See Murnane, "It Is the Simple Life," SM4. On October 21, 1912, the *Chicago Tribune* reported that Wood made $13,500 in salary and endorsements that year. Joe remembered that he received $1,000 for his newspaper byline, ghostwritten by Jim O'Leary of the *Globe*, and for the famous Regal shoe advertisement he got $25 in shoes, about five pairs. He also received a gold pocket watch from a "millionaire," which he considered his greatest gift, and it became the central object in Roger Angell's story "The Web of the Game." See chapter 11.

15. With some of his World Series money, Joe bought ninety-seven acres across from the family homestead, where he and Laura would live late the next year. See chapter 6.

16. After the World Series Joe became more popular in Kansas when he traveled there late in 1912 for pool playing and shooting: "With all his success and fame, Joe Wood never forgot where he came from and maintained close ties to Hutchinson and Ness City. His fans in Kansas likewise followed their hero." Hutchinson proclaimed Joe Wood's birthday a public holiday. "In Ness City a celebration was held with a post card shower to be sent to Joe's home in Pennsylvania. On November 10, Joe came to Hutchinson, met with friends at the Brunswick Smoker pool hall, and then went home to Ness City to visit, shoot pool, and hunt jack rabbits." See http://funvalleysports.com/history/smoky_joe_wood.shtml, par. 24.

17. It didn't help calm fears when Speaker was quoted as saying that the victory in the last game was on "nerve alone" because he had an "agonizing" "lame arm." See Ryan, "Holy Smoky," E1.

6. Playing with Pain

1. In addition to helping construct Joe's house, brother Pete pitched in the Class B New England League for the Brockton Shoemakers, the New Bedford Whalers,

and the Lowell Grays. His combined record in twenty-five games was 6-5. Pete batted .327. In 1914 Pete was 3-8 with the Trenton Tigers of the Class B Tri-State League, batting .107. In 1916 Pete played in A A ball, going 0-1 for the Newark Indians of the International League.

2. Such self-pampering typified Leonard's career and would contribute to the controversy of 1926–27. See chapter 9.

3. An article in the *Atlanta Constitution* on October 25, 1916, argued that Joe's arm problems began in this series when he and Claude Hendrix competed to throw faster in a game that the Red Sox finally won, 5 to 4. But no extant box scores show them pitching against each other or a 5–4 game. Hendrix had an off year in 1913, going 14-15.

4. In an interview in the J W A, he said of Byrne, "I don't think he ever played much after that, and I was awfully sorry." See Alvarez, "Interview with Smokey Joe Wood," 55. Actually Bobby played 113 games for the Pirates in 1913, hitting .270, more than fifteen points higher than his average. He later played as a Philly in the 1915 World Series. Joe also worried about hitting Red Davis in the Western Association.

5. "Revival of Ancient Fake Angers Red Sox," *Boston Globe*, March 23, 1913, 11.

6. According to Charles Alexander in *Spoke*, Wood and Speaker were often visited by Harry Hooper and his wife, Esther. President McAleer took out twenty-five thousand dollars of life insurance on the roommates (59, 62).

7. J W A.

8. J W A. See Green, "Joe Wood," 15.

9. Joe often mentioned Jake Stahl bringing him back too early after the second injury in Detroit. But Carrigan had replaced Stahl by then. This is the injury from which Joe returned too early.

10. Although the earlier injury to his thumb was the beginning of his arm problems, Joe dated them from this day in Detroit.

11. While Joe was recovering, on August 24, 1913, his brother, Pete, pitched for Berkeley, Rhode Island, of the Intercity League in an exhibition against the Boston Braves and lost to Bill James, 8–3. Pete got a hit but gave up six hits and eight walks.

12. The day before, August 28, 1913, at Fenway, Walter Johnson had failed to win his second number sixteen. That day Ray Collins pitched a seven-hitter, and Boston won in the eleventh inning. The Big Train only gave up three hits but lost 1–0.

13. Alexander, *Spoke*, 65.

14. Although confusing, public records on the O'Sheas are helpful. Laura's birth certificate, no. 7667, file B 26, gives her birth as May 4, 1890, in Kansas City, Missouri, with no address. Her full name is written as Laura Tereasa [*sic*] O'Shea. Laura's father was named Charles Francis O'Shea, born June 30, 1860, in Missouri, the son of Charles Carl O'Shea and Margaret Gaynon, both from Ennis, Ireland. Laura's mother, Ella (sometimes Ellen) Begley, was born on February 2, 1862, in Illinois (or Indiana), to Bernard Begley and Arlissie Summers Begley, both of whom had emigrated from Dublin, Ireland. At the time of the marriage, Edith was probably twenty-six.

15. Joe and Laura were married in a Methodist church, the affiliation of Rebecca Stephens Wood. But no records show that they joined the Milford United Methodist Church.

16. The word *skimmerton*, or *skimmington*, is taken from an English ritual in which someone, or a couple, is ridiculed for their public misconduct, usually involving infidelity or abuse. Such a parade had become ironic in the colonies, an occasion for any rowdy public display for couples.

17. Unidentified article, McGreevey Collection, Boston Public Library. Dr. Frank Edward Gessner trained at Bellevue Hospital in New York and graduated in 1903. He also interned at St. Michael's Hospital in Newark, New Jersey, before settling in Port Jervis in August 1904. Sadly, he died after a "short illness" at Interpines Sanitarium, Goshen, New York, at only thirty-five years old — suffering from what reporters then called "lunacy."

18. According to an article released from Boston on March 17 and recorded in "Brothers of Stars to Play" in the *Chicago Daily Tribune* on March 18, 1914, p. 13, Pete was projected to pitch and Hank Mathewson to play outfield for Lawrence, Massachusetts, in the New England League. But neither played for the Lawrence Barristers that year. Like his brother, Hank Mathewson attended Bucknell University. He pitched in three games for the Giants in 1906 and 1907; he made his debut on September 28 against the Cardinals, relieving Christy and protecting an 8–1 lead. On October 5, 1906, Hank walked a record fourteen batters. He never returned to the Majors.

19. Lardner's joke is based on the fact that Smoky Joe Wood appeared slim and fragile, though he was five feet eleven inches tall and weighed around 180 pounds. Such a misconception was based on his wearing baggy uniforms, his boyish face, and his history of injury. Joe's body was like that of today's Pedro Martinez and Tim Lincecum, but Smoky Joe was heavier than both of them.

20. Throughout early 1914 rumors continued about Joe joining the Federal League, though he denied the stories, saying because of the appendicitis he "wasn't even offered a contract" with the Federals. Some papers reported that he was loyal to the Red Sox; others listed him as eligible for the lucrative offer made to Walter Johnson. See also Murdock, interview with Joe Wood.

21. Alexander, *Spoke*, 75.

22. Dr. Gessner, his wife, and Laura (who spent much of her summer with Mrs. Gessner) were the box-seat guests of the Red Sox during this road trip. The doctor reported that Joe wasn't strong enough to pitch "every day," and "the pitching hand which was injured last July sometimes goes back on him." At games Laura often held the wallets and rings of Joe and Tris for safety.

23. Rather than report to Cleveland, Rankin Johnson skipped to the Federal League, where he was 9-5 with an ERA of 1.58 for the ChiFeds. Coumbe was an Indian with Joe 1917–19.

24. Among players who used the services of Reese were Cy Young, Christy

Mathewson, Walter Johnson, Ed Walsh, Addie Joss, Chief Bender, Stan Coveleski, Frank Chance, Eddie Collins, Napoleon Lajoie, Frank Baker, Jimmy Collins, Honus Wagner, Ty Cobb, Shoeless Joe Jackson, and Tris Speaker. For Bonesetter's interesting life, see Anderson, "Bonesetter Reese"; and Strickler, *Child of Moriah*.

25. Alexander, *Spoke*, quotes Bill Carrigan as admitting that some of Wood's success in 1914 was due to using emery paper in his glove for roughing the ball (77).

26. Richard Wood, telephone interview with the author, June 12, 2007.

27. Gregg, a left-hander, pitched in eighteen games that year and returned in 1916 for the Red Sox. In 1918 he returned with the A's and in 1925, as a forty-year-old, posted a 4.12 ERA for Washington.

28. See Douskey, "Smoky Joe Wood's Last Interview," 70.

29. Alexander, in *Spoke* (98–99), notes that Joe was involved in the Series and received a twenty-five-dollar fine from the commission for verbal abuse of Erskine Mayer in Game Two.

30. In mid-February Baker was sent for $37,500 to the Yankees, where he played through 1922.

31. Speaker was sold to Cleveland for $55,000 and Sam Jones and Roy Thomas. With Dunn, Speaker signed a two-year contract for $15,000 a year and a $2,500 signing bonus. See Alexander, *Spoke*, 99–102; and Gay, *Tris Speaker*, 160–64.

32. Ryan, "Holy Smoky," E1.

33. Ritter, "Joe Wood," 167.

34. Although the chiropractor's name is spelled "Crucius" in Foster, "Boston: Joe Wood," 443, in tapes Joe spelled it with an *s*, not a *c*, in the middle. See also Douskey, "Smoky Joe Wood's Last Interview," 71; Green, "Joe Wood," 16.

35. Andy Coakley pitched Game Three of the 1905 World Series for the Athletics and lost to Christy Mathewson. But he is most famous for fisticuffs with Rube Waddell, which kept Rube out of that Series. Coakley also recruited Eddie Collins for Connie Mack. See Huhn, *Eddie Collins*, 32; and Macht, *Connie Mack*, 356, 369.

36. Ritter, "Joe Wood," 167.

37. Sutton, *Wayne County Sports History*, 124.

7. Indian Outfielder and Utility Man

1. Green, "Joe Wood—Waiting for Cooperstown," 34. See also Franz Douskey, "Smoky Joe Wood's Last Interview," 70.

2. JWA. Joe also summarized the Boston years in the videotape made at Opening Day 1982, Fenway Park: "In 1912 was the only big year I ever had, which was the 34 and 5. After that it was a question of a sore arm and just getting in as often as I could in order to get my salary and that was it. Then I would have small-time wins and losses. But only two years that I pitched was I all together for the whole season."

3. Longert, *Addie Joss*, 39–40; and Mansch, *Rube Marquard*, 20–22.

4. Longert, *Addie Joss*, 40, 50–51; and Mansch, *Rube Marquard*, 20–22.

5. Fleitz, *Shoeless*, 92; Longert, *Addie Joss*, 50–51; Mansch, *Rube Marquard*, 20–22; and Alexander, *Spoke*, 87.

6. Constantelos, "Cleveland," 637–38; and Alexander, *Spoke*, 101–2, 105–6, 109, 112–13.

7. Murdock, interview with Joe Wood. For a good summary of Joe's years in Cleveland, see Huhn, "It Was 'Smoky' in Cleveland."

8. In the JWA tapes Joe explained that they were "drilled every day" in uniform during World War I by a "Captain Baker." The players, he explained, were "about as serious as any could be.... When their number came up, they were going. That's all there was to it."

9. Joe was required by law to register for the draft on June 5, 1917, as were all men between twenty-one and thirty-one. But as a married man, and with a dependent child, he was exempt.

10. "Fisk Employees Have Athletic Association," *Atlanta Constitution*, July 8, 1917, A5.

11. Harry Hooper, George Sisler, and Ty Cobb, as well as Ruth, started as pitchers. Indian Jack Graney was a pitcher in the Minors until converted to the outfield by Lee Fohl in Columbus.

12. It was reported, and catcher Steve O'Neill believed, that the second child was named after O'Neill. But Laura told Bob that Steve was named for a family friend.

13. JWA; and Alvarez, "Interview with Smokey Joe Wood," 53. See also Douskey, "Smoky Joe Wood's Last Interview," 71; Green, "Joe Wood," 16.

14. Wood's play inspired a Cleveland poet to craft a limerick from such defensive prowess,

> There was a young fellow
> named Wood;
> In the shoes of Tris Speaker
> he stood.
> The fans laughed at "Smoke"
> In the brogans of "Spoke,"
> But right off the reel he made good. (JWA)

15. Accounts varied on whether the last homer was to left or right. I have used the most immediate one, from the New York papers. Joe recollected "one in left and one in right." See Green, "Joe Wood," 18.

16. The last two stanzas of a poem on the same theme, also written at the time, declare:

> Afield, on bases or at bat,
> In fact, wherever he is at,
> Josephus sure is making good;
> He's proving he's a regular guy,

Therefore our tip to keep an eye
Upon the smoke of Joey Wood.

Out there in left he fields like Tris
And you should see Josephus kiss
    The apple for a solid smash.
Tho he may never pitch again
We'll bet a goodly bunch of yet
    On smoky Joseph Wood to cash. (JWA)

17. Unidentified articles in JWA.

18. Hugh Fullerton, "Left Fielders Far below Standards of Past Years," *Atlanta Constitution*, April 9, 1919, 15.

19. Even when Speaker became the manager, he and Joe Wood remained roommates. Spoke had a democratic style; an article in the *Atlanta Constitution* on July 30, 1919, noted that Tris continued to seek advice from his players and refused a position of authority on the bench, moving randomly among his teammates.

20. Pete Wood again played with the Fisk Red Tops late in the summer of 1919, winning games on July 28 against the Hartford Polis, named for the Police Department, in Hartford and the Comstock Cheney team on September 1 in Ivoryton, Connecticut.

8. Glory Revisited

1. Though the erudite tone suggests it was ghostwritten, an article in the McGreevey collection at the Boston Public Library describes Joe's reflections on the weakening of pitchers at the end of the second decade of the twentieth century. One reason was the banning of doctored pitches and "limitation of the use of the spitball to those who already were in the major leagues." Also there was the effect of two wars: "First, we had the federal league war [which] cut the number of bush circuits from forty to twenty [and] the great war," when "most of the minor leagues went out of business."

2. Given his miniscule lifetime ERA, the damage was significant. On the basis of this one outing, a 22.5 ERA, his overall ERA in the Major Leagues went from 2.00 to 2.03.

3. Alexander, *Spoke*, 156–57; and Sowell, *Pitch That Killed*, 174.

4. Alexander, *Spoke*, 157–58; and Sowell, *Pitch That Killed*, 175–84. The Indians won the game of Chapman's injury, 4–3, though the Yankees scored three times in the ninth. See Green, "Joe Wood," 21.

5. See, for example, audiotapes in JWA; and Alexander, *Spoke*, 156–60; Ritter, "Joe Wood" audiocassette; and Murdock, interview with Joe Wood, Eugene Murdock Baseball Collection.

6. Alexander, *Spoke*, 158; and Sowell, *Pitch That Killed*, 189–90.

7. Sowell, *Pitch That Killed*, xiii; Alexander, *Spoke*, 161; and Felber, *Under Pallor, under Shadow*, 131.

8. Sowell, *Pitch That Killed*, 207–8. Harry Lunte was Chappy's initial replacement at shortstop. But before the end of the season Cleveland took a chance on a youngster from the University of Alabama, Joe Sewell, who hit well that year, .329 in twenty-two games. But his defense was shaky. Joe said only that Sewell "fit in well."

9. Bagby was the seventh to win thirty games in the twentieth century: Cy Young, Jack Chesbro, Ed Walsh, Jack Coombs, Walter Johnson, and Smoky Joe Wood in 1912.

10. It was a very potent offensive outfield that year. In addition to the combination of Wood/Smith, Speaker hit .388, Evans .349, Graney .296, and Jamieson .319. The 1920 Indians hit .303, with a slugging percentage of .417.

11. See, for example, Sowell, *Pitch That Killed*, 263.

12. Spink, *Judge Landis*, 205. The 1920 Series was studied during the Black Sox investigation in New York and Illinois. See Asinof, *Eight Men Out*, 214.

13. Sowell, *Pitch That Killed*, 274.

14. In interviews Joe didn't confirm reports that Speaker ran to his mother, declaring the championship was his birthday present to her. But Joe said Tris's mom was present at the game.

15. Pitchers to win three games in previous World Series: Bill Dinneen (1901), Christy Mathewson (1905), Babe Adams (1909), Jack Coombs (1910), and Smoky Joe Wood (1912).

16. Sowell, *Pitch That Killed*, 277–79; and Alexander, *Spoke*, 174.

17. The original deed to Indian Camp was between James and Bridgett (his wife) McConnell and Joseph Wood of Township Shohola, on November 22, 1919, for "One Dollar and divers other good and lawful considerations" on "approximately One Acre" just off Dingman Turnpike st. Road 739, in back of McConnell Pond. Joe said Jimmy McConnell also rented the hunting land for seventy-five dollars over the two weeks. "Old Jimmy McConnell," described by Joe as "quite a character" and in good shape because he would "tramp around in the woods," also drove into the wilderness to flush out deer and other animals for the hunters. According to Bob Wood the group often "included Steve O'Neill, Elmer Smith, Bill Wambsganss, Charlie Jamieson, Stanley Coveleski, George Burns, Doc Johnston, plus Clyde Engle of the Red Sox and about five local guys." At the opening of "the hunting season, always the first two weeks of December," Cubby "the chef, 12–14 hunters and 6 kegs of beer" would gather there and hunt on the adjacent one thousand acres. See "Smoky Joe's Café," par. 18–20; Green, "Joe Wood," 21.

18. Alexander, *Spoke*, 178.

19. Alexander, *Spoke*, 181; Bob Wood, interview with the author.

20. Joe Wood and Joe E. Brown became good friends. See chapters 9–11.

21. Sowell, *Pitch That Killed*, 283–85.

22. Alexander, *Spoke*, 189.

23. Alexander, *Spoke*, 190.

24. Alexander, *Spoke*, 191.

25. Alexander, *Spoke*, 197; Green, "Joe Wood," 21.

26. Alvarez, "Interview with Smokey Joe Wood," 56. See also Ritter, "Joe Wood" audiocassette, and Murdock, interview with Joe Wood, Murdock Baseball Collection, as well as tapes in the J W A and Douskey, "Smoky Joe Wood's Last Interview," 71.

27. Ritter, "Joe Wood," 169.

28. Members of S A B R have established Wood's 92 R B I in his last year as significant. Although Dave Orr had 124 in 1890 and Joe Jackson and Happy Felsch had 121 and 115 for the White Sox in 1920, Wood's total stood first in the twentieth century among Major Leaguers *who retired voluntarily* until Dave Kingman had 94 in 1986, followed by Kirby Puckett (99 in 1995), and finally Albert Belle (103 in 2000).

29. Pete was still in semipro ball as Joe's career moved to a conclusion. He lost in Bristol, Connecticut, to the New Departure team 2–0 on August 28, 1921. He also pitched for All-Insurance of Hartford.

30. Green, "Joe Wood — Still Waiting for Cooperstown," 34, 36.

9. The Yale Years

1. Gehrig signed with the Yankees on April 30, 1923, and reported to them on June 11. Joe also saw Gehrig play for Hartford of the Eastern League

2. Even after Joe's pro career ended, his brother played in semipro leagues, playing for the Fisk Red Tops, Portsmouth, New Hampshire, and in the Connecticut League. In 1928 Pete was still with Fisk.

3. According to Carl Vogt Joe was low key in Shohola. But John F. was not. When the Wood patriarch bought his first car from Carl's father, a Dodge dealer, Vogt Sr. offered to teach John to drive. Instead John F. chugged down the street in high gear.

4. Locals in Shohola want to believe that Babe Ruth came to the Wood farm during Joe's Yale years. The fantasy developed from the fact that Ruth often exited the train at Shohola and stayed at the Fauchere Hotel in Milford, Pennsylvania, and various places in upstate New York. More sensationally, Joe remembered the Babe often traveling to the New Jersey farm of Harry Clayton Harper, identified by Joe as a "big left-handed pitcher," who started Game Six of the 1921 Series. In Joe's suggestive words, Ruth "never came alone" when the ostensible reason was to hunt birds.

5. There was another death in Yale baseball that year. On June 12 a centerfielder on the 1925 team, William Harvey Cushing, and three others were killed in a late-night automobile crash.

6. See, for example, the following discussions: Gay, *Tris Speaker*, 224–48; Blaisdell, "Cobb-Speaker Scandal"; Alexander, *Ty Cobb*, 180–95; Alexander, *Spoke*, 233–52; Stump, *Cobb*, 368–85; R. Smith, *Baseball in the Afternoon*, 232–35; Spink, *Judge Landis*, 154–63; Ginsburg, *The Fix Is In*, 196–212; Seymour, *Baseball*, 382–87; Murdock, *Ban Johnson*, 205–25; G. C. Wood, "Doctor Smoke"; Alvarez, "Say It Ain't So, Ty"; and Pietrusza, *Judge and Jury*, 284–311.

7. Alexander, *Ty Cobb*, 185.

8. Both letters in, for example, Stump, Cobb, 375 (Cobb's), 376 (Wood). The numbers add up. At 10–7 odds, the $420 would be 70 percent of the $600. The $420 divided three ways would be $140. Minus $10 "service fee" is $130 to each.

9. About that time, showing no integrity, West released the story that he had placed the money on a horse race, not the ball game. See Alexander, *Spoke*, 245.

10. Speaker and Cobb sought congressional support for their cause. However, baseball's preferred status on trade blocked the move. See Alexander, *Ty Cobb*, 191; and Alexander, *Spoke*, 245.

11. JWA.

12. Gambling has always been an issue in baseball. In Joe's time it was common for players to wager on games, even their own, without reprisal. Post–World War I baseball was especially susceptible because of widespread gambling and the moneygrubbing of owners. See R. Smith, *Baseball in Afternoon*, 44–47, 163–67; Abrams, *Dark Side of the Diamond*; Ginsburg, *Fix Is In*; Hartley, *Christy Mathewson*, 50; Pietrusza, *Rothstein*, 148–50; Asinof, *Eight Men Out*, 13; Blaisdell, "Cobb-Speaker Scandal," 56, 58; and Stump, *Cobb*, 373.

13. See Gay, *Tris Speaker*, 241; and Blaisdell, "Cobb-Speaker Scandal," 65.

14. Bruce Caldwell's first Major League game was on June 30, 1928. He played eighteen games that year, primarily in the outfield. He had one more shot, in 1932, when he played seven games, six at first, for the Dodgers. Later Bruce studied law at Yale.

15. After the season Joe pursued another interest, golf, and reached the finals of the Wolf Hollow Golf Club Championship, in Delaware Gap, Pennsylvania; he lost one-up on August 1.

16. On one of these trips Joe killed a 185-pound bear, which he had made into a rug, later stolen from Joe's Pennsylvania home.

17. Albie Booth, the "Little Boy Blue" of Yale football, against Army on October 26, 1929, scored two touchdowns from scrimmage and another on a punt return as Yale won 21–13.

18. In a phone interview with the author on December 12, 2006, Fay Vincent Jr. said that his father told him Joe would whistle, once for Fay Sr. to talk to the pitcher and twice to take him out. See also Fay Vincent, *The Last Commissioner* (New York: Simon & Schuster, 2002), 101.

19. See Alexander, *Spoke*, 283; and Zingg, *Harry Hooper*, 218.

20. Zingg, *Harry Hooper*, 215–16. McInnis coached against Yale but not against Joe Wood. Stuffy was at Harvard between 1949 and 1954.

21. Some sources list Robert Wagner Jr., son of the senator from New York and himself later mayor of New York, as one of Joe's players. Wagner was a manager of the 1933 team.

22. Devens pitched only fourteen games that year and one more in 1934 before ending his Major League career with a 5-3 record and an ERA of 3.73.

23. Also at exhibitions was comedian Joe E. Brown, dressed in a Yale uniform. See chapter 11.

24. Yale considered an invitation to play in Japan that August. It declined in 1933 because of scheduling for classes in September. The team made the trip in 1935. See discussion later in the chapter.

25. Broaca posted good years with the Yankees in 1934–36, winning thirty-nine games, but he continued to be trouble. He jumped from the Yankees during the 1937 season and claimed to be going into boxing.

26. Joe and Laura emphasized their children's education. Joe Frank and Steve went to Nathan Hale in Morris Cove and Hillhouse School. The twins attended New Haven Junior High before Bob went on to Hopkins Preparatory for two years, as had his older brothers. And all the boys eventually attended Deerfield Academy; Joe graduated in 1937, Steve in 1938, and Bob in 1939.

27. Joe's recollections of the Japan trip from JWA.

28. On April 28, 1937, Steve Wood, Joe's second son, pitched for Hopkins but walked thirteen. He lost to the Yale freshmen 4–3.

29. Both Booth and Kelley were inducted into the College Football Hall of Fame. Joe respected Kelley's ability but wasn't impressed with his effort. Joe said, "As a college ball player, he was just as good as he wanted to be. Never did put out" (JWA).

30. Unlike Horton, Klimczak continued with eight other Minor League teams and finished back in Toronto in 1941. A catcher, he hit .381 for the Greenville Spinners of the South Atlantic League.

31. Joe became a scratch player using a baseball grip. In an article in the *Chicago Tribune* on March 21, 1921, Robert Edgren explored Cobb's complaint that golf "interferes with batting. A golf stroke is a long, easy, carefully timed swing, and a batting stroke is a short, jerky chop," noting Ty's one exception. In Cobb's words, "Joe Wood was the only ball player I ever knew who could play a good game of golf and drive the ball with a baseball swing. He hit a golf ball with a short, snappy chop, and he was the most tremendous driver I ever saw."

32. Actors like John Gilbert and Clara Bow frequented Rohman's. Over the years the bar has continued to attract celebrities like Robert De Niro, Paul Newman, and the racing Andrettis. While women were welcome, Laura didn't accompany Joe to Rohman's.

33. Joe Frank Wood was named captain of the Yale freshman team after their debut against Milford Prep. He struck out ten in five innings and hit two singles as Yale won 10–4.

34. In Bob's judgment the Northern League was a good semipro circuit (superior to the Cape Cod League) with teams like Burlington, Plattsburgh, and Merrimack Lake. Mostly college players, they took no money but got room, board, and perks.

35. Swint, "Don't Forget 'Smoky' Joe Wood," par. 30.

36. Scher, "Case for Ouray's Smoky Joe Wood," 16.

37. From his playing days Joe had three watch fobs with diamonds in the middle. He gave each boy a ring refitted with one of these diamonds to present to his fiancée.

38. Sawyer didn't become the coach. The appointment went to Red Rolfe, a four-time All-Star third baseman in his ten years with the New York Yankees. Only thirty-three in 1942, he played in that year's World Series, hitting .353. By then, on September 10, 1942, he had been announced as Yale's baseball and basketball coach. He was at Yale through 1945.

39. Joe Wood papers in Yale University Sports Archives.

40. Ted Harrison, who also played football and hockey, was stationed at Fort Sill, Oklahoma. The most valuable ROTC candidate at Yale, he was commissioned as a second lieutenant. After the war he played with the Lawrence Millionaires of the New England League and later taught English at Andover's Phillips Academy.

41. Joe Wood papers, Yale University Sports Archives; *Yale Baseball Media Guide*, 1999, 17.

42. See the Goodwin tape in the JWA and Ritter, "Joe Wood," audiocassette.

43. Joe's identification with workers is evident in the interview in the *Baseball Research Journal* by Mark Alvarez: "That's one thing they can blame for some of the things that they thought were crooked, like that 1919 Black Sox scandal. There's no question about it. Players weren't getting any money, especially the Chicago White Sox players" ("Interview with Smokey Joe Wood," 56).

44. Fay Vincent Jr., telephone interview with the author, December 12, 2006; and his *Last Commissioner*, 101.

10. Final Innings

1. Tom Bergin, telephone interview with the author, December 13, 2006; John Bergin, telephone interview with the author, December 12, 2006.

2. Joe's epitaph for his father: a "brilliant man but never cashed in on it."

3. From records gathered by Mike McConnell of Fort Myers, Florida. Matt McConnell, Mike's great-great-uncle, was a recently divorced boxer and one of Joe's sporting pals in Lord's Valley. Matt's most notable venture was a training camp at a nearby lake where such famous pugilists as Abe Simon, Max Baer, and "Two Ton" Tony Galento worked out. Pictures confirm the memory of Lois Sooley, who lived across the highway, was a great niece of the boxer, and visited the cabin at "six or so" in the mid-1930s (and now resides in Lakeland, Florida): "It was really rustic! The walls (unfinished) were covered with pictures of the players. They practiced on . . . property right along the road that . . . wasn't a real baseball field, just a place to hit and run."

4. Gay, *Satch, Dizzy & Rapid Robert*, 217. As members of the Baseball Players Federation, Joe's friends Ty Cobb, Larry Gardner, and Edd Roush worked to establish a pension for ballplayers. Early on, Bob Feller opposed such efforts, which deeply disappointed Joe Wood.

5. See audiotapes in the JWA and the biography of ex–Minor Leaguer and later actor Pat Flaherty, whose daughter took lessons from Joe, in SABR BioProject at

http://bioproj.sabr.org/ bioproj.cfm?=v&v=17pid=169407bid=1183. Thanks to Richard Wood for the last reference.

6. See also Alvarez, "Interview with Smokey Joe Wood," 56.

7. A rumor in baseball circles said Cobb cooled toward Wood because Joe wouldn't invest in Coca-Cola with Ty. Wood denied the story but said Cobb "was so mixed up in the stock market he had lines running right to his room in the hotel when he was playing."

8. From 1947 to 1951 (and as early as 1942), Pete and Stella lived at 1538 S. Canfield Avenue, nearly five miles east of the golf range. No address is listed for Joe Wood until 1952, when new ones are noted for Pete and Joe. Pete and Stella relocated that year to 11146 Montana in West Los Angeles, just over a mile north and west of the golfing establishment. Joe and Laura spent their last two years in LA at 1622 Veteran Avenue, a half-mile (and thus an easy walk) to the southeast of the range.

9. Bob Wood remained at the New Haven Hospital a year. In 1958 he moved to one in Springfield, Massachusetts, where he stayed four years. In 1962 he transferred to Keene, New Hampshire, where he worked twelve years before entering the sports memorabilia business.

10. His son David remembers carrying a lot of water and making trips to Scranton, Pennsylvania, for meat by-products to feed the mink. In 1959 Joe Frank's family relocated to Clinton, Connecticut.

11. At one point all brothers lived in a town called Milford: Steve in Massachusetts, Bob in Connecticut, and Joe in Pennsylvania.

12. Alvarez, "Interview with Smokey Joe," 55.

13. Richard Wood, email to the author, July 20, 2008.

14. Richard Wood, email to the author, July 20, 2008. Joe Wood supported local brewers. Horlacher and Kaier's were German-influenced beers from Pennsylvania, Horlacher in Allentown and Kaier's at Mahanoy City.

15. JWA. Mercifully, Joe Wood didn't experience the loss of the homestead. It was destroyed by fire in 1991, with arson suspected.

16. Richard Wood remembers Joe was so concerned with money that he even stopped buying ice cream when the price rose above a dollar.

17. Richard Wood, email to the author, July 20, 2008. Richard also noted that his father, Joe Frank Wood, inherited his father's care with money: "My father, . . . having lost $5.00, . . . never gambled or waged a bet again."

18. Richard Wood, email to the author, July 20, 2008.

19. In Joe's words "details" would reveal "too much" about an episode that "stinks." See Felder, *Under Pallor, under Shadow*, 205, 229.

20. Runyon, "Interview with Dutch Leonard," 4. Leonard also said he had other evidence (possibly "lost" by Johnson and Landis) which documented betting by key players. Ironically, similar evidence was held in a Cleveland bank by Speaker and Cobb. Joe confirmed: "My greatest friends, Spoke and Cobb . . . got a bunch of stuff

written up and typewritten that they deposited it in a vault in a bank in Cleveland. And if they would've chased Cobb and Speaker out of baseball, this would've all come out." See Stump, *Cobb*, 383.

21. The proceedings were couched in legalese language — with Landis using words like "I hand you," "Exhibit 1," "to-wit," and "inclusive" — and notarized by John A. Witt, who wrote at the end of the transcript: "[The] witnesses, Cobb, Wood, Speaker and West, took oath and made affidavit to the truth of the statements made and testimony given by them as above written." But Landis was not serving as a judge, and thus there was no legal authority. Leonard's absence made all statements inadmissible evidence. Transcript of hearings courtesy of Roger Abrams.

22. The chronology doesn't support this explanation. Cobb resigned in early November, well before Landis exhausted attempts at summoning Leonard. As Mark Alvarez asserts in "Say It Ain't So, Ty," the explanations were passed to the public by a cooperative press (23).

23. Blaisdell, "Cobb-Speaker Scandal," 58, and Alvarez, "Say It Ain't So, Ty," 23. The absence of betting in the Landis judgment suggests that he found cause for implicating the two active players but was more committed to ending the national obsession with wagering. That is why, in Alvarez's words, "there was no weighing of testimony," "no explanation of why it had taken so long to arrive at this simple decision," and "reasons for Ban Johnson's original finding of guilt were never detailed or specifically refuted by the Commissioner's Office," (27).

24. Fullerton, "Are Baseball Games Framed?," 85.

25. Wood in the Ritter tapes: "I was at a World Series with Landis down in New York [in 1926 or 1927]. He says, 'Joe, are we going to have any trouble over this thing?' And I says, 'I don't think so.' He says, 'Well, let me know if you do.' 'Well,' I says, 'I'll let you know,' but, of course, I knew I was in the clear." Joe called Landis a friend and "for me" in proceedings.

26. Leonard slipped to over a 4.00 ERA in 1924 and 1925 and incurred Cobb's wrath for not playing hard, was put on waivers, and not picked up by Speaker (Alexander, *Ty Cobb*, 187). For his abrasive personality, see Blaisdell, "Cobb-Speaker Scandal," 60.

27. See Runyon, "Interview with Dutch Leonard," 4.

28. Others did their part. Roger Henn, originally from Ouray, Colorado, worked on Joe's candidacy in Chicago, and Alex Preutz led attempts in eastern Pennsylvania.

29. "Smoky Joe Wood" [Interview with Bob Wood by Parker Livermore], *Forever Baseball*, February 9, 1991, from JWA. After Joe's death the group redoubled efforts, culminating in a videotape *"Smoky" Joe Wood: A Cornerstone Legend of Baseball* (JWA). Interviewees noted his low lifetime ERA, winning streak, and the support of Ted Williams, favorably comparing Joe with Dizzy Dean, Sandy Koufax, Addie Joss, and Lefty O'Doul (similarly excluded from the Hall of Fame). The most passionate support came from Geoff Zonder, sports archivist at Yale, who said Joe "belongs with the greats because he played against the greats. He beat the greats. He did

everything he had to do against the greats," and Tip O'Neill, who declared, "As you measure a ball player, he had everything." "He's done nothing but brought fame and honor to baseball. How you can let a man like that slide back? It is sacrilegious, to be perfectly truthful." Joe appeared briefly on the veterans ballot in the early years of the twenty-first century (2 votes on the final ballot in 2005 and a nomination in 2007) but remains outside the hall.

30. Joe was a bit embarrassed by the hall activities. But goaded by the entry of inferior players, he showed some bitterness, saying he "wouldn't give a nickel" to be in because he would seem to be begging. See Green, "Joe Wood — Still Waiting for Cooperstown," 37; and Douskey, "Smoky Joe Wood's Last Interview," 70, 72–73. Joe told Murdock he worried that Leonard's accusations hurt his own chances.

31. See James, *Politics of Glory*, 38–52, 143–71, 291–307; and K. Smith, *Baseball's Hall of Fame.*

32. Gary Whitney, telephone interview with the author, July 25, 2007. By the end of the 1960s Joe had given up hunting and fishing, saying he wanted to protect, not kill animals. But he still allowed friends to hunt around his Pennsylvania home.

33. Bob Duda, interview with the author, October 15, 2005. Mr. Duda suffered from Parkinson's disease. But he summoned the strength to control tremors as he talked, a tear coursing down his right cheek as he considered his loss of a good neighbor.

34. Robert Wood, interview with the author, October 14, 2005.

35. See Whaley, "Smokey Joe Wood Looks Back," 41–42.

36. Joe declared that he didn't "even want to hear the name of Jimmy Carter." Because he was so money conscious, Joe was outraged at double-digit inflation during the Carter years.

37. JWA.

38. Even as an old man, Joe could recite the history of his autos: an Oakland roadster (a yellow one that "wouldn't run downhill in high"), a seven-passenger Oakland, a Buick, a Ford Maxwell, one of the first Chrysler roadsters (a "beautiful car"), a six- or seven-passenger Nash, and "Chryslers from then on."

39. Since Joe wasn't giving interviews, Roger Angell was pleased to meet him in the old dining room. When asked about opening day at Fenway, Joe responded, "I don't remember a goddamn thing about it, except that I wasn't pitching that day." Joe struck Angell as small, "very direct," and "not very happy," but "stalwart." Angell, telephone interview with the author; and JWA.

40. Carl Vogt, interview with the author, April 17, 2007.

41. Ironically, when Joe first came up with the Sox, he was also incorrectly called a left-hander.

42. Durinda, a granddaughter of Joe Wood, remembered "granddaddy's" weeping as "adorable." Son Bob represented his father at the regular graduation ceremony, on May 24, 1985.

everything he had to do against the greats," and Tip O'Neill, who declared, "As you measure a ball player, he had everything." "He's done nothing but brought fame and honor to baseball. How you can let a man like that slide back? It is sacrilegious, to be perfectly truthful." Joe appeared briefly on the veterans ballot in the early years of the twenty-first century (2 votes on the final ballot in 2005 and a nomination in 2007) but remains outside the hall.

30. Joe was a bit embarrassed by the hall activities. But goaded by the entry of inferior players, he showed some bitterness, saying he "wouldn't give a nickel" to be in because he would seem to be begging. See Green, "Joe Wood — Still Waiting for Cooperstown," 37; and Douskey, "Smoky Joe Wood's Last Interview," 70, 72–73. Joe told Murdock he worried that Leonard's accusations hurt his own chances.

31. See James, *Politics of Glory*, 38–52, 143–71, 291–307; and K. Smith, *Baseball's Hall of Fame.*

32. Gary Whitney, telephone interview with the author, July 25, 2007. By the end of the 1960s Joe had given up hunting and fishing, saying he wanted to protect, not kill animals. But he still allowed friends to hunt around his Pennsylvania home.

33. Bob Duda, interview with the author, October 15, 2005. Mr. Duda suffered from Parkinson's disease. But he summoned the strength to control tremors as he talked, a tear coursing down his right cheek as he considered his loss of a good neighbor.

34. Robert Wood, interview with the author, October 14, 2005.

35. See Whaley, "Smokey Joe Wood Looks Back," 41–42.

36. Joe declared that he didn't "even want to hear the name of Jimmy Carter." Because he was so money conscious, Joe was outraged at double-digit inflation during the Carter years.

37. JWA.

38. Even as an old man, Joe could recite the history of his autos: an Oakland roadster (a yellow one that "wouldn't run downhill in high"), a seven-passenger Oakland, a Buick, a Ford Maxwell, one of the first Chrysler roadsters (a "beautiful car"), a six- or seven-passenger Nash, and "Chryslers from then on."

39. Since Joe wasn't giving interviews, Roger Angell was pleased to meet him in the old dining room. When asked about opening day at Fenway, Joe responded, "I don't remember a goddamn thing about it, except that I wasn't pitching that day." Joe struck Angell as small, "very direct," and "not very happy," but "stalwart." Angell, telephone interview with the author; and JWA.

40. Carl Vogt, interview with the author, April 17, 2007.

41. Ironically, when Joe first came up with the Sox, he was also incorrectly called a left-hander.

42. Durinda, a granddaughter of Joe Wood, remembered "granddaddy's" weeping as "adorable." Son Bob represented his father at the regular graduation ceremony, on May 24, 1985.

written up and typewritten that they deposited it in a vault in a bank in Cleveland. And if they would've chased Cobb and Speaker out of baseball, this would've all come out." See Stump, *Cobb*, 383.

21. The proceedings were couched in legalese language — with Landis using words like "I hand you," "Exhibit 1," "to-wit," and "inclusive" — and notarized by John A. Witt, who wrote at the end of the transcript: "[The] witnesses, Cobb, Wood, Speaker and West, took oath and made affidavit to the truth of the statements made and testimony given by them as above written." But Landis was not serving as a judge, and thus there was no legal authority. Leonard's absence made all statements inadmissible evidence. Transcript of hearings courtesy of Roger Abrams.

22. The chronology doesn't support this explanation. Cobb resigned in early November, well before Landis exhausted attempts at summoning Leonard. As Mark Alvarez asserts in "Say It Ain't So, Ty," the explanations were passed to the public by a cooperative press (23).

23. Blaisdell, "Cobb-Speaker Scandal," 58, and Alvarez, "Say It Ain't So, Ty," 23. The absence of betting in the Landis judgment suggests that he found cause for implicating the two active players but was more committed to ending the national obsession with wagering. That is why, in Alvarez's words, "there was no weighing of testimony," "no explanation of why it had taken so long to arrive at this simple decision," and "reasons for Ban Johnson's original finding of guilt were never detailed or specifically refuted by the Commissioner's Office," (27).

24. Fullerton, "Are Baseball Games Framed?," 85.

25. Wood in the Ritter tapes: "I was at a World Series with Landis down in New York [in 1926 or 1927]. He says, 'Joe, are we going to have any trouble over this thing?' And I says, 'I don't think so.' He says, 'Well, let me know if you do.' 'Well,' I says, 'I'll let you know,' but, of course, I knew I was in the clear." Joe called Landis a friend and "for me" in proceedings.

26. Leonard slipped to over a 4.00 ERA in 1924 and 1925 and incurred Cobb's wrath for not playing hard, was put on waivers, and not picked up by Speaker (Alexander, *Ty Cobb*, 187). For his abrasive personality, see Blaisdell, "Cobb-Speaker Scandal," 60.

27. See Runyon, "Interview with Dutch Leonard," 4.

28. Others did their part. Roger Henn, originally from Ouray, Colorado, worked on Joe's candidacy in Chicago, and Alex Preutz led attempts in eastern Pennsylvania.

29. "Smoky Joe Wood" [Interview with Bob Wood by Parker Livermore], *Forever Baseball*, February 9, 1991, from JWA. After Joe's death the group redoubled efforts, culminating in a videotape *"Smoky" Joe Wood: A Cornerstone Legend of Baseball* (JWA). Interviewees noted his low lifetime ERA, winning streak, and the support of Ted Williams, favorably comparing Joe with Dizzy Dean, Sandy Koufax, Addie Joss, and Lefty O'Doul (similarly excluded from the Hall of Fame). The most passionate support came from Geoff Zonder, sports archivist at Yale, who said Joe "belongs with the greats because he played against the greats. He beat the greats. He did

11. Legend and Legacy

1. Spatz, SABR *Baseball List*, 202–3, 219, 224, 234, 239, 241, 243, 271.

2. http://www.baseball-reference.com and JWA.

3. Quoted in Lawrence Ritter, "Joe Wood," 154. Wood was always deferential to Walter Johnson but was quoted in his Associated Press biography, "'Smokey Joe' Wood," as believing his fastball "was about as fast, if not as fast, as Johnson's."

4. JWA. See also the AP biography "'Smokey Joe' Wood," where Lajoie also is quoted as saying Joe Wood "had everything . . . superb stamina, iron nerve, brains and natural pitching skill."

5. Ritter, "Harry Hooper," 147.

6. JWA. Bob Wood often repeated a baseball joke that Joe Wood and Jim Thorpe were the two most natural athletes of their time, but Thorpe couldn't hit a curve ball. As Mike Sowell notes in *The Pitch That Killed*, 116, "Wood was widely regarded as the best pool player in baseball; Jamey [Charlie Jamieson] liked to brag he was the second best."

7. JWA.

8. JWA.

9. JWA.

10. Lane, "Extraordinary Career of Smokey Joe Wood," 493, 494. The previous year, in another article by Lane, Joe claimed, "The greatest satisfaction is the thought that after I was read out of baseball as a poor old pitcher who was all through, I was able to make myself over into an outfielder at least good enough to stick with a winning club. To me, there is some satisfaction in fooling the fates when they seem dead set against you." Lane, "Flashback . . . 'Smoky Joe' Wood," 47.

11. "Spotlight" in the *New York Tribune*, JWA. See also Green, in "Joe Wood — Still Waiting for Cooperstown," 37.

12. Sobol, *Babe Ruth and the American Dream*, quoted in Scher, "Case for Ouray's Smoky Joe Wood," 11; and Vaccaro, *First Fall Classic*, 200.

13. Murdock, interview with Joe Wood, Cleveland Public Library. Unless otherwise noted, direct quotes from Joe Wood in the following paragraphs are from the JWA.

14. Ritter, "Joe Wood," audiocassette.

15. Sterling, Interview; http://www.cmgww.com/ baseball/wood.

16. Cascade was distilled in Coffee County, Tennessee, southeast of Nashville; its popularity resulted from creative marketing distributor George A. Dickel. Today's Dickel uses a Cascade recipe. See Gaston, "Tennessee Distilleries."

17. JWA; and Douskey, "Smoky Joe Wood's Last Interview," 73.

18. Alvarez, "Interview with Smokey Joe Wood," 54. Transcript of hearing courtesy of Roger Abrams.

19. Ritter, "Joe Wood," audiocassette.

20. See Alexander, *Spoke*, 80.

21. In the Ritter audiotape, Joe describes young Babe Ruth as having piano legs but also being slender, "well built," and loving baseball. See also Alvarez, "Interview with Smokey Joe," 54. Baseball historians compare Joe Wood with pitchers with shortened careers, like Addie Joss, Dizzy Dean, and Sandy Koufax. But the best comparison may be Ruth. Both had two twenty-win seasons; Ruth's winning percentage, .671, was almost identical to Joe's, .672; and Babe's ERA was just .25 higher.

22. Ritter, "Joe Wood," audiocassette.

23. See Douskey, "Smoky Joe Wood's Last Interview," 71–72.

24. Wood had some of the stereotypical views of African Americans. But some sports cartoons (like those by Wallace Goldsmith), with thick-lipped, naive, and dialect-spewing characters, were even more aggressively racist.

25. Joe remembered that Eppa Rixey didn't even appear in the 1915 World Series, with the implication that Rixey wasn't good enough to play. In fact, Rixey pitched six and two-thirds innings of relief in the final game, giving up three runs and taking the loss.

26. JWA.

27. JWA.

28. Durinda Wood, interview with the author, June 7, 2007.

29. JWA.

30. JWA.

31. Ritter and Honig, "'Smokey' Joe Wood," 56–57.

32. *Baseball*, dir. Ken Burns (Florentine Films, 1994).

33. Society for American Baseball Research electronic newsletters.

34. Lardner, *You Know Me Al*, 64.

35. Grey, *Young Pitcher*, 76–77, 109, and 196.

36. Even though probably ghosted, "His Success is Due to Speed," *Washington Post*, December 8, 1912, reflected Joe's belief: "I bring my arm over at full length, with the hand more or less upright, and throw with all the energy I have. As the arm comes very nearly as far as it will go, the wrist does the rest." The ball then "takes a jump before it reaches the plate."

37. Baer, "Crambury Tiger," 314.

38. There are many inaccuracies: Wood wasn't living on a farm when he joined the Bloomer Girls, his father supported his career, he didn't wear a wig and didn't always pitch, and there were no games against Major League teams.

39. See Ritter, "Joe Wood," 154.

40. Farrell, *My Baseball Diary*, 35–36.

41. Angell, "Web of the Game," 17.

42. Angell, "Web of the Game," 9, 23.

43. Greenberg, *Celebrant*, 180–81, 196, 235.

44. Soos, *Murder at Fenway Park*, 39; see also 5, 53, 121, 149, 151, 173, 174–75, 188–94, and 221; Soos, *Hanging Curve*, 69. In 2004 a blues band in the Los Angeles area,

Smokey Joe Wood, produced the CD titled *Throwback*. One player, Van Holmes, is the grandson of another "Ducky" Holmes, Russell Holmes, a catcher in the Red Sox organization in the second decade of the last century.

45. J. S. Winter, *Murder on Mount Monadnock* (Keene NH: Surry Cottage Books, 2008), 20, 92–96, 229, 276.

46. Donald Hall, "Ninth Inning," in *The Museum of Clear Ideas* (Boston: Ticknor & Fields, 1993).

47. Donald Hall, "The Radio Red Sox," in *Here at Eagle Pond* (Boston: Moriner, 1990), 68.

48. *Elmer the Great*, directed by Mervyn Leroy, starring Joe E. Brown and Patricia Ellis (Warner Brothers, 1933). See J. E. Brown, *Laughter Is a Wonderful Thing*, 202–3, 212–13.

49. Brown played semipro baseball in New York and Ohio when Wood was a young Boston Red Sox player. Crucial to their friendship was the night of April 22, 1921, in Cleveland when the team celebrated their championship at the Hanna Theatre and were entertained by Joe E. Brown, touring in his revue "Jim, Jam, Jems" (J. E. Brown, *Laughter Is a Wonderful Thing*, 111; Gehring, *Joe E. Brown*, 16, 24, 27, 33–34; and Alexander, *Spoke*, 181). Also key was their mutual friendship with Tris Speaker. Brown and Speaker were partners in the purchase of the Kansas City Blues, Wood's old team, in January 1933 (Alexander, *Spoke*, 284–86; and J. E. Brown, *Laughter Is a Wonderful Thing*, 220, 223). Wood gave Brown a 1912 uniform, which either became part of a sports collection in the LA area or burned with Joe E.'s home in Bel Air, on November 7, 1961.

50. There are possible connections between Joe E. Brown and Wood in the third film of Brown's baseball trilogy, and the best, titled *Alibi Ike* (directed by Ray Enright, starring Joe E. Brown, Olivia de Havilland, Ruth Donnelly, Roscoe Karns, and William Frawley [Warner Brothers, 1935]). The main character is from Kansas and a pool expert like Joe Wood.

51. *Fireman, Save My Child*, directed by Lloyd Bacon, starring Joe E. Brown, Evalyn Knapp, Lilian Bond, and Guy Kibbee (First National, 1932). Brown may have been offered a contract with the Boston Red Sox in 1911; see Rob Edelman, "Joe E. Brown," 130.

52. *Field of Dreams*, directed by Phil Alden Robinson, Kevin Costner, Amy Madigan, James Earl Jones, Burt Lancaster. Universal, 1989.

53. Author's telephone interviews with Phil Robinson and Durinda Wood, who worked on *Star Trek: The Next Generation*, *The Sure Thing*, *Back to School*, and *Mighty Wind*.

54. JWA. See overthemonster.com.

Bibliography

Archival Sources

Eugene C. Murdock Baseball Collection. Cleveland Public Library. Cleveland, Ohio. Interview with Joe Wood by Eugene Murdock.

Joe E. Brown files. Margaret Herrick Library of the Academy of Motion Picture Arts and Sciences. Beverly Hills CA.

SABR Archives, Phoenix AZ. 1991. Interview with Joe Wood Jr. by Pete Zanardi.

Yale University Sports Archives. New Haven CT. Joe Wood Papers.

Published Sources

Abrams, Roger I. *The Dark Side of the Diamond: Gambling, Violence, Drugs and Alcoholism in the National Pastime.* Burlington MA: Rounder, 2007.

Alexander, Charles C. *Spoke: A Biography of Tris Speaker.* Dallas: Southern Methodist University Press, 2007.

———. *Ty Cobb.* Dallas: Southern Methodist University Press, 2006. First published 1984 by Oxford University Press.

Alvarez, Mark. "An Interview with Smokey Joe Wood." *Baseball Research Journal* 16 (1987): 53–56.

———. "Say It Ain't So, Ty: The Cobb-Speaker Scandal." *The National Pastime: A Review of Baseball History* 13 (1994): 21–28.

Anderson, David. "Bonesetter Reese." http://bioproj.sabr. org.

Angell, Roger. "The Web of the Game." In *The Armchair Book of Baseball*, edited by John Thorn, 7–23. New York: Charles Scribner's Sons, 1985. First published July 20, 1981, in *New Yorker*.

Asinof, Eliot. *Eight Men Out: The Black Sox and the 1919 World Series.* Introduced by Stephen Jay Gould. New York: Henry Holt, 1987. First published 1963 by Holt, Rinehart, & Winston.

Baer, Arthur "Bugs". "The Crambury Tiger." In *Baseball's Best Short Stories*, edited by Paul D. Staudohar, 311–21. Chicago: Chicago Review Press, 1995.

Bibliography

"The Ball Parks of Kansas City, Part 1." *American Association Almanac* 4, no. 3 (Summer 2005): 1–33.

Berlage, Gai. *Women in Baseball*. Westport CT: Praeger, 1994.

Blaisdell, Lowell L. "The Cobb-Speaker Scandal: Exonerated but Probably Guilty." *Nine: A Journal of Baseball History and Culture* 13, no. 2 (Spring 2005): 54–70.

Booth, Malcolm A. "A Short History of Orange County New York." http://www.co.orange.ny.us-documentView.aspdocID= 2432.url.

Brown, Joe E., with Ralph Hancock. *Laughter Is a Wonderful Thing*. New York: A. S. Barnes, 1956.

Browne, Lois. *Girls of Summer*. New York: HarperCollins, 1993.

Constantelos, Steve. "Cleveland." In *Deadball Stars of the American League*, edited by David Jones, 641–43. Dulles VA: Potomac, 2006.

Corning, A. Elwood. *The Concise History of Orange County*. Saugerties NY: Hope Farm Press, 1993. First published 1946 by Lewis Historical Publishing.

Douskey, Franz. "Smoky Joe Wood's Last Interview." *The National Pastime: A Review of Baseball History* 27 (2007): 69–73.

Duren, Don. *Boiling Out at the Springs*. Dallas: Hodge, 2006.

Edelman, Rob. "Joe E. Brown: A Clown Prince of Baseball." *The National Pastime: A Review of Baseball History* 27 (2007): 127–31.

Farrell, James T. *My Baseball Diary*. New York: A. S. Barnes, 1957.

Felber, Bill. *Under Pallor, under Shadow: The 1920 American League Pennant Race That Rattled and Rebuilt Baseball*. Lincoln: University of Nebraska Press, 2011.

Fleitz, David. *Shoeless: The Life and Times of Joe Jackson*. Jefferson NC: McFarland, 2001.

Foster, Michael. "Boston: Joe Wood." In *Deadball Stars of the American League*, edited by David Jones, 441–44. Dulles VA: Potomac, 2006.

Fullerton, Hugh. "Are Baseball Games Framed? The Story of Spoke and Smoky Joe." *Liberty*, April 2, 1927, 83–86.

Gaston, Kay Baker. "Tennessee Distilleries: Their Rise, Fall, and Re-emergence." *Border States: Journal of the Kentucky-Tennessee American Studies Association* 12 (1999). http://spider.georgetowncollege.edu/htallant/border/bs12tabl.htm.

Gay, Timothy M. *Satch, Dizzy & Rapid Robert*. New York: Simon & Schuster, 2010.

———. *Tris Speaker: The Rough-and-Tumble Life of a Baseball Legend*. Lincoln: University of Nebraska Press, 2005.

Gehring, Wes. *Joe E. Brown: Film Comedian and Baseball Buffoon*. Jefferson NC: McFarland, 2006.

Giamatti, A. Bartlett. *A Great and Glorious Game*. Chapel Hill NC: Algonquin, 1998.

Ginsburg, Daniel E. *The Fix Is In: A History of Baseball Gambling and Game Fixing Scandals*. Jefferson NC: McFarland, 1995.

The Glory of Their Times. Directed by Bud Greenspan. Discovery Channel, March 20, 1977. Videocassette recording in JWA.

Green, Paul. "Joe Wood." In *Forgotten Fields*, 6–24. Waupaca WI: Parker, 1984.

———. "Joe Wood—Still Waiting for Cooperstown." *Sports Collectors Digest*, November 26, 1982, 28, 32, 34, 36–37.

Greenberg, Eric Rolfe. *The Celebrant*. Lincoln: University of Nebraska Press, 1993. First published 1983 by Everest House.

Gregorich, Barbara. "Blues, Bloomers, and Bobbies." *Pennsylvania Heritage*, Summer 1998, 32–37.

———. *Women at Play*. New York: Harcourt, Brace, 1993.

Gregory, Doris. *History of Ouray: A Heritage of Mining and Everlasting Beauty*. Vol. 1. Ouray CO: Cascade, 1995.

Grey, Zane. "The Knocker." In *The Redheaded Outfield and Other Baseball Stories*. Whitefish MT: Kessinger, 2005. Story first published in August 1910. Volume first published 1920 by Grosset & Dunlap.

———. *The Shortstop*. Foreword by John Thorn. New York: Morrow Junior Books, 1992. First published 1909 by A. C. McClurg.

———. *The Young Pitcher*. Foreword by John Thorn. New York: Morrow Junior Books, 1992. First published 1911 novel by Harper & Brothers.

Hall, Mary L. *Requiem II*. Spearville KS: Spearville News, 1985.

Hartley, Michael. *Christy Mathewson: A Biography*. Jefferson NC: McFarland, 2004.

Holway, John B. *Smokey Joe and the Cannonball*. Washington DC: Capital Press, 1985.

Honig, Donald. "Joe Wood." In *The October Heroes*, 164–81. New York: Simon & Schuster, 1979.

———. "Smokey Joe Wood." In *Baseball America*, 75–88. New York: Macmillan, 1985.

Huhn, Rick. *Eddie Collins: A Baseball Biography*. Jefferson NC: McFarland, 2008.

———. "It Was 'Smoky' in Cleveland." In *Batting Four Thousand: Baseball in the Western Reserve*, edited by Brad Sullivan, 28–30. Cleveland: SABR, 2008.

James, Bill. *The Politics of Glory: How Baseball's Hall of Fame Really Works*. New York: Macmillan, 1994.

Jedick, Peter. *League Park*. Cleveland: SABR, 1990.

Johnson, Lloyd. "Baseball in Kansas City," In *Unions to Royals: The Story of Professional Baseball in Kansas City*, edited by Lloyd Johnson, Steve Garlick, and Jeff Magalif, 2–3. Manhattan KS: AG Press, 1996.

Johnson, Richard. *Field of Our Fathers: An Illustrated History of Fenway Park*. Chicago: Triumph Books, 2011.

Jorgensen, Joyce. "Smoky Joe Wood." *Ouray County (CO) Plaindealer* July 31, 1980.

Lane, F. C. "The Extraordinary Career of Smokey Joe Wood." *Baseball Magazine*, October 1921, 493–94.

———. "Flashback . . . Smokey Joe Wood." *Baseball Magazine*, August 1954, 19, 26, 47. First published in September 1920 *Baseball Magazine*.

Lardner, Ring. *You Know Me Al*. New York: Charles Scribner's Sons, 1988. First published 1914 by Curtis.

Leek, Thomas. "Gravestones Back in Right Place." *Tri-State Gazette*, July 24, 1989.

Leslie, Vernon. *The Battle of Minisink: A Revolutionary War Engagement in the Upper Delaware Valley.* Middletown NY: T. Emmett Henderson, 1975.

Longert, Scott. *Addie Joss: King of the Pitchers.* Cleveland: SABR, 1998.

Macht, Norman. *Connie Mack and the Early Years of Baseball.* Lincoln: University of Nebraska Press, 2007.

Mansch, Larry. *Rube Marquard: The Life and Times of a Baseball Hall of Famer.* Jefferson NC: McFarland, 1998.

Markson, David. "A Day for Addie Joss." *Atlantic Monthly,* August 1975, 36–40.

Mathews, Alfred. *History of Wayne, Pike and Monroe Counties, Pennsylvania.* Philadelphia: R. T. Peck, 1886.

Moss, Irvin, and Mark Foster. *Home Run in the Rockies: The History of Baseball in Colorado.* NC: Publication Design, 1994.

Murdock, Eugene C. *Ban Johnson: Czar of Baseball.* Westport CT: Greenwood, 1982.

Murnane, T. H. "It Is the Simple Life for Farmer Joe Wood in the Winter Time." *Boston Daily Globe,* February 2, 1913.

Nowlin, Bill. *The Great Red Sox Spring Training Tour of 1911.* Jefferson NC: McFarland, 2010.

Pembleton, Luke, et al. *Ness County History, 1870–1910.* Compiled and edited by Helen Pembleton French. Ness City NS: n.p., 1990.

Pietrusza, David. *Judge and Jury: The Life and Times of Kenesaw Mountain Landis.* South Bend IN: Diamond Communications, 1998.

———. *Rothstein: The Life, Times, and Murder of the Criminal Genius Who Fixed the 1919 World Series.* New York: Carroll & Graf, 2003.

Riess, Steven A. *Touching Base: Professional Baseball and American Culture in the Progressive Era.* Champaign: University of Illinois Press, 1999.

Ritter, Lawrence S. "Harry Hooper." In *The Glory of Their Times: The Story of the Early Days of Baseball Told by the Men Who Played It,* 138–53. New York: Harper Collins, 1992. Enlarged edition of 1966 printing by Macmillan.

———. "Joe Wood." In *The Glory of Their Times,* 154–69.

———. "Joe Wood." *The Glory of Their Times.* Audiocassette. St. Paul MN: HighBridge Company, 1998.

Ritter, Lawrence, and Donald Honig. "'Smokey' Joe Wood." In *The 100 Greatest Baseball Players of All Time,* 56–57. New York: Crown, 1981.

Runyon, Damon. "Interview with Dutch Leonard. *Cleveland Plain Dealer,* December 22, 1926.

Ryan, Bob. "Holy Smoky: Wood Had Season for Ages." *Boston Globe,* December 21, 1999.

———. *When Boston Won the World Series.* Philadelphia: Running Press, 2003.

Scher, Zeke. "The Case for Ouray's Smoky Joe Wood. *Empire* [Sunday magazine of the *Denver Post*], July 27, 1980, 10–13, 16.

Seymour, Harold. *Baseball: The Golden Age.* New York: Oxford University Press, 1971.

Smith, Duane. "Nothing but Baseball on His Mind." In *Above the Fruited Plain:*

Bibliography

Baseball in the Rocky Mountain West, edited by Thomas L. Altherr, 77–80. Denver: SABR, 2003.

Smith, Ken. *Baseball's Hall of Fame*. New York: Grosset & Dunlap, 1981. First published 1947 by A. S. Barnes.

Smith, Robert. *Baseball in the Afternoon*. New York: Simon & Schuster, 1993.

"'Smokey Joe' Wood." *Associated Press Biographical Service*, 3813 (June 1, 1953): n.p.

"Smoky Joe Wood" [interview with Bob Wood by Parker Livermore]. *Forever Baseball*, February 9, 1991.

"Smoky Joe's Café [interview with Bob Wood]." June 2001. http://www.thediamondangle.com/archive/june01/woodint.html.

Sobol, Ken. *Babe Ruth and the American Dream*. New York: Random House, 1974.

Soos, Troy. *Hanging Curve*. New York: Kensington Books, 1999.

———. *Murder at Fenway Park*. New York: Kensington Books, 1994

Sowell, Mike. *The Pitch That Killed: Carl Mays, Ray Chapman, and the Pennant Race of 1920*. New York: Macmillan, 1989.

Spatz, Lyle, ed. *The SABR Baseball List & Record Book*. New York: Scribner, 2007.

Spink, J. G. Taylor. *Judge Landis and Twenty-Five Years of Baseball*. New York: Thomas Y. Crowell, 1947.

Stout, Glenn. *Fenway 1912: The Birth of a Ballpark, a Championship Season, and Fenway's Remarkable First Year*. Boston: Houghton Mifflin Harcourt, 2011.

———, ed. *Impossible Dreams: A Red Sox Collection*. Boston: Houghton Mifflin, 2003.

Stout, Glenn, and Richard A. Johnson. *Red Sox Century: The Definitive History of Baseball's Most Storied Franchise*. Boston: Houghton Mifflin, 2005.

Strickler, David L. *Child of Moriah: A Biography of John D. "Bonesetter" Resse, 1855–1931*. Chapel Hill NC: Four Corners Press, 1984.

Stump, Al. *Cobb*. Chapel Hill NC: Algonquin, 1996.

Sutton, Keith. *Wayne County Sports History, 1871–1972*. Honesdale PA: Wayne Independent, 1972.

Swint, Jim. "Don't Forget 'Smoky' Joe Wood, You Were Some Kind of Ballplayer." http://www.funvalleysports.com/history /smokey_joe_wood.shtml.

———. "A History of Baseball in Hutchinson, Kansas." http:/ /funvalleysports.com/ history/history_baseball.shtml.

———. "A History of Baseball in Hutchinson, Kansas." *Legacy: The Journal of the Reno County Historical Society* 3, no. 2 (Spring 1991): 11–14, 17–18.

———. "'Smoky' Joe Wood, You Were Some Kind of Ballplayer." *Legacy: The Journal of the Reno County Historical Society* 5, no. 1 (Winter 1993): 2, 5–6, 9–10; and 5, no. 2 (Spring 1993): 2, 5–6.

Vaccaro, Mike. *The First Fall Classic: The Red Sox, the Giants, and the Cast of Players, Pugs, and Politicos Who Reinvented the World Series in 1912*. New York: Doubleday, 2009.

Ward, John J. "Joseph Wood, Esq., Pitcher." *Baseball Magazine* 10, no. 1 (November 1912): 49–54.

Bibliography

Whalen, Thomas J. *When the Red Sox Ruled: Baseball's First Dynasty, 1912–1918.* Chicago: Ivan R. Dee, 2011.

Whaley, Joan. "Smokey Joe Wood Looks Back on His Baseball Career." *Baseball Digest* 40 (May 1981): 40–44.

Wiggins, Robert Peyton. *The Federal League of Base Ball Clubs.* Jefferson NC: McFarland, 2009.

Wood, Francis, and Dorothy Wood. *I Hauled These Mountains in Here.* Caldwell ID: Caxton, 1977.

Wood, Gerald C. "Doctor Smoke: Joe Wood, Yale University, and the 1926 Baseball Controversy." In *Baseball/Literature/ Culture: Essays 2006–2007*, edited by Ronald E. Kates and Warren Tormey, 130–38. Jefferson NC: McFarland, 2008.

Wood, Joe. "Doing the Comeback Stunt." *Baseball Magazine* 19, no. 4 (August 1917): 425–26.

"Wood's Strong Wrist Great Aid in Pitching." *Sporting Life*, November 30, 1912, 12.

Yale Baseball Media Guide, 1991.

Yale Baseball Media Guide, 1999.

Zingg, Paul J. *Harry Hooper: An American Baseball Life.* Urbana: University of Illinois Press, 1993.

Audiovisual Sources

The following audiotapes and videotapes in the Joe Wood archives, some made in conjunction with the campaign for Joe's election to the Hall of Fame, were useful in capturing Joe's voice and views. They were identified and provided by Bob Wood.

Amoruso, Marino, and Frank Williams. Interview with Joe Wood and Bob Wood. Audiocassette recording. October 18, 1983.

Anonymous interviewers. Interview with Joe Wood. Audiocassette recording. September 16, 1982.

Boston Red Sox Old-Timers' Game. Videocassette recording. May 27, 1984.

Colcord, Elmer. Videotaped interview. May 1993.

Colorado Sports Hall of Fame Award Banquet. Videocassette recording. Denver CO. February 6, 1995.

Derba, Joe. Videotaped interview. May 1993.

Draudt, John. Interview by Joe Wood and Bob Wood about Jake Beckley. Audiocassette recording. February 2, 1984.

Finn, Jack "Huck." Interview with Joe Wood, Bob Wood, and Virginia Wood Whitney. Audiocassette recording. March 20, 1980.

Geer, George. Interview with Joe Wood. Audiocassette recording. May 16, 1979.

Goodwin, Lee. Interview with Joe and Bob Wood. Audiocassette recording. December 23, 1980.

Green, Paul, and Dave Moriah. Interview with Bob Wood and Joe Wood. Audiocassette recording. August 16, 1983.

Bibliography

Halper, Barry. Videotaped interview. Yankee Stadium Executives Offices. July 25, 1999.

Halper, Barry, and Geoff Zonder. Audiotaped interview by Doug Roberts and Bob Wood. Yankee Stadium. September 1999.

Harmon, Mike, and Joe Martin. Interview with Joe Wood, Virginia Wood Whitney, and Bob Wood. For "Sports Spotlight" show on WADS radio. Audiocassette recording. June 18, 1980.

Hill, R. Craig. Audiotape of questions answered by Joe Wood and Bob Wood. February 2, 1984.

Lee, Dick, Bill Ryan, Frank Williams, and Ed Walton. Conversation with Joe Wood, Bob Wood, and Virginia Wood Whitney. Audiocassette recording. February 1980.

McGorry, Mark. Interview for ESPN and Southern Connecticut State College. Audiocassette recording. October 27, 1981.

Northeastern University. Interview with Joe Wood for World Series room. Audiocassette recording. September 10, 1980.

Presentation of Doctor of Humane Letters Degree to Joe Wood. Audiocassette recording. January 3, 1985.

Ritter, Lawrence. Videotaped interview. Yankee Stadium Executive Offices. July 25, 1999.

Ryan, Bill, and "Huck" Finn. Interview with Joe Wood, Virginia Wood Whitney, and Bob Wood. Audiocassette recording. April 17 1980.

SABR Convention, Baltimore MD. Conversations with Joe Wood. Audiocassette recording. June 25–27, 1982.

Shirley, Dan, Frank Williams, Joe Wood, Bob Wood. Audiotaped interview. February 15, 1983.

Smoky Joe Wood [interview on Opening Day, Fenway Park, 1982]. Produced and directed by Paul Zuckoski and Joseph Leary. Owl Video Productions.

"Smoky Joe Wood" [interview with Bob Wood about Joe and Hall Candidacy on August 8, 1995]. NESN's Front Row. October 1995. Audiocassette recording.

"Smoky" Joe Wood: A Cornerstone Legend of Baseball. Videotape in support of Joe Wood's entry into Hall of Fame. N.d.

Soolman, Harvey, Bob Wood, and Joe Wood. Interview. Audiocassette recording. May 25, 1983.

Sterling, John. Interview with Joe Wood. Audiocassette recording. June 24, 1981.

Theimer, Zoë, Ruth Meranda, Walt Theimer, Joe Wood, and Bob Wood. Interview. Audiocassette recording. August 19, 1982.

Walton, Ed, Frank Williams, Virginia Whitney, Joe Wood, Harriet Rice Wood, Bob Wood, Chuck Polka. Interview. Audiocassette recording. May 22, 1980.

Williams, Frank. Interview with Joe Wood and Bob Wood. Audiocassette recording. October 26, 1982.

Williams, Frank and Harvey Soolman. Interview with Joe Wood and Bob Wood. Audiocassette recording. January 18, 1984.

Bibliography

Wood, Bob. Interview with Joe Wood on 1912 World Series for Wichita ĸs, Fan. Audiocassette recording. December 22, 1981.

Wood, Joe, and Bob Wood. Discussion of Forrest "Hick"" Cady. Audiocassette recording. November 11, 1983.

Wood, Richard. "Smoky Joe Wood Reminisces." Audiotaped interview with Joe Wood, by his grandson. August 1979.

Yale University Athletic Department interviews. Coordinated by Debbie Sterling. Audiocassette recording. November 9, 1993.

Zonder, Geoff. Videotaped interview. Yankee Stadium Executive Offices. July 25, 1999.

Interviews by Author

Angell, Roger. Telephone interview. December 13, 2006.

Bergin, John. Telephone interview. December 12, 2006.

Bergin, Tom. Telephone interview. December 13, 2006.

Cooney, Leo. Personal interview. June 11, 2006.

Duda, Bob and Pauline. Personal interview. October 15, 2005.

Durham, Frank. Telephone interview. June 27, 2006.

Fluhr, George. Telephone interview. December 30, 2006.

Henn, Roger. Telephone interview. June 4, 2007.

McConnell, Mike. Telephone interview. March 7, 2008.

Moncrieff, Robert P. Telephone interview. November 14, 2006.

Robinson, Phil Alden Robinson. Telephone interview. January 8, 2008.

Scott, Tris Speaker. Personal interview. October 22, 2005.

Theimer, Sandy. Telephone interview. January 4, 2010.

Travis, Levi. Telephone interview. June 7, 2007.

Vincent, Fay, Jr. Telephone interview. December 12, 2006.

Vogt, Carl. Personal interview. April 17, 2007. Telephone interview. December 30, 2006

Whitney, Gary. Telephone interview. July 25, 2007.

Whitney, Virginia Wood. Telephone interview. July 6, 2006.

Wood, Carol. Telephone interview. July 16, 2007.

Wood, David J. Telephone interview. January 3, 2007.

Wood, Durinda. Telephone interviews. June 7, 2007; September 19, 2008.

Wood, Richard. Email correspondences. October 6, 2007; June 28, 2008; July 20, 2008; August 19, 2008. Telephone interviews. June 12, 2007; August 20, 2008.

Wood, Robert K. Personal interview. October 14, 2005.

Websites

www.ballparksofbaseball.com
www.baseball-almanac.com
www.baseball-reference.com
www.baseballalmanac.com

Bibliography

www.baseballchronology.com
www.baseballindex.org
www.baselllibrary.com
www.baseballrace.com
www.cmgww.com/baseball/wood
www.overthemonster.com
www.retrosheet.com
www.sabr.org
www.shohola.com/township
www.thebaseballpage.com

Newspapers

Atlanta Constitution
Boston American
Boston Globe
Boston Post
Chicago Defender
Chicago Tribune
Christian Science Monitor
Cleveland Plain Dealer
Cleveland Press
Denver Post
Ellinwood (KS) Leader
Great Bend (KS) Daily Item
Hartford Courant
Hutchinson (KS) Daily News
Indianapolis Star
Kansas City Post
Kansas City Star
Kansas City Times
Los Angeles Times
Ness City (KS) Times
Ness County (KS) News
New Haven Register
New York Daily News
New York Herald Tribune
New York Times
Ouray (CO) Herald
Ouray County (CO) Plaindealer
Ouray (CO) Times
Washington Post

Index